Movie Musicals
on Record

Recent Titles in
Discographies

Women in Jazz
Jan Leder, compiler

The King Labels: A Discography
Michel Ruppli, compiler

Thank You Music Lovers:
A Bio-Discography of Spike Jones and His City Slickers, 1941-1965
Jack Mirtle, compiler

John McCormack: A Comprehensive Discography
Paul W. Worth and Jim Cartwright, compilers

Count Basie: A Bio-Discography
Chris Sheridan, compiler

The Symphonies of Gustav Mahler
Lewis M. Smoley, compiler

V-Discs: First Supplement
Richard S. Sears, compiler

French Horn Discography
Michael Hernon, compiler

The Clef/Verve Labels: A Discography
Michel Ruppli, compiler

The Cliff Edwards Discography
Larry F. Kiner, compiler

Broadway on Record: A Directory of New York Cast Recordings
of Musical Shows, 1931-1986
Richard Chigley Lynch, compiler

The Blue Note Label: A Discography
Michael Cuscuna and Michel Ruppli, compilers

His Master's Voice/La Voce Del Padrone
Alan Kelly, compiler

Irish Folk Music: A Selected Discography
Deborah L. Schaeffer, compiler

MOVIE MUSICALS ON RECORD

*A Directory of Recordings
of Motion Picture Musicals,
1927-1987*

Compiled by
Richard Chigley Lynch

Discographies, Number 32

Greenwood Press
New York • Westport, Connecticut • London

Library of Congress Cataloging-in-Publication Data

Lynch, Richard Chigley, 1932-
 Movie musicals on record : a directory of recordings of motion
picture musicals, 1927-1987 / compiled by Richard Chigley Lynch.
  p. cm.—(Discographies, ISSN 0192-334X ; no. 32)
 Companion vol. to: Broadway on record. 1987.
 Bibliography: p.
 Filmography: p.
 Includes indexes.
 ISBN 0-313-26540-2 (lib. bdg. : alk. paper)
 1. Motion picture music—Discography. 2. Musical films—
Discography. I. Lynch, Richard Chigley, 1932-   Broadway on
record. II. Title. III. Series.
ML156.4.M6L9 1989
016.7821'4'0266—dc20   89-2137

British Library Cataloguing in Publication Data is available.

Library of Congress Catalog Card Number: 89-2137
ISBN: 0-313-26540-2
ISSN: 0192-334x

First published in 1989

Greenwood Press, Inc.
88 Post Road West, Westport, Connecticut 06881

Printed in the United States of America

The paper used in this book complies with the
Permanent Paper Standard issued by the National
Information Standards Organization (Z39.48-1984).

10 9 8 7 6 5 4 3 2

This volume is dedicated to all
lovers of the film musical, and
particularly those who assisted
me in its preparation.

Contents

Introduction

The purpose of this discography is to provide a listing of the songs and the singers who performed them as recorded on commercially available albums of motion picture musicals. Chronologically it covers the period from <u>The Jazz Singer</u> in 1927 to <u>Three Amigos!</u> in 1987, a span of sixty years. There are 666 film albums included with some 6500 song titles represented. This volume is intended as a companion to my previous <u>Broadway on Record</u> (Greenwood Press, 1987) and is arranged in exactly the same manner.

What is a motion picture musical? In my research for this discography I have come across numerous definitions. Most agree, however, that musical numbers must actually be performed in the film and must in some way be concerned with the film's plot. For the purposes of this volume, at least three musical numbers must be included on the album (to avoid the many single recordings issued) and must have been performed in the film (as opposed to being heard only on the soundtrack). There are some exceptions. Generally not included are albums of concert documentaries, short films, dance and opera films. Also not included are albums that were not generally available to the record buying public. While the scope is primarily American, some foreign film albums are included, usually those that were popular in this country.

The entries are arranged alphabetically by film title with the name of the company that presented it and the year that it was first released. Musical films that were re-made (and recorded) are arranged chronologically. The original label and number are given, as well as information on the most recent reissue. 'Soundtrack' indicates that it is not a studio recording. Whether the recording is in mono or stereo or available as a compact disc (CD) is also indicated. Major composer, lyricist and musical conductor credits are given. Cast members who sing on the recording are listed alphabetically. (The voice of) indicates that the person was not in the film, but his or her voice was heard, frequently singing the title song over the film credits. When the entire cast is so indicated, it denotes an animated film. (Not in film) is used to indicate that the vocalist was not involved in the actual film

and sings on the recording as a studio cast member. (For Rita
Hayworth) indicates that the person sang for (called 'dubbed')
the star named. In the cases where it is not known who actually
dubbed for a star, the star is listed.

All the songs included on the album are then listed in the order
they are presented on the recording, followed by the name of the
artist(s) who performed them. The broken lines (---) separate
the different sides of the record. Additional composers and lyricists are also listed when several different persons contributed
to the film's score. All of this information is occasionally
followed by a note of interest to the reader, including single
recordings not included on the album.

Following the alphabetical discography is a chronological
listing of the films, alphabetically by year, indicating the studio
that presented the film. The occasional foreign film is indicated
here by the name of the country of origin. There are two separate
indexes. The first lists performers in alphabetical order, each
performer followed by the titles of all the albums he or she sings
on, which are also listed alphabetically. The second, the technical
index, is a listing of composers, lyricists, and musical directors,
again in alphabetical order with the film titles following. A
song title index having proved unwieldy, the researcher is referred
to two detailed song indexes:

Hirschhorn, Clive. The Hollywood Musical (Crown, 1981).
Shapiro, Nat and Pollack, Bruce. Popular Music, 1920-1979
    (with supplements) (Gale Research, 1985).

Of the many reference sources consulted in the compilation of
this discography, the two most invaluable were:

Green, Stanley. Encyclopedia of the Musical Film (Oxford
    University Press, 1981).
Raymond, Jack. Show Music on Record (Frederick Unger Press, 1982)

I would also like to acknowledge the aid and assistance given to
me by the staff of the Performing Arts Research Center, The New
York Public Library at Lincoln Center. Because it was not possible
to actually locate and listen to each and every album included in
this discography, I am indebted to the following individuals who
have assisted me in preparing the entries for this volume:

Rex Bunnett (England)   Barry Monush (New Jersey)
Jay Burk (Arkansas)   Jim Moody (Arkansas)
Joan Baxter (North Carolina)   Tom Oliver (Arkansas)
Roy Cooke (England)   Dennis Preato (New York)
Bob Davenport (Arkansas)   Margie Schultz (Ohio)
Peter Hoggett (England)   Serge Trepanier (Canada)
Jack Kabin (New York)   Joseph Yranski (New York)
Tom Lynch (New Jersey)

Discography

AARON SLICK FROM PUNKIN CRICK (Paramount, 1952)

RCA LPM 3006 mono

Music, lyrics: Jay Livingston, Ray Evans; musical direction:
Henri Rene, others

Cast: Robert Merrill, Dinah Shore, Alan Young

Songs: Saturday Night in Punkin Crick (Shore, chorus)
       My Beloved (Merrill) musical direction: Hugo Winterhalter
       Purt 'Nigh but Not Plumb (Shore, Young)
       Marshmallow Moon (Shore, chorus)
       Why Should I Believe in Love (Shore)
       Chores (Shore, Young)
       Still Water (Merrill, chorus) musical direction: Hugo
            Winterhalter
       Life Is A Beautiful Thing (Shore, chorus)

AARON SLICK FROM PUNKIN CRICK (Paramount, 1952)

Motion Picture Tracks International MPT - 4 (soundtrack) mono

Musical direction: Robert Emmett Dolan

Cast: Veda Ann Borg, Chick Chandler, Robert Merrill, Dinah
         Shore, Martha Stewart, Minerva Urecal, Alan Young

Songs: Opening Titles (orchestra)
       Chores (Shore, Young)
       My Beloved (Merrill)
       Saturday Night in Punkin Crick (Shore, Young)
       Marshmallow Moon (chorus)
       Step Right Up (Chandler, Borg)
       Soda Shop (Young, Shore, cast)
       Why Should I Believe in Love? (Shore)
       Still Water (Merrill, Shore, cast)
       Purt 'Nigh but Not Plumb (Shore, Young)
       Life Is A Beautiful Thing (Shore, Urecal)
       I'd Like to Baby You (Stewart, cast)
       Saturday Night in Punkin Crick (reprise) (cast)
       Step Right Up (reprise) (Merrill, Stewart)
       Saturday Night in Punkin Crick (finale) (cast)

AN AFFAIR TO REMEMBER (Twentieth Century-Fox, 1957)

Columbia CL 1013 (soundtrack) mono

Music for songs: Harry Warren; lyrics: Harold Adamson, Leo McCarey; musical score: Hugo Friedhofer; musical direction: Lionel Newman

Cast: (the voice of) Vic Damone, Marni Nixon (for Deborah Kerr)

Songs: Main Title: An Affair to Remember (Our Love Affair)
      (Damone, chorus)
      Continue (orchestra)
      Villefranche (orchestra)
      In the Chapel (orchestra)
      Tomorrowland (Nixon)
      Pink Champagne (orchestra)
      Revelation (orchestra)
      You Make It Easy to Be True (orchestra)
      Proposal (orchestra)
---   Continue (reprise) (Nixon)
      Night Club Affair (Our Love Affair) (Nixon)
      Empire State Montage (orchestra)
      Return to Villefranche (orchestra, Nixon, chorus)
      The Tiny Scout (He Knows You Inside Out) (Nixon,
        children's chorus)
      Ballet (orchestra)
      End Title: An Affair to Remember (Our Love Affair)
        (chorus)

ALEXANDER'S RAGTIME BAND (Twentieth Century-Fox, 1938)

Hollywood Soundstage 406 (soundtrack) mono

Music, lyrics: Irving Berlin; musical direction: Alfred Newman

Cast: Don Ameche, Chick Chandler, Donald Douglas, Dixie Dunbar, Alice Faye, Jack Haley, Ethel Merman, Wally Vernon

Songs: Opening Credits (orchestra)
      Alexander's Ragtime Band (Faye)
      Ragtime Violin (men)
      The International Rag (Faye, Haley, Chandler)
      Everybody's Doin' It (Vernon, Dunbar, Faye, chorus)
      Now It Can Be Told (Ameche)
      Now It Can Be Told (reprise) (Faye)
      This Is the Life (Vernon)
      When the Midnight Choo Choo Leaves for Alabam' (Faye)
      For Your Country and My Country (Douglas)
      In the YMCA (chorus)
      Oh, How I Hate to Get Up in the Morning (Haley, chorus)
      We're On Our Way to France (chorus)
---   Say It with Music (Merman)

A Pretty Girl Is Like A Melody (Merman)
Blue Skies (Merman, Faye)
Pack Up Your Sins and Go to the Devil (Merman)
What'll I Do? (chorus)
My Walking Stick (Merman)
Remember (Faye)
Everybody Step (Merman)
All Alone (Faye)
Marie (orchestra)
Easter Parade (Ameche)
Heat Wave (Merman)
Alexander's Ragtime Band (reprise) (Faye, chorus)
End Titles (orchestra)

Note: The above recording includes spoken dialog.

ALICE IN WONDERLAND (Disney, 1951)

RCA (78rpm) Y-437 mono (LP: LY-1 with 'Treasure Island')

Music: Sammy Fain, others; lyrics: Bob Hilliard, others;
musical direction: Norman Leyden

Cast: (the voices of) Kathryn Beaumont, Jerry Colonna, Sterling
        Holloway, Arnold Stang(not from film), Ed Wynn, others

45-5296 In A World of My Own (Beaumont)
        I'm Late (Stang)
---   The Caucus Race (The Dodo)
45-5297 How Do You Do and Shake Hands (Tweedledee, Tweedledum)
            music: Cy Cohen; lyrics: Oliver Wallace
        The Walrus and the Carpenter (Tweedledee, Tweedledum)
        All in A Golden Afternoon (chorus)
---   The Unbirthday Song (Wynn, Colonna) music: Al Hoffman,
45-5297   Jerry Livingston; lyrics: Mack David
        Very Good Advice (Beaumont)
        'Twas Brillig (Holloway) music: Gene de Paul; lyrics:
            Don Raye
---   Painting the Roses Red (chorus)
45-5296 March of the Cards (orchestra)
        In A World of My Own (reprise) (Beaumont)

Note: The above recording includes spoken dialog and narration.
        Disneyland Records (1208) contains the above songs per-
        formed by a studio cast with Darlene Gillespie as Alice.

ALICE'S ADVENTURES IN WONDERLAND (American National Enterprises,
1972)

Warner Bros BS 2671 (soundtrack) stereo

Music: John Barry; lyrics: Don Black, others; musical direction:

John Barry

Cast: Peter Bull, Michael Crawford, Fiona Fullerton, Robert
        Helpmann, Michael Hordern, Davy Kaye, Spike Milligan,
        Dudley Moore, Flora Robson, Peter Sellers

Songs: Overture (orchestra)
        Curiouser and Curiouser (Fullerton)
        You've Gotta Know When to Stop (Kaye)
        The Royal Procession (orchestra)
        The Last Word Is Mine (Crawford, Fullerton)
        Dum and Dee Dance (Fullerton) lyrics: Lewis Carroll
        The Pun Song (Helpmann, Sellers, Moore)
        I've Never Been This Far Before (orchestra)
---   Curiouser and Curiouser (reprise) (orchestra)
        I've Never Been This Far Before (reprise) (Fullerton)
        Off with Their Heads (Robson)
        The Croquet Game (orchestra)
        Off with Their Heads (reprise) (Robson)
        The Moral Song (Bull)
        Off with Their Heads (reprise) (Robson)
        The Me I Never Knew (orchestra)
        The Lobster Quadrille (orchestra)
        Will You Walk A Little Faster? (Hordern, Milligan)
           lyrics: Lewis Carroll
        They Told Me (Crawford) lyrics: Lewis Carroll
        The Me I Never Knew (reprise) (Fullerton)

ALICE'S RESTAURANT (United Artists, 1969)

United Artists UAS 5195 stereo

Music, lyrics: Arlo Guthrie, others; musical direction: Garry
Sherman

Cast: Arlo Guthrie, Tigger Outlaw (not in film), Al Schackman

Songs: Traveling Music (orchestra)
        Alice's Restaurant Massacee, part I (Guthrie)
        The Let Down (orchestra) music: Garry Sherman
        Songs to Aging Children (Outlaw) music, lyrics: Joni
           Mitchell
        Amazing Grace (chorus) arr: Arlo Guthrie, Garry Sherman
---   Trip to the City (orchestra)
        Alice's Restaurant Massacree, part II (Guthrie)
        Crash Pad Improvs (guitar)
        You're A Fink (Schackman, chorus) music, lyrics: Arlo
           Guthrie, Garry Sherman
        Harps and Marriage (orchestra) music: Garry Sherman

ALL HANDS ON DECK (Twentieth Century-Fox, 1961)

Dot (45/EP) DEP 1098 (soundtrack) stereo

Music, lyrics: Jay Livingston, Ray Evans; musical direction:
Lionel Newman

Cast: Pat Boone

songs: All Hands on Deck (Boone)
       There's No One Like You (Boone)
       I've Got It Made (Boone)
       Somewhere There's Home (Boone)

ALL THAT JAZZ (Twentieth Century Fox / Columbia, 1979)

Casablanca NBLP 7198 (soundtrack) stereo

Music, lyrics for songs: various; musical score, direction:
Ralph Burns

Cast: (the voices of Peter Allen, George Benson), Sandahl
       Bergman, Erzsebet Foldi, Leland Palmer, Ann Reinking,
       Roy Scheider, Ben Vereen

Songs: Main Title (orchestra)
       On Broadway (Benson) music, lyrics: Barry Mann, Cynthia
           Weil, Jerry Leiber, Mike Stoller
       Michelle (orchestra)
       Take Off with Us (Bergman, chorus) music, lyrics:
           Stanley Lebowsky, Fred Tobias
       Concerto in G (bit -orchestra) music: Antonio Vivaldi
       Ponte Vecchio (orchestra)
       Everything Old Is New Again (Allen) music: Peter Allen;
           lyrics: Carole Bayer Sager
---   South Mt Sinai Parade (orchestra)
       After you've Gone (Palmer, chorus) music: Turner Layton;
           lyrics: Henry Creamer
       There'll Be Some Changes Made (Reinking, chorus) music:
           W B Overstreet; lyrics: Billy Higgins
       Who's Sorry Now (chorus) music: Ted Snyder; lyrics:
           Bert Kalmar, Harry Ruby
       Some of These Days (Foldi, chorus) music, lyrics:
           Sheldon Brooks
       Going Home Now (orchestra)
       Bye Bye Love (Vereen, Scheider, chorus) music, lyrics:
           Felice and Boudleaux Bryant

AN AMERICAN IN PARIS (MGM, 1951)

MGM E 93 (soundtrack) mono reissued: MCA 1427

Music: George Gershwin; lyrics: Ira Gershwin; musical direction:
Johnny Green

Cast: Georges Guetary, Gene Kelly

Songs: 's Wonderful (Kelly, Guetary)
        Love Is Here to Stay (Kelly)
        I'll Build A Stairway to Paradise (Guetary)
        I Got Rhythm (Kelly, children)
        An American in Paris Ballet (orchestra)

Note: Additional soundtrack selection, cut from film:

        I've Got A Crush on You (Kelly) LP: Out Takes OTF-2

AN AMERICAN TAIL (Universal, 1986)

MCA 39096 (soundtrack) stereo CD

Music: James Horner, Barry Mann; lyrics: Cynthia Weil; musical
direction: James Horner

Cast: (the voices of) Betsy Cathcart, Dom DeLuise, Phillip
        Glasser, John Guarnieri, Warren Hays, James Ingram,
        Nehemiah Persoff, Christopher Plummer, Linda Ronstadt

Songs: Main Title (orchestra)
       The Cossack Cats (orchestra)
       There Are No Cats in America (Persoff, Guarnieri, Hays)
       The Storm (orchestra)
       Give Me Your Tired, Your Poor (orchestra)
       Never Say Never (Plummer, Glasser)
       The Market Place (orchestra)
       Somewhere Out There (Glasser, Cathcart)
---   Somewhere Out There (reprise) (Ronstadt, Ingram)
       Releasing the Secret Weapon (orchestra)
       A Duo (DeLuise, Glasser)
       The Great Fire (orchestra)
       Reunited (orchestra)
       Flying Away and End Credits (orchestra)

ANCHORS AWEIGH (MGM, 1945)

Curtain Calls 100/17 (soundtrack) mono also: Sandy Hook SH 2024

Music: Jule Styne; lyrics: Sammy Cahn; musical direction: George
Stoll

Cast: Kathryn Grayson, Jose Iturbi (piano), Gene Kelly, Frank
        Sinatra

Songs: Main Title (orchestra)
   We Hate to Leave (Sinatra, Kelly, chorus)
   Lullaby (Sinatra) music: Brahms
   I Begged Her (Sinatra, Kelly)
   If You Knew Susie (Sinatra, Kelly) music: Joseph Meyer;
    lyrics: Buddy DeSylva
   Jealousy (Grayson) music: Jacob Gade; lyrics: Vera Bloom
   What Makes the Sunset (Sinatra)
---   All of A Sudden My Heart Sings (Grayson) music: Herpin;
    lyrics: Harold Rome
   Donkey Serenade (Iturbi, piano) music: Rudolf Friml
   The Worry Song (Kelly) music: Sammy Fain; lyrics: Ralph
    Freed
   The Charm of You (Sinatra)
   I Fall in Love Too Easily (Sinatra)
   Anchors Aweigh - Finale (Sinatra, chorus) music: Alfred
    Miles; lyrics: Charles Zimmerman

Note: Studio recordings by cast members:

MGM (78rpm) 30073 All of A Sudden My Heart Sings (Grayson)
       Jealousy (Grayson)
Columbia (78rpm) 36774 I Begged Her (Sinatra) LP: CL 2913
       What Makes the Sunset (Sinatra) LP: CL 2913
Columbia (78rpm) 36830 I Fall in Love Too Easily (Sinatra) CL 2913
       The Charm of You (Sinatra) LP: CL 2913

AND THE ANGELS SING (Paramount, 1944)

Legends 1000/4 (soundtrack) mono 'Dorothy Lamour'

Music: Jimmy Van Heusen; lyrics: Johnny Burke

Cast: Mimi Chandler, Julie Gibson (for Diana Lynn), Betty Hutton,
   Dorothy Lamour

Songs: Knocking On Your Own Front Door (Chandler, Gibson, Hutton,
    Lamour)
   It Could Happen to You (Lamour)
   For the First Hundred Years (Chandler, Gibson, Hutton,
    Lamour)

Note: Betty Hutton studio recording:

   Capitol (78rpm) 155 His Rocking Horse Ran Away

ANNIE (Columbia, 1982)

Columbia JS 38000 (soundtrack) stereo CD

Music: Charles Strouse; lyrics: Martin Charnin; musical direction:
Ralph Burns

Cast: Carol Burnett, Lois deBanzie, Tim Curry, Albert Finney,
        Toni Ann Gisondi, Edward Herrmann, Geoffrey Holder,
        Lu Leonard, Peter Marshall, Roger Minami, Bernadette
        Peters, Aileen Quinn, Ann Reinking

Songs: Tomorrow (Quinn, girls)
        It's the Hard-Knock Life (Quinn, Gisondi, chorus)
        Maybe (Quinn)
        Dumb Dog (Quinn)
        Sandy (Quinn, girls)
        I Think I'm Gonna Like It Here (Quinn, Reinking)
        Little Girls (Burnett)
        We Got Annie (Reinking, Leonard, Holder, Minami)
---   Let's Go to the Movies (Quinn, Reinking, Finney, chorus)
        Sign (Brunett, Finney)
        You're Never Fully Dressed without A Smile (Marshall,
            chorus)
        Easy Street (Burnett, Curry, Peters)
        Tomorrow (White House Version) (Quinn, Finney, deBanzie,
            Herrmann)
        Maybe (reprise) (Quinn, Finney)
        Finale: I Don't Need Anything But You (Quinn, Finney,
                    chorus)
                We Got Annie (chorus)
                Tomorrow (chorus)

ANNIE GET YOUR GUN (MGM, 1950)

Sound/Stage 2302 (soundtrack) mono also: Sandy Hook SH 2053

Music, lyrics: Irving Berlin; musical direction: Adolph Deutsch

Cast: Howard Keel, Judy Garland, Frank Morgan, Benay Venuta,
        Keenan Wynn

Songs: Colonel Buffalo Bill (Wynn, Venuta, Keel, chorus)
        Doin' What Comes Natur'lly (Garland, children)
        The Girl That I Marry (Keel)
        You Can't Get A Man with A Gun (Garland)
        There's No Business Like Show Business (Wynn, Morgan,
            Keel, Garland)
        They Say It's Wonderful (Keel, Garland)
        They Say It's Wonderful (reprise) (Garland)
---   There's No Business Like Show Business (reprise) (Garland)
        My Defenses Are Down (Keel)
        I'm An Indian Too (Garland, chorus)
        The Girl That I Marry (reprise) (Garland)
        I Got the Sun in the Morning (Garland, chorus)
        Let's Go West Again (Garland, chorus)
        Anything You Can Do (Garland, Keel)
        There's No Business Like Show Business (finale) (Garland,
            Morgan, Keel, Wynn)

Note: The above recording is the soundtrack of an unfinished
        version of this film. MGM Records also issued:

        You Can't Get A Man with A Gun (Garland)
           LP: MGM E 4005P 'The Judy Garland Story, vol 2'

ANNIE GET YOUR GUN (MGM, 1950)

MGM E 509 (soundtrack) mono reissued: MGM 2-SES-42ST

Music, lyrics: Irving Berlin; musical direction: Adolph Deutsch

Cast: Louis Calhern, Betty Hutton, Howard Keel, Keenan Wynn

Songs: I've Got the Sun in the Morning (Hutton, chorus)
        They Say It's Wonderful (Hutton, Keel)
        You Can't Get A Man with A Gun (Hutton)
        My Defenses Are Down (Keel, chorus)
        Doin' What Comes Natur'lly (Hutton, children)
        The Girl That I Marry (Keel)
        Anything You Can Do (Hutton, Keel)
        There's No Business Like Show Business (Hutton, Keel,
           Calhern, Wynn)

Note: The following additional selection was not used in the film:

        Let's Go West Again (Hutton) LP: Out Takes OTF - 2

ANY WHICH WAY YOU CAN (Warner Bros, 1980)

Warner Bros HS 3499 (soundtrack) stereo

Music, lyrics: various; musical direction: Steve Dorff

Cast: Glen Campbell, Ray Charles, Cliff Crofford, Fats Domino,
        Johnny Duncan, John Durrill, Clint Eastwood, David Frizzell,
        Sondra Locke, Jim Stafford, The Texas Opera Company (group),
        Gene Watson, Shelly West

Songs: Beers to You (Charles, Eastwood) music, lyrics: Steve
           Dorff, John Durrill, S Pinkard, Snuff Garrett
        Any Which Way You Can (Campbell) music, lyrics: M Brown,
           Steve Dorff, Snuff Garrett
        You're the Reason God Made Oklahoma (Frizzell, West)
           music, lyrics: L Collins, S Pinkard
        Whiskey Heaven (Domino) music, lyrics: Cliff Crofford,
           John Durrill, Snuff Garrett
        One Too Many Women in Your Life (Locke) music, lyrics:
           John Durrill, P Everly
        Cow Patti (Stafford) music, lyrics: Jim Stafford
---   Acapulco (Duncan) music, lyrics: L Collins, M Leath
        Any Way You Want Me (Watson) music, lyrics: L Ofman

> Cotton-Eyed Clint (The Texas Opera Company) music, lyrics:
>   adapted by Steve Dorff, Snuff Garrett
> Orangutan Hall of Fame (Crofford) music, lyrics: Cliff
>   Crofford, Snuff Garrett
> Too Loose (Locke) music, lyrics: M Brown, Steve Dorff,
>   Snuff Garrett
> The Good Guys and the Bad Guys (Durrill) music, lyrics:
>   John Durrill, Snuff Garrett

ANYTHING GOES (Paramount, 1936)

Decca DL 4251 mono 'Bing's Hollywood - Pennies from Heaven'

Music, lyrics: various; musical direction: Georgie Stoll

Cast: Bing Crosby

Songs: Moonburn (Crosby) music: Hoagy Carmichael; lyrics: Edward
           Heyman
       My Heart and I (Crosby) music: Frederick Hollander;
           lyrics: Leo Robin
       Sailor Beware (Crosby) music: Richard Whiting; lyrics:
           Leo Robin

Note: Additional soundtrack selections on:

Encore Records ST 101 (soundtrack) mono 'Merman in the Movies'

Music, lyrics: Cole Porter, others; musical direction: Victor
Young

Cast: Bing Crosby, Ethel Merman

Songs: You're the Top (Merman, Crosby)
       Shanghi-De-Ho (Merman) music: Frederick Hollander; lyrics:
           Leo Robin
       End Title (Merman, Crosby)

ANYTHING GOES (Paramount, 1956)

Decca DL 8318 (partial soundtrack) mono

Music, lyrics: Cole Porter, others; musical direction: Joseph
Lilley

Cast: Bing Crosby, Mitzi Gaynor, Jeanmaire, Donald O'Connor

Songs: Ya Gotta Give the People Hoke (Crosby, O'Connor) music:
           James Van Heusen; lyrics: Sammy Cahn
       Anything Goes (Gaynor)
       I Get A Kick Out of You (Jeanmaire)
       You're the Top (Crosby, Gaynor)

Dream Ballet (Let's Do It, All Through the Night)
      (orchestra)
---   It's De-Lovely (Gaynor, O'Connor)
      All Through the Night (Crosby)
      A Second Hand Turban and A Crystal Ball (Crosby, O'Connor)
            music: James Van Heusen; lyrics: Sammy Cahn
      You Can Bounch Right Back (O'Connor) music: James Van
            Heusen; lyrics: Sammy Cahn
      Blow Gabriel Blow (Crosby, O'Connor, Gaynor, Jeanmaire)

APRIL IN PARIS (Warner Bros, 1952)

Columbia (45/EP) B 1581 mono

Music: Vernon Duke; lyrics: Sammy Cahn, others; musical direction:
Paul Weston, others

Cast: Doris Day

Songs: April in Paris (Day, chorus) lyrics: E Y Harburg; musical
            direction: Percy Faith
       I'm Gonna Ring the Bell Tonight (Day, chorus)
       I Know A Place (Day)
       That's What Makes Paris Paree (Day, chorus)

APRIL LOVE (Twentieth Century-Fox, 1957)

Dot DLP 9000 (soundtrack) mono

Music: Sammy Fain; lyrics: Paul Francis Webster; musical direction:
Lionel Newman

Cast: Pat Boone, Shirley Jones

Songs: Main Title (orchestra)
       Clover in the Meadow (Boone)
       Tugfire (orchestra)
       Give Me A Gentle Girl (Boone)
       First Meeting (orchestra)
       Give Me A Gentle Girl (reprise) (Jones)
       April Love (Boone)
       Tugfire's Escape (orchestra)
---   April Love (reprise) (Boone, Jones)
       The Sulky Race (orchestra)
       Do It Yourself (Boone, Jones, ensemble)
       Lovers' Quarrel (orchestra)
       Tugfire's Illness (orchestra)
       The Bentonville Fair (Boone, Jones, ensemble)
       Finale: April Love (Boone, ensemble)

THE ARISTOCATS (Disney, 1969)

Disneyland DQ 1333 stereo

Music, lyrics: Richard M Sherman, Robert B Sherman, others;
musical direction: Mike Sammes

Cast: (the voices of) Phil Harris, Robie Lester, Gregory Novack,
        Susan Novack, Victor Sweier

Songs: The Aristocats (chorus)
        Scales and Arpeggios (Lester, S Novack, G Novack, Sweier,
           chorus)
        She Never Felt Alone (Lester)
        Thomas O'Malley Cat (Harris) music, lyrics: Terry Gilkyson
        Ev'rybody Wants to Be A Cat (Harris, chorus) music, lyrics:
           Floyd Huddleston, Al Rinker

Note: Phil Harris is the only film voice used on this recording.

ARTISTS AND MODELS (Paramount, 1955)

Capitol (45/EP) EAP 1-702 mono

Music: Harry Warren; lyrics: Jack Brooks; musical direction:
Dick Stabile

Cast: Dean Martin

Songs: Inamorata (Martin)
        The Lucky Song (Martin)
        You Look So Familiar (Martin)
        When You Pretend (Martin)

AS LONG AS THEY'RE HAPPY (Rank, 1954)

HMV (British) DLPC 1001 mono

Music, lyrics: Sam Coslow; musical direction: Stanley Black

Cast: Jack Buchanan, Jean Carson, Diana Dors, Jerry Wayne

Songs: You Started Something (Wayne)
        I Don't Know Whether to Laugh or to Cry Over You (Wayne)
        Be My Guest (Wayne)
        Liza's Eyes (Wayne)
        Quiet Little Rendezvous (Carson)
        Crazy Little Mixed-Up Heart (Carson)
        Hokey-Pokey Polka (Dors, Buchanan)
        Cry (Buchanan)
        I Don't Know Whether to Laugh or to Cry Over You (reprise)
           (Buchanan)

AT LONG LAST LOVE (Twentieth Century-Fox, 1975)

RCA ABL2-0967 (two records - soundtrack) stereo

Music, lyrics: Cole Porter; musical direction: Lionel Newman

Cast: Eileen Brennan, Duilio Del Prete, John Hillerman, Madeline
        Kahn, Mildred Natwick, Burt Reynolds, Cybill Shepherd

Songs: Overture (orchestra)
        Which (Shepherd, Brennan)
        Poor Young Millionaire (Reynolds, Hillerman)
        You're the Top (Reynolds, Kahn, Del Prete, Shepherd)
---   Find Me A Primitive Man (Kahn)
        Friendship (Kahn, Shepherd, Reynolds, Del Prete)
        But in the Morning, No (Brennan, Hillerman, Reynolds,
          Shepherd)
        At Long Last Love (Del Prete, Kahn, Reynolds, Shepherd)
---   Well, Did You Evah? (Reynolds, Kahn, Shepherd, Del Prete,
          Natwick, chorus)
        From Alpha to Omega (Del Prete, Kahn)
        Let's Misbehave (Shepherd, Reynolds)
        It's De-Lovely (Reynolds, Shepherd)
        But in the Morning, No (reprise) (Hillerman, Brennan)
        It's De-Lovely (reprise) (Shepherd, Reynolds)
        Let's Misbehave (reprise) (Shepherd, Reynolds)
---   Just One of Those Things (Reynolds, Shepherd, Del Prete)
        I Get A Kick Out of You (Shepherd)
        Most Gentlemen Don't Like Love (Brennen, Shepherd, Kahn)
        I Loved Him (But He Didn't Love Me) (Kahn, Shepherd)
        A Picture of Me without You (Reynolds, Shepherd, Kahn,
          Del Prete)
        At Long Last Love (reprise) (orchestra)
        Finale (orchestra)

ATHENA (MGM, 1954)

Mercury MG 25202 (soundtrack) mono

Music, lyrics: Hugh Martin, Ralph Blane; musical direction:
George Stoll

Cast: Vic Damone, Jane Powell, Debbie Reynolds

Songs: Vocalize (Powell)
        The Girl Next Door (Damone)
        I Never Felt Better (Reynolds)
        Love Can Change the Stars (Powell)
---   Love Can Change the Stars (reprise) (Damone)
        Imagine (Reynolds, Damone)
        Venezia (Damone)
        The Daughter of the Regiment: Chancun le Sait (Powell)

        music: Donizetti

ATHENA (MGM, 1954)

Motion Picture Tracks International MPT - 2 (soundtrack) mono

Cast: Louis Calhern, Vic Damone, Jane Powell, Debbie Reynolds

Songs: Overture (orchestra)
       The Girl Next Door (Damone)
       Vocalize (Powell)
       Imagine (Powell, Reynolds)
       Faster than Sound (Damone) cut from film
       Harmonize (Calhern, Powell, Damone, Reynolds, chorus)
       Imagine (reprise) (Damone, Reynolds)
---   Love Can Change the Stars (Reynolds, Powell)
       I Never Felt Better (Reynolds, Powell, chorus)
       The Daughter of the Regiment: Chancun le Sait (Powell)
           music: Donizetti
       Venezia (Damone)
       Love Can Change the Stars (reprise) (Damone)
       Harmonize (reprise) (Powell, Reynolds, Damone, cast)
       End Title (Love Can Change the Stars) (Powell, Reynolds,
           Damone, cast)

BABES IN ARMS (MGM, 1939)

Curtain Calls 100/6 (soundtrack) mono also: Sandy Hook SH 2077

Music: Richard Rodgers, others; lyrics: Lorenz Hart, others;
musical direction: George Stoll

Cast: Judy Garland, Betty Jaynes, Douglas McPhail, Mickey Rooney

Songs: Main Title (orchestra)
       Good Morning (Garland, Rooney) music: Nacio Herb Brown;
           lyrics: Arthur Freed
       I Like Opera / I Like Swing (Garland, Jaynes) music,
           lyrics: Roger Edens
       Babes in Arms (McPhail, Garland, Rooney, chorus)
       Where or When (McPhail, Jaynes, Garland)
---   I Cried for You (Garland) music: Abe Lyman, Gus Arnheim;
           lyrics: Arthur Freed
       Minstrel Show:
           Daddy Was A Minstrel Man (Garland) music, lyrics:
             Roger Edens
           Oh Susannah(Garland, Rooney, chorus) music, lyrics:
             Stephen Foster
           Ida, Sweet As Apple Cider (Rooney) music, lyrics:
             Eddie Leonard
           Moonlight Bay (chorus) music: Percy Wenrich; lyrics:

Edward Madden
I'm Just Wild About Harry (Garland, Rooney, chorus)
music: Eubie Blake; lyrics: Noble Sissle
God's Country (Garland, Rooney, McPhail, Jaynes) music:
Harold Arlen; lyrics: E Y Harburg

Note: The above recording includes spoken dialog. Studio
recordings by Judy Garland:

Decca (78rpm) 2873 Figaro (LP: Stanyan 10095)
Brunswick (British 78rpm) 02969 I'm Just Wild About Harry

BABES IN TOYLAND (Disney, 1961)

Disney 1219 stereo   reissued: Buena Vista 4022

Music: Victor Herbert, arranged by George Bruns; lyrics: Mel
Levin; musical direction: George Bruns

Cast: Annette Funicello, Ray Bolger, Henry Calvin, Ann Jilliann,
Mary McCarty, Tommy Sands, Ed Wynn

Songs: Babes in Toyland Overture (orchestra) arranged: Camarata
Mother Goose Village and Lemonade (chorus)
We Won't Be Happy Till We Get It (Bolger, Calvin)
Just A Whisper away (Sands, Funicello)
Slowly He Sank to the Bottom of the Sea (Calvin)
Castle in Spain (Dolger)
Never Mind Bo Peep (Jilliann, Funicello, McCarty, chorus)
I Can't Do the Sum (Funicello)
---   Floretta (Sands, chorus)
Forest of No Return (chorus)
Go to Sleep (Sands, Funicello)
Toyland (children's chorus)
Workshop Song (Wynn, children)
Just A Toy (Sands, Funicello)
March of the Toys (orchestra)
Tom and Mary (chorus)

BABES ON BROADWAY (MGM, 1941)

Curtain Calls 100/7 (soundtrack) mono

Music, lyrics: various; musical direction: George Stoll

Cast: Judy Garland, Ray MacDonald, Richard Quine, Annie Rooney,
Mickey Rooney, Virginia Weidler

Songs: Main Title (orchestra) introduction by Alexander Woolcott
Anything Can Happen in New York (M Rooney, MacDonald,

           Quine) music: Burton Lane; lyrics: E Y Harburg
       How About You (Garland, M Rooney) music: Burton Lane;
           lyrics: Ralph Freed
       Hoe Down (Garland, M Rooney, chorus) music: Roger Edens;
           lyrics: Ralph Freed
       Chin Up, Cheerio, Carry On (Garland, chorus) music:
           Burton Lane; lyrics: E Y Harburg
---   Star Medley:
           Mary's A Grand Old Name (Garland, chorus) music,
               lyrics: George M Cohan
           She Is Ma Daisy (M Rooney) music, lyrics: Harry Lauder
           Rings On My Fingers (Garland, chorus) music: Maurice
               Scott; lyrics: F J Barnes, R P Weston
           Sarah Bernhardt Impression (Garland) spoken
           I'm A Yankee Doodle Dandy (M Rooney, Garland, chorus)
               music, lyrics: George M Cohan
           Bombshell from Brazil (Garland, chorus) music, lyrics:
               Roger Edens
           Mama Yo Quiero (M Rooney, chorus) music, lyrics: Al
               Stillman, Jararaca and Vincente Paiva
           Blackout Over Broadway (Garland, M Rooney, cast)
       Minstrel Medley:
           By the Light of the Silvery Moon (chorus) music: Gus
               Edwards; lyrics: Edward Madden
           F D R Jones (Garland, chorus) music, lyrics: Harold Rome
           Ring, Ring the Banjo (chorus) music, lyrics: Stephen
               Foster
           The Old Folks at Home (banjo solo) music: Stephen Foster
           Alabama Bound (banjo solo) music: Ray Henderson
           Waitin' for the Robert E Lee (Garland, M Rooney,
               chorus) music: Lewis F Muir; lyrics: F Wolfe Gilbert
       Babes on Broadway (Garland, M Rooney, Weidler, MacDonald,
           Quine, A Rooney, chorus) music: Burton Lane; lyrics:
           Ralph Freed

Note: The above recording includes spoken dialog. Studio
       recordings by Judy Garland:

       Decca (78rpm) 4072 How About You (LP: MCA 4046)
       Decca (78rpm) 4199 F D R Jones (LP: MCA 4003)

BACK TO THE BEACH (Paramount, 1987)

Columbia SC 40892 (soundtrack) stereo CD

Music, lyrics: various

CAst: Frankie Avalon, Pato Banton, Dave Edmunds, Fishbone,
       Annette Funicello, Pee-Wee Herman, Marti Jones, Almee
       Mann, Eddie Money, Private Domain

Songs: Catch A Ride (Money) music, lyrics: David Kahne
      Pipeline (instrumental) music, lyrics: B Spickard, B Carmen
      Sign of Love (Mann) music, lyrics: Mark Goldenberg, J Condos
      Absolute Perfection (Private Domain, Banton) music,
        lyrics: Jack Butler, Paul Shaffer
      Surfin' Bird (Herman) music, lyrics: A Frazier, C White,
        J Harris, T Wilson, Jr
---   Sun, Sun, Sun, Sun, Sun (Jones) music, lyrics: David Kahne
      Jamaica Ska (Funicello, Fishbone) music, lyrics: B Lee
      Wipe Out (instrumental) music, lyrics: R Berryhill, P
        Connolly, J Fuller, R Wilson
      California Sun (Avalon) music, lyrics: H Glover, M Levy
      Wooly Bully (Edmunds, chorus) music, lyrics: D Samodio

LA BAMBA (Columbia, 1987)

Slash / Warner Bros 1-25605 (soundtrack) stereo   CD

Music, lyrics: Richie Valens, others

Cast: Marshall Crenshaw, Bo Diddley (not in film), David
      Hidalgo (for Lou Diamond Phillips), Howard Huntsberry,
      Los Lobos, Brian Setzer

Songs: La Bamba (Hidalgo, Los Lobos) arr: Valens
      Come On, Let's Go (Hidalgo, Los Lobos)
      Ooh! My Head (Hidalgo, Los Lobos)
      We Belong Together (Hidalgo, Los Lobos) music, lyrics:
        S Weiss, Robert Carr, Johnny Mitchell
      Framed (Hidalgo, Los Lobos) music, lyrics: Jerry Leiber,
        Mike Stoller
      Donna (Hidalgo, Los Lobos)
---   Lonely Teardrops (Huntsberry, chorus) music, lyrics:
        Berry Gordy, Jr, Tyran Carlo, Gwen Gordy
      Crying, Waiting, Hoping (Crenshaw) music, lyrics: Buddy
        Holly
      Summertime Blues (Setzer) music, lyrics: Eddie Cochran,
        Jerry Capehart
      Who Do You Love (Diddley) music, lyrics: Ellas McDaniel
      Charlena (Los Lobos) music, lyrics: M G Chavez
      Goodnight My Love (Hidalgo, Los Lobos) music, lyrics:
        George Motola, John Marascalco

BAMBI (Disney, 1942)

Disneyland DQ 1203 (soundtrack) mono   CD

Music: Frank Churchill, Ed Plumb; lyrics: Larry Morey; musical
direction: Alexander Steinert

Cast: Unidentified

Songs: Main Title (orchestra)
      Little April Shower (chorus)
      Gallop of the Stags (orchestra)
      Love Is A Song (tenor, chorus)
---   Wintry Winds (orchestra)
      Let's Sing A Gay Little Spring Song (chorus)
      I Bring You A Song (baritone, chorus)
      Finale (orchestra)

THE BAND WAGON (MGM, 1953)

MGM E 3051 (soundtrack) mono reissued: MCA 25015 CD

Music: Arthur Schwartz; lyrics: Howard Dietz; musical direction:
Adolph Deutsch

Cast: India Adams (for Cyd Charisse), Fred Astaire, Jack
      Buchanan, Nanette Fabray, Oscar Levant

Songs: A Shine On Your Shoes (Astaire)
      By Myself (Astaire)
      Dancing in the Dark (orchestra)
      Triplets (Astaire, Fabray, Buchanan)
      New Sun in the Sky (Adams)
      I Guess I'll Have to Change my Plan (Astaire, Buchanan)
      Louisiana Hayride (Fabray, chorus)
---   I Love Louisa (Astaire, chorus)
      That's Entertainment (Astaire, Fabray, Buchanan, Adams,
        Levant, chorus)
      The Girl Hunt Ballet (Astaire) spoken (musical adaption:
        Roger Edens; narration written by Alan Jay Lerner)

Note: The following selections were not used in the film, but
      released on other albums:

Out Takes OTF - 1 Gotta Bran' New Suit (Fabray, Astaire)
              You Have Everything (orchestra)
Out Takes OTF - 2 Sweet Music to Worry the Wolf Away (Fabray,
                              Levant)

THE BARKLEYS OF BROADWAY (MGM, 1949)

MGM L-8 (78 rpm - soundtrack) mono reissued: MGM 2-SES-51 ST

Music: Harry Warren; lyrics: Ira Gershwin; musical direction:
Lennie Hayton

Cast: Fred Astaire, Ginger Rogers

MGM (78rpm) 50016 You'd Be Hard to Replace (Astaire)
              My One and Only Highland Fling (Astaire, Rogers)
MGM (78rpm) 50017 Shoes with Wings On (Astaire)

They Can't Take That Away from Me (Astaire) music:
George Gershwin; lyrics: Ira Gershwin

THE BARKLEYS OF BROADWAY (MGM, 1949)

Sountrak STK -116 (soundtrack) mono

Cast: Fred Astaire, Oscar Levant, Ginger Rogers

Songs: Overture (Swing Trot) (chorus)
       Sabre Dance (Levant, piano) music: Khatchaturian
       You'd Be Hard to Replace (Astaire)
       Bouncin' the Blues (orchestra)
       My One and Only Highland Fling (Astaire, Rogers)
       A Weekend in the Country (Astaire, Rogers, Levant)
       Shoes with Wings On (Astaire)
---   Piano Concerto (Levant, piano) music: Tchaikovsky
       They Can't Take That Away from Me (Astaire)
       Sarah Bernhardt Audition (Rogers) spoken
       Manhattan Downbeat (Astaire, chorus)
       Finale (orchestra)

Note: The above recording includes spoken dialog.

BEACH BLANKET BINGO (American International, 1965)

Capitol T 2323 stereo

Music, lyrics: Guy Hemrick, Jerry Styner, others

Cast: Donna Loren

Songs: Cycle Set (Loren) music, lyrics: Gary Usher, Roger
          Christian
       I Think, You Think (Loren)
       It Only Hurts When I Cry (Loren)
       These Are the Good Times (Loren)
       I'll Never Change Him (Loren)
---   Fly Boy (Loren)
       New Love (Loren)
       I Am My Ideal (Loren)
       Beach Blanket Bingo (Loren)
       Freeway (orchestra) music: Mike Curb

BEACH PARTY (American International, 1963)

Vista BV 3316 stereo

Music, lyrics: various

Cast: Annette Funicello

Songs: Beach Party (Funicello, chorus) music, lyrics: Gary Usher,
            Roger Christian
        Treat Him Nicely (Funicello) music, lyrics: Guy Hemrick,
            Jerry Styner
        Don't Stop Now (Funicello, chorus) music, lyrics: Robert
            Marcucci, Russell Faith
        Promise Me Anything (Funicello, chorus) music, lyrics:
            Guy Hemrick, Jerry Styner
        Secret Surfin' Spot (Funicello, chorus) music, lyrics:
            Gary Usher, Roger Christian
        Song of the Islands (Funicello, chorus) music, lyrics:
            Charles E King (not from film)
---   California Sun (Funicello) music, lyrics: M Glover
            (not from film)
        The Battle of San Orofre (Funicello, chorus) music,
            lyrics: Zino, Crawford (not from film)
        Swingin' and Surfin' (Funicello) music, lyrics: Gary
            Usher, Roger Christian
        (Every Night Is) Date Night in Hawaii (Funicello, chorus)
            music, lyrics: The Sherman Brothers (not from film)
        Surfin' Luau (Cha-Cha-Cha) (Funicello, chorus) music,
            lyrics: The Sherman Brothers (not from film)
        Pineapple Princess (Funicello, chorus) music, lyrics:
            The Sherman Brothers (not from film)

BEAU JAMES (Paramount, 1957)

Imperial 9041 (soundtrack) mono

Music, lyrics: various; musical direction: Joseph J Lilley

Cast: Jimmy Durante, Bob Hope, Imogene Lynn (for Vera Miles)

Songs: Manhattan (orchestra) music: Richard Rodgers
        Will You Love Me in December As You Do in May (orchestra)
            music: Ernest R Ball (narration: Hope, Walter Winchell)
        Will You Love Me in December As You Do in May (reprise)
            (Hope) music: Ernest R Ball; lyrics: James J Walker
        Manhattan (reprise) (Lynn) music: Richard Rodgers;
            lyrics: Lorenz Hart
        Manhattan (reprise) (Lynn, Hope)
        Someone to Watch Over Me (Lynn) music: George Gershwin;
            lyrics: Ira Gershwin
        Will You Love Me in December...(reprise) (Hope)
---   When We're Alone (Penthouse Serenade) (Lynn, chorus)
            music, lyrics: Will Jason, Val Burton
        His Honor, the Mayor of New York (Durante) music: Joseph
            J Lilley; lyrics: Sammy Cahn
        Sidewalks of New York (Hope, Durante, chorus) music:
            Charles B Lawlor; lyrics: James W Blake
        Tammany Parade March (orchestra)

Manhattan - End Title (orchestra) narration: Walter Winchell

BECAUSE YOU'RE MINE (MGM, 1952)

RCA LM 7015 mono

Music, lyrics: various; musical direction: Constantine Callincos

Cast: Mario Lanza

Songs: Cavalleria Rusticana: Addio Alla madre (Lanza) music:
       Pietro Mascagni
       Granada (Lanza) music: Augustin Lara
       Mamma mia che vo' sape? (Lanza) music: Emanuelle Nutile
       The Lord's Prayer (Lanza, choir) music: Alfred Hay
       Malotte; musical direction: Ray Sinatra
---   Because You're Mine (Lanza) music: Nicholas Brodszky;
       lyrics: Sammy Cahn
       The Song Angels Sing (Lanza) music: Irving Aaronson;
       lyrics: Paul Francis Webster
       You Do Something to Me (Lanza) music, lyrics: Cole Porter
       Lee-Ah-Loo (Lanza) music: Ray Sinatra; lyrics: John
       Lehmann

BEDKNOBS AND BROOMSTICKS (Disney, 1971)

Buena Vista STER 5003 (soundtrack) stereo

Music, lyrics: Richard M Sherman, Robert B Sherman; musical
direction: Irwin Kostel

Cast: Angela Lansbury, David Tomlinson

Songs: Overture (chorus)
       The Old Home Guard (chorus)
       The Age of Not Believing (Lansbury)
       With A Flair (Tomlinson)
       A Step in the Right Direction (Lansbury)
       Eglantine (Tomlinson)
       Don't Let Me Down (Lansbury)
       Eglantine (reprise) (Tomlinson, Lansbury)
---   Portobello Road (Tomlinson, children, chorus)
       Portobello Street Dance (Tomlinson)
       The Beautiful Briny (Tomlinson, Lansbury, children)
       Substitutiary Locomotion (Tomlinson, Lansbury, children)
       Eglantine (reprise) (Lansbury)
       Portobello Road (reprise) (Tomlinson)
       Finale (chorus)

THE BELLE OF NEW YORK - see page 359

BELLE OF THE NINTIES (Paramount, 1934)

Rosetta RR 1315 (soundtrack) mono 'Mae West'

Music, lyrics: various; musical direction: Duke Ellington

Cast: Duke Ellington Orchestra, Mae West

Songs: Memphis Blues (West, Ellington Orchestra) music: W C
           Handy; lyrics: George A Norton
       My Old Flame (West, Ellington Orchestra) music: Arthur
           Johnston; lyrics: Sam Coslow
       St Louis Woman (West, Ellington Orchestra) music:
           Arthur Johnston; lyrics: Sam Coslow

Note: Additional (soundtrack ?) recording:

Cosmopolitan (78rpm) 7501 My Old Flame (West, Ellington Orchestra)

BELLS ARE RINGING (MGM, 1960)

Capitol SW 1435 (soundtrack) stereo

Music: Jule Styne; lyrics: Betty Comden, Adolph Green; musical
direction: Andre Previn

Cast: Eddie Foy, Jr, Judy Holliday, Hal Linden, Dean Martin

Songs: Overture / Bells Are Ringing (orchestra / chorus)
           It's A Perfect Relationship (Holliday)
           Do It Yourself (Martin)
           It's A Simple Little System (Foy, chorus)
           Better Than A Dream (Holliday, Martin)
           I Met A Girl (Martin, chorus)
---   Just in Time (Martin, Holliday, chorus)
           Drop That Name (Holliday, chorus)
           The Party's Over (Holliday, chorus)
           The Midas Touch (Linden, girls)
           I'm Going Back (Holliday)
           Finale (chorus)

Note: Additional soundtrack selections cut from film:

        Is It A Crime? (Holliday) LP: Out Takes OTF - 1
        My Guiding Star (Martin) SPO (45rpm) 145 B

THE BELLS OF ST MARY'S (RKO, 1945)

Decca DL 4258 mono 'Bing's Hollywood - Accentuate the Positive'

Music, lyrics: various; musical direction: John Scott Trotter

Cast: Bing Crosby

Songs: The Bells of St Mary's (Crosby) music: A Emmett Adams;
       lyrics: Douglas Furber
       Adeste Fideles (Crosby, chorus) anon
       Aren't You Glad You're You? (Crosby) music: James Van
       Heusen; lyrics: John Burke
       In the Land of Beginning Again (Crosby) music: George
       W Meyer; lyrics: Grant Clarke

THE BEST LITTLE WHOREHOUSE IN TEXAS (Universal / RKO, 1982)

MCA 6112 (soundtrack) stereo CD

Music, lyrics: Carol Hall, others; musical direction: Gregg Perry

Cast: Dom DeLuise, Charles Durning, Teresa Merritt, Jim Nabors,
      Dolly Parton, Burt Reynolds

Songs: 20 Fans (Nabors, chorus)
       A Lil' Ole Bitty Pissant Country Place (Parton, Merritt,
       girls, customers)
       Sneakin' Around (Parton, Reynolds) music, lyrics: Dolly
       Parton
       Watchdog Report (chorus)
       Texas Has A Whorehouse in It (DeLuise, chorus)
       Courtyard Shag (orchestra)
---   The Aggie Song (chorus)
       The Sidestep (Durning)
       Hard Candy Christmas (Parton, girls)
       I Will Always Love You (Parton) music, lyrics: Dolly Parton

THE BEST THINGS IN LIFE ARE FREE (Twentieth Century-Fox, 1956)

Capitol T 765 mono

Music: Ray Henderson; lyrics: B G De Sylva, Lew Brown; musical
direction: Van Alexander

Cast: Gordon MacRae

Songs: The Best Things in Life Are Free (MacRae, chorus)
       Black Bottom (chorus)
       Button Up Your Overcoat (MacRae, chorus)
       It All Depends on You (MacRae)
       Sonny Boy (MacRae, chorus) additional lyrics: Al Jolson
       Just A Memory (MacRae, chorus)
       One More Time (MacRae)
---   The Birth of the Blues (MacRae)
       Together (MacRae, chorus)
       You Try Somebody Else (MacRae, chorus)
       Without Love (MacRae, chorus)

You're the Cream of My Coffee (MacRae)
The Best Things in Life Are Free (reprise) (MacRae, chorus)

THE BIG BEAT (Universal, 1958)

RCA (45/EP) EPA 4185 mono

Music: Irving Fields, others; lyrics: Bernard Gasso, others

Cast: Gogi Grant

Songs: Lazy Love (Grant)
       Call Me (Grant)
       You've Never Been in Love (Grant) music, lyrics: Jack
          Lloyd, Alan Copeland
       I Waited So Long (Grant) music, lyrics: Jay Livingston,
          Ray Evans

BIG BOY (Warner Bros, 1930)

A-Jay 3749 (soundtrack) mono 'Al Jolson - The Vitaphone Years'

Music: Sammy Stept, others; lyrics: Bud Green, others

Cast: Al Jolson

Songs: Liza Lee (Jolson)
       Hooray for Baby and Me (Jolson) music, lyrics: Sidney D
          Mitchell, Archie Gottler, George W Meyer
       Tomorrow Is Another Day (Finale) (Jolson, chorus)

THE BIG BROADCAST (Paramount, 1932)

Sountrak ST 101 (soundtrack) mono also: Sandy Hook SH 2007

Music: Ralph Rainger, others; lyrics: Leo Robin, others

Cast: Gracie Allen, The Boswell Sisters, George Burns, Cab
       Calloway, Bing Crosby, Vincent Lopez Orchestra, The Mills
       Brothers, Donald Novis, Kate Smith, Arthur Tracy

Songs: Overture (montage of film cast: The Boswell Sisters, Cab
          Calloway, The Mills Brothers, Arthur Tracy, George
          Burns, Gracie Allen)
       Dinah (Crosby) music: Harry Akst; lyrics: Sam M Lewis,
          Joe Young
       Take A Letter (Burns, Allen) spoken
       Where's Bing Crosby? (chorus)
       Here Lies Love (Crosby)
       Money Making Brother (Burns, Allen) spoken
       Please (Crosby, Eddie Lang on guitar)

Tiger Rag (The Mills Brothers) music, lyrics: B J LaRocca
--- I'm the Drummer (chorus, Vincent Lopez Orchestra)
Trees (Novis) music: Oscar Rasbach; lyrics: Joyce Kilmer
Crazy People (The Boswell Sisters) music: Jimmy Monaco;
    lyrics: Edgar Leslie
It Was So Beautiful (intro: When the Moon Comes Over the
    Mountain) (Smith) music: Harry Barris; lyrics: Arthur
    Freed
Minnie the Moocher (Calloway, chorus) music, lyrics: Cab
    Calloway, Barney Bigard, Irving Mills
Please (reprise) (Crosby)
End Credits (orchestra)

Note: Studio recordings by cast members:

Brunswick (78rpm) 6240 Dinah (Crosby, The Mills Brothers)
Brunswick (78rpm) 6394 Please (Crosby)
Brunswick (78rpm) 6406 Here Lies Love (Crosby)
  (three above on LP: Columbia C2L 43 'Bing Crosby in Hollywood')
Brunswick (78rpm) 6216 Marta (Tracy)
Brunswick (78rpm) 6847 Crazy People (The Boswell Sisters)

THE BIG BROADCAST OF 1938 (Paramount, 1938)

Radiola 2MR 1718 (soundtrack) mono 'Hollywood Is on the Air'

Music: Ralph Rainger; lyrics: Leo Robin; musical direction:
Boris Morros

Cast: Shep Fields Orchestra, W C Fields, Bob Hope, Shirley Ross

Songs: This Little Ripple Has Rhythm (Shep Fields Orchestra)
        Thanks for the Memory (Hope, Ross)
        Comedy Routine (W C Fields, Hope) spoken (not from film)

Note: The above recording includes a narration for radio spoken
        by Bob Hope. Additional recordings by cast members:

Brunswick (78rpm) 8017 You Took the Words Right Out of My Heart
                       (Dorothy Lamour) LP: West Coast 14002
Bluebird (78rpm) 7318 Thanks for the Memory (Fields Orchestra)
                       Mama, That Moon Is Here Again (Fields
                       Orchestra)
Decca (78rpm) 2219 Thanks for the Memory (Hope, Ross) LP: Decca 7-1

BIG CITY (MGM, 1948)

MGM (78rpm) 23 mono

Music, lyrics: various

Cast: Betty Garrett, Frankie Lester (not in film), Art Lund
        (not in film), Kate Smith (not in film)

MGM (78rpm) 30100 Ok'l Baby Dok'l (Garrett) music: Sidney Miller;
                  lyrics: Inez James
                  Don't Blame Me (Garrett) music: Jimmy McHugh;
                  lyrics: Dorothy Fields
MGM (78rpm) 30101 What'll I Do? (Lund) music, lyrics: Irving
                  Berlin
                  God Bless America (Smith) music, lyrics:
                  Irving Berlin
MGM (78rpm) 30102 I'm Gonna See A Lot of You (Garrett) music:
                  Fred Spielman; lyrics: Janice Torre
                  Don't Blame Me (Lester) music: Jimmy McHugh;
                  lyrics: Dorothy Fields

BIG CITY (MGM, 1948)

RCA (78rpm) MO 226 mono

Musical direction: Robert Armbruster

Cast: Lotte Lehman

Songs: Lullaby (Lehman) music: Brahms
        Traumere (Lehman) music: Schumann
        God Bless America (Lehman, chorus) music, lyrics:
           Irving Berlin
        The Kerry Dance (Lehman) music, lyrics: J L Molloy

BILLY ROSE'S JUMBO (MGM, 1962)

Columbia OS 2260 (soundtrack) stereo

Music: Richard Rodgers, others; lyrics: Lorenz Hart, others;
musical direction: George Stoll

Cast: Doris Day, Jimmy Durante, James Joyce (for Stephen Boyd),
        Martha Raye

Songs: The Circus on Parade (Day, Raye, Durante)
        Over and Over Again (Day, chorus)
        Why Can't I? (Day, Raye)
        This Can't Be Love (Day)
---   The Most Beautiful Girl in the World (Joyce)
        My Romance (Day)
        The Most Beautiful Girl in the World (reprise) (Durante)
        Little Girl Blue (Day)
        Sawdust, Spangles and Dreams (Day, Joyce, Raye, Durante,
           chorus) music, lyrics: Roger Edens

BIRTH OF THE BLUES (Paramount, 1941)

Decca DL 4255 mono 'Bing's Hollywood - Only Forever'

Music, lyrics: Various; musical direction: John Scott Trotter

Cast: Bing Crosby, Mary Martin, Jack Teagarden

Songs: The Birth of the Blues (Crosby) music: Ray Henderson;
          lyrics: B G DeSylva, Lew Brown; musical direction:
          Jack Teagarden
       Wait Till the Sun Shines, Nellie (Crosby, Martin) music:
          Harry Von Tilzer; lyrics: Andrew B Sterling
       My Melancoly Baby (Crosby) music: Ernie Burnett; lyrics:
          George A Norton
       The Waiter and the Porter and the Upstairs Maid (Crosby,
          Martin, Teagarden) music, lyrics: Johnny Mercer;
          musical direction: Jack Teagarden

BLACK ORPHEUS (Orfeu Negro) (Lopert, 1959) Brazil

Fontana SRF 67520 (soundtrack) stereo (re-processed)

Music, lyrics: Luiz Bonfa, Antonio Carlos Jobim

Cast: Marpessa Dawn, Breno Mello

Songs: Generique (street sounds) trad
       Felicidade (male vocal)
       Frevo (street sounds)
       O Nosso Amor (chorus, carnival bands)
       O Nosso Amor (reprise) (tambourine, accordion)
       Manha de Carnaval (Mello)
       Scene du Lever du Soleil (guitar)
       Manha de Carnaval (reprise) (guitar)
---   Scenes de la Macumba (street sounds) trad
       O Nosso Amor (reprise) (street sounds)
       Manha de Carnaval (reprise) (Dawn)
       Samba de Orfeu (chorus, guitar)
       Batterie de Cappella (drums, flute) trad

BLAZING SADDLES (Warner Bros, 1974)

Asylum 5E-501 (soundtrack) stereo 'High Anxiety'

Music, lyrics: Mel Brooks, others; musical direction: John Morris

Cast: Madeline Kahn, (the voice of) Frankie Laine

Songs: Blazing Saddles (Laine, chorus) music: John Morris
       The French Mistake (men)
       I'm Tired (Kahn, men)

BLOOD AND SAND (Twentieth Century-Fox, 1941)

Decca DL 5380 mono   reissued: Varese STV 81117

Music, lyrics, musical direction: Vincente Gomez

Cast: Graciela Parraga (for Rita Hayworth)

Songs: Sangre Y Arena (Parraga)
        Verde Luna (Green Moon) (Parraga)
        Chi Qui Chi (Parraga)
---   Romance de Amor (Parraga)
        Torero (Parraga)
        Pirate (Parraga, chorus)

THE BLUE ANGEL (Paramount / UFA, 1930) Germany

HMV (45/EP) 7EG 8257 mono

Music, lyrics: Frederick Hollander (English translations by
Sammy Lerner); musical direction: Frederick Hollander

Cast: Marlene Dietrich

Songs: Falling in Love Again (Dietrich)
        Blonde Women (Dietrich)
        This Evening, Children (Dietrich)
        Lola (Dietrich)

Note: These four English language recordings have also been
        available on the British LP: Regal EMI 1078. The German
        language versions have been available on the German LP:
        Historia H 607, with the following titles:

        Ich bin von Kopf bis Fuss auf Liebe eingestellt
        Nimm dich in acht vor blonden Frauen
        Kinder, heut' Abend such' ich mir was aus
        Ich bin die fesche Lola

THE BLUE ANGEL (Twentieth Century-Fox, 1959)

Fox (45 rpm) 163 (soundtrack) stereo

Music, lyrics: various; musical direction: Lionel Newman

Cast: May Britt

Songs: Lola-Lola (Britt, girls) music, lyrics: Ray Evans, Jerry
            Livingston
        Falling in Love Again (Britt) music: Frederick Hollander;
            lyrics: Sammy Lerner

BLUE HAWAII (Paramount, 1961)

RCA LSP 2426 (soundtrack) stereo reissued: AYL 1-3683 CD

Music: Roy C Bennett, others; lyrics: Sid Tepper, others

Cast: Elvis Presley

Songs: Blue Hawaii (Presley) music: Ralph Rainger; lyrics: Leo
          Robin
       Almost Always True (Presley) music: Ben Weisman; lyrics:
          Fred Wise
       Aloha Oe (Presley) music, lyrics: Queen Liliuokalani
       No More (Presley) music: Hal Blair; lyrics: Don Robertson
       Can't Help Falling in Love (Presley) music, lyrics:
          Hugh Peretti, Luigi Creatore, George David Weiss
       Rock-A-Hula Baby (Presley) music: Ben Weisman; lyrics:
          Fred Wise, Dolores Fuller
       Moonlight Swim (Presley) music: Ben Weisman; lyrics:
          Sylvia Dee
---   Ku-u-i-po (Presley) music, lyrics: Hugh Peretti, Luigi
          Creatore, George David Weiss
       Ito Eats (Presley)
       Slicin' Sand (Presley)
       Hawaiian Sunset (Presley)
       Beach Boy Blues (Presley)
       Island of Love (Presley)
       Hawaiian Wedding Song (Presley) music, lyrics: Charles E
          King

BLUE SKIES (Paramount, 1946)

Decca DL 4259 mono 'Bing's Hollywood - Blue Skies'

Music, lyrics: Irving Berlin; musical direction: John Scott Trotter

Cast: Fred Astaire, Bing Crosby, Trudy Erwin (not in film)

Songs: Blue Skies (Crosby, chorus)
       All By Myself (Crosby)
       A Couple of Song and Dance Men (Astaire, Crosby)
       I've Got My Captain Working for Me Now (Crosby)
       I'll See You in C-U-B-A (Crosby, Erwin)
       Getting Nowhere (Crosby, quartet)
---   Everybody Step (Crosby)
       You Keep Coming Back Like A Song (Crosby, quartet)
       A Serenade to An Old Fashioned Girl (Crosby, chorus)

Note: An additional studio recording:

       Puttin' on the Ritz (Astaire) LP: Vocalion VL 3716

BLUE SKIES (Paramount, 1946)

Sountrak STK - 104 (soundtrack) mono

Musical direction: Robert Emmett Dolan

Cast: Fred Astaire, Joan Caulfield, Bing Crosby, Billy DeWolfe,
       Olga San Juan

Songs: Everybody Step (Crosby)
       A Couple of Song and Dance Men (Astaire, Crosby)
       I've Got My Captain Working for Me Now (Crosby, DeWolfe)
       Getting Nowhere (Crosby)
       Say It Isn't So (Crosby)
       I'll See You in C-U-B-A (Crosby, San Juan)
       You'd Be Suprised (San Juan)
       Puttin' on the Ritz (Astaire)
---   Heat Wave (San Juan, chorus)
       Blue Skies (Crosby)
       You Keep Coming Back Like A Song (Crosby)
       What'll I Do? (Crosby, chorus)
       All Alone (Crosby, chorus)
       Remember (Crosby, chorus)
       I'm Putting All My Eggs in One Basket (Crosby)
       Cheek to Cheek (Crosby)
       All By Myself (Crosby, Caulfield)
       Any Bonds Today (Crosby)
       This Is the Army (Crosby)
       White Christmas (Crosby)
       God Bless America (Crosby)
       A Serenade to An Old Fashioned Girl (Caulfield, chorus)
       The Little Things in Life (Crosby)
       Not for All the Rice in China (Crosby)
       Russian Lullaby (Crosby)
       You Keep Coming Back Like A Song (Crosby, Caulfield, chorus)

THE BLUES BROTHERS (Universal, 1980)

Atlantic SD 16017 (soundtrack) stereo   CD

Music, lyrics: various; musical direction: Ira Newborn

Cast: Dan Aykroyd, John Belushi, James Brown, Cab Calloway,
       Ray Charles, Aretha Franklin

Songs: She Caught the Katy (Belushi) music, lyrics: Taj Mahal,
          Yank Rachel
       Peter Gunn Theme (orchestra) music: Henry Mancini
       Gimme Some Lovin' (Belushi, chorus) music, lyrics: Steve
          Winwood, Muff Winwood, Spencer Davis

Shake A Tail Feather (Charles, Belushi, Aykroyd) music,
lyrics: Otis Hayes, Andre Williams, Verlie Rice
Everybody Needs Somebody to Love (Belushi, Aykroyd, girls)
music, lyrics: Jerry Wexler, Bert Berns, Solomon Burke
The Old Landmark (Brown, choir) music, lyrics: A M Brunner
--- Think (Franklin, girls) music, lyrics: Ted White, Aretha
Franklin
Theme from Rawhide (Belushi, Aykroyd, chorus) music:
Dimitri Tiomkin; lyrics: Ned Washington
Minnie the Moocher (Calloway, chorus) music, lyrics: Cab
Calloway, Barney Bigard, Irving Mills
Sweet Home Chicago (Belushi, Aykroyd) music, lyrics:
Woody Payne
Jailhouse Rock (Belushi) music, lyrics: Jerry Leiber, Mike
Stoller

BOMBAY TALKIE (Merchant Ivory, 1970) India

EMI Odeon (India) MOCE 4006 (soundtrack) mono

Music: Shankar Jaikishan; lyrics: Usha Iyer, others

Cast: (the voice of) Asha Bhosie, Usha Iyer, (the voice of)
Kishore Kumar, (the voice of) Mohd. Rafi

Songs: Main Titles / Bombay Talkie Theme (orchestra, chorus)
Tum Mere Pyar Ki Duniyamen (Rafi) lyrics: Hasrat Jaipuri
Theme and Variations (orchestra):
Incidental Music
Devotion
Rajput Suite
Now I Shall Call You 'Ma'
More Incidental Music
Hari Om Tat Sat (Iyer, chorus) disc version
--- Hari Om Tat Sat (Iyer, chorus)
Theme and Variations (orchestra):
Picnic in the Cave
Birthday Party I
Typewriter Tip, Tip, Tip (Kumar, Bhosie) lyrics: Hasrat
Jaipuri
Theme and Variations (orchestra):
Meeting
Birthday Party II
Good Times, Bad Times (Iyer)

BORN TO DANCE (MGM, 1936)

Classic International Filmusicals C I F 3001 (soundtrack) mono
also: Sandy Hook SH 2088

32 Discography

Music, lyrics: Cole Porter; musical direction: Alfred Newman

Cast: Virginia Bruce, Buddy Ebsen, Frances Langford, Una Merkel,
       Eleanor Powell, Sid Silvers, James Stewart, Raymond Walburn

Songs: Title Music (orchestra)
        Rolling Home (Stewart, Ebsen, Silvers, male quartet, chorus)
        Rap-Tap on Wood (Powell, male quartet)
        Hey, Babe, Hey (Stewart, Powell, Merkel, Langford, Silvers,
          Ebsen, chorus)
        Love Me, Love My Pekinese (Bruce, Walburn, chorus)
        Easy to Love (Stewart, Powell)
---   I've Got You Under My Skin (Bruce)
        Easy to Love (reprise) (Langford)
        Dance (orchestra)
        Swingin' the Jinx Away (Langford, Ebsen, ensemble)
        Easy to Love (reprise) (Stewart, chorus)
        Finale (orchestra)

Note: The above recording includes spoken dialog. Studio
        recordings by cast members:

Vocalion (78rpm) 523 I've Got You Under My Skin (Bruce)
                      Easy to Love (Bruce)
Decca (78rpm) 939   Rap-Tap on Wood (Langford)
                      I've Got You Under My Skin (Langford)
                        (LP: Take Two TT 214)
Decca (78rpm) 940   Easy to Love (Langford) (LP: Take Two TT 214)
                      Swingin' the Jinx Away (Langford)
                        (LP: Take Two TT 214)

BOUND FOR GLORY (United Artists, 1976)

United Artists UA LA 695-H stereo

Music, lyrics for songs: Woody Guthrie, others; background score,
musical direction: Leonard Rosenman

Cast: David Carradine

Songs: Hard Travelin' (Carradine)
        This Train Is Bound for Glory (orchestra)
        The Drifters (orchestra)
        I Ain't Got No Home (orchestra)
        So Long It's Been Good to Know Yuh (orchestra)
        Hobo's Lullaby (Carradine) music, lyrics: G Reeves
        Dust Storm (orchestra)
        Pastures of Plenty (orchestra)
        Do Re Mi (Carradine)
        Running for the Train (orchestra)
        So Long It's Been Good to Know Yuh (reprise) (orchestra)

This Train Is Bound for Glory (reprise) (orchestra)
Arrival in Los Angeles (orchestra)
Oklahoma Hills (Carradine) music, lyrics: Jack, Woody Guthrie
--- So Long It's Been Good to Know Yuh (reprise) (Carradine)
Howdido (Carradine)
So Long It's Been Good to Know Yuh (reprise) (orchestra)
Pastures of Plenty (orchestra)
Hitchhiking (orchestra)
Ramshackle (orchestra)
Pastures of Plenty (reprise) (Carradine)
Curly Headed Baby (orchestra)
Talking Dust Bowl Blues (orchestra)
This Land Is Your Land (orchestra)
Deportee (Carradine) music, lyrics: M Hoffman, Woody Guthrie
Hobo's Lullaby (reprise) (orchestra)
On the Road Again (orchestra)
Going Down the Road (orchestra)
This Land Is Your Land (reprise) (Carradine, chorus)

THE BOY FRIEND (MGM, 1972)

MGM 1SE-32ST (soundtrack) stereo   reissued: MCA 39069

Music, lyrics: Sandy Wilson, others; musical direction: Peter
Maxwell Davies

Cast: Max Adrian, Graham Armitage, Sally Bryant, Antonia Ellis,
       Moyra Fraser, Christopher Gable, Georgina Hale, Caryl
       Little, Murray Melvin, Brian Murphy, Bryan Pringle,
       Tommy Tune, Twiggy, Barbara Windsor

Songs: Overture (orchestra)
       The Boy Friend (Windsor, boys and girls)
       Perfect Young Ladies (Windsor, Ellis, Hale, Bryant, Little)
       I Could Be Happy with You (Twiggy, Gable)
       Fancy Forgetting (Pringle, Fraser)
       Sur le Plage (Windsor, company)
       You Are My Lucky Star (Twiggy) music: Nacio Herb Brown;
          lyrics: Arthur Freed
       It's Never Too Late to Fall in Love (Adrian, Hale)
       Won't You Charleston with Me? (Tune, Ellis, boys and girls)
--- The You-Don't-Want-to-Play-with-Me Blues (Fraser, Pringle,
          boys and girls)
       A Room in Bloomsbury (Twiggy, Gable)
       It's Nicer in Nice (Windsor, company)
       All I Do Is Dream of You (Twiggy) music: Nacio Herb
          Brown; lyrics: Arthur Freed
       Safety in Numbers (Ellis, Tune, Murphy, Armitage, Melvin)
       Poor Little Pierrette (Twiggy, Fraser, girls)
       The Riviera (company)
       The Boy Friend (Finale) (company)

A BOY NAMED CHARLIE BROWN (National General, 1969)

Columbia OS 3500 (soundtrack) stereo

Music, lyrics: Rod McKuen, others; musical direction: John Scott Trotter

Cast: (the voices of) Anne Altieri, Sally Dryer, Pamela Ferdin, Andy Forsich, Glenn Gilger, Rod McKuen, Peter Robbins, Erin Sullivan

Songs: A Boy Named Charlie Brown (McKuen)
        Cloud Dreams (Ferdin, Gilger, Robbins)
        Charlie Brown and His All-Stars (the team)
        We Lose Again (Robbins, Gilger)
        Blue Charlie Brown (Robbins, Ferdin)
        Time to Go to School (Gilger, Ferdin)
        I Only Dread One Day at A Time (Robbins, Gilger, Ferdin, Altieri, Dryer)
        Failure Face (Ferdin, Altieri, Dryer)
        By Golly I'll Show 'Em (Robbins, friends)
        Class Champion (Robbins, Gilger)
        'I' Before 'E' (Robbins, Gilger)
        School Spelling Bee (Robbins, Gilger, Ferdin)
        Champion Charlie Brown (gang)
---   Start Boning Up on Your Spelling, Charlie Brown (Robbins, friends)
        You'll Either Be A Hero - or A Goat (Robbins, Gilger, Sullivan)
        Bus Station (gang)
        Bus Wheel Blues (orchestra)
        Do Piano Players Make A Lot of Money (Ferdin, Forsich)
        I've Got to Get My Blanket Back (Gilger, Ferdin)
        Big City (Robbins, Gilger)
        Snoopy on Ice (orchestra)
        Found Blanket (Robbins, Gilger)
        National Spelling Bee (Robbins, friends)
        B-E-A-G-E-L (Robbins, friends)
        Bus Wheel Blues (reprise) (orchestra)
        Homecoming (Robbins, Gilger)
        I'm Never Going to School Again (Robbins, Gilger, Sullivan)
        Welcome Home Charlie Brown (Robbins, Ferdin)
        A Boy Named Charlie Brown (reprise) (McKuen)

THE BOYS FROM SYRACUSE (Universal, 1940)

Legends 1000/5-6 (soundtrack) mono 'Martha Raye'

Music: Richard Rodgers; lyrics: Lorenz Hart; musical direction: Charles Previn

Cast: Joe Penner, Martha Raye

Songs: The Greeks Have No Word for It (Raye)
       Sing for Your Supper (Raye)
       He and She (Raye)

Note: Studio recordings by Allan Jones:

Victor (78rpm) 4525 Falling in Love with Love (LP: Camden CAL 2256)
                    Who Are You?

BRIGADOON (MGM, 1954)

MGM E 3135 (soundtrack) mono reissued: MCA 39062 CD

Music: Frederick Loewe; lyrics: Alan Jay Lerner; musical
direction: Johnny Green

Cast: John Gustafson (for Jimmy Thompson), Van Johnson, Gene
       Kelly, Carole Richards (for Cyd Charisse)

Songs: Prologue (orchestra)
       Once in the Highlands (chorus)
       Brigadoon (chorus)
       Down on MacConnachy Square (chorus)
       The Heather on the Hill (Kelly)
       Waitin' for My Dearie (Richards)
       I'll Go Home with Bonnie Jean (Gustafson, Johnson, chorus)
---   Come to Me, Bend to Me (Gustafson)
       Almost Like Being in Love (Kelly)
       The Heather on the Hill (reprise) (orchestra)
       There But for You Go I (Kelly)
       Brigadoon (reprise) (chorus)

BROADWAY GONDOLIER (Warner Bros, 1935)

Columbia C2L 44 mono 'Dick Powell in Hollywood'

Music: Harry Warren; lyrics: Al Dubin; musical direction:
Victor Arden

Cast: Dick Powell

Songs: Outside of You (Powell)
       Lulu's Back in Town (Powell)
       The Rose in Her Hair (Powell)
       Lonely Gondolier (Powell)

Note: Additional recordings:

Brunswick (78rpm) 02093 (British) Sweet and Slow (The Mills Bros)
Radiola LP: 17-18 (soundtrack) Lulu's Back in Town (Powell)

THE BROADWAY MELODY (MGM, 1929)

Mark 56-847 (two records - soundtrack) mono

Music: Nacio Herb Brown, others; lyrics: Arthur Freed, others;
musical direction: Arthur Lange

Cast: The Biltmore Trio, James Burrows, Charles King, Bessie
        Love, Anita Page

Songs: Broadway Melody (King)
       Broadway Melody (reprise) (King, Page, Love)
       Harmony Babies (Page, Love)
       Love Boat (Burroughs, chorus)
       You Were Meant for me (King)
       Truthful Parson Brown (The Biltmore Trio) music, lyrics:
           Willard Robinson
       The Wedding of the Painted Doll (Burrows)
       The Boy Friend (Page, Love)

Note: The above recording includes the entire film soundtrack,
        with all the dialog. Studio recordings by Charles King:

        Victor (78rpm) 21964 Broadway Melody (LP: RCA 538)
                             The Wedding of the Painted Doll
        Victor (78rpm) 21965 You Were Meant for Me
                             The Love Boat

BROADWAY MELODY OF 1938 (MGM, 1937)

Motion Picture Tracks - 3 (soundtrack) mono

Music: Nacio Herb Brown, others; lyrics: Arthur Freed, others;
musical direction: Georgie Stoll

Cast: Buddy Ebsen, Judy Garland, Charles Igor Gorin, George
        Murphy, Eleanor Powell, Sophie Tucker

Songs: Overture (Broadway Melody) (chorus)
       Yours and Mine (Garland)
       Carmen: Toreador Song (Gorin) music: Bizet
       Follow in My Footsteps (Murphy, Ebsen, Powell)
       Yours and Mine (reprise) (Powell)
       Everybody Sing (Garland, Tucker, chorus)
       Some of These Days (Tucker) music, lyrics: Shelton Brooks
       I'm Feelin' Like A Million (Garland) not in film
---   I'm Feelin' Like A Million (Powell, Murphy)
       (Dear Mr Gable) You Made Me Love You (Garland) music:
           James Monaco; lyrics: Joseph McCarthy, Roger Edens
       Finale: Your Broadway and My Broadway (orchestra, Tucker,
           Gorin, cast) incorporates 'Broadway Melody' and other
           songs

Note: The above recording includes spoken dialog.   Studio
        recordings by cast members:

Decca (78rpm) 1463 (Dear Mr Gable) You Made Me Love You
                        (Garland) LP: Decca DXB 172
Decca (78rpm) 1472 Some of These Days (Tucker)

BROADWAY MELODY OF 1940 (MGM, 1940)

Classic International Filmusicals C I F 3002 (soundtrack) mono

Music, lyrics: Cole Porter; musical direction: Alfred Newman

Cast: Fred Astaire, Lois Hodnett, Douglas McPhail, George
        Murphy, Eleanor Powell

Songs: Opening Titles (orchestra)
       Please Don't Monkey with Broadway (Astaire, Murphy)
       I Am the Captain (Rocked in the Cradle of the Deep)
          (Powell, men) music, lyrics: Roger Edens
       Between You and Me (Murphy)
       I've Got My Eyes on You (Astaire)
---   Juke Box Dance (Astaire, Powell)
       I Concentrate on You (McPhail)
       Begin the Beguine (Hodnett, chorus)
       I've Got My Eyes on You (chorus)
       End Titles (orchestra)

BROADWAY SERENADE (MGM, 1939)

Sunbeam P 514 (soundtrack) mono 'Jeanette MacDoanld Sings!'

Music: Ed Ward, others; lyrics: Bob Wright, Chet Forrest, others;
musical direction: Herbert Stothart

Cast: Jeanette MacDonald

Songs: High Flyin' (MacDonald, chorus)
       One Look at You (MacDonald)
       For Every Lonely Heart (MacDonald, chorus) music: Herbert
          Stothart (from Tchaikovsky's 'None but the Lonely
          Heart'); lyrics: Gus Kahn

Note: The above recording includes a narration for radio.

BROADWAY THROUGH A KEYHOLE (Twentieth Century, 1933)

Golden Legends 2000/1 (soundtrack) mono 'Films of Russ Columbo'

Music: Harry Revel; lyrics: Mack Gordon; musical direction:
Alfred Newman

Cast: Russ Columbo, Constance Cummings, Eddie Foy, Jr, Frances
        Williams

Songs: Main Title (orchestra)
        Doing the Uptown Lowdown (Williams) intro: Texas Guinan
        When You Were A Girl on A Scooter and I Was A Boy on A
            Bike (Cummings, Foy, chorus) intro: Texas Guinan
        You're My Past, Present and Future (Columbo, Cummings,
            Foy, chorus)
        I Love You Prince Pizzicato (Columbo, Cummings) musical
            direction: Abe Lyman
        End Titles (Give My Regards to Broadway) (orchestra)

Note: The above recording includes spoken dialog.

BRONCO BILLY (Warner Bros, 1980)

Elektra 512 (soundtrack) stereo

Music, lyrics: various; musical direction: Steve Dorff

Cast: Penny De Haven, Clint Eastwood, Merle Haggard, Ronnie
        Milsap, The Reinsmen

Songs: Cowboys and Clowns (Milsap) music, lyrics: Steve Dorff,
            G Harju, Larry Herbstritt, Snuff Garrett
        Bayou Lullaby (De Haven) music, lyrics: Cliff Crofford,
            Snuff Garrett
        Misery and Gin (Haggard) music, lyrics: John Durrill,
            Snuff Garrett
        The Not So Great Train Robbery (orchestra) music: Steve
            Dorff, Snuff Garrett
        Bar Room Buddies (Haggard, Eastwood) music, lyrics:
            M Brown, Cliff Crofford, Steve Dorff, Snuff Garrett
  ---   Thunderer's March (orchestra) music: John Philip Sousa
        Stardust Cowboy (The Reinsmen) music, lyrics: Cliff
            Crofford, Snuff Garrett
        Love Theme: Cowboys and Clowns (reprise) (orchestra)
        Stars and Stripes Forever (orchestra) music: John Philip
            Sousa
        Bronco Billy (Milsap) music, lyrics: M Brown, Steve Dorff,
            Snuff Garrett

THE BUDDY HOLLY STORY (Columbia, 1978)

Epic PE 35412 (soundtrack) stereo CD

Music, lyrics: Charles Hardin, Norman Petty, others; musical
direction: Joe Rentzetti

Cast: Gary Busey

Songs: Rave On (Busey) music, lyrics: Sonny West, Bill Tilghman,
            Norman Petty

It's So Easy (Busey) music, lyrics: Buddy Holly, Norman
    Petty
True Love Ways (Busey) music, lyrics: Buddy Holly, Norman
    Petty
That'll Be the Day (Busey) music, lyrics: Norman Petty,
    Buddy Holly, Jerry Allison
Oh Boy! (Busey) music, lyrics: Sonny West, Bill Tilghman,
    Norman Petty
Peggy Sue (Busey) music, lyrics: Jerry Allison, Norman
    Petty, Buddy Holly
Maybe Baby (Busey)
Not Fade Away (Busey)
I'm Gonna Love You Too (Busey) music, lyrics: J Mauldin,
    N Sullivan, Norman Petty
--- Whole Lot of Shakin' Goin' On (Busey) music, lyrics:
    Dave Williams, Sunny David
Well All Right (Busey) music, lyrics: Norman Petty, Buddy
    Holly, Jerry Allison, J Mauldin
Listen to Me (Busey)
Maybe Baby (reprise) (Busey)
Everyday (Busey)
Rock Around with Ollie Vee (Busey) music, lyrics: Sonny
    Curtis
That'll Be the Day (reprise) (Busey)

BUGSY MALONE (Paramount, 1976)

RSO RS 1-3501 (soundtrack) stereo

Music, lyrics, musical direction: Paul Williams

Cast: (the voices of) Archie Hahn, Julie McWirder, Liberty
      Williams, Paul Williams

Songs: Bugsy Malone
      Fat Sam's Grand Slam
      Tomorrow
      Bad Guys
      I'm Feeling Fine
---   My Name Is Tallulah
      So You Wanna Be A Boxer
      Ordinary Fool
      Down and Out
      You Give A Little Love

Note: Vocals on above recording are uncredited. This is a live
      action film with a cast of children, with film vocals dubbed.

BUNDLE OF JOY (RKO, 1956)

RCA LPM 1399 mono

Music; Josef Myrow; lyrics: Mack Gordon; musical direction:
Hugo Winterhalter, others

Cast: Eddie Fisher, Debbie Reynolds, Nita Talbot

Songs: Bundle of Joy Overture (orchestra)
       Worry About Tomorrow - Tomorrow (Fisher)
       What's So Good About Good Morning (Reynolds, Talbot)
       Worry About Tomorrow - Tomorrow (reprise) (Reynolds,
          Talbot)
       Some Day Soon (Fisher)
       Some Day Soon Fantasy (orchestra) musical direction:
          Walter Scharf
       All About Love (Fisher, chorus)
---   Lullaby in Blue (Reynolds, Fisher)
       New Year's Eve on Times Square (Auld Lang Syne) (chorus)
       I Never Felt This Way Before (Fisher)
       Tempo Fugit (orchestra) musical direction: Walter Scharf
       Bundle of Joy (Fisher)
       Finale: All About Love (reprise) (chorus)
               Some Day Soon (reprise) (chorus)
               Lullaby in Blue (reprise) (chorus)
               Bundle of Joy (reprise) (Fisher)

BY THE LIGHT OF THE SILVERY MOON (Warner Bros, 1953)

Columbia CL 6248 mono   reissued: CBS P 18421

Music, lyrics: various; musical direction: Paul Weston

Cast: Doris Day

Songs: By the Light of the Silv'ry Moon (Day, chorus) music:
          Gus Edwards; lyrics: Edward Madden
       Your Eyes Have Told Me So (Day) music: Walter Blaufuss,
          Egbert Van Alstyne; lyrics: Gus Kahn
       Just One Girl (Day, chorus) music: Lyn Udall; lyrics:
          Karl Kennett
       Ain't We Got Fun? (Day, chorus) music: Richard Whiting;
          lyrics: Gus Kahn, Raymond B Egan
---   If You Were the Only Girl (Day) music: Nat D Ayer;
          lyrics: Clifford Grey
       Be My Little Baby Bumble Bee (Day, chorus) music: Henry
          I Marshall; lyrics: Stanley Murphy
       I'll Forget You (Day) music: Ernest R Ball; lyrics:
          Annelu Burns
       King Chanticleer (Day, chorus) music: Nat D Ayer; lyrics:
          A S Brown

BY THE LIGHT OF THE SILVERY MOON (Warner Bros, 1953)

Capitol H 422 mono

Musical direction: Axel Stordahl

Cast: June Hutton (not in film), Gordon MacRae

Songs: My Home Town Is A One Horse Town (MacRae, chorus)
            music: Abner Silver; lyrics: Alex Gerber
        Your Eyes Have Told Me So (MacRae, Hutton)
        Be My Little Baby Bumble Bee (Hutton, MacRae, chorus)
        I'll Forget You (Hutton)
---   Just One Girl (MacRae)
        By the Light of the Silvery Moon (MacRae, Hutton, chorus)
        Ain't We Got Fun? (Hutton, MacRae, chorus)
        If You Were the Only Girl (MacRae, Hutton)

BYE BYE BIRDIE (Columbia, 1963)

RCA LSO 1081 RE (soundtrack) stereo

Music: Charles Strouse; lyrics: Lee Adams; musical direction:
Johnny Green, others

Cast: Ann-Margret, Mary La Roche, Janet Leigh, Paul Lynde,
        Jesse Pearson, Bryan Russell, Bobby Rydell, Maureen
        Stapleton, Dick Van Dyke

Songs: Bye Bye Birdie (Ann-Margret, girls)
        Main Titles (orchestra)
        We Love You, Conrad (girls)
        How Lovely to Be A Woman (Ann-Margret)
        The Telephone Hour (Rydell, teenagers)
        Put On A Happy Face (Van Dyke, Leigh)
        Honestly Sincere (Pearson, girls)
        Hymn for A Sunday Evening (Ann-Margret, Lynde, La Roche,
            Russell)
---   One Last Kiss (Pearson, girls) musical direction: Hank
            Levine (not soundtrack)
        One Boy (Ann-Margret, Leigh, Rydell)
        Kids (Van Dyke, Lynde, Stapleton, Russell)
        A Lot of Livin' to Do (Pearson, Ann-Margret, Rydell,
            chorus)
        Rosie (Van Dyke, Leigh, Ann-Margret, Rydell)
        Bye Bye Birdie (reprise) (Ann-Margret)

Note: Bobby Rydell recorded an additional album (Cameo 1043) of
        songs from this score with musical direction by Jack Pleis:

        Honestly Sincere
        Kids
        One Special Girl
        A Lot of Living to Do
        Bye Bye Birdie

     We Love You, Conrad
     How Lovely to Be A Woman
     One Last Kiss
     The Telephone Hour
     Put On A Happy Face
     Rosie

CABARET (Allied Artists, 1972)

ABC Records ABCD 752 (soundtrack) stereo   reissued: MCA 37125

Music: John Kander; lyrics: Fred Ebb; musical direction:
Ralph Burns

Cast: Joel Grey, (the voice of) Greta Keller, Angelika
       Koch, Mark Lambert (for Oliver Collignon), Liza
       Minnelli, Louise Quick

Songs: Willkommen (Grey, chorus)
       Mein Herr (Minnelli, chorus) introduction by Grey
       Two Ladies (Grey, Koch, Quick)
       Maybe This Time (Minnelli)
       Sitting Pretty (orchestra)
       Variations on Two Ladies (Tiller Girls) (orchestra)
       Money, Money (Minnelli, Grey)
       Heiraten (Married) (Keller)
       If You Could See Her (Grey)
       Tomorrow Belongs to Me (Lambert, chorus)
       Cabaret (Minnelli)
       Finale (Willkommen) (Grey)

CABIN IN THE SKY (MGM, 1943)

Hollywood Soundstage 5003 (soundtrack) mono

Music: Harold Arlen, Vernon Duke; lyrics: E Y Harburg, John
Latouche; musical direction: George Stoll

Cast: Eddie 'Rochester' Anderson, Lena Horne, John W (Bubbles)
       Sublett, Ford L (Buck) Washington, Ethel Waters

Songs: Title Music (chorus, orchestra)
       Little Black Sheep (Walers, Hall Johnson Choir) music:
          Arlen; lyrics: Harburg
       Happiness Is A Thing Called Joe (Waters) music: Arlen;
          lyrics: Harburg
       Cabin in the Sky (Waters, Anderson, chorus) music: Duke;
          lyrics: Latouche
       Trumpet Solo (Louis Armstrong)
       Ain't It the Truth (Horne) music: Arlen; lyrics: Harburg

        (cut from film)
        Happy Birthday (Anderson, chorus)
        Taking A Chance on Love (Waters) music: Duke; lyrics:
           Ted Fetter, Latouche
---   Consequence (Anderson, Horne) music: Arlen; lyrics:
           Harburg
        Happiness Is Just A Thing Called Joe (reprise) (Waters)
        Duke Ellington Orchestra Medley:
           Things Ain't What They Used to Be
           Going Up
        Shine (Buck & Bubbles, chorus, Ellington Orchestra)
           music: Fred Dabney; lyrics: Cecil Mack
        Honey in A Honeycomb (Horne, Ellington Orchestra) music:
           Duke; lyrics: Latouche
        Honey in A Honeycomb (reprise) (Waters, Ellington Orchestra)
        Taking A Chance on Love (reprise) (Waters, chorus)

Note: The above recording includes spoken dialog. Additional
      recording:

      V Disc (78rpm) 172 Consequence (Horne, Anderson)

CAIRO (MGM, 1942)

Sunbeam P 514 (soundtrack) mono 'Jeanette MacDonald Sings!'

Music: Arthur Schwartz, others; lyrics: E Y Harburg, others;
musical direction: Georgie Stoll

Cast: Jeanette MacDonald, Ethel Waters

Songs: Main Titles (orchestra)
       Cairo (MacDonald, chorus)
       Buds Won't Bud (Waters) music: Harold Arlen
       To A Wild Rose (MacDonald, chorus) music, lyrics: Edward
          MacDowell
       From the Land of the Sky Blue Water (MacDonald, chorus)
          music: Charles Wakefield Cadman; lyrics: Nell Richmond
          Eberhart
       Beautiful Ohio (MacDonald, chorus) music: Robert A King;
          lyrics: Ballard MacDonald
       Waiting for the Robert E Lee (Waters) music: Lewis Muir;
          lyrics: L Wolfe Gilbert
       Home Sweet Home (MacDonald, chorus) music: Sir Henry
          Bishop; lyrics: John Howard Payne
       Keep A Light Burning Bright (MacDonald, chorus)

Note: The above recording includes a narration for radio.

CALAMITY JANE (Warner Bros, 1953)

Columbia CL 6273 (soundtrack) mono reissued: CBS P 19011

Music: Sammy Fain; lyrics: Paul Francis Webster; musical
direction: Ray Heindorf

Cast: Doris Day, Howard Keel

Songs: The Deadwood Stage (Whip-Crack-Away) (Day)
       I Can Do Without You (Day, Keel)
       The Black Hills of Dakota (Day, quartet)
       Just Blew In from the Windy City (Day)
       A Woman's Touch (Day)
       Higher Than A Hawk (Deeper Than A Well) (Keel)
       'Tis Harry I'm Plannin' to Marry (Day, quartet)
       Secret Love (Day)

CALL ME MADAM (Twentieth Century-Fox, 1953)

Decca 5465 (soundtrack) mono reissued: STET DS 25001

Music, lyrics: Irving Berlin; musical direction: Alfred Newman

Cast: Ethel Merman, Donald O'Connor, Carole Richards (for
       Vera-Ellen), George Sanders

Songs: The Hostess with the Mostes' on the Ball (Merman)
       Can You Use Any Money Today? (Merman)
       Marrying for Love (Sanders)
       It's A Lovely Day Today (O'Connor, Richards)
       The International Rag (Merman)
       You're Just in Love (Merman, O'Connor)
       The Ocarina (Richards)
       What Chance Have I with Love (O'Connor)
       Something to Dance About (O'Connor, Richards)
       The Best Thing for You (Merman, Sanders)
       Finale (Merman, Sanders, chorus):
          You're Just in Love (reprise)
          Something to Dance About (reprise)

CAMELOT (Warner Bros, 1967)

Warner Bros BS 1712 (soundtrack) stereo CD

Music: Frederick Loewe; lyrics: Alan Jay Lerner; musical
direction: Alfred Newman

Cast: Peter Bromilow, Richard Harris, Gary Marshal, Gene Merlino
       (for Franco Nero), Vanessa Redgrave, Anthony Rogers

Songs: Overture (orchestra)
   I Wonder What the King Is Doing Tonight (Harris)
   The Simple Joys of Maidenhood (Redgrave)
   Camelot (Harris, chorus)
   C'est Moi (Merlino)
   The Lusty Month of May (Redgrave, chorus)
   Follow Me (chorus)
   How to Handle A Woman (Harris)
---   Take Me to the Fair (Redgrave, Bromilow, Marshal, Rogers)
   If Ever I Would Leave you (Merlino)
   What Do Simple Folk Do? (Harris, Redgrave)
   I Loved You Once in Silence (Redgrave, Merlino)
   Guenevere (chorus)
   Finale Ultimo (Camelot) (Harris, chorus)

...CAN HEIRONYMUS MERKIN EVER FORGET MERCY HUMPPE AND FIND TRUE
HAPPINESS? (Universal, 1969)

Kapp KRS 5509 (soundtrack) stereo

Music: Anthony Newley; lyrics: Herbert Kretzmer

Cast: Joan Collins, Bruce Forsythe, Stubby Kaye, Anthony
   Newley, Ron Rubin

Songs: Overture (orchestra)
   If All the World's A Stage (Newley)
   Piccadilly Lily (Newley)
   Oh, What A Son of A Bitch I Am (Newley, Rubin, Kaye)
   Sweet Love Child (Newley)
   Astrological Ballet (orchestra)
   Chalk and Cheese (Collins)
   I'm All I Need (Newley)
---   On the Boards (Forsythe)
   Lullaby (Newley)
   Piccadilly Lily (reprise) (Newley)
   Once Upon A Time (Newley)
   When You Gotta Co (Newley)
   I'm All I Need (reprise) (Newley)
   Finale (If All the World's A Stage) (chorus)

CAN-CAN (Twentieth Century-Fox, 1960)

Capitol SW 1301 (soundtrack) stereo

Music, lyrics: Cole Porter; musical direction: Nelson Riddle

Cast: Maurice Chevalier, Louis Jourdan, Shirley MacLaine, Frank
   Sinatra

Songs: Main Title (orchestra)

  I Love Paris (chorus)
  Montmart' (Sinatra, Chevalier, chorus)
  C'est Magnifique (Sinatra)
  Maidens Typical of France (chorus)
  Just One of Those Things (Chevalier)
  I Love Paris (Sinatra, Chevalier)
  Can-Can (orchestra)
--- Entr'acte (orchestra)
  It's All Right with Me (Sinatra)
  Come Along with Me (MacLaine)
  Live and Let Live (Chevalier, Jourdan)
  You Do Something to Me (Jourdan)
  Let's Do It (Sinatra, MacLaine)

CAN'T HELP SINGING (Universal, 1944)

Decca A-387 (78rpm) mono

Music: Jerome Kern; lyrics: E Y Harburg; musical direction:
Edgar Fairchild

Cast: Deanna Durbin, Robert Paige

Decca (78rpm) 23388 Can't Help Singing (Durbin, Paige, chorus)
        Californ-i-ay (Durbin, Paige, chorus)
Decca (78rpm) 23389 More and More (Durbin)
        Any Moment Now (Durbin)
Decca (78rpm) 23390 Elbow Room (Paige, chorus)
        Swing Your Sweetheart (chorus)

Note: First four selections included on British LP,
   Ace of Hearts (AH 60) 'Deanna Durbin - Can't Help Singing'

CAN'T STOP THE MUSIC (EMI, 1980)

Casablanca NBLP 7220 (soundtrack) stereo

Music: Jacques Morali; lyrics: various; musical direction:
Horace Ott

Cast: (the voice of) David London, The Ritchie Family, The
   Village People

Songs: Can't Stop the Music (The Village People) lyrics: Henri
   Belolo, Phil Hurtt, Beauius Whitehead
   Samantha (London) lyrics: Henri Belolo, Phil Hurtt
   Give Me A Break (The Ritchie Family) lyrics: Henri Belolo,
    The Ritchie Family
   Liberation (The Village People) lyrics: Henri Belolo,
    Phil Hurtt, Beauius Whitehead

     Magic Night (The Village People) lyrics: Henri Belolo,
        V Willis
--- The Sound of the City (London) lyrics: Henri Belolo, Phil
        Hurtt
     Milkshake (The Village People) lyrics: Henri Belolo,
        V Willis
     YMCA (The Village People) lyrics: Henri Belolo, V Willis
     I Love You to Death (The Village People) lyrics: Henri
        Belolo, Phil Hurtt, Beauius Whitehead
     Sophistication (The Ritchie Family) lyrics: Horace Ott,
        Henri Belolo, Phil Hurtt

CAPTAIN JANUARY (Twentieth Century-Fox, 1936)

Fox 103-2 (two records - soundtrack) mono 'Shirley Temple Songbook'

Music: Lew Pollack; lyrics: Jack Yellen; musical direction:
Louis Silvers

Cast: Guy Kibbee, Slim Summerville, Shirley Temple

Songs: The Right Somebody to Love (Temple)
       Sextet from Lucia (Temple, Kibbee, Summerville)
       At the Codfish Ball (Temple)
       Early Bird (Temple)

CAREFREE (RKO, 1938)

Classic International Filmusicals C I F 3004 (soundtrack) mono
also: Sandy Hook SH 2010

Music, lyrics: Irving Berlin; musical direction: Victor Baravalle

Cast: Fred Astaire, Ginger Rogers

Songs: Main Title (orchestra)
       Since They Turned Loch Lomond into Swing (orchestra)
       I Used to Be Color Blind (Astaire, chorus)
       The Yam (Rogers, Astaire)
       Change Partners (Astaire)
       Change Partners (reprise) (chorus)
       End Titles (orchestra)

Note: The above recording includes spoken dialog. Studio
       recordings by Astaire, all on Col LP: SG 32472:

       Brunswick (78rpm) 8189 I Used to Be Color Blind
                              Change Partners
       Brunswick (78rpm) 8190 The Yam
                              The Yam Step

Ginger Rogers studio recordings:

Bluebird (78rpm) 7981 I Used to Be Color Blind (LP: RCA
The Yam   LPV-579)

CARMEN JONES (Twentieth Century-Fox, 1954)

RCA LM 1881 (soundtrack) mono   reissued RCA ARL1-0046 CD

Music: Georges Bizet; lyrics: Oscar Hammerstein II; musical
direction: Herschel Burke Gilbert

Cast: Pearl Bailey, Joe Crawford (for Nick Stewart), Marvin
        Hayes (for Joe Adams), Marilyn Horne (for Dorothy Dandridge),
        LeVern Hutcherson (for Harry Belafonte), Olga James,
        Brock Peters (for Roy Glenn), Bernice Peterson (for
        Diahann Carroll)

Songs: Overture (orchestra)
        Opening Medley (Send Them Along; Lift 'em Up and Put
          'em Down) (chorus)
        Dat's Love (Habanera) (Horne, chorus)
        You Talk Jus' Like My Maw (Hutcherson, James)
        Dere's A Cafe on de Corner (Horne)
        Dis Flower (Hutcherson)
        Beat Out Dat Rhythm on A Drum (Bailey, chorus)
---   Stan' Up an' Fight (Hayes, chorus)
        Quintet: Wizzin' Away Along de Track (Horne, Crawford,
          Peterson, Peters, Bailey)
        Card Song (Horne, Bailey, cast)
        My Joe (James)
        Duet (Horne, Hutcherson, chorus)
        Finale (chorus)

Note: The voices of Dandridge and Belafonte are heard briefly
        in spoken dialog.

CARNEGIE HALL - see page 359

CAROUSEL (Twentieth Century-Fox, 1956)

Capitol SW 694 (soundtrack) stereo CD

Music: Richard Rodgers; lyrics: Oscar Hammerstein II; musical
direction: Alfred Newman

Cast: Shirley Jones, Gordon MacRae, Cameron Mitchell, Robert
        Rounseville, Barbara Ruick, Claramae Turner

Songs: The Carousel Waltz (orchestra)
        You're A Queer One, Julie Jordan! (Ruick, Jones)

Mr Snow (Ruick)
If I Loved You (Jones, MacRae)
When the Children Are Asleep (Rounseville, Ruick)
June Is Bustin' Out All Over (Turner, Ruick, chorus)
--- Soliloquy (MacRae)
Blow High, Blow Low (Mitchell, men's chorus)
A Real Nice Clambake (Ruick, Turner, Rounseville,
   Mitchell, chorus)
Stonecutters Cut It on Stone (Mitchell, chorus)
What's the Use of Wondrin' (Jones, girls' chorus)
You'll Never Walk Alone (Turner)
If I Loved You (reprise) (MacRae)
You'll Never Walk Alone (Finale) (Jones, chorus)

CASBAH (Universal, 1948)

RCA Victor (not issued as an album) mono

Music: Harold Arlen; lyrics: Leo Robin; musical direction:
Earle Hagen

Cast: Tony Martin

RCA (78rpm) 20-2689 For Every Man There's A Woman (Martin)
                   What's Good About Goodbye (Martin)
RCA (78rpm) 20-2690 Hooray for Love (Martin)
                   It Was Written in the Stars (Martin)

THE CAT AND THE FIDDLE (MGM, 1934)

Hollywood Soundstage 5015 (soundtrack) mono

Music: Jerome Kern; lyrics: Otto Harbach; musical direction:
Herbert Stothart

Cast: Jeanette MacDonald, Ramon Novarro, Earl Oxford, Vivianne
       Segal

Songs: Opening Music (orchestra)
       The Night Was Made for Love (MacDonald, Novarro)
       One Moment Alone (Novarro, chorus)
       The Night Was Made for Love (reprise) (MacDonald)
       Concertina Melody (and) Poor Pierrot (chorus)
       She Didn't Say 'Yes' (MacDonald, chorus)
       Don't Ask Me Not to Sing (chorus)
       The Night Was Made for Love (reprise) (MacDonald, chorus)
       I Watch the Love Parade (MacDonald, Novarro)
       A New Love Is Old (Segal)
       A New Love Is Old (reprise) (Novarro)
       Ha! Cha! Cha! (Oxford, Segal, chorus)
       Try to Forget (MacDonald)
       This Is the Day for the Masses (chorus)
       A New Love Is Old (reprise) (MacDonald)

> I Bring You A Song in the Springtime (MacDonald, chorus)
> Waltz (orchestra)
> Try to Forget (reprise) (Novarro, MacDonald, male chorus)
> I Watch the Love Parade (reprise) (Novarro, MacDonald)
> Poor Pierrot (Long Long Ago) (MacDonald, Novarro, chorus)
> One Moment Alone (reprise) (MacDonald, Novarro, chorus)
> Finale (orchestra)

Note: The above recording includes spoken dialog. Jeanette MacDonald studio recording:

Victor (78rpm) 24754 Try to Forget

CATCH MY SOUL (Cinerama, 1974)

Metromedia BML 1-0176 (soundtrack) stereo

Music: Tony Joe White, others; lyrics: Jack Good, others

Cast: Bonnie Bramlett, Delaney Bramlett, Richie Havens, Lance Le Gault, Susan Tyrrell, Tony Joe White

Songs: Othello (White, chorus) music, lyrics; Tony Joe White
Wash Us Clean (White, chorus)
Catch My Soul (Le Gault, chorus)
Working on A Building (Havens, chorus) music, lyrics: Tony Joe White
Othello (part 2) (White, chorus)
Catch My Soul (part 2) (Le Gault, chorus)
Open Our Eyes (Havens) music, lyrics: Leon Lumkins
Backwoods Preacherman (White, chorus) music, lyrics: Tony Joe White
Looking Back (White, chorus) lyrics: Delaney Bramlett
Eat the Bread - Drink the Wine (Le Gault, chorus)
That's What God Said (D Bramlett, chorus) music, lyrics: Delaney Bramlett
--- Chug A Lug (The Drinking Song) (B Bramlett) music, lyrics: Delaney Bramlett
I Found Jesus (D Bramlett, chorus) music, lyrics: Delaney Bramlett
Run Shaker Run (Havens, chorus) trad
Catch My Soul (part 3) (Le Gault, chorus)
Book of Prophecy (Havens) music: Richie Havens
Othello (part 3) (White, chorus)
Lust of the Blood (Le Gault) music: Ray Pohlman
Tickle His Fancy (Tyrrell) music, lyrics: Allene Lubin
Why (Havens) music: Emile Dean Zoghby
Othello (part 4) (White, chorus)
Catch My Soul (part 4) (Le Gault, chorus)
Put Out the Light (Havens) music: Ray Pohlman
Othello (part 5) (White, chorus)

CENTENNIAL SUMMER (Twentieth Century-Fox, 1946)

Classic International Filmusicals C I F 3009 (soundtrack) mono

Music: Jerome Kern; lyrics: Leo Robin, others; musical direction: Alfred Newman

Cast: Walter Brennan, Linda Darnell, Eddie Dunn, William Eythe, Louanne Hogan (for Jeanne Crain), Kathleen Howard, Avon Long, Larry Stevens, Harry Strang, Cornel Wilde

Songs: Overture: Centennial - Long Live Our Free America (chorus)
        Railroad Song (Brennan, Strang, Dunn, Hogan, chorus)
        The Right Romance (Hogan)
        Up with the Lark (Howard, Hogan, Darnell, Brennan, cast)
        In Love in Vain (Hogan, Eythe, chorus)
        All Through the Day (Stevens, cast) lyrics: Oscar
            Hammerstein II
        Cinderella Sue (Long, children) lyrics: E Y Harburg
        Up with the Lark (reprise) (Hogan, Wilde)
        Finale: Up with the Lark (chorus)

Note: The above recording includes spoken dialog. Louanne Hogan recorded four songs for Musicraft Records (78rpm).

CHARLIE CHAN AT THE OPERA (Twentieth Century-Fox, 1936)

Medallion ML 310 (soundtrack) mono 'Oscar Levant - For the Record'

Music: Oscar Levant; lyrics: William Kernall (Italian translation by Alfredo Sabato); musical direction: Samuel Kaylen

Cast: Zarubi Elmassian (for Margaret Irving), Enrico Ricardi (for Gregory Gaye), Tudor Williams (for Boris Karloff)

Songs: Then Farewell (Williams)
        King and Country Call (Ricardi)
        Ah! Romantic Love Dream (Elmassian)
        Then Farewell (reprise) (Williams, Elmassian)

Note: According to liner notes by Michael Feinstein, 'Much of the opera was cut from the film but it is contained intact on this recording.'

CHARLOTTE'S WEB (Paramount, 1973)

Paramount PAS 1008 (soundtrack) stereo

Music, lyrics: Richard M Sherman, Robert B Sherman; musical direction: Irwin Kostal

Cast: (the voices of) Pam Ferdin, Henry Gibson, Paul Lynde,
        Agnes Moorehead, Debbie Reynolds

Songs: Main Title (orchestra)
        There Must Be Something More (Ferdin)
        I Can Talk (Gibson, Moorehead)
        Chin Up (Reynolds, Gibson)
        Mother Earth and Father Time (Reynolds)
        We've Got A Lot in Common (Gibson, Reynolds, chorus)
        A Veritable Smorgasbord (Lynde, Moorehead)
        Deep in the Dark (Reynolds, male choir)
        Chin Up March (orchestra)
        Zuckerman's Famous Pig (quartet, chorus)
        Charlotte's Farewell (Mother Earth and Father Time)
          (Reynolds)
        End Title (orchestra)

CHITTY CHITTY BANG BANG (United Artists, 1968)

United Artists UAS 5188 (soundtrack) stereo

Music, lyrics: Richard M Sherman, Robert B Sherman; musical
direction: Irwin Kostal

Cast: Gert Frobe, Adrian Hall, Sally Ann Howes, Lionel Jeffries,
        Anna Quayle, Heather Ripley, Dick Van Dyke

Songs: Chitty Chitty Bang Bang (orchestra)
        You Two (Van Dyke, Hall, Ripley)
        Toot Sweets (Van Dyke, Howes, Hall, Ripley, cast)
        Hushabye Mountain (Van Dyke)
        Me Ol' Bam-Boo (Van Dyke, chorus)
        Chitty Chitty Bang Bang (Van Dyke, Hall, Ripley)
        Truly Scrumptious (Howes, Hall, Ripley)
        Chitty Chitty Bang Bang (reprise) (Van Dyke, Howes,
          Hall, Ripley)
---   Lovely Lonely Man (Howes)
        Posh! (Jeffries)
        Hushabye Mountain (reprise) (Van Dyke, Howes)
        The Roses of Success (Jeffries, men)
        Chu-Chi Face (Frobe, Quayle)
        Doll on A Music Box (Howes)
        Truly Scrumptious (reprise) (Van Dyke)
        Chitty Chitty Bang Bang (finale) (Van Dyke, Howes, chorus)
        Chitty Chitty Bang Bang (reprise) (orchestra)
        The Roses of Success (reprise) (orchestra)

THE CHOCOLATE SOLDIER (MGM, 1941)

Columbia ML 4060 mono   reissued: CSP P-13707

Music: Oscar Straus, others; lyrics: Stanislaus Stange, others;
musical direction: Robert Armbruster

Cast: Nelson Eddy, Rise Stevens

Songs: My Hero (Stevens, Eddy)
       While My Lady Sleeps (Eddy, chorus) music: Bronislaw
           Kaper; lyrics: Gus Kahn
       The Chocolate Soldier (Stevens, Eddy)
       Forgive (Stevens, Eddy, chorus)
       Ti-Ra-La-La (Stevens, chorus)
       Sympathy (Stevens, Eddy)

A CHORUS LINE (Columbia, 1985)

Casablanca 826 306-1 M-1 (soundtrack) stereo CD

Music: Marvin Hamlisch; lyrics: Edward Kleban; musical direction:
Ralph Burns

Cast: Yamil Borges, Gregg Burge, Cameron English, Vicki
        Frederick, Michelle Johnston, Pam Klinger, Audrey
        Landers, Charles McGowan, Alyson Reed

Songs: I Hope I Get It (ensemble)
       Who Am I Anyway? (English)
       I Can Do That (McGowan)
       At the Ballet (Frederick, Johnston, Klinger)
       Suprise, Suprise (Burge)
       Nothing (Borges)
---   Let Me Dance for You (Reed)
       Dance: Ten; Looks: Three (Landers)
       One (rehearsal) (ensemble)
       What I Did for Love (Reed)
       One (finale) (ensemble)

THE CHRISTMAS THAT ALMOST WASN'T (Childhood Productions, 1966)

RCA Camden CAS 1086 (soundtrack) stereo

Music, lyrics: Ray Carter, Paul Tripp; musical direction:
Bruno Nicolai

Cast: Rosanno Brazzi, Paul Tripp, others

Songs: The Christmas That Almost Wasn't (Tripp, chorus)
       Kids Get All the Breaks (Brazzi)
       Why Can't Every Day Be Christmas? (Tripp, children)
       Christmas Is Coming (Mrs Santa)
       Hustle Bustle (men)
       I'm Bad (Brazzi, chorus)

          The Name of the Song Is Prune (men)
          What Are the Children Like? (Santa)
          Why Can't Every Day Be Christmas? (reprise) (children)
---   Time for Christmas (Tripp)
          I've Got A Date with Santa (children)
          Santa Claus Round (children)
          Nothing to Do but Wait (Brazzi)
          Why Can't Every Day Be Christmas? (reprise) (Brazzi,
            chorus)
          The Christmas That Almost Wasn't (reprise) (Tripp)

Note: The above recording includes a narration by Paul Tripp.

CINDERELLA (Disney, 1949)

Disneyland DQ 1207 (soundtrack) mono

Music: Al Hoffman, Jerry Livingston, others; lyrics: Mack David;
musical direction: Oliver Wallace, Paul Smith

Cast: Don Barclay, Verna Felton, Ilene Woods

Songs: Cinderella (chorus)
       A Dream Is A Wish Your Heart Makes (Woods)
       Oh Sing Sweet Nightingale (Woods)
       The Work Song (Jaq and Gus)
       A Dream Is A Wish Your Heart Makes (reprise) (chorus)
---   Bibbidi-Bobbidi-Boo (Felton, chorus)
       Cinderella Arrives at the Ball (orchestra) music: Paul
         J Smith
       So This Is Love (Woods, Barclay)
       Finale (orchestra) music: Oliver Wallace, Paul J Smith
         A Dream Is A Wish Your Heart Makes (reprise) (chorus)

CINDERFELLA (Paramount, 1960)

Dot DLP 38001 stereo

Music: Walter Scharf, Harry Warren; lyrics: Jack Brooks; musical
direction: Walter Scharf

Cast: Bill Lee (not in film), Jerry Lewis, Del Moore (not in
      film), Loulie Jean Norman (not in film), Max Smith (not
      in film), Salli Terri (not in film)

Songs: Overture (orchestra)
       Let Me Be A People (Lewis) music: Warren
       Tick-A-Dee (Lewis) music: Scharf
       I'm Part of A Family (Lewis) music: Scharf
       Turn It On (Lewis, choir) music: Warren
---   We're Going to the Ball (Terri, Lee, Smith) music: Scharf

Somebody (Lewis) music: Warren
The Princess Waltz (Lewis, Norman, choir)
Turn It On (Lewis, Moore, choir)

Note: The above recording includes spoken dialog and a narration
        by Bill Lee.

CLAMBAKE (United Artists, 1967)

RCA LSP 3893 stereo   reissued: APL 1-2565

Music: Roy C Bennett, others; lyrics: Sid Tepper, others

Cast: Elvis Presley

Songs: Clambake (Presley) music: Ben Weisman; lyrics: Sid Wayne
       Who Needs Money? (Presley, unidentified voice) music,
           lyrics: Randy Starr
       A House That Has Everything (Presley)
       Confidence (Presley)
       Hey, Hey, Hey (Presley) music, lyrics: Joy Byers
       You Don't Know Me (Presley) music: Eddy Arnold; lyrics:
           Andy Walker
       The Girl I Never Loved (Presley) music, lyrics: Randy
           Starr

C'MON LET'S LIVE A LITTLE (Paramount, 1967)

Liberty LST 7430 (soundtrack) stereo

Music, lyrics: Don Crawford, others; musical direction: Don
Ralke

Cast: Don Crawford, Jackie DeShannon, Eddie Hodges, Suzie Kaye,
        The Pair, Ethel Smith, Bobby Vee

Songs: C'mon Let's Live A Little (orchestra)
       Instant Girl (Vee)
       Baker Man (DeShannon)
       C'mon Let's Live A Little (reprise) (Kaye)
       What Fool This Mortal Be (Vee)
       Tonight's the Night (The Pair)
---   For Granted (DeShannon)
       Back Talk (Vee, DeShannon)
       Over and Over (Vee, DeShannon)
       Let's Go-Go (Hodges) music, lyrics: James Pinkard, Melvin
           Brown
       Way Back Home (Smith, Crawford)
       C'mon Let's Live A Little (reprise) (orchestra)

COAL MINER'S DAUGHTER (Universal, 1980)

MCA 1699 (soundtrack) stereo

Music, lyrics: Loretta Lynn, others

Cast: Beverly D'Angelo, Levon Helm, Sissy Spacek

Songs: The Great Titanic (Spacek) trad
        Blue Moon of Kentucky (Helm) music, lyrics: Bill Monroe
        There He Goes (Spacek) music, lyrics: Eddie Miller, Durwood
            Haddock, W S Stevenson, Eddie Miller
        I'm A Honky Tonk Girl (Spacek)
        Amazing Grace (choir) trad
        Walking After Midnight (D'Angelo) music: Alan Block;
            lyrics: Don Hecht
        Crazy (D'Angelo) music, lyrics: Willie Nelson
---   I Fall to Pieces (Spacek) music: Harlan Howard; lyrics:
            Hank Cochran
        Sweet Dreams (D'Angelo) music, lyrics: Don Gibson
        Back in Baby's Arms (Spacek, D'Angelo) music, lyrics:
            Bob Montgomery
        One's On the Way (Spacek) music, lyrics: Shel Silverstein
        You Ain't Woman Enough to Take My Man (Spacek)
        You're Looking at Country (Spacek)
        Coal Miner's Daughter (Spacek)

THE COCOANUTS (Paramount, 1929)

Sountrak 108 (soundtrack) mono also: Sandy Hook SH 2059

Music, lyrics: Irving Berlin; musical direction: Frank Teurs

Cast: Mary Eaton, The Marx Brothers (Groucho, Chico, Harpo,
        Zeppo), Oscar Shaw

Songs: Overture (orchestra)
        Florida by the Sea (chorus)
        When My Dreams Come True (Shaw, Eaton)
        Groucho Romances Margaret Dumont (spoken)
        When My Dreams Come True (reprise) (H Marx - harp solo)
        Groucho and Chico Make A Deal (spoken)
        Monkey-Doodle-Do (Eaton)
---   Groucho and Chico at the Auction (spoken)
        Dance of the Cocoanuts (orchestra)
        When My Dreams Come True (reprise) (Eaton)
        The Tale of A Shirt (Marx Brothers, cast) Carmen:
            Toreador Song; music: Bizet
        Gypsy Love Song (C Marx - piano solo) music: Victor Herbert
        End Titles (orchestra)

Note: The above recording includes spoken dialog.

COLLEGE HUMOR (Paramount, 1933)

Columbia C2L 43 mono 'Bing Crosby in Hollywood'

Music: Arthur Johnston; lyrics: Sam Coslow; musical direction:
Jimmie Grier

Cast: Bing Crosby

Songs: Learn to Croon (Crosby)
       Moonstruck (Crosby)
       Down the Old Ox Road (Crosby)

A CONNECTICUT YANKEE IN KING ARTHUR'S COURT (Paramount, 1949)

Decca DL 4261 mono 'Bings Hollywood - Sunshine Cake'

Music: James Van Heusen; lyrics: John Burke; musical direction:
Victor Young

Cast: William Bendix, Bing Crosby, Rhonda Fleming, Sir Cedric
       Hardwicke

Songs: Once and for Always (Crosby, chorus)
       If You Stub Your Toe on the Moon (Crosby, Rhythmaires)
       Busy Doing Nothing (Crosby, Bendix, Hardwicke)
       Once and for Always (reprise) (Crosby, Fleming)

THE COTTON CLUB (Orion, 1984)

Geffen Records GHS 24062 (soundtrack) stereo

Music: John Barry, Duke Ellington, others; lyrics: Ted Koehler,
Irving Mills, others; musical direction: Bob Wilbur

Cast: Priscilla Baskerville, Dave Brown, Gregory Hines, Lonette
       McKee, Larry Marshall

Songs: The Mooche (orchestra) music: Ellington, Irving Mills
       Cotton Club Stomp #2 (orchestra) music: Ellington
       Drop Me Off in Harlem (orchestra) music: Ellington
       Creole Love Call (Baskerville) music, lyrics: Ellington
       Ring dem Bells (Brown) music: Ellington, Mills
       East St Louis Toodle-o (orchestra) music: Ellington
       Truckin' (orchestra) music: Rube Bloom
---   Ill Wind (McKee) music: Harold Arlen; lyrics: Ted Koehler
       Cotton Club Stomp #1 (orchestra) music: Ellington
       Mood Indigo (orchestra) music: Ellington
       Minnie the Moocher (Marshall) music, lyrics: Cab Calloway,
          Irving Mills
       Copper Colored Gal (Hines) music: J Fred Coots; lyrics:
          Benny Davis

     Dixie Kidnaps Vera (orchestra) music: Barry
     The Depression Hits / Best Beats Sandman (orchestra)
        music: Barry
     Daybreak Express Medley (orchestra) music: Ellington
        Wall Street Wail
        Slippery Horn
        High Life

THE COUNTRY GIRL (Paramount, 1954)

Decca DL 4264 mono 'Bing's Hollywood - Anything Goes'

Music: Harold Arlen; lyrics: Ira Gershwin; musical direction:
Joseph Lilley

Cast: Patty Andrews (not in film), Bing Crosby

Songs: It's Mine, It's Yours (The Pitchman) (Crosby, girls trio)
      Dissertation on the State of Bliss (Love and Learn)
        (Crosby, Andrews)
      The Search Is Through (Crosby)
      The Land Around Us (Crosby, chorus)

THE COURT JESTER (Paramount, 1956)

Decca DL 8212 mono

Music, lyrics: Sylvia Fine, Sammy Cahn; musical direction:
Vic Schoen

Cast: Danny Kaye

Songs: Overture (orchestra)
      Life Could Not Better Be (Kaye)
      Outfox the Fox (Kaye, chorus)
      I'll Take You Dreaming (Kaye, chorus)
      My Heart Knows A Lovely Song (Kaye)
---   I Live to Love (Kaye)
      Willow, Willow Waley (Kaye)
      Pass the Basket (Kaye, chorus)
      The Maladjusted Jester (Kaye, chorus)
      Where Walks My True Love (Kaye, chorus)
      Life Could Not Better Be (reprise) (Kaye, chorus)

COVER GIRL (Columbia, 1944)

Curtain Calls CC 100/24 (soundtrack) mono

Music: Jerome Kern, others; lyrics: Ira Gershwin, others;

musical direction: Morris Stoloff

Cast: Leslie Brooks, Gene Kelly, Phil Silvers, Nan Wynn (for
        Rita Hayworth)

Songs: Main Title (orchestra)
        The Show Must Go On (Wynn, Brooks, girls)
        Who's Complaining (Silvers, girls)
        Sure Thing (Wynn, chorus)
        Make Way for Tomorrow (Kelly, Wynn, Silvers) lyrics:
           E Y Harburg
        Put Me to the Test (Kelly)
        Long Ago and Far Away (Kelly, Wynn)
        Poor John! (Wynn) music, lyrics: H E Pether, Fred W Leigh
        Cover Girl (chorus)
        Finale: Long Ago and Far Away (Wynn, Kelly)
                Make Way for Tomorrow (Silvers, Wynn, Kelly, chorus)

DAMES (Warner Bros, 1934)

Warner Bros 3XX2736 (soundtrack) mono 'Fifty years of Film Music'

Music: Harry Warren; lyrics: Al Dubin; musical direction: Leo F
Forbstein

Cast: Joan Blondell, Dick Powell

Songs: I Only Have Eyes for You (Powell, chorus)
        Dames (Powell, chorus)
        The Girl at the Ironing Board (Blondell, chorus)

Note: An additional soundtrack recording:

        I Only Have Eyes for You (Dick Powell, Ruby Keeler, chorus)
           UA LA215-H 'The Golden Age of the Hollywood Musical'

DAMN YANKEES (Warner Bros, 1958)

RCA LOC 1047 (soundtrack) mono

Music, lyrics: Richard Adler, Jerry Ross; musical direction:
Ray Heindorf

Cast: Rae Allen, Shannon Bolin, Russ Brown, Bob Fosse, Nathaniel
        Frey, Tab Hunter, Jimmie Komack, Albert Linville, Robert
        Shafer, Gwen Verdon, Ray Walston

Songs: Overture (orchestra)
        Six Months Out of Every Year (Bolin, Shafer, chorus)
        Goodbye, Old Girl (Shafer, Hunter)
        Heart (Brown, Komack, Linville, Frey)
        Shoeless Joe from Hannibal, Mo (Allen, men)

        There's Something About An Empty Chair (Bolin) music,
           lyrics: Richard Adler
        Whatever Lola Wants (orchestra)

---   A Little Brains, A Little Talent (Verdon)
        Whatever Lola Wants (reprise) (Verdon)
        Those Were the Good Old Days (Walston)
        Who's Got the Pain (Verdon, Fosse)
        Two Lost Souls (Verdon, Hunter)
        There's Something About An Empty Chair (reprise)
           (Bolin, Shafer)

A DAMSEL IN DISTRESS (RKO, 1937)

Curtain Calls CC 100/19 (soundtrack) mono

Music: George Gershwin, others; lyrics: Ira Gershwin, others;
musical direction: Victor Baravalle

Cast: Gracie Allen, Fred Astaire, Mario Berini (for Reginald
       Gardiner), George Burns

Songs: Main Title (orchestra)
      Comedy Routine (Burns, Allen) spoken
      I Can't Be Bothered Now (Astaire)
      The Jolly Tar and the Milkmaid (Astaire, madrigal singers)
      Put Me to the Test (I've Just Begun to Live) (orchestra)
      Stiff Upper Lip (Allen)
      Things Are Looking Up (Astaire)
      A Foggy Day (Astaire)
      Nice Work If You Can Get It (Astaire, trio)
---   Marta: Ah, che a voi perdoni iddio (Berini) music; Flotow
      Nice Work If You Can Get It (reprise) (orchestra)
      Finale (orchestra)

Note: The above recording contains spoken dialog, including the
      voices of Joan Fontaine and Reginald Gardiner. Studio
      recordings by Fred Astaire:

      Brunswick (78rpm) 7982 I Can't Be Bothered now
                       A Foggy Day
      Brunswick (78rpm) 7983 Things Are Looking Up
                       Nice Work If You Can Get It

      The above four studio recorings are included on the
      Columbia LP: SG 32472 'Starring Fred Astaire'

DANCING LADY (MGM, 1933)

Curtain Calls CC 100/23 (soundtrack) mono 'Joan Crawford'

Music: Burton Lane; lyrics: Harold Adamson; musical direction:

Lou Silvers

Cast: Fred Astaire, Joan Crawford, Art Jarrett

Songs: Everything I Have Is Yours (Jarrett, Crawford)
       Heigh-Ho the Gangs All Here (Crawford, Astaire, chorus)
       Let's Go Bavarian (Crawford, Astaire, chorus)

DARLING LILI (Paramount, 1969)

RCA LSPX-1000 stereo

Music: Henry Mancini; lyrics: Johnny Mercer; musical direction:
Henry Mancini

Cast: Julie Andrews, Gloria Paul

Songs: Overture (chorus)
       Whistling Away the Dark (Andrews)
       The Little Birds (Les P'tits Oiseaux) (children's chorus)
       The Girl in No Man's Land (Andrews)
       Gypsy Violin (orchestra)
       I'll Give You Three Guesses (Andrews, chorus)
---   Darling Lili (chorus)
       Smile Away Each Rainy Day (Andrews, chorus)
       The Can-Can Cafe (orchestra)
       I'll Give You Three Guesses (reprise) (Andrews)
       Skal (Let's Have Another on Me) (chorus)
       Your Good-Will Ambassador (Paul)
       Whistling Away the Dark (reprise) (chorus)

A DATE WITH JUDY (MGM, 1948)

Curtain Calls CC 100/4 (soundtrack) mono 'Jane Powell'

Music, lyrics: various; musical direction: George Stoll

Cast: Scotty Beckett, Jane Powell

Songs: It's A Most Unusual Day (Powell) music: Gene dePaul;
          lyrics: Don Raye
       Through the Years (Powell, Beckett) music: Vincent Youmans;
          lyrics: Edward Heyman
       Love Is Where You Find It (Powell) music: Nacio Herb
          Brown; lyrics: Earl Brent
       I'm Strictly on the Corny Side (Powell, Beckett) music:
          Alec Templeton; lyrics: Stella Unger

Note: A soundtrack excerpt with various members of the cast is
       included on MCA 2-11002 'That's Entertainment'

Carmen Miranda studio recording:

Decca (78rpm) 24479 Cuanto La Gusta (recorded 11/29/47)
music: Gabriel Ruiz; lyrics: Ray
Gilbert

THE DAY OF THE LOCUST (Paramount, 1974)

London PS 912 (soundtrack) stereo

Music, lyrics for songs: various; score, musical direction:
John Barry

Cast: (the voice of) Louis Armstrong, Michael Dees, Paul Jabara,
        (the voice of) Nick Lucas, Pamela Myers

Songs: Jeepers Creepers (Armstrong) music: Harry Warren; lyrics:
           Johnny Mercer (recorded 1938)
       The Storyteller / Garden of the Locust (orchestra)
       Isn't It Romantic (Dees) music: Richard Rodgers; lyrics:
           Lorenz Hart (musical direction: Pete King)
       The Flying Carpet (orchestra)
       A Picture of Love (orchestra)
       I Wished on the Moon (Lucas) music: Ralph Rainger; lyrics:
           Dorothy Parker
       Soft Shoe Salesman (orchestra)
---   Fire and Passion (orchestra)
       Hot Voodoo (Jabara) music: Ralph Rainger; lyrics: Sam
           Coslow (musical direction: Pete King)
       Fashion and Fantasy (orchestra)
       Sing You Sinners (Myers) music: W Franke Harling; lyrics:
           Sam Coslow
       The Day of the Locust (orchestra)
       Theme from 'The Day of the Locust' / Finale (orchestra)

THE DAYDREAMER (Embassy, 1966)

Columbia OS 2940 (soundtrack) stereo

Music: Maury Laws; lyrics: Jules Bass

Cast: Ray Bolger, (the voices of Patty Duke, Robert Goulet,
        Robert Harter, Hayley Mills), Paul O'Keefe, (the voice
        of Ed Wynn)

Songs: Daydreamer (Goulet)
       Overture (orchestra)
       Wishes and Teardrops (Mills)
       Happy Guy (Duke, chorus)
       Isn't It Cozy (trio)
       Tivoli Bells (orchestra)

---   Daydreamer (reprise) (chorus)
        Luck to Sell (O'Keefe)
        Who Can Tell (Bolger, Harter, chorus)
        Waltz for A Mermaid (chorus)
        Simply Wonderful (Wynn, men)
        Voyage of the Walnut Shell (chorus)
        Finale (Daydreamer) (orchestra)

DEEP IN MY HEART (MGM, 1954)

MGM E 3153 (soundtrack) mono   reissued: MCAD 5949 (CD)

Music: Sigmund Romberg; lyrics: Dorothy Donnelly, Roger Edens, Oscar Hammerstein II, Otto Harbach, Ballard MacDonald, Herbert Reynolds, Cyrus Wood, Rida Johnson Young; musical direction: Adolph Deutsch

Cast: Rosemary Clooney, Vic Damone, Jose Ferrer, Howard Keel, Fred Kelly, Gene Kelly, Tony Martin, Ann Miller, William Olvis, Jane Powell, Helen Traubel

Songs: Overture: Will You Remember, The Desert Song, One Kiss
      (orchestra), Deep in My Heart (chorus) lyrics: Donnelly
     Leg of Mutton (Some Smoke) (Ferrer, Traubel) lyrics: Edens
     Your Land and My Land (Keel, chorus) lyrics; Donnelly
     You Will Remember Vienna (Traubel) lyrics: Hammerstein
     It (Miller, chorus) lyrics: Harbach, Hammerstein
     Auf Wiedersehn (Traubel) lyrics: Reynolds
     Serenade (Olvis, chorus) lyrics: Donnelly
---   Softly As in A Morning Sunrise (Traubel) lyrics:
       Hammerstein
     Road to Paradise (Damone) lyrics: Young
     Will You Remember (Sweetheart) (Powell, Damone) lyrics:
       Young
     Mr and Mrs (Ferrer, Clooney) lyrics: Wood
     I Love to Go Swimmin' with Wimmen (Gene Kelly, Fred Kelly,
       girls) lyrics: MacDonald
     Lover Come Back to Me (Martin) lyrics: Hammerstein
     Stout Hearted Men (Traubel) lyrics: Hammerstein
     When I Grow Too Old to Dream (Ferrer, chorus) lyrics:
       Hammerstein

Note: The above recording includes spoken dialog and a narration. The following selections were not used in the film, but released on other recordings (Cut! Out Takes OTF - 3):

      One Kiss (Powell) lyrics: Hammerstein
      Dance My Darlings (Traubel) lyrics: Hammerstein

DELIGHTFULLY DANGEROUS (United Artists, 1945)

Curtain Calls CC 100/4 (soundtrack) mono 'Jane Powell'

Music: Morton Gould; lyrics: Edward Heyman; musical direction: Morton Gould

Cast: Constance Moore, Jane Powell

Songs: In A Shower of Stars (Powell)
        Once Upon A Song (Powell)
        Through Your Eyes to Your Heart (Powell)

Note: The following additional soundtrack selection is included
        on Legends 1000/2 'Ladies of Burlesque'

        I'm Only Teasin' (Moore)

THE DESERT SONG (Warner Bros, 1943)

Columbia ML 4272 mono

Music: Sigmund Romberg; lyrics: Otto Harbach, Oscar Hammerstein
II; musical direction: Edgar Roemheid

Cast: Dennis Morgan

Songs: The Desert Song (Morgan, chorus)
        One Flower Grows Alone in Your Garden (Morgan, chorus)
        One Alone (Morgan, chorus)
        The Riff Song (Morgan, chorus)

THE DESERT SONG (Warner Bros, 1953)

RCA LPM 3105 mono

Music: Sigmund Romberg, others; lyrics: Otto Harbach, Oscar
Hammerstein II, others; musical direction; Arthur Fiedler

Cast: Kathryn Grayson, Tony Martin (not in film)

Songs: The Riff Song (Martin, chorus)
        Gay Parisienne (Grayson, Martin) music: Sergai Walter;
          lyrics: Jack Scholl
        Long Live the Night (Grayson, Martin) lyrics: Mario Sylva
        Romance (Grayson)
---   The Desert Song (Grayson, Martin)
        One Flower Grows Alone in Your Garden (Grayson, chorus)
        One Alone (Grayson, Martin)
        The Night Is Young (Martin) not from film

THE DESERT SONG (Warner Bros, 1953)

Capitol T 384 mono

Music: Sigmund Romberg; lyrics: Otto Harbach, Oscar Hammerstein II; musical direction: George Greeley

Cast: Gordon MacRae, Lucille Norman (not in film), Thurl
        Ravenscroft (not in film), Bob Sands (not in film)

Songs: Overture (orchestra)
       Prologue (Sands, male chorus)
       Riff Song (MacRae, male chorus)
       Why Did We Marry Soldiers (girls' chorus)
       French Military Marching Song (Norman, girls' chorus)
       Romance (Norman)
       Then You'll Know (MacRae, Norman, chorus)
       The Desert Song (MacRae)
       Let Love Come (Ravenscroft)
       One Flower (Sands)
       One Alone (MacRae)
       Duet (MacRae, Norman)
       Sabre Song (Norman)
       Finale: The Desert Song (MacRae, chorus)
               The Riff Song (MacRae, chorus)
               One Alone (Norman, MacRae, chorus)

DICK DEADEYE (Intercontinental, 1975)

GM Records GML 1018 (British) (soundtrack) stereo

Music: Arthur Sullivan; lyrics: W S Gilbert; new lyrics: Robin Miller; musical direction: Jimmy Horowitz

Cast: (the voice of) John Baldry, Barry Cryer, Miriam Karlin,
        Casey Kelly, Linda Lewis, Peter Reeves, Ian Samwell,
        Victor Spinetti, Liza Strike

Songs: Overture (Iolanthe, Act I) (orchestra)
       Peers March (chorus)
       Here's A How D'ye Do (Mikado, Act II) (Spinetti, Reeves)
       Modern Major General (Pirates, Act I) (Baldry, ladies)
       I Am A Pirate King (Pirates, Act I) (pirates)
       Willow Waley (Patience, Act II) (Spinetti, Strike)
       John Wellington Wells (Sorcerer, Act I) (Reeves)
       Policeman's Lot (Pirates, Act II) (policemen)
       All Hail Great Judge (Trial by Jury, Act I) (chorus)
       From Bias Free (Trial by Jury, Act I) (Cryer, ladies)
       A Wandering Minstrel I (Mikado, Act I) (Kelly)
       A Most Intense Young Man (Patience, Act II) (Kelly,
           Cryer, jury)
 ---   For I Am A Judge (Trial by Jury) (Cryer, chorus)

        Farewell the World (Kelly)
        Moon and I (Mikado, Act II) (Lewis)
        I Am the Monarch of the Sea (Pinafore, Act I) (Baldry,
           ladies)
        The Flowers That Bloom in the Spring (Mikado, Act II)
           (Kelly, Samwell, prisoners)
        When I Was A Lad (Pinafore, Act I) (Baldry, ladies)
        Captain of the Pinafore (Pinafore, Act I) (Reeves,
           Spinetti, sailors)
        When the Pirate Bares His Steel - Tarantara (Pinafore,
           Act I) (chorus)
        A Many Years Ago (Pinafore, Act II) (Karlin, sailors)
        Hail Hail (chorus)
        Finale: Ultimate Secret Song (Nothing Venture) (chorus)
               My Love and I (Lewis, Kelly)
               Here's A How D'ye Do (reprise) (chorus)
               Ultimate Secret Song (Nothing Venture) (reprise)
                  (chorus)
               Willow Waley (reprise) (Spinetti, Strike)
               Ultimate Secret Song (Nothing Venture) (reprise)
                  (chorus)

DIMPLES (Twentieth Century-Fox, 1936)

Dox 3045 (soundtrack) mono 'More Little Miss Wonderful'

Music: Jimmy McHugh; lyrics: Ted Koehler; musical direction:
Louis Silvers

Cast: Shirley Temple

Songs: Hey! What Did the Bluejay Say? (Temple)
       Picture Me Without You (Temple)
       He Was A Dandy (Temple)

DOCTOR DOLITTLE (Twentieth Century-Fox, 1967)

Fox DTCS 5101 (soundtrack) stereo

Music, lyrics: Leslie Bricusse; musical direction: Lionel Newman

Cast: Richard Attenborough, William Dix, Samantha Eggar, Rex
      Harrison, Anthony Newley

Songs: Overture (orchestra)
       My Friend the Doctor (Newley)
       The Vegetarian (Harrison)
       Talk to the Animals (Harrison)
       At the Crossroads (Egger)
       I've Never Seen Anything Like It (Attenborough)
       Beautiful Things (Newley, Eggar)

```
         When I Look in Your Eyes (Harrison)
---      Like Animals (Harrison)
         After Today (Newley)
         Fabulous Places (Eggar, Harrison, Newley)
         Where Are the Words (Newley)
         I Think I Like You (Harrison, Eggar)
         Doctor  Dolittle (Newley, Dix, children)
         Something in Your Smile (Harrison)
         My Friend the Doctor (reprise) (chorus)
```

Note: Anthony Newley also recorded an album of this score on
        RCA LSP 3839

DOCTOR RHYTHM (Paramount, 1938)

Decca DL 4253 mono 'Bing's Hollywood – East Side of Heaven'

Music: James V Monaco; lyrics: John Burke; musical direction:
John Scott Trotter

Cast: Bing Crosby

Songs: On the Sentimental Side (Crosby)
        My Heart Is Taking Lessons (Crosby)
        This Is My Night to Dream (Crosby)

THE DOLLY SISTERS (Twentieth Century-Fox, 1945)

Classic International Filmusicals C I F 3010 (soundtrack) mono

Music: James Monaco, others; lyrics: Mack Gordon, others;
musical direction: Charles Henderson, Alfred newman

Cast: Betty Grable, June Haver, John Payne

Songs: Opening and Titles (orchestra)
        Vamp (Grable, Haver) music, lyrics: Byron Gay
        I Can't Begin to Tell You (Payne)
        Give Me the Moonlight (Payne, Crable, chorus) music:
           Albert Von Tilzer; lyrics: Lew Brown
        We've Been Around (Grable, Haver) music: Charles Henderson
        Carolina in the Morning (Grable, Haver) music: Walter
           Donaldson; lyrics: Gus Kahn
        Don't Be Too Old Fashioned (Grable, Haver, chorus)
        Powder, Lipstick and Rouge (Grable, Haver, girls) music:
           Harry Revel
        I'm Always Chasing Rainbows (Payne, Grable) music: Harry
           Carroll; lyrics: Joseph McCarthy
---   Dark Town Strutters Ball (Grable, Haver, girls) music,
           lyrics: Shelton Brooks (sung in French and English)
        I Can't Begin to Tell You (reprise) (Grable)
```
```

          Arrah Go On, I'm Gonna Go Back to Oregon (men) music:
               Bert Grant; lyrics: Joe Young, Sam Lewis
          Smiles (men) music: Lee Roberts; lyrics: J Will
               Callahan
          Oh Frenchie (chorus) music: Con Conrad; lyrics: Sam
               Ehrlich
          Medley: I'm Always Chasing Rainbows (reprise) (Payne)
                    Arrah Go On, I'm Gonna Go Back to Oregon (reprise)
                       (Payne)
                    I Can't Begin to Tell You (reprise) (Payne)
          Hindustan (orchestra) music: Harold Weeks
          The Sidewalks of New York (Grable, Haver) music: Charles
               B Lawlor; lyrics: James W Blake
          I'm Always Chasing Rainbows (reprise) (Payne)
          I Can't Begin to Tell You (reprise) (Payne, Grable,
               Haver)

Note: The above recording includes spoken dialog. Betty Grable
        made her only studio recording (as 'Dolly Haag') from
        the score of this film:

        Columbia (78rpm) 36867 I Can't Begin to Tell You
                             (LP: Columbia CL 2534)

DOUBLE DYNAMITE! (RKO, 1951)

Motion Picture Tracks M P T - 7 (soundtrack) mono

Music: Jule Styne; lyrics: Sammy Cahn

Cast: Groucho Marx, Jane Russell, Frank Sinatra

Songs: Opening Title - It's Only Money (orchestra)
        It's Only Money (Sinatra, Marx)
        Kisses and Tears (Russell, Sinatra)
        It's Only Money (reprise) (Sinatra, Marx, Russell)

Note: Studio recording by cast members:

        Columbia (78rpm) 38790 Kisses and Tears (Russell, Sinatra)
                             (LP: Columbia CL 2530)

DOUBLE OR NOTHING (Paramount, 1937)

Decca DL 4252 mono 'Bing's Hollywood - Pocket Full of Dreams'

Music: Arthur Johnston; lyrics: John Burke; musical direction:
John Scott Trotter

Cast: Bing Crosby

Songs: It's the Natural Thing to Do (Crosby)
       (You Know It All) Smarty (Crosby) music: Burton Lane;
           lyrics: Ralph Freed
---   The Moon Got in My Eyes (Crosby)
       All You Want to Do Is Dance (Crosby)

Note: Additional soundtrack recordings are included on Legends
      1000/15-16, 'Martha Raye'

      Listen My Children (Raye)
      After You (Crosby, Raye, Frances Faye)

DOUBLE TROUBLE (MGM, 1967)

RCA LSP 3787 stereo   reissued: APL 1-2564

Music, lyrics: Randy Starr, others

Cast: Elvis Presley

Songs: Double Trouble (Presley) music: Mort Shuman; lyrics:
           Doc Pomus
       Could I Fall in Love (Presley)
       Baby, If You'll Give Me All of Your Love (Presley)
           music, lyrics: Joy Byers
       Long Legged Girl (Presley) music: Winfield Scott; lyrics:
           J Leslie McFarland
       City by Night (Presley) music: Florence Kaye; lyrics:
           Bill Giant, Bernie Baum
       I Love Only One Girl (Presley) music: Roy C Bennett;
           lyrics: Sid Tepper
       Old MacDonald (Presley)
       There Is So Much World to See (Presley) music: Ben
           Weisman; lyrics: Sid Tepper

DOWN ARGENTINE WAY (Twentieth Century-Fox, 1940)

Hollywood Soundstage 5013 (soundtrack) mono

Music: Harry Warren, others; lyrics: Mack Gordon, others;
musical direction: Emil Newman

Cast: Carlos Albert (for Don Ameche in Spanish), Don Ameche,
      Bando Da Lua, Betty Grable, Charlotte Greenwood, Pepe

Guizar, Leonid Kinsky, Chris-Pin Martin, Carmen Miranda,
J Carrol Naish, Harold Nicholas, Henry Stephenson

Songs: Opening Credits: Down Argentina Way (chorus)
South American Way (Miranda, Bando Da Lua, chorus)
   music: Jimmy McHugh; lyrics: Al Dubin
Down Argentina Way (Albert / Ameche, Grable, chorus)
Musical Montage (chorus)
Down Argentina Way (reprise) (Nicholas)
Nenita (Kinsky, trio)
Doin' the Conga (orchestra) music: Gene Rose
Mamae eu Quero (Miranda, Bando Da Lua) music, lyrics:
   Al Stillman, Jararaca and Vincente Paiva
Bambu, Bambu (Miranda, Bando Da Lua) music, lyrics:
   Patricia Teixeira, Donga
Fiesta Time (orchestra)
Sing for Your Senorita (Greenwood, chorus)
Two Dreams Met (Guizar, chorus, Grable, Ameche)
Mamae eu Quero (reprise) (orchestra)
Finale: Down Argentina Way (Naish, Martin, Nicholas)
      Sing to Your Senorita (Greenwood, chorus)
      Down Argentina Way (Stephenson, Kinsky, Greenwood,
      chorus)
      Two Dreams Met (Ameche, Grable, chorus)
End Credits (orchestra)

Note: The above recording includes spoken dialog. Carmen Miranda
studio recordings:

Decca (78rpm) 23130 South American Way (LP: AH 99)
Decca (78rpm) 23132 Mamae eu Quero (LP: AH 69)
                  Bambu, Bambu

DOWN TO EARTH (Columbia, 1947)

Curtain Calls CC 100/22 (soundtrack) mono 'Rita Hayworth'

Music, lyrics: Doris Fisher, Allen Roberts; musical direction:
Morris Stoloff

Cast: Anita Ellis (for Rita Hayworth), Larry Parks

Songs: Let's Stay Young Forever (Ellis)
They Can't Convince Me (Parks, Ellis)
People Have More Fun than Anyone (Ellis, chorus)

THE DUKE WORE JEANS (Insignia, 1958) British

Decca (British) LF 1308 (soundtrack) mono

Music, lyrics: Lionel Bart, Jimmy Bennett, Michael Pratt;
musical direction: Roland Shaw

Cast: June Laverick, Tommy Steele

Songs: It's All Happening (Steele)
        What Do You Do (Steele)
        Family Tree (Steele)
        Happy Guitar (Steele)
---   Hair-Down Hoe-Down (Steele, chorus)
        Princess (Steele)
        Photograph (Steele, Laverick)
        Thanks A Lot (Steele)

Note: 'Jimmy Bennett' is a pseudonym for Tommy Steele.

DUMBO (Disney, 1941)

Disneyland 1204 (soundtrack) mono

Music: Frank E Churchill; lyrics: Ned Washington, others

Cast: Betty Noyes

Songs: Main Title (orchestra)
        Look Out for Mr Stork (chorus)
        Casey Jr (chorus)
        Song of the Roustabouts (chorus)
        It's Circus Day Again (orchestra)
        Dumbo Theme (orchestra)
        Baby Mine (Noyes)
---   Pink Elephants on Parade (chorus) lyrics: Oliver Wallace
        Dumbo and Timothy (orchestra)
        Pyramid of Elephants (orchestra)
        Dumbo Disgraced (orchestra)
        When I See An Elephant Fly (crow quintet) lyrics: Oliver
            Wallace
        Dumbo's Triumph (orchestra)
        Finale (orchestra)

EAST SIDE OF HEAVEN (Universal, 1939)

Decca DL 4253 mono 'Bing's Hollywood - East Side of Heaven'

Music: James V Monaco; lyrics: John Burke; musical direction:
John Scott Trotter

Cast: Bing Crosby

Songs: East Side of Heaven (Crosby)
        That Sly Old Gentleman (from Featherbed Lane) (Crosby)

       Hang Your Heart on A Hickery Limb (Crosby)
       Sing A Song of Sunbeams (Crosby)

EASTER PARADE (MGM, 1948)

MGM E 502 (soundtrack) mono reissued: MCA 1459 CD

Music, lyrics: Irving Berlin; musical direction: John Green

Cast: Fred Astaire, Judy Garland, Peter Lawford, Ann Miller

Songs: Steppin' Out with My Baby (Astaire, chorus)
       A Fella with An Umbrella (Garland, Lawford)
       Shaking the Blues Away (Miller, chorus)
       I Love A Piano (Garland)
       Snooky Ookums (Garland, Astaire)
       When the Midnight Choo Choo Leaves for Alabam' (Garland,
         Astaire)
\---   A Couple of Swells (Garland, Astaire)
       It Only Happens When I Dance with You (Astaire)
       Better Luck Next Time (Garland)
       Easter Parade (Garland, Astaire, chorus)

Note: An additional selection, cut from final film:

       Mr Monotony (Garland) LP: Out Takes OTF-1

EASY COME, EASY GO (Paramount, 1967)

RCA (45/EP) EPA 4387 stereo

Music, lyrics: various

Cast: Elvis Presley

Songs: Easy Come, Easy Go (Presley) music: Ben Weisman; lyrics:
       Sid Wayne
       The Love Machine (Presley) music, lyrics: Gerald Nelson,
       Fred Burch, Chuck Taylor
       Yoga Is As Yoga Does (Presley) music, lyrics: Gerald
       Wilson, Fred Burch
\---   You Gotta Stop (Presley) music, lyrics: Bill Grant, Bernie
       Baum, Florence Kaye
       Sing You Children (Presley) music, lyrics: Gerald Nelson,
       Fred Burch
       I'll Take Love (Presley) music, lyrics: Dolores Fuller,
       Mark Barkan

THE EDDIE CANTOR STORY (Warner Bros, 1954)

Capitol L-467 (soundtrack) mono

Music, lyrics: various; musical direction: Ray Heindorf

Cast: Eddie Cantor (for Keefe Brasselle)

Songs: Now's the Time to Fall in Love (Cantor) music, lyrics:
            Al Lewis, Al Sherman
        When I'm the President (Cantor, chorus) music, lyrics:
            Al Lewis, Al Sherman
        If You Knew Susie (Cantor) music: Joseph Meyer; lyrics:
            Buddy DeSylva
        Ida! Sweet As Apple Cider (Cantor) music: Eddie Leonard;
            lyrics: Eddie Munson
        Josephine Please No Lean on the Bell (Cantor) music,
            lyrics: Edward Nelson, Harry Pease, Duke Leonard
        Pretty Baby (Cantor) music: Tony Jackson, Egbert Van
            Alstyne; lyrics: Gus Kahn
        You Must Have Been A Beautiful Baby (Cantor) music:
            Harry Warren; lyrics: Johnny Mercer
        Yes Sir, That's My Baby (Cantor) music: Walter Donaldson;
            lyrics: Gus Kahn
---   Makin' Whoopee (Cantor) music: Walter Donaldson; lyrics:
            Gus Kahn
        Ma (He's Making Eyes at Me) (Cantor, chorus) music: Con
            Conrad; lyrics: Sidney Clare
        Bye, Bye, Blackbird (Cantor) music: Ray Henderson; lyrics:
            Mort Dixon
        Margie (Cantor) music: Con Conrad, J Russell Robinson;
            lyrics: Benny Davis
        Row, Row, Row (Cantor) music: James V Monaco; lyrics:
            William Jerome
        How 'Ya Gonna Keep 'em Down on the Farm (Cantor) music:
            Walter Donaldson; lyrics: Sam M Lewis, Joe Young
        One Hour with You (Each Sunday with You) (Cantor) music:
            Richard Whiting; lyrics: Leo Robin

THE EMPEROR WALTZ (Paramount, 1948)

Decca DL 4260 mono 'Bing's Hollywood But Beautiful'

Music: various; lyrics: John Burke, others; musical direction:
Victor Young

Cast: Bing Crosby

Songs: Friendly Mountains (Crosby, chorus) music: arranged by
            Joseph Lilley
        I Kiss Your Hand, Madame (Crosby) music: Ralph Erwin;
            lyrics: Sam M Lewis, Joe Young
        The Kiss in Your Eyes (Crosby) music: Richard Heuberger
        Emperor Waltz (Crosby) music: Johann Strauss

EVERGREEN (Gaumont-British, 1934)

Music for Pleasure (British) MFP 1127 mono 'Jessie Matthews'

Music, lyrics: Harry M Woods, others

Cast: Jessie Matthews

Songs: Tinkle, Tinkle, Tinkle (Matthews)
       Over My Shoulder (Matthews)
       When You've Got A Little Springtime in Your Heart
         (Matthews)
       Just By Your Example (Matthews)
       Dancing on the Ceiling (Matthews) music: Richard Rodgers;
         lyrics: Lorenz Hart

EVERY DAY'S A HOLIDAY (Grand National, 1964) British

Decca (British 45/EP) DFE 8606 (soundtrack) mono

Music, lyrics: various

Cast: The Baker Twins, Granzina Frame, Ron Moody, Michael Ripper

Songs: Every Day's A Holiday (Frame) music, lyrics: Mort Shuman,
         Clive Westlake
       Romeo Jones (The Baker Twins) music, lyrics: Mort Shuman,
         McFarland
---   Second Time Around (Frame) music, lyrics: Clive Westlake
       Now Ain't That Somethin' Caw (Moody, Ripper) music,
         lyrics: Mort Shuman, McFarland

Note: A Second soundtrack album was issued by Mercury Records
       under the American title of this film. See:

       SEASIDE SWINGERS (Avco Embassy, 1965)

EVERY NIGHT AT EIGHT (Twentieth Century-Fox, 1935)

Take Two TT 214 mono 'Frances Langford'

Music: Jimmy McHugh, others; lyrics: Dorothy Fields, others;
musical direction: Mahon Merrick, others

Cast: Frances Langford

Songs: I Feel A Song Coming On (Langford) co-lyr: George Oppenheim
       Then You've Never Been Blue (Langford) music: Ted Fio Rito;
         lyrics: Sam L Lewis, Joe Young
       Speaking Confidentially (Langford)

I'm In the Mood for Love (Langford)
It's Like Reaching for the Moon (Langford) music, lyrics:
  Al Lewis, Al Sherman, Marqusee; musical direction:
  Victor Young

Note: Additional recordings, with Alice Faye and Patsy Kelly:

  Speaking Confidentially (Faye) LP: CL 3068 'Alice Faye'
  I Feel A Song Coming On (Faye, Kelly, Langford) (sound-
    track) LP: Curtain Calls CC 100/3 'Alice Faye'

EVERY WHICH WAY BUT LOOSE (Warner Bros, 1978)

Elektra 5E-503 (soundtrack) stereo

Music, lyrics: various; musical direction: Steve Dorff

Cast: Carol Chase, Larry Collins, Cliff Crofford, Phil Everly,
     Sondra Locke, Eddie Rabbitt, Charlie Rich, Hank Thompson,
     Mel Tillis

Songs: Every Which Way but Loose (Rabbitt) music, lyrics: Steve
     Dorff, M Brown, T Garrett
     Send Me Down to Tucson (Tillis) music, lyrics: Cliff
      Crofford, T Garrett
     I Seek the Night (Locke) music, lyrics: Neil Diamond
     Coca-Cola Cowboy (Tillis) music, lyrics: Steve Dorff,
      S Alchley, S Pinkard, I Dain
     Monkey See, Monkey Do (Crofford) music, lyrics: Cliff
      Crofford, T Garrett
     Salty Dog Blues (orchestra) music adapted: Steve Dorff,
      T Garrett
     I'll Wake You When I Get Home (Rich) music, lyrics:
      Steve Dorff, M Brown
     Red Eye Special (Collins) music, lyrics: Larry Collins,
      S Pinkard, T Garrett
     Eastwood's Alley Walk (orchestra) music: Steve Dorff,
      T Garrett
     Behind Closed Doors (Rich) music, lyrics: K O'Dell
     I Can't Say No to A Truck Drivin' Man (Chase) music,
      lyrics: Cliff Crofford
     Under the Double Eagle (orchestra) music adapted: Steve
      Dorff, T Garrett
     Biker's Theme (orchestra) music: Steve Dorff, T Garrett
     Don't Say You Don't Love Me No More (Locke, Everly) music:
      lyrics: Phil Everly, J Paige
     A Six Pack to Go (Thompson) music, lyrics: Hank Thompson,
      J Lowe, D Hart
     Overture (orchestra):
      Every Which Way but Loose
      I Seek the Night
      I'll Wake You Up When I Get Home

EVERYTHING I HAVE IS YOURS (MGM, 1952)

MGM E 187 (soundtrack) mono reissued: MCA 39081 CD

Music, lyrics: various; musical direction: David Rose, others

Cast: Gower Champion, Marge Champion, Monica Lewis

Songs: Like Monday Follows Sunday (Marge and Gower Champion)
            music, lyrics: Johnny Mercer, C Grey, R Newman, Douglas
            Furber
       Everything I Have Is Yours (Lewis) music: Burton Lane;
            lyrics: Harold Adamson
       Seventeen Thousand Telephone Poles (Lewis, chorus) music,
            lyrics: Saul Chaplin
       Derry Down Dilly (Marge Champion) music: Johnny Green;
            lyrics: Johnny Mercer
       Serenade for A New Baby (orchestra) music, musical
            direction: Johnny Green

EVERYTHING IS RHYTHM (Astor, 1936) British

World Records (British) SH 197 (soundtrack) mono 'Bands on Film'

Music: Cyril Ray, others; lyrics: Jack Meskill, others; musical
direction: Harry Roy

Cast: Bill Currie, Mabel Mercer, Ivor Moreton, Mr and Mrs Harry
       Roy, Phyllis Thackery

Songs: You're the Last Word in Love (orchestra)
       Cheerful Blues (Harry Roy) music, lyrics: Harry Roy
       You're the Last Word in Love (reprise) (Harry Roy,
            Thackery, Moreton)
       Black Minnie's Got the Blues (Harry Roy, Mercer, chorus)
       Make Mine Music (Harry Roy, chorus)
       Man of My Dreams (Mrs Harry Roy) not from soundtrack
       Life Is Empty without Love (Mr and Mrs Harry Roy)
       The Internationalle (Harry Roy)
---   No Words Nor Anything (Harry Roy, Moreton, Currie)
       Life Is Empty without Love (reprise) (Harry Roy)
       Sky High Romance (Mr and Mrs Harry Roy, ensemble)

EXPRESSO BONGO (British Lion, 1959) British

Columbia (British 45/EP) SEG 7971 stereo

Music, lyrics: Robert Farnon, Val Guest, Norrie Paramor, Bunny
Lewis, Paddy Roberts, others

Cast: Cliff Richard

Songs: Love (Richard)
      A Voice in the Wilderness (Richard)
---   The Shrine on the Second Floor (Richard) music: David
         Heneker, Monty Norman; lyrics: Julian More, David
         Heneker, Monty Morman
      Bongo Blues (Richard)

A FACE IN THE CROWD (Warner Bros, 1957)

Capitol W 872 (soundtrack) mono

Music: Tom Glazer; lyrics: Budd Schulberg

Cast: Andy Griffith

Songs: Main Title (A Face in the Crowd) (orchestra)
      Free Man in the Morning (Griffith)
      Fruit Salad Ferryboat (orchestra)
      Old Fashioned Marriage (female trio)
      Just Plain Folks (male group)
      Medley: Free Man in the Morning; Just Plain Folks (piano)
      Mama Guitar (Griffith)
---   Rock-A-Billy Rock (orchestra)
      Just A Closer Walk with Thee (Griffith) trad
      March Montage (orchestra)
      Vitajex Jingle (female trio)
      Rain Fever (orchestra)
      Elevator (orchestra)
      A Face in the Crowd (reprise) (Griffith)

FAME (MGM, 1980)

RSO RX 1-3080 (soundtrack) stereo CD

Music: Michael Gore, others; lyrics: Dean Pitchford, others;
musical direction: Michael Gore

Cast: Irene Cara, (the voice of) Linda Clifford, Paul McCrane

Songs: Fame (Cara, chorus)
      Out Here on My Own (Cara) lyrics: Lesley Gore
      Hot Lunch Jam (Cara, chorus) lyrics: Lesley Gore, Robert
        F Colesberry
      Dogs in the Yard (McCrane) music, lyrics: Dominic Bugatti,
        Frank Musker
---   Red Light (Clifford, chorus)
      Is It Okay If I Call You Mine? (McCrane) music, lyrics:
        Paul McCrane
      Never Alone (chorus) music: Anthony Evans
      Ralph and Monty (dressing room piano)
      I Sing the Body Electric (cast)

THE FASTEST GUITAR ALIVE (MGM, 1967)

MGM SE 4475 (soundtrack) stereo reissued: MCA 1437

Music, lyrics: Bill Dees, Roy Orbison

Cast: Roy Orbison

Songs: Whirlwind (Orbison)
       Medicine Man (Orbison)
       River (Orbison)
       The Fastest Guitar Alive (Orbison)
       Rollin' On (Orbison)
---   Pistolero (Orbison)
       Good Time Party (Orbison)
       Heading South (Orbison)
       Best Friend (Orbison)
       There Won't Be Many Coming Home (Orbison)

FIDDLER ON THE ROOF (United Artists, 1971)

United Artists UAS 10900 (two records - soundtrack) stereo CD

Music: Jerry Bock; lyrics: Shelton Harnick; musical direction:
John Williams (violin solos: Isaac Stern)

Cast: Patience Collier, Norma Crane, Leonard Frey, Michael
       Glaser, Rosalind Harris, Ruth Madoc, Paul Mann, Michele
       Marsh, Molly Picon, Shimen Ruskin, Neva Small, Topol

Songs: Prologue (Stern, orchestra)
       Tradition (Topol, chorus)
       Main Title (Stern, orchestra)
       Matchmaker (Harris, Marsh, Small)
---   If I Were A Rich Man (Topol)
       Sabbath Prayer (Topol, Crane, chorus; Stern)
       To Life (Topol, Mann, chorus)
       Miracle of Miracles (Frey)
---   Tevye's Dream (Topol, Crane, Collier, Madoc, chorus)
       Sunrise, Sunset (Topol, Crane, Glaser, Marsh, chorus; Stern)
       Wedding Celebration and 'The Bottle Dance' (chorus)
---   Do You Love Me? (Topol, Crane)
       Far from the Home I Love (Marsh, Topol)
       Chava Ballet Sequence (Topol; Stern)
       Anatevka (Topol, Crane, Mann, Picon, Ruskin, chorus; Stern)
       Finale (orchestra; Stern)

Note: The above recording includes spoken dialog.

FINIAN'S RAINBOW (Warner Bros, 1968)

Warner Bros BS 2550 (soundtrack) stereo

Music: Burton Lane; lyrics: E Y Harburg; musical direction:
Ray Heindorf

Cast: Brenda Arnau, Fred Astaire, Petula Clark, Don Francks,
        Roy Glenn, Barbara Hancock, Jester Hairston, Avon Long,
        Tommy Steele, Keenan Wynn

Songs: Prelude: Look to the Rainbow (Main Title) (Clark, chorus)
        This Time of the Year (chorus)
        How Are Things in Glocca Morra? (Clark, Astaire)
        Look to the Rainbow (Clark, Francks, Astaire)
        If This Isn't Love (Francks, Clark, Astaire, chorus)
        Something Sort of Grandish (Steele, Clark)
        That Great Come-and-Get-It Day (Francks, Clark, chorus)
---   Old Devil Moon (Francks, Clark)
        When the Idle Poor Become the Idle Rich (Astaire, Clark,
            chorus)
        When I'm Not Near the Girl I Love (Steele)
        Necessity (Arnau, chorus)
        Rain Dance Ballet (chorus)
        The Begat (Wynn, Long, Hairston, Glenn)
        How Are Things in Glocca Morra? (Finale) (Clark, Francks,
            Steele, Hancock, chorus)

Note: The above recording includes spoken dialog.

FIRST LOVE (Universal, 1939)

Decca (78rpm) 75 mono 'Deanna Durbin Souvenir Album No 2'

Music, lyrics: various

Cast: Deanna Durbin

Decca (78rpm) 15044 Spring in My Heart (Durbin) based on a melody
                    by Johann Strauss, adapted by Hans J Salter
                    and Ralph Freed (LP: Ace of Hearts 60)
                    Madama Butterfly: One Fine Day (Durbin) music:
                    Puccini (LP: Ace of Hearts 93)
Decca (78rpm) 2758 Home, Sweet Home (Durbin) music: Sir Henry
                    Bishop; lyrics: John Howard Payne (LP: AH 60)

Note: Other recordings:

Decca (78rpm) 3063 Amapola (Durbin) music: Joseph M Lacalle;
                    lyrics: Reginald Connelly
Decca (LP) DL 75289 Spring in My Heart (soundtrack) (Durbin)

THE FIRST NUDIE MUSICAL (Northal, 1977)

Varese Sarabande VC 81028 (soundtrack) stereo

Music, lyrics: Bruce Kimmel; musical direction: Rene Hall

Cast: Diana Canova, Valerie Gillett, Bruce Kimmel, Alexandra
       Morgan, Stephen Nathan, Annette O'Toole (for Leslie
       Ackerman), Debbie Shapiro, Cindy Williams

Songs: Overture (orchestra)
       The First Nudie Musical (Nathan, chorus)
       The Lights and the Smiles (O'Toole)
       Orgasm ('Mr Tux')
       Lesbian, Butch, Dyke (Shapiro)
       Dancing Dildos (Morgan, chorus)
---   Perversion (Canova, chorus)
       Where Is A Man? (Gillett) cut from film
       Honey, What Ya Doin' Tonight? (girls)
       Let 'em Eat Cake (Nathan, Williams, chorus)
       I Don't Have to Hide Anymore (Kimmel, chorus)

THE FIVE PENNIES (Paramount, 1959)

Dot 29500 (soundtrack) stereo

Music, lyrics: Sylvia Fine, others; musical direction: Leith
Stevens

Cast: Louis Armstrong, Susan Gordon, Danny Kaye, Eileen Wilson
       (for Barbara Bel Geddes)

Songs: Main Title (orchestra)
       The Five Pennies (Kaye)
       After You've Gone (orchestra) music: Turner Layton
       Bill Bailey, Won't You Please Come Home (Armstrong, Kaye)
          music, lyrics: Hughie Cannon
       Indiana Radio Montage: Back Home Again in Indiana
          (unidentified vocals) music: James F Hanley; lyrics:
          Ballard MacDonald
       Back Home Again in Indiana (reprise) (orchestra)
       Goodnight, Sleep Tight (Wilson)
       Lullaby in Ragtime (Kaye) with reprise of Wilson singing
          'Goodnight, Sleep Tight' contrapuntally
       Battle Hymn of the Republic (Armstrong) trad
---   The Five Pennies Saints (Kaye, Armstrong) trad (S Fine
          version of 'When the Saints Go Marchin' In')
       College Montage: Washington and Lee Swing (orchestra)
                        music: Thornton Allen, M W Sheafe
                   Runnin' Wild (orchestra) music:
                   A Harrington Gibbs
                   Follow the Leader (Kaye, chorus)
       Medley: Goodnight, Sleep Tight (Armstrong)
               Lullaby in Ragtime (Kaye)
               The Five Pennies (Gordon) all sung contrapuntally
       Just the Blues (orchestra) music: Leith Stevens

Carnival in Venice (Kaye) music: Pietro Frosini
The Music Goes 'Round and 'Round (Kaye, Gordon) music,
    lyrics: Ed Farley, Mike Riley, Red Hodgson
Wail of the Winds (orchestra) music: Harry Warren
Jingle Bells (Kaye) trad
Finale: The Five Pennies (Wilson)
        Battle Hymn of the Republic (orchestra)

Note: The above recording includes spoken dialog.

FLAME AND THE FLESH (MGM, 1954)

MGM (45/EP) X 1080 (soundtrack) mono

Music: Nicholas Brodszky; lyrics: Jack Lawrence; musical direction:
George Stoll

Cast: Carlos Thompson

Songs: No One but You (Thompson)
        Languida (Thompson)
---   Peddler Man (Ten I Loved) (Thompson)
        By Candlelight (Thompson)

Note: MGM also released a single soundtrack recording of
        instrumental music from this film, George Stoll conducting:

        MGM (78rpm) 30851 Antonia
                        Fisherman Song
                ---   Peddler Man (Ten I Loved)

THE FLEET'S IN (Paramount, 1942)

Hollywood Soundstage 405 (soundtrack) mono

Music: Victor Schertzinger; lyrics: Johnny Mercer; musical
direction: Victor Young

Cast: Eddie Bracken, Cass Daley, Bob Eberly, Betty Hutton,
        Dorothy Lamour, Helen O'Connell, Betty Jane Rhodes

Songs: Opening Titles (orchestra)
        The Fleet's In (Rhodes)
        Anchors Aweigh (orchestra) music: Alfred Marks
        The Fleet's In (reprise) (chorus)
        Contrasts (Jimmy Dorsey Orchestra)
        Tangerine (Eberly, O'Connell, Dorsey Orchestra) lyrics:
            Frank Loesser
        When You Hear the Time Signal (Lamour, chorus) (Bracken,
            dialog)
        If You Build A Better Mousetrap (Hutton)
        Not Mine (Lamour, Hutton, Bracken, Dorsey Orchestra)

        I Remember You (Lamour, chorus, Dorsey Orchestra)
---   If You Build A Better Mousetrap (reprise) (Eberly,
            O'Connell, Dorsey Orchestra)
        Arthur Murray Taught Me Dancing in A Hurry (Hutton)
        I Remember You (reprise) (Dorsey Orchestra)
        Tomorrow You Belong to Uncle Sammy (Daley)
        Finale (orchestra)

Note: The above recording includes spoken dialog. Studio
        recordings by Jimmy Dorsey Orchestra:

Decca (78rpm) 4122 Not Mine
                   Arthur Murray Taught Me Dancing in A Hurry
Decca (78rpm) 4123 Tangerine
Decca (78rpm) 4132 I Remember You
                   If You Build A Better Mousetrap

FLOWER DRUM SONG (Universal, 1961)

Decca DL 79098 (soundtrack) stereo reissued: MCA 2069

Music: Richard Rodgers; lyrics: Oscar Hammerstein II; musical
direction: Alfred Newman

Cast: Patrick Adiarte, B J Baker (for Nancy Kwan), John Dodson
        (for Kam Tong), Benson Fong, Juanita Hall, Marilyn Horne
        (for Reiko Sato), James Shigeta, Jack Soo, Miyoshi Umeki,
        Victor Sen Yung

Songs: Main Title - Overture: Flower Drum Song (orchestra)
        A Hundred Million Miracles (Umeki, Dodson, chorus)
        The Other Generation (Fong, Hall, Adiarte)
        I Enjoy Being A Girl (Baker)
        I Am Going to Like It Here (Umeki)
        Chop Suey (Shigeta, Hall, Adiarte, chorus)
        Grant Avenue (Baker, chorus)
---   Dream Ballet (orchestra)
        Gliding Through My Memories (Yung, cast)
        Fan Tan Fanny (Baker, chorus)
        Love Look Away (Horne)
        Sunday (Soo, Umeki)
        You·Are Beautiful (Shigeta)
        Don't Marry Me (Soo, Umeki)
        Finale: Wedding Procession - Wedding Ceremony - End Title
           (Umeki, Baker, chorus)

FLYING DOWN TO RIO (RKO, 1933)

Classic International Filmusicals C I F 3004 (soundtrack) mono
also: Sandy Hook SH 2010

Music: Vincent Youmans; lyrics: Edward Eliscu, Gus Kahn; musical
direction: Max Steiner

Cast: Fred Astaire, Etta Moten, Ginger Rogers, Raul Roulien

Songs: Main Title (orchestra)
        Music Makes Me (Rogers)
        Carioca (Moten, unidentified vocalist)
        Orchids in the Moonlight (Roulien)
        Music Makes Me (reprise) (orchestra)
        Flying Down to Rio (Astaire)
        End Titles (orchestra)

Note: The above recording includes spoken dialog. Fred Astaire
        studio recordings, on Monmouth Evergreen LP: MES 7036
        and British World LP: H 124:

        Columbia (78rpm) 2912 Flying Down to Rio
                              Music Makes Me

FOLIES-BERGERE (Films-Around-the-World, 1958)   France

Philips (French 45/EP) 432.140 BE mono

Music, lyrics: various; musical direction: Andre Popp

Cast: Zizi Jeanmaire

Songs: La Croqueuse de Diamant (Jeanmaire) music, lyrics: J M
            Damase, Roland Petit, R Queneau
        Paris-Boheme (Jeanmaire) music, lyrics: Ph Gerard, R
            Rouzaud, J Larue
---   La Java (Jeanmaire) music, lyrics: Maurice Yvain, Albert
            Willemetz, Jacques Charles
        Ca, C'est Paris (Jeanmaire) music, lyrics: Jose Padilla,
            Lucien Boyer, Jacques Charles

FOLLOW A STAR (Rank, 1959) British

Top Rank (British 45/EP) JKP 2052 mono

Music, lyrics: Norman Wisdom, others; musical direction: Malcolm
Lockyer

Cast: Norman Wisdom

Songs: Follow A Star (Wisdom)
        Give Me A Night in June (Wisdom, chorus) music, lyrics:
            Miller, Green

>   I Love You (Wisdom, chorus)
>   The Bath Song (Wisdom, chorus)

FOLLOW THAT DREAM (United Artists, 1962)

RCA (45/EP) EPA 4368 stereo

Cast: Elvis Presley

Songs: Follow That Dream (Presley) music, lyrics: Fred Wise,
            Ben Weisman
        Angel (Presley) music: Roy C Bennett; lyrics: Sid Tepper
        What A Wonderful Life (Presley) music, lyrics: Sid Wayne,
            Jerry Livingston
        I'm Not the Marrying Kind (Presley) music: Sherman
            Edwards; lyrics: Hal David

FOLLOW THE BOYS (Universal, 1944)

Hollywood Soundstage 5012 (soundtrack) mono

Music, lyrics: various

Cast: The Andrews Sisters, The Delta Rhythm Boys, Louis Jordan,
        Ted Lewis, Jeanette MacDonald, Donald O'Connor, Artur
        Rubinstein, Peggy Ryan, Dinah Shore, Freddie Slack
        Orchestra, Charlie Spivak, Sophie Tucker

Songs: Opening Titles (orchestra)
        Goodnight (Lewis)
        I Feel A Song Coming On (orchestra) music: Jimmy McHugh;
            lyrics: George Oppenheim, Dorothy Fields
        Tonight (chorus) music: Walter Donaldson; lyrics: Kermit
            Goell
        Furlough Fling (Freddie Slack Orchestra) music, lyrics:
            Charles Weintraub, Frank Davenport
        The Bigger the Army and the Navy (Tucker) music, lyrics:
            Jack Yellen
        Medley (The Andrews Sisters):
            Bei Mir Bist Du Schoen (music: Sholom Secunda; lyrics:
                Saul Chaplin, Sammy Cahn)
            Well, All Right
            Beer Barrel Polka (music: Jaramir Vejvoda; lyrics: Lew
                Brown, Waldimir A Timm)
            I'll Be With You in Apple Blossom Time (music: Albert
                Von Tilzer; lyrics: Neville Fleeson)
            Pennsylvania Polka (music, lyrics: Lester Lee, Zeke
                Manners)
            Vict'ry Polka (music: Jule Styne; lyrics: Sammy Cahn)

Swing Low Sweet Chariot (Charlie Spivak Orchestra) anon
Kitten with Mittens Laced (O'Connor, Ryan) music, lyrics:
    Sidney Miller, Inez James
Beyond the Blue Horizon (MacDonald) music: Richard Whiting,
    W Franke Harling; lyrics: Leo Robin
--- I'll Walk Alone (Shore) music: Jule Styne; lyrics: Sammy
    Cahn
Liebestraum (Rubinstein, piano) music: Liszt
Besame Mucho (Charlie Spivak Orchestra) music: Consuelo
    Velazquez; lyrics: Sunny Skylar
I'll Get By (Shore) music: Fred E Ahlert; lyrics: Roy Turk
Is You Is or Is You Ain't My Baby (Jordan) music, lyrics:
    Louis Jordan, Billy Austin
Sweet Georgia Brown (Louis Jordan Orchestra) music,
    lyrics: Ben Bernie, Maceo Pinkard, Kenneth Casey
Alegrias (orchestra) music: Sabicas
I'll See You in My Dreams (MacDonald) music: Isham Jones;
    lyrics: Gus Kahn
The House I Live In (Delta Rhythm Boys) music: Earl
    Robinson; lyrics: Lewis Allen
Shoo-Shoo Baby (Andrews Sisters, Freddie Slack Orchestra)
    music, lyrics: Phil Moore
A Better Day Is Coming (chorus) music: Jule Styne; lyrics:
    Sammy Cahn
End Credits (orchestra)

Note: The above recording includes spoken dialog. Studio
      recordings by cast members:

Capitol (78rpm) 146 Furlough Fling (Freddie Slack Orchestra)
Decca (78rpm) 18572 Shoo-Shoo Baby (The Andrews Sisters)
Victor (78rpm) 20-1586 I'll Walk Alone (Shore)

FOLLOW THE BOYS (MGM, 1963)

MGM 4123 stereo

Music, lyrics: Benny Davis, Ted Murry, others; musical direction:
LeRoy Holmes

Cast: Connie Francis

Songs: Follow the Boys (Francis)
      Tonight's My Night (Francis)
      Intrigue (Francis)
      Waiting for Billy (Francis)
      Italian Lullaby (Francis) music, lyrics: Connie Francis
      Intrigue (Dixieland version)

Note: The above album also includes songs not from the film.

FOLLOW THE FLEET (RKO, 1936)

Sountrak STK - 118 (soundtrack) mono

Music, lyrics: Irving Berlin; musical direction: Max Steiner

Cast: Fred Astaire, Betty Grable, Jeanne Gray, Harriet Hilliard,
        Joy Hodges, Ginger Rogers

Songs: Main Title (orchestra)
       We Saw the Sea (Astaire, sailors)
       Let Yourself Go (Rogers, Gray, Grable, Hodges)
       Get Thee Behind Me, Satan (Hilliard)
       Dance Contest (orchestra)
       I'd Rather Lead A Band (Astaire)
---   But Where Are You? (Hilliard)
       I'm Putting All My Eggs in One Basket (Astaire, piano)
       I'm Putting All My Eggs in One Basket (reprise) (Astaire,
          Rogers)
       Let's Face the Music and Dance (Astaire)
       Finale: We Saw the Sea (orchestra)

Note: The above recording includes spoken dialog. Studio
        recordings by cast members:

Brunswick (78rpm) 7608 Let Yourself Go (Astaire)
                    Let's Face the Music and Dance (Astaire)
Brunswick (78rpm) 7609 We Saw the Sea (Astaire)
                    I'm Putting All My Eggs...(Astaire)
Brunswick (78rpm) 7610 I'd Rather Lead A Band (Astaire)
      (all of the above on LP: Columbia SG 32472)
Brunswick (78rpm) 7607 But Where Are You? (Hilliard)
                    Get Thee behind Me, Satan (Hilliard)
Decca (Br) (78rpm) 5963 I'm Putting All My Eggs...(Rogers)
                    Let Yourself Go (Rogers) LP: Ace of
                    Hearts AH 67

FOOTLIGHT PARADE (Warner Bros, 1933)

Columbia C2L 44 mono 'Dick Powell in Hollywood'

Music: Sammy Fain, Harry Warren; lyrics: Al Dubin, Irving Kahal

Cast: Dick Powell

Songs: By A Waterfall (Powell) music: Fain; lyrics: Kahal
       Ah! The Moon Is Here (Powell) music: Fain; lyrics: Kahal
       Honeymoon Hotel (Powell) music: Warren; lyrics: Dubin

Note: The following soundtrack selection was issued on United
        Artists 'Golden Age of the Hollywood Musical' (UA-LA 215-H)

with James Cagney, Ruby Keeler and Dick Powell; musical
direction: Leo F Forbstein:

By A Waterfall (Powell, Keeler, chorus)
Shanghai Lil (Cagney, Keeler, chorus) music: Warren;
    lyrics: Dubin

FOR ME AND MY GAL (MGM, 1942)

Sountrak STK 107 (soundtrack) mono

Music, lyrics: various; musical direction: George Stoll

Cast: Ben Blue, Marta Eggerth, Judy Garland, Gene Kelly, Ben
        Lesey, Lucille Norman, George Murphy

Songs: Overture (Orchestra):
            For Me and My Gal (music: George W Meyer)
            Over the Waves (music: Juventino Rosas)
        Oh Johnny (orchestra) music: Abe Olman
        They Go Wild, Simply Wild, Over me (orchestra) music:
            Fred Fisher
        Oh, You Beautiful Doll (Murphy, Norman) music: Nat D Ayer;
            lyrics: A Seymour Brown
        Don't Leave Me Daddy (Garland) music, lyrics: J M Verges
        Oh, You Beautiful Doll (reprise) (Murphy)
        Shanty Dance (orchestra)
        By the Beautiful Sea (Garland, Murphy, girls) music:
            Harry Carroll; lyrics: Harold Atteridge
        For Me and My Gal (Garland, Kelly) music: George M Meyer;
            lyrics: Edgar Leslie, E Ray Goetz
        When You Wore A Tulip (Garland, Kelly) music: Percy
            Wenrich; lyrics: Jack Mahoney
        Do I Love You (Eggerth) music: Henri Christine; lyrics:
            E Ray Goetz
---   After You've Gone (Garland) music: Turner Layton; lyrics:
            Henry Creamer
        Tell Me (Norman, men) music, lyrics: Max Kortlander
        Till We Meet Again (Norman, chorus, Garland) music:
            Richard Whiting; lyrics: Raymond B Egan
        We Don't Want the Bacon (Lesey) music, lyrics: Carr,
            Russell, Havens
        Ballin' the Jack (Garland, Kelly) music; Chris Smith;
            lyrics: Jim Burris
        What Are You Going to Do for Uncle Sammy (quartet) music,
            lyrics: Tom Waring
        How Ya Gonna Keep Them Down on the Farm (Garland, quartet)
            music: Walter Donaldson; lyrics: Sam M Lewis, Joe Young
        Where Do We Go from Here (Garland, quartet) music: Percy
            Wenrich; lyrics: Howard Johnson
        Over There (orchestra) music: George M Cohan

It's A Long Way to Tipperary (Garland, chorus) music:
    Jack Judge; lyrics: Harry Williams
Goodbye Broadway, Hello France (chorus) music: Billy
    Baskette; lyrics: C Francis Reisner, Benny Davis
Smiles (Garland) music: Lee M Roberts; lyrics: J Will
    Callahan
Oh Frenchy (Kelly, Blue) music: Con Conrad; lyrics: Sam
    Ehrlich
Pack Up Your Troubles (Garland) music: Felix Powell;
    lyrics: George Asaf
March Medley (orchestra)
When Johnny Comes Marching Home (Garland, chorus) music,
    lyrics: Patrick S Gilmore
Finale: For Me and My Gal (Garland, Kelly, chorus)

Note: The above recording includes spoken dialog. A different
        version of the finale was included on Out Takes OTF-3:

        Finale: For Me and My Gal (Garland, Kelly, Murphy)

        Judy Garland, Gene Kelly studio recordings, included on
        Decca LP: DXB 172 'The Best of Judy Garland'

Decca (78rpm) 18480 For Me and My Gal (Garland, Kelly)
                    When You Wore A Tulip (Garland, Kelly)

FOR THE FIRST TIME (MGM, 1959)

RCA LSC 2338 (soundtrack) stereo reissued: AGL 1-3977

Music, lyrics: various; musical direction: Carlo Savina, others

Cast: Mario Lanza

Songs: Come Prima (Lanza) music, lyrics: Panzeri, Taccani,
            Di Paola
        Tarantella (Lanza) music: George Stoll
        O Sole Mio (Lanza) music, lyrics: Russo, Di Capua
        Neopolitan Dance (Lanza) music, lyrics: George Stoll
        Hofbrauhaus Song (Lanza) music, lyrics: Betti, Hauff;
            musical direction: Johannes Rediske Band
        O Mon Amour (Lanza) music: Marguerite Monnot; lyrics:
            Raymond Asso
        Mazurka (Lanza) music: George Stoll
        Pineapple Pickers (Lanza) music: George Stoll
            musical direction: Johannes Rediske Band
---   Pagliacci: Vesti La Giubba (Lanza) music: Leoncavallo
            musical direction: Constantine Callincos
        Otello: Finale (Lanza) music: Verdi
            musical direction: Constantine Callincos

Aida: Act I (Lanza) music: Verdi
    musical direction: Constantine Callincos
Ich Liebe Dich (Lanza) music: Edvard Grieg
    musical direction: Constantine Callincos
Ave Maria (Lanza) music: Franz Schubert
    musical direction; George Stoll

42nd STREET (Warner Bros, 1933)

United Artists LA 361-H (soundtrack) mono 'Hooray for Hollywood'

Music: Harry Warren; lyrics: Al Dubin; musical direction:
Leo F Forbstein

Cast: Bebe Daniels, Ruby Keeler, Una Merkel, Clarence Nordstrom,
       Dick Powell, Ginger Rogers

Songs: You're Getting to Be A Habit with Me (Daniels)
       Shuffle Off to Buffalo (Keeler, Nordstrom, Merkel, Rogers,
           chorus)
       Young and Healthy (Powell, chorus)

Note: The above recording includes spoken dialog. An additional
       soundtrack selection was included on the LP: 'The Golden
       Age of the Hollywood Musical' UA LA 215-H:

       42nd Street (Keeler, Powell, chorus)

FOUR JILLS IN A JEEP (Twentieth Century-Fox, 1944)

Hollywood Soundstage 407 (soundtrack) mono

Music: Jimmy McHugh, others; lyrics: Harold Adamson, others;
musical direction: Emil Newman

Cast: The Jimmy Dorsey Orchestra, Alice Faye, Kay Francis,
       Betty Grable, Dick Haymes, George Jessel, Carole Landis,
       Mitzi Mayfair, Carmen Miranda, Martha Raye, Phil Silvers

Songs: Opening Music (orchestra)
       Cuddle Up A Little Closer (Grable) music: Karl Hoschna;
           lyrics: Otto Harbach
       Radio Scene (Francis, Raye, Mayfair, Landis) spoken
       The Champ (Dorsey Orchestra)
       (If You Can't Sing It) You'll Have to Swing It (Raye,
           chorus) music, lyrics: Sam Coslow
       How Blue the Night (Haymes, chorus)
       Ohio (Dorsey Orchestra)
---   Command Performance Broadcast (Jessel) spoken
       You'll Never Know (Faye) music: Harry Warren; lyrics:
           Mack Gordon

                    I, Yi, Yi, Yi, Yi I Like You Very Much (Miranda,
                        chorus) music: Harry Warren; lyrics: Mack Gordon
            You Send Me (Haymes, chorus)
            No Love No Nothing (Silvers, Dorsey Orchestra) music:
                Harry Warren; lyrics: Leo Robin
            How Many Times Do I Have to Tell You? (Haymes)
            Boogie Woogie Dance (orchestra)
            Crazy Me (Landis)
            Finale (The Caissons Go Rolling Along) (chorus) music,
                lyrics: Edmund L Gruber

Note: The above recording includes spoken dialog. Studio
         recordings by cast members:

Decca (78rpm) 18593 Ohio (Jimmy Dorsey Orchestra)
Decca (78rpm) 18556 You'll Never Know (Haymes)
Decca (78rpm) 18604 How Blue the Night (Haymes)
                    How Many Times Do I Have to Tell You? (Haymes)

         The following selection was cut from the film, but issued
         on another recording:

         S.N A.F.U. (Raye, Landis, Mayfair) LP: Choice Cuts ST 500/1

FRANKIE AND JOHNNY (United Artists, 1966)

RCA LSP 3553 stereo

Music: Roy C Bennett, others; lyrics: Sid Tepper, others

Cast: Elvis Presley

Songs: Frankie and Johnny (Presley) music: Ben Weisman; lyrics:
            Alex Gottlieb, Fred Karger
        Come Along (Presley) music, lyrics: David Hess
        Petunia, the Gardner's Daughter (Presley)
        Chesay (Presley) music: Ben Weisman; lyrics: Fred Karger,
            Sid Wayne
        What Every Woman Lives For (Presley) music, lyrics: Doc
            Pomus, Mort Shuman
        Look Out, Broadway (Presley) music: Randy Starr; lyrics:
            Fred Wise
---   Beginner's Luck (Presley)
        Down by the Riverside (Presley) trad
        When the Saints Go Marching In (Presley) trad
        Shout It Out (Presley) music: Florence Kaye; lyrics: Bill
            Giant, Bernie Baum
        Hard Luck (Presley) music: Ben Weisman; lyrics: Sid Wayne
        Please Don't Stop Loving Me (Presley) music, lyrics: Joy
            Byers
        Everybody Come Aboard (Presley) music: Florence Kaye;
            lyrics: Bill Giant, Bernie Baum

THE FRENCH LINE (RKO, 1954)

Mercury MG 25182 (soundtrack) mono

Music: Walter Scharf; lyrics: Ralph Blane, Robert Wells; musical direction: Constantin Bakaleinkoff

Cast: Mary McCarty, Gilbert Roland, Jane Russell

Songs: The French Line (chorus)
       Well I'll Be Switched (Russell)
       With A Kiss (Roland)
       Wait Till You See Paris (Roland)
---   What Is This That I Feel? (Russell)
       Comment Allez-Vous - How Are Things with You? (Roland)
       Any Gal from Texas (Russell, McCarty)
       Lookin' for Trouble (Russell)

FRIENDLY PERSUASION (Allied Artists, 1956)

Dot (45/EP) 1054 mono

Music: Dimitri Tiomkin; lyrics: Paul Francis Webster

Cast: (the voice of) Pat Boone

Songs: Coax Me A Little (Boone)
       The Mocking Bird in the Willow Tree (Boone)
---   Indiana Holiday (Boone)
       Marry Me, Marry Me (Boone)

Note: Additional studio recordings:

       Dot (45rpm) 15490 Friendly Persuasion (Boone)
       Epic (45rpm) 5-9181 Friendly Persuasion (Anthony Perkins)

FUN AND FANCY FREE (Disney, 1947)

Columbia JL 8503 mono 'Bongo'

Music, lyrics: Eliot Daniel, Buddy Kaye, others

Cast: Dinah Shore

Songs: Lazy Countryside (Shore) music, lyrics: Bobby Worth
       Say It with A Slap (Shore)
       Too Good to Be True (Shore)

Note: Other studio recordings by cast members:

Capitol (78rpm) 466 Fun and Fancy Free (The Dinning Sisters)

music, lyrics: Bennie Benjamin, George Weiss
Capitol (78rpm) CCX 67 (two record set) mono 'Mickey and the
        Beanstalk' musical direction: Billy May

Cast: Bobby Driscoll (not in film), Jim MacDonald, Johnny
        Mercer (not in film), Clarence Nash, Luana Patten

FUN IN ACAPULCO (Paramount, 1963)

RCA LSP 2756 stereo   reissued: AFL 1-2756

Music: Roy C Bennett, others; lyrics: Sid Tepper, others

Cast: Elvis Presley

Songs: Fun in Acapulco (Presley) music: Ben Weisman; lyrics:
            Sid Wayne
        Vino, Dinero y Amor (Presley)
        Mexico (Presley)
        El Torro (Presley) music: Florence Kaye; lyrics: Bill
            Giant, Bernie Baum
        Marguerita (Presley) music, lyrics: Don Robertson
        The Bullfighter Was A Lady (Presley)
        (There's) No Room to Rhumba in A Sports Car (Presley)
            music: Dick Manning; lyrics: Fred Wise
        I Think I'm Gonna Like It Here (Presley) music: Hal
            Blair; lyrics: Don Robertson
        Bossa Nova, Baby (Presley) music, lyrics: Jerry Leiber,
            Mike Stoller
        You Can't Say No in Acapulco (Presley) music: Feller;
            lyrics: Doris Fuller, Lee Morris
        Guadalajara (Presley) music, lyrics: Pepe Guizar

FUNNY FACE (Paramount, 1957)

Verve 15001 (soundtrack) mono   reissued: DRG 15001 CD

Music: George Gershwin, others; lyrics: Ira Gershwin, others;
musical direction: Adolph Deutsch

Cast: Fred Astaire, Audrey Hepburn, Kay Thompson

Songs: Overture: Funny Face (Astaire)
        'S Wonderful (chorus)
        Think Pink! (Thompson, chorus) music: Roger Edens; lyrics:
            Leonard Gershe
        How Long Has This Been Going On? (Hepburn)
        How Long Has This Been Going On? (reprise) (orchestra)
        Funny Face (reprise) (Astaire)
        Bonjour Paris! (Hepburn, Astaire, Thompson, chorus) music:

Roger Edens; lyrics: Leonard Gershe
--- Clap Yo Hands (Thompson, Astaire)
He Loves and She Loves (Astaire)
Bonjour Paris! (reprise) (orchestra)
On How to Be Lovely (Thompson, Hepburn) music: Roger Edens;
    lyrics: Leonard Gershe
Basal Mentabolism (How Long Has This Been Going On; Funny
    Face) (orchestra)
Let's Kiss and Make Up (Astaire)
'S Wonderful (reprise) (Astaire, Hepburn)

FUNNY GIRL (Columbia, 1968)

Columbia BOS 3220 (soundtrack) stereo CD

Music: Jule Styne, others; lyrics: Bob Merrill, others;
musical direction: Walter Scharf

Cast: Kay Medford, Mae Questel, Omar Sharif, Barbra Streisand

Songs: Overture (orchestra)
    I'm the Greatest Star (Streisand)
    If A Girl Isn't Pretty (Questal, Medford)
    Roller Skate Rag (girls)
    I'd Rather Be Blue Over You (Streisand) music: Fred
      Fisher; lyrics: Billy Rose
    His Love Makes Me Beautiful (chorus, Streisand)
--- People (Streisand)
    You Are Woman, I Am Man (Sharif, Streisand)
    Don't Rain on My Parade (Streisand)
    Sadie, Sadie (Streisand, Sharif)
    The Swan (Streisand)
    Funny Girl (Streisand)
    My Man (Streisand) music: Maurice Yvain; lyrics: Channing
      Pollock
    Finale (orchestra)

FUNNY LADY (Columbia, 1975)

Arista AL 9004 (soundtrack) stereo

Music: John Kander, others; lyrics: Fred Ebb, others; musical
direction: Peter Matz

Cast: James Caan, Barbra Streisand, Ben Vereen

Songs: How Lucky Can You Get (Streisand, men)
    So Long Honey Lamb (Caan, Streisand, chorus)
    I Found A Million Dollar Baby (in A Five and Ten Cent
      Store) (Streisand) music: Harry Warren; lyrics: Billy

                    Rose, Mort Dixon
            Isn't This Better (Streisand)
            Me and My Shadow (Caan) music: Al Jolson, Dave Dreyer;
                lyrics: Billy Rose
            If I Love Again (Streisand) music: Ben Oakland; lyrics:
                J P Murray
            I Got A Code in My Doze (Streisand) music, lyrics: Billy
                Rose, Arthur Fields, Fred Hall
            (It's Gonna Be A) Great Day (Streisand, chorus) music:
                Vincent Youmans; lyrics: Billy Rose, Edward Eliscu
    ---   Blind Date (Streisand, chorus)
            Am I Blue (Streisand) music: Harry Akst; lyrics: Grant
                Clarke
            It's Only A Paper Moon (chorus) music: Harold Arlen;
                lyrics: Billy Rose, E Y Harburg
            I Like Him (Streisand)
            It's Only A Paper Moon (reprise) (Caan)
            I Like Her (reprise) (Caan)
            More Than You Know (Streisand) music: Vincent Youmans;
                lyrics: Billy Rose, Edward Eliscu
            Clap Hands Here Comes Charley (Vereen, chorus) music:
                Joseph Meyer; lyrics: Billy Rose, Ballard MacDonald
            Let's Hear It for Me (Streisand)

A FUNNY THING HAPPENED ON THE WAY TO THE FORUM (United Artists,
                                                            1966)
United Artists UAS 5144 (soundtrack) stereo reissued: UA LA-284

Music, lyrics: Stephen Sondheim; background score, musical
direction: Ken Thorne

Cast: Annette Andre, Michael Crawford, Jack Gilford, Leon
        Greene, Michael Hordern, Zero Mostel, Phil Silvers

Songs: Tiba Solo (orchestra) music: Thorne
        Comedy Tonight (Mostel, company)
        Search for Mare's Sweat (orchestra) music: Thorne
        Lovely (Andre, Crawford)
        Tintinabula's Dance (orchestra) music: Thorne
        Vibrata's Dance (orchestra) music: Thorne
        Roman Emissary (orchestra) music: Thorne
        Everybody Ought to Have A Maid (Hordern, Mostel, Gilford,
            Silvers)
        Riot at the Funeral (orchestra)
        Domina Returns (Fanfare) (orchestra) music: Thorne
        My Bride (Greene, company)
    --- Erronius Returns (orchestra) music: Thorne
        Orgy Music - Roman Style (orchestra) music: Thorne
        Lovely (reprise) (Mostel, Gilford)
        In the Arena (orchestra) music: Thorne

>The Dirge (Greene, company)
>The Rescue of Philia (orchestra) music: Thorne
>The Chase (orchestra)
>Comedy Tonight (reprise) (Mostel, cast)
>Playout (orchestra)

G I BLUES (Paramount, 1960)

RCA LSP 2256 stereo   reissued: AYL 1-3735 CD

Music: Sherman Edwards, others; lyrics: Sid Wayne, others

Cast: Elvis Presley

Songs: Tonight Is So Right for Love (Presley) music, lyrics:
>>Sid Wayne, Abner Silver (Offenbach's 'Baccarolle')
>What's She Really Like (Presley) music, lyrics: Sid
>>Wayne, Abner Silver
>Frankfort Special (Presley)
>Wooden Heart (Presley) music, lyrics: Frank Wise, Ben
>>Wiseman, Kay Twomey, Berthold Kaempfer ('Muss I Denn')
>G I Blues (Presley) music: Roy C Bennett; lyrics:
>>Sid Tepper
>Pocketful of Rainbows (Presley) music: Ben Wiseman;
>>lyrics: Fred Wise
>Shoppin' Around (Presley) music: Roy C Bennett; lyrics:
>>Sid Tepper
>Big Boots (Presley)
>Didja' Ever (Presley)
>Blue Suede Shoes (Presley) music, lyrics: Carl Perkins
>Doin' the Best I Can (Presley) music, lyrics: Doc Pomus,
>>Mort Shuman

GAILY, GAILY (United Artists, 1969)

United Artists UAS 5202 (soundtrack) stereo

Music: Henry Mancini; lyrics: Alan and Marilyn Bergman; musical
direction: Henry Mancini

Cast: Melina Mercouri, Anita Nye, (the voice of) Jimmie Rodgers

Songs: Tomorrow Is My Friend (Rodgers)
>>Good Morning, Mr Ransehoff (orchestra)
>>Sentimental Dream (orchestra)
>>Christmas Eve on Skid Row (Mercouri) spoken
>>There's Enough to Go Around (orchestra)
>>Tomorrow Is My Friend (reprise) (orchestra)
>>There's Enough to Go Around (reprise) (chorus)
>>Sentimental Dream (reprise) (Nye)
>>Gaily, Gaily (orchestra)
>>The Tango I Saved for You (orchestra)

        Tomorrow Is My Friend (reprise) (chorus)

THE GANG'S ALL HERE (Twentieth Century-Fox, 1943)

Classic International Filmusicals C I F 3003 (soundtrack) stereo
                                    also: Sandy Hook SH 2009
Music: Harry Warren, others; lyrics: Leo Robin, others; musical
direction: Alfred Newman, Charles Henderson

Cast: Phil Baker, Alice Faye, Benny Goodman, Carmen Miranda

Songs: Opening Titles:
            Let's Begin (orchestra) music: Gregory Stone, Joe
               Bonimo, Fanny May Balridge
            The Gang's All Here (chorus) adapted by Theodore F
               Morse from a melody by Arthur Sullivan
            Paducah (orchestra)
            Brazil (unidentified tenor, chorus, Miranda, chorus)
               music: Ary Barroso; lyrics: S K Russell
            You Discover You're in New York (Miranda, Faye, girls,
               chorus, Baker)
            Let's Dance (Benny Goodman Orchestra)
            Minnie's in the Money (Goodman)
            The Lady in the Tutti-Frutti Hat (Miranda, chorus)
            A Journey to A Star (Faye, chorus)
            Rhythm Number (Benny Goodman Orchestra)
---   No Love No Nothing (Faye)
            No Love No Nothing (reprise) (chorus)
            Minnie's in the Money (reprise) (Benny Goodman Orchestra)
            Paducah (Goodman, Miranda)
            A Journey to A Star (reprise) (Faye, chorus)
            Polka-Dot Polka (Faye, chorus)
            A Journey to A Star (reprise) (Eugene Paulette, Charlotte
               Greenwood, Edward Everett Horton, Baker, Miranda,
               Faye, chorus)
            End Titles (orchestra)

Note: The above recording includes spoken dialog.

THE GAY DIVORCEE (RKO, 1934)

EMI (British) EMTC 101 (soundtrack) mono also: Sountrak STK-105

Music: Con Conrad, Cole Porter, Harry Revel; lyrics: Mack
Gordon, Herb Magidson, Cole Porter; musical direction: Max Steiner

Cast: Fred Astaire, Betty Grable, Edward Everett Horton, Lillian
        Miles, Erik Rhodes, Ginger Rogers

Songs: Overture (orchestra)
        Don't Let It Bother You (female chorus) music: Revel;
           lyrics: Gordon

A Needle in A Haystack (Astaire) music: Conrad; lyrics:
    Magidson
Let's K-nock K-nees (Grable, Horton) music: Revel; lyrics:
    Gordon
Night and Day (Astaire) music, lyrics: Cole Porter
The Continental (Rogers, Rhodes, Miles, chorus) music:
    Conrad; lyrics: Magidson

Note: The above recording includes spoken dialog.

GAY PURR-EE (Warner Bros, 1962)

Warner Bros BS 1479 (soundtrack) stereo

Music: Harold Arlen; lyrics: E Y Harburg; musical direction:
Mort Lindsay

Cast: (the voices of) Red Buttons, Paul Frees, Judy Garland,
        Robert Goulet

Songs: Overture: Take My Hand Paree (Garland)
                 Mewsette (chorus)
                 Little Drops of Rain (Garland)
                 Bubbles (chorus)
                 Paris Is A Lonely Town (Garland)
                 Roses Red, Violets Blue (Garland, chorus)
        Mewsette (Goulet)
        Little Drops of Rain (Garland)
        The Money Cat (Frees, men)
        Portrait of Mewsette (orchestra)
        Take My Hand Paree (Garland)
---   Paris Is A Lonely Town (Garland)
        Bubbles (Goulet, Buttons, men)
        Roses Red, Violets Blue (Garland)
        Little Drops of Rain (reprise) (Goulet)
        Variation: Paris Is A Lonely Town (orchestra)
        The Horse Won't Talk (Frees)
        Finale: Mewsette (Goulet, Garland, chorus)

GENTLEMEN MARRY BRUNETTES (United Artists, 1955)

Coral CRL 57013 (partial soundtrack) mono

Music: Richard Rodgers, others; lyrics: Lorenz Hart, others;
musical direction: Robert Farnon

Cast: Jeanne Crain, Johnny Desmond (not in film), Anita Ellis
        (most vocals for Jeanne Crain), Robert Farnon (for Scott
        Brady), Jane Russell, Rudy Vallee, Alan Young

Songs: Gentlemen Marry Brunettes (Desmond) music, lyrics:

            Herbert Spencer, Earle Hagen, Robert Sale
        You're Driving Me Crazy (Russell, Ellis) music, lyrics:
            Walter Donaldson
        Miss Annabelle Lee (orchestra) music: Lew Pollack, Harry
            Richman, Sidney Clare
        Have You Met Miss Jones? (Russell, Ellis, Vallee, Farnon,
            Young, chorus)
        My Funny Valentine (Ellis, Young, chorus)
        I've Got Five Dollars (Farnon, Russell)
---   I Wanna Be Loved by You (Vallee, Crain, Russell, chorus)
            music: Harry Ruby, Herbert Stothart; lyrics: Bert
            Kalmar
        Daddy (Russell, Ellis) music, lyrics: Bobby Troup
        Ain't Misbehavin' (Young, Russell, Ellis) music: Fats
            Waller, Harry Brooks; lyrics: Andy Razaf
        Finale: My Funny Valentine (reprise) (Young)
                I've Got Five Dollars (reprise) (Russell)
                Gentlemen Marry Brunettes (reprise) (Desmond)

Note: The above recording includes spoken dialog.

GENTLEMEN PREFER BLONDES (Twentieth Century-Fox, 1953)

MGM E 208 (soundtrack) mono   reissued: DRG DS 15005

Music: Jule Styne, others; lyrics: Leo Robin, others; musical
direction: Lionel Newman

Cast: Marilyn Monroe, Jane Russell

Songs: Bye Bye Baby (Russell, chorus)
        A Little Girl from Little Rock (Russell, Monroe)
        Diamonds Are A Girl's Best Friend (Monroe)
        Ain't There Anyone Here for Love? (Russell) music:
            Hoagy Carmichael; lyrics: Harold Adamson
        When Love Goes Wrong (Nothing Goes Right) (Russell,
            Monroe) music: Carmichael; lyrics: Adamson
        Bye Bye Baby (reprise) (Monroe, chorus)

Note: An additional soundtrack excerpt is included on:

        Legends 1000/1 Marilyn Monroe

        A Little Girl from Little Rock (Russell, Monroe, chorus)
            complete version with Main Title and End Title

MARILYN (Fox FXG 5000) contains the following selections
        with the voice of Eileen Wilson substituting for Jane
        Russell:

        A Little Girl from Little Rock (Monroe, Wilson)
        When Love Goes Wrong (Monroe, Wilson)

Diamonds Are A Girl's Best Friend (Monroe)
Bye Bye Baby (Monroe, chorus)

GET YOURSELF A COLLEGE GIRL (MGM, 1964)

MGM SE 4273 (soundtrack) stereo

Music, lyrics: various

Cast: The Animals, Freddie Bell and the Bell Boys, The Dave
      Clark Five, Stan Getz, Astrud Gilberto, Roberta Linn,
      Mary Ann Mobley, The Standells, The Jimmy Smith Trio

Songs: Whenever You're Around (Dave Clark Five) music, lyrics:
      Dave Clark, Mike Smith
      The Girl from Ipanema (Getz, Gilberto) music: Antonio
      Carlos Jobim; English lyrics: Norman Gimbel
      Around and Around (The Animals) music, lyrics: Chuck Berry
      The Sermon (Jimmy Smith Trio)
      Get Yourself A College Girl (Mobley) music, lyrics: Fred
      Karger, Sidney Miller
      Bony Moronie (The Standells)
---   Thinking of You Baby (Dave Clark Five) music, lyrics:
      Dave Clark, Mike Smith
      Sweet Rain (Getz) music: Mike Gibbs
      Blue Feeling (The Animals) music, lyrics: Marion Motter
      Comin' Home Johnny (Jimmy Smith Trio)
      Talkin' About Love (Bell, Bell Boys, Linn)
      The Swim (The Standells)

GIGI (MGM, 1958)

MGM E 3641 ST (soundtrack) mono   reissued: MCA 39045

Music: Frederick Loewe; lyrics: Alan Jay Lerner; musical
direction: Andre Previn

Cast: Maurice Chevalier, Hermione Gingold, Louis Jourdan,
      Betty Wand (for Leslie Caron)

Songs: Overture (orchestra)
      Thank Heaven for Little Girls (Chevalier)
      It's A Bore (Chevalier, Jourdan)
      The Parisians (Wand)
      Waltz at Maxim's (She Is Not Thinking of Me) (Jourdan)
      The Night They Invented Champagne (Wand, Gingold, Jourdan)
---   I Remember It Well (Chevalier, Gingold)
      Say A Prayer for Me Tonight (Wand)
      I'm Glad I'm Not Young Any More (Chevalier)
      Gigi (Gaston's Soliloquy) (Jourdan)
      Finale: Thank Heaven for Little Girls (Chevalier, chorus)

GILDA (Columbia, 1946)

Curtain Calls CC 100/22 (soundtrack) mono 'Rita Hayworth'

Music, lyrics: Doris Fisher, Allan Roberts; musical direction: Morris Stoloff

Cast: Anita Ellis (for Rita Hayworth), Rita Hayworth

Songs: Put the Blame on Mame (slow version) (Hayworth)
       Amado Mio (Ellis)
       Put the Blame on Mame (nightclub version) (Ellis)

GIRL CRAZY (MGM, 1943)

Decca DL 5412 mono

Music: George Gershwin; lyrics: Ira Gershwin; musical direction: Georgie Stoll

Cast: Judy Garland, Mickey Rooney

Songs: Embraceable You (Garland, male quintet)
       Could You Use Me? (Rooney, Garland)
       But Not for Me (Garland)
---   Treat Me Rough (Rooney)
       Bidin' My Time (Garland, male quintet)
       I Got Rhythm (Garland)

GIRL CRAZY (MGM, 1943)

Hollywood Soundstage HS 5008 (soundtrack) mono also: Curtain Calls 100/9-10

Cast: June Allyson, Tommy Dorsey Orchestra, Judy Garland, Rags
        Ragland, Mickey Rooney, Nancy Walker

Songs: Overture (orchestra)
       Treat Me Rough (Allyson, Rooney, chorus)
       Bidin' My Time (Garland, men)
       Could You Use Me (Rooney, Garland)
       Bronco Busters (Garland, Rooney, Walker, chorus) cut from
          film
---   Happy Birthday, Ginger (Ragland, chorus) music, lyrics:
          Roger Edens
       Embraceable you (Garland, chorus)
       Comedy Routine (Rooney) spoken
       Fascinating Rhythm (Tommy Dorsey Orchestra)
       But Not for Me (Ragland, Garland)
       I Got Rhythm (Garland, Rooney, chorus)

Note: The above recording includes spoken dialog.

GIRL HAPPY (MGM, 1965)

RCA LSP 3338 stereo   reissued: AFL 1-3338

Music: Florence Kaye, others; lyrics: Bill Giant, Bernie Baum, others

Cast: Elvis Presley

Songs: Girl Happy (Presley) music: Norman Meade; lyrics: Doc
          Pomus
        Spring Fever (Presley)
        Fort Lauderdale Chamber of Commerce (Presley) music: Roy
          C Bennett; lyrics: Sid Tepper
        Startin' Tonight (Presley) music, lyrics: Lenore Rosenblatt,
          Victor Millrose
        Wolf Call (Presley)
        Do Not Disturb (Presley)
---   Cross My Heart and Hope to Die (Presley) music, lyrics:
          Sid Wayne, Ben Weisman
        The Meanest Girl in Town (Presley) music, lyrics: Joy
          Byers
        Do the Clam (Presley) music: Ben Weisman; lyrics: Sid
          Wayne, Dolores Fuller
        Puppet on A String (Presley) music: Roy C Bennett;
          lyrics: Sid Wayne
        I've Got to Find My Baby (Presley) music, lyrics: Joy
          Byers
        You'll Be Gone (Presley) music, lyrics: Elvis Presley,
          Charlie Hodge, Red West

Note: Additional soundtrack selection on LP: Legends 1000/2
        'Ladies of Burlesque'

        I Got News for You (Nita Talbot)

THE GIRL MOST LIKELY (RKO, 1957)

Capitol W 930 (soundtrack) mono

Music, lyrics: Hugh Martin, Ralph Blane, others; musical
direction: Nelson Riddle

Cast: Keith Andes, Kaye Ballard, Kelly Brown, Tommy Noonan,
        Jane Powell, Cliff Robertson

Songs: Main Title: The Girl Most Likely (chorus) music: Nelson
          Riddle; lyrics: Bob Russell
        We Gotta Keep Up with the Joneses (Powell, Noonan,
          ensemble)
        I Don't Know What I Want (Powell)
        Beach Party (orchestra)

        Travelogue (Where Do You Come From?) (Powell, Robertson,
            Ballard, Brown, ensemble)
        Balboa (Powell, Robertson, Ballard, Brown, ensemble)
---   I Like the Feeling (Powell, Robertson)
        Pink Cloud Music (orchestra)
        Crazy Horse (Powell, children's chorus)
        All the Colors of the Rainbow (Powell, Andes, Ballard,
            Brown, ensemble)
        End Title: I Know Now What I Want (Powell)

LES GIRLS (MGM, 1957)

MGM E 3590 (soundtrack) mono reissued: MCA 1426 CD

Music, lyrics: Cole Porter; musical direction: Adolph Deutsch

Cast: Taina Elg, Mitzi Gaynor, Gene Kelly, Kay Kendall

Songs: Les Girls (Kelly, Gaynor, Kendall, Elg)
       You're Just Too, Too! (Kelly, Kendall)
       Ca, C'est L'Amour (Elg)
       Ladies in Waiting (Gaynor, Kendall, Elg)
       Why Am I So Gone (About That Gal) (Kelly)

GIRLS! GIRLS! GIRLS! (Paramount, 1962)

RCA LSP 2621 stereo reissued: AFL 1-2621

Music: Roy C Bennett, others; lyrics: Sid Tepper, others

Cast: Elvis Presley

Songs: Girls! Girls! Girls! (Presley) music, lyrics: Jerry
           Leiber, Mike Stoller
       I Don't Want to Be Tied (Presley) music: Florence Kaye;
           lyrics: Bill Giant, Bernie Baum
       Where Do You Come From (Presley) music: Bob Roberts;
           lyrics: Ruth Batchelor
       I Don't Want To (Presley) music: Fred Spielman; lyrics:
           Janice Torre
       We'll Be Together (Presley) music: Dudley Brooks; lyrics:
           Charles O'Curran
       A Boy Like Me, A Girl Like You (Presley)
       Earth Boy (Presley)
---   Return to Sender (Presley) music: Winfield Scott; lyrics:
           Otis Blackwell
       Because of Love (Presley) music: Bob Roberts; lyrics:
           Ruth Batchelor
       Thanks to the Rolling Sea (Presley) music: Bob Roberts;
           lyrics: Ruth Batchelor
       Song of the Shrimp (Presley)

The Walls Have Ears (Presley)
We're Coming In Loaded (Presley) music: Winfield Scott;
      lyrics: Otis Blackwell

GO INTO YOUR DANCE (Warner Bros, 1935)

Hollywood Soundstage 402 (soundtrack) mono   also: Golden Legends
                                                          2000/2
Music: Harry Warren, others; lyrics: Al Dubin, others; musical
direction: Leo F Forbstein

Cast: Al Jolson, Ruby Keeler, Helen Morgan

Songs: Opening Music (orchestra)
        Cielito Lindo (Jolson, chorus) music, lyrics: Fernandez,
            Yradier, Ramirez
        A Good Old Fashioned Cocktail (Keeler, chorus)
        Mammy, I'll Sing About You (Jolson)
        About A Quarter to Nine (Jolson, chorus)
        The Little Things You Used to Do (Morgan)
        Casino De Paree (Jolson)
        She's A Latin from Manhattan (Jolson, chorus)
        Go Into Your Dance (Jolson)
        About A Quarter to Nine (reprise) (Jolson)

Note: The above recording includes spoken dialog. Helen Morgan
        made the following studio recording:

Brunswick (78rpm) 7424 The Little Things you Used to Do
                  LP: Audio 2330

GODSPELL (Columbia, 1973)

Arista AL 5-8071 (soundtrack) stereo

Music, lyrics: Stephen Schwartz; musical direction: Stephen
Reinhardt

Cast: Victor Garber, Katie Hanley, David Haskell, Merrell
        Jackson, Joanne Jonas, Richard LaBonte, Robin Lamont,
        Gilmer McCormick, Jeffrey Mylett, Stephen Reinhardt,
        Jerry Sroka, Lynne Thigpen

Songs: Prepare Ye (The Way of the Lord) (Haskell, company)
        Save the People (Garber, company)
        Day by Day (Lamont, company)
        Turn Back, O Man (Jonas, Garber, company)
        Bless the Lord (Thigpen, company)
        All for the Best (Garber, Haskell, company)
        All Good Gifts (Jackson, company)
---   Light of the World (Sroka, McCormick, Mylett, Lamont,
        company)

> Alas for You (Garber)
> By My Side (Hanley, company) music: Peggy Gordon; lyrics:
>   Jay Hamburger
> Beautiful City (company)
> On the Willows (Reinhardt, LaBonte, Garber)
> Finale (Garber, company)

GOING HOLLYWOOD (MGM, 1933)

Columbia C2L 43 mono 'Bing Crosby in Hollywood'

Music: Nacio Herb Brown, others; lyrics: Arthur Freed, others;
musical direction: Lennie Hayton

Cast: Bing Crosby

Songs: Just An Echo in the Valley (Crosby) music, lyrics:
            Reginald Connelly, Jimmy Campbell, Harry Woods
        Beautiful Girl (Crosby)
        After Sundown (Crosby)
        We'll Make Hay While the Sun Shines (Crosby)
        Temptation (Crosby)
        Our Big Love Scene (Crosby)

Note: The following additional soundtrack selection is included
        on another recording:

        Going Hollywood (Crosby, chorus) LP: MCA 2-11002 'That's
            Entertainment'

GOING MY WAY (Paramount, 1944)

Decca DL 4257 mono 'Bing's Hollywood - Swinging On A Star'

Music: James Van Heusen, others; lyrics: Johnny Burke, others;
musical direction: John Scott Trotter, others

Cast: Bing Crosby, The Williams Brothers (not in film)

Songs: Going My Way (Crosby)
        Swinging On A Star (Crosby, The Williams Brothers)
        The Day After Forever (Crosby)
        Too-Ra-Loo-Ra-Loo-Ral (Crosby) music, lyrics: James
            Royce Shannon
        Ave Maria (Crosby, choir) music: Franz Schubert; musical
            direction: Victor Young
        Silent Night (Crosby, chorus) music: Franz Gruber

Note: Rise Stevens studio recording:

        Columbia (78rpm) 71192-D Carmen: Habanera; music: Bizet

GOLD DIGGERS OF BROADWAY (Warner Bros, 1929)

Take Two 110 (soundtrack) mono 'Lost Films - Trailers...'

Music: Joe Burke; lyrics: Al Dubin

Cast: Winnie Lightner, Nick Lucas, Nancy Welford

Songs: Tip-Toe Through the Tulips (Lucas)
       In A Kitchenette (Lucas)
       Painting the Clouds with Sunshine (Lucas)
       Tip-Toe Through the Tulips (reprise) (piano)
       Mechanical Man (Lightner)
       Song of the Gold Diggers (Welford)
       Song of the Gold Diggers (reprise) (cast)

Note: The above recording includes a narration and cast inter-
        views. Additional recordings by Nick Lucas:

Take Two (LP) 104 Tip-Toe Through the Tulips (Lucas, chorus)

Brunswick (78rpm) 4418 Painting the Clouds with Sunshine
                       Tip-Toe Through the Tulips (LP: DEcca 7-1)

GOLD DIGGERS OF 1933 (Warner Bros, 1933)

United Artists UA-LA215-H (soundtrack) mono 'The Golden Age..'

Music: Harry Warren; lyrics: Al Dubin; musical direction: Leo F
Forbstein

Cast: Joan Blondell, Ruby Keeler, Dick Powell, Ginger Rogers

Songs: Main Titles: We're in the Money (orchestra)
                    I've Got to Sing A Torch Song (orchestra)
                    We're in the Money (chorus)
       My Forgotten Man (Blondell, chorus)
       Shadow Waltz (Powell, Keeler, chorus)

Warner Bros 3XX2736 (additional soundtrack selection) mono

       We're in the Money (Rogers, chorus)

Note: Dick Powell made the following studio recordings, all
        included on the Columbia LP: C2L 44, 'Dick Powell in
        Hollywood'

       Perfect (78rpm) 12919 We're in the Money
                             I've Got to Sing A Torch Song
       Perfect (78rpm) 12920 Pettin' in the Park
                             Shadow Waltz

GOLD DIGGERS OF 1935 (First National, 1935)

Columbia C2L 44 mono 'Dick Powell in Hollywood'

Music: Harry Warren; lyrics: Al Dubin; musical direction:
Jimmie Grier

Cast: Dick Powell

Brunswick (78rpm) 7374 Lullaby of Broadway (Powell)
Brunswick (78rpm) 7407 I'm Goin' Shoppin' with You (Powell)
                      The Words Are in My Heart (Powell)

Note: The following soundtrack selections, with Dick Powell,
       Wini Shaw and musical direction by Leo F Forbstein, are
       included on the following albums:

       The Words Are in My Heart (Powell) UA-LA361-H 'Hooray
          for Hollywood'
       Lullaby of Broadway (Shaw, Powell, chorus) UA-LA 215-H
          'The Golden Age of the Hollywood Musical'

       In addition, several soundtrack excerpts of 'Lullaby of
       Broadway' are included on WB 3XX2736 'Fifty Years of Film
       Musicals', and one other studio recording was issued:

Decca (78rpm) 408 Lullaby of Broadway (Shaw) LP: Decca DEA 7-1
                  I'm Goin' Shoppin' with You (Shaw)

GOLD DIGGERS OF 1937 (First National, 1936)

United Artists UA-LA361-H (soundtrack) mono 'Hooray for Hollywood'

Music: Harry Warren; lyrics: Al Dubin; musical direction: Leo F
Forbstein

Cast: Joan Blondell, Lee Dixon, Rosalind Marquis, Dick Powell

Song: All's Fair in Love and War (Blondell, Dixon, Marquis,
          Powell, chorus)

Additional studio recordings by Dick Powell:

Decca (78rpm) 1067 With Plenty of Money and you (LP: MCA 1511)
                   Speaking of the Weather (LP: MCA 1511) music:
                   Harold Arlen; lyrics: E Y Harburg

Decca (78rpm) 1068 All's Fair in Love and War (LP: MCA 1691)
                   Let's Put Our Heads Together (music: Harold
                   Arlen; lyrics: E Y Harburg)

THE GOOD COMPANIONS (Associated British, 1957)

Parlophone (British 45/EP) GEP 8604 (soundtrack) mono

Music, lyrics: various; musical direction: Lou Levy

Cast: John Fraser, Janette Scott

Songs: Good Companions (chorus)
       This Kind of Love (Scott)
       Where There's You There's Me (Fraser)
       If Only (Scott, chorus)
---   Round the World in Eighty Minutes (Scott, chorus) music,
          lyrics: Rossi, Roberts, Parsons

GOOD NEWS (MGM, 1947)

MGM E 504 (soundtrack) mono reissued: MCA 39083 CD

Music: Ray Henderson, others; lyrics: B G De Sylva, Lew Brown,
others; musical direction: Lennie Hayton

Cast: June Allyson, Tom Dugan, Peter Lawford, Joan McCracken,
        Ray MacDonald, Pat Marshall, Lou Tindall, Mel Torme

Songs: Good News (Tait College) (McCracken, chorus)
       Be A Ladies' Man (Lawford, MacDonald, Dugan, Tindall,
          Torme)
       Lucky in Love (Marshall, Lawford, Allyson, chorus)
       The French Lesson (Lawford, Allyson) music: Roger Edens;
          lyrics: Betty Comden, Adolph Green
---   The Best Things in Life Are Free (Allyson, Lawford)
       Pass That Peace Pipe (McCracken, chorus) music: Roger
          Edens; lyrics: Hugh Martin, Ralph Blane
       Just Imagine (Allyson)
       The Varsity Drag (Allyson, Lawford, chorus)

GOOD NEWS (MGM, 1947)

Sunbeam STK 111 (soundtrack) mono

Songs: Main Titles: Good News (chorus)
                    The Best Things in Life Are Free (chorus)
       Be A Ladies' Man (Lawford, MacDonald, Dugan, Tindall,
          Torme)
       Lucky in Love (Marshall, McCracken, Torme, Allyson,
          Lawford, chorus)
       The French Lesson (Allyson, Lawford)
       The Best Things in Life Are Free (Allyson)
----   Pass That Peace Pipe (McCracken, chorus)
       Just Imagine (Allyson)

The Best Things in Life Are Free (reprise) (Torme,
   Lawford)
The Varsity Drag (Allyson, Lawford, chorus)
Finale: The French Lesson (chorus)

Note: Both of the above recordings include spoken dialog. The
following additional selection was not used in the film,
but released on another album:

An Easier Way (Allyson, Marshall) music: Roger Edens;
   lyrics: Betty Comden, Adolph Green; LP: Cut! OTF - 1

Mel Torme studio recording:

Musicraft (78rpm) 15118 The Best Things in Life Are Free

GOOD TIMES (Columbia, 1967)

ATCO 33-214 stereo

Music, lyrics: Sonny Bono

Cast: Sonny & Cher

Songs: I Got You Babe (opening scene and instrumental)
       It's the Little Things
       Good Times
       Trust Me
---   I Don't Talk to Strangers
       I'm Gonna Love You
       Just A Name
       I Got You Babe (reprise)

GOODBYE, MR CHIPS (MGM, 1969)

MGM S1E-19 STX (soundtrack) stereo   reissued: MCA 39066

Music, lyrics: Leslie Bricusse; musical direction: John Williams

Cast: Petula Clark, Peter O'Toole

Songs: Overture (orchestra)
       Fill the World with Love (boys)
       Where Did My Childhood Go? (O'Toole)
       London Is London (Clark, chorus)
       And the Sky Smiled (Clark)
       Apollo (Clark)
       When I Am Older (boys)
       Walk Through the World (Clark)
---   Entr'Acte (orchestra)
       What Shall I Do with Today? (Clark)

What A Lot of Flowers! (O'Toole)
Schooldays (Clark, boys)
When I Was Younger (O'Toole)
You and I (Clark)
Fill the World with Love (reprise) (O'Toole, boys)
You and I (reprise) (orchestra)

GREASE (Paramount, 1978)

RSO RS-2-4002 (two records - soundtrack) stereo

Music, lyrics: Jim Jacobs, Warren Casey, others; musical
direction: Bill Oakes

Cast: Frankie Avalon, Cindy Bullens, Stockard Channing, Jeff
        Conaway, Olivia Newton-John, Louis St Louis, Sha-Na-Na,
        John Travolta, (the voice of) Frankie Valli

Songs: Grease (Valli, chorus) music, lyrics: Barry Gibb
       Summer Nights (Travolta, Newton-John, cast)
       Hopelessly Devoted to You (Newton-John, chorus) music,
          lyrics: John Farrar
       You're the One That I Want (Travolta, Newton-John, chorus)
          music, lyrics: John Farrar
       Sandy (Travolta) music: Louis St Louis; lyrics: Scott
          Simon
---   Beauty School Dropout (Avalon, chorus)
       Look at Me, I'm Sandra Dee (Channing, chorus)
       Greased Lightnin' (Travolta, Conaway, chorus)
       It's Raining on Prom Night (Bullens, chorus)
       Alone at A Drive-In Movie (orchestra)
       Blue Moon (Sha-Na-Na) music: Richard Rodgers; lyrics:
          Lorenz Hart
---   Rock n' Roll Is Here to Stay (Sha-Na-Na) music, lyrics:
          D White
       Those Magic Changes (Sha-Na-Na)
       Hound Dog (Sha-Na-Na) music, lyrics: Jerry Leiber, Mike
          Stoller
       Born to Hand-Jive (Sha-Na-Na)
       Tears on My Pillow (Sha-Na-Na) music: S Bradford; lyrics:
          A Lewis
       Mooning (St Louis, Bullens, chorus)
---   Freddy My Love (Bullens, chorus)
       Rock n' Roll Party Queen (St Louis, chorus)
       There Are Worse Things I Could Do (Channing)
       Look at Me, I'm Sandra Dee (reprise) (Newton-John)
       We Go Together (Travolta, Newton-John, cast)
       Love Is A Many Splendored Thing (chorus) music: Sammy
          Fain; lyrics: Paul Francis Webster
       Grease (reprise) (Valli, chorus)

GREASE 2 (Paramount, 1982)

RSO RS 1-3803 (soundtrack) stereo

Music: Louis St Louis, others; lyrics: Howard Greenfield,
others; musical direction: Louis St Louis

Cast: Maxwell Caulfield, The Four Tops (not in film), Peter
        Frechette, Tab Hunter, Lorna Luft, Michelle Pfeiffer,
        Alison Price, Maureen Teefy, Adrian Zmed

Songs: Back to School Again (The Four Tops)
        Cool Rider (Pfeiffer) music, lyrics: Dennis Linde
        Score Tonight (cast) music: Dominic Bugatti; lyrics:
           Frank Musker
        Girl for All Seasons (Teefy, Luft, Price, Pfeiffer)
           music: Dominic Bugatti; lyrics: Frank Musker
        Do It for Our Country (Frechette) music, lyrics: Bob
           Hegel
        Who's That Guy (cast)
---   Prowlin' (Frechette, gang) music: Dominic Bugatti; lyrics:
           Frank Musker, Christopher Cert
        Reproduction (Hunter, cast) music, lyrics: Dennis Linde
        Charades (Caulfield) lyrics: Michael Gibson
        (Love Will) Turn Back the Hands of Time (Caulfield,
           Pfeiffer)
        Rock-A-Hula-Luau (Summer Is Coming) (cast) music:
           Dominic Bugatti; lyrics: Frank Musker
        We'll Be Together (Caulfield, Pfeiffer, Zmed, Luft,
           Frechette, Teefy, cast) music: Bob Morrison;
           lyrics: Johnny MacRae

THE GREAT AMERICAN BROADCAST (Twentieth Century-Fox, 1941)

Citadel 6004 (soundtrack) mono 'Alice Faye Sings the Songs of
Harry Warren'

Music: Harry Warren; lyrics: Mack Gordon; musical direction:
Alfred Newman

Cast: Alice Faye

Songs: It's All in A Lifetime (Faye)
        Long Ago Last Night (Faye)
        I Take to You (Faye)
        Where Are You (Faye)

Note: Additional soundtrack recordings on Radiola LP: 17-18:

        Alabamy Bound (The Ink Spots) music: Ray Henderson;
           lyrics: Buddy DeSylva, Bud Green
        The Great American Broadcast (James Newell, chorus)

THE GREAT CARUSO (MGM, 1951)

RCA LM 1127 mono

Music, lyrics: various; musical direction: Constantine Callinicos

Cast: Mario Lanza

Songs: Rigoletto: Questa O Quella (Lanza) music: Verdi
                  La Donna e Mobile (Lanza)
                  Parmi Veder Le Lagrime (Lanza)
           Tosca: Recondita Armonia (Lanza) music: Puccini
---   E Lucevan Le Stelle (Lanza)
           L'Elisir D'Amore: Una Furtiva Lagrima (Lanza) music:
              Donizetti
           La Gioconda: Cielo E Mar! (Lanza) music: Ponchielli
           Pagliacci: Vesti La Giubba (Lanza) music: Leoncavallo

Note: Additional cast recordings:

MGM (78rpm) 30352 The Loveliest Night of the Year (Ann Blyth)
                  music: adapted by Irving Harrison; lyrics:
                  Paul Francis Webster (LP: Lion L 70108)

RCA (45rpm) 49-3435 Marechiare (Lanza)
                    'A Vucchella (Lanza)

THE GREAT MUPPET CAPER! (Universal, 1981)

Atlantic SD 16047 (soundtrack) stereo

Music, lyrics, musical direction: Joe Raposo

Cast: Dave Goelz, Jim Henson, Richard Hunt, Jerry Nelson, Frank
       Oz, Steve Whitmire

Songs: Hey, A Movie! (Henson, Oz, Goelz, Hunt, chorus)
       The Big Red Bus (orchestra)
       Happiness Hotel (Henson, Oz, Goelz, Nelson, Whitmire,
          Hunt, chorus)
       Lady Holiday (orchestra)
       Steppin' Out with A Star (Henson, Oz, Goelz)
       The Apartment (orchestra)
       Night Life (Henson)
---   The First Time It Happens (Henson, Oz, chorus)
       Couldn't We Ride (Henson, Oz, Goelz, Hunt, chorus)
       Piggy Fantasy (Henson, unidentified voice)
       The Great Muppet Caper:
          a) The Heist (orchestra)
          b) The Muppet Fight Song (chorus)
          c) Muppets to the Rescue (orchestra)
       Homeward Bound (orchestra)

          Finale: Hey, A Movie! (cast)
                  The First Time It Happens (cast)

THE GREAT WALTZ (MGM, 1938)

Sountrak STK 109 (soundtrack) mono

Music: Johann Strauss II (adapted and arranged by Dimitri
Tiomkin); lyrics: Oscar Hammerstein II; musical direction:
Arthur Gutmann

Cast: Curt Bois, Fernand Gravet, George Houston, Leonid Kinsky,
        Miliza Korjus, Christian Rub, Al Shean

Songs: Overture (orchestra)
        I'm in Love with Vienna (Bois, Kinsky, Shean, Houston,
            chorus)
        There'll Come A Time (Korjus)
        Medley: Introduction to Tales of the Vienna Woods,
                Revolutionary March (chorus)
---   Tales of the Vienna Woods (Gravet, Korjus, Rub)
        Tales of the Vienna Woods (Korjus)
        One Day When We Were Young (Gravet)
        Only You (Korjus, Houston, chorus)
        One Day When We Were Young (reprise) (Korjus)
        Finale: I'm in Love with Vienna (chorus)
                One Day When We Were Young (Korjus, chorus)
                The Blue Danube (orchestra)
                Tales of the Vienna Woods (chorus)

Note: The above recording includes spoken dialog. Studio
        recordings by Miliza Korjus (LP: Camden CAL 279):

        Victor (78rpm) 4410 Tales of the Vienna Woods
        Victor (78rpm) 4411 There'll Come A Time
                            One Day When We Were Young

THE GREAT WALTZ (MGM, 1972)

MGM 1SE-39ST (soundtrack) stereo

Music: Johann Strauss and Sons; lyrics: Robert Craig Wright,
George Forrest; musical direction: Roland Shaw

Cast: Ken Barrie (for Horst Bucholz), Joan Baxter (for Yvonne
        Mitchell), Mary Costa, (the voice of) Kenneth McKellar

Songs: Crystal and Gold (McKellar)
        Nightfall (McKellar, chorus)
        Warm (Barrie, Baxter)
        Wine, Women and Song (orchestra) violin: Carlos Villa

Love Is Music (Costa, chorus)
Louder and Faster (Costa, Barrie)
---   With You Gone (McKellar)
Through Jerry's Eyes (Costa, McKellar, chorus)
Say Yes (Baxter, chorus)
Six Drinks (Barrie, chorus)
Schani Gives Chase (orchestra)
Who Are You? (Costa)
The Great Waltz in Boston (Blue Danube) (chorus)

THE GREAT ZIEGFELD (MGM, 1936)

Classic International Filmusicals C I F 3005 (soundtrack) mono

Music: Walter Donaldson, others; lyrics: Harold Adamson, others;
musical direction: Arthur Lange

Cast: Ray Bolger, Fanny Brice, Virginia Bruce, Buddy Doyle,
Allan Jones (for Dennis Morgan), Luise Rainer

Songs: Overture (orchestra)
Won't You Come and Play with Me? (Rainer)
It's Delightful to Be Married (Rainer, chorus) music:
    Vincent Scotto; lyrics: Anna Held
If You Knew Susie (Doyle) music: Joseph Meyer; lyrics:
    B G DeSylva
A Pretty Girl Is Like A Melody (Jones, chorus) music,
    lyrics: Irving Berlin
You Gotta Pull Strings (chorus)
She's A Follies Girl (Bolger, girls) You (chorus)
---   You Never Looked So Beautiful Before (Bruce, chorus)
Yiddle on the Fiddle (Brice) music, lyrics: Irving Berlin
Queen of the Jungle (Brice, girls)
My Man (Brice) music: Maurice Yvain; lyrics: Channing
    Pollock
Look for the Silver Lining (men) music: Jerome Kern;
    lyrics: Buddy DeSylva
Telephone Scene (Rainer) spoken
A Circus Must Be Different in A Ziegfeld Show (chorus)
    music: Con Conrad; lyrics: Herb Magidson
Finale (Ziegfeld Medley) (chorus)

Note: The above recording includes spoken dialog.

GROUNDS FOR MARRIAGE (MGM, 1950)

MGM E 536 (soundtrack) mono

Music, lyrics: various; musical direction: Johnny Green

Cast: Richard Atckison, Kathryn Grayson, Stephen Kemalyan

        (for Van Johnson), Gilbert Russell (for Van Johnson)

Songs: Carmen: Prelude (orchestra) music: Bizet
                Habanera (Grayson)
                Micaela's Aria (Grayson)
                Toreador Song (Grayson, Kemalyan)
                Finale (Grayson, Russell)
---   La Boheme: O Soave Fanciulla (Grayson, Atchison) music:
           Puccini
        Le Coq D'Or: Hymn to the Sun (Grayson) music: Rimsky-
           Korsakoff
        Toy Concertino (orchestra) music: David Raksin

GUYS AND DOLLS (GOLDWYN, 1955)

Motion Picture Tracks M P T - 1 (soundtrack) mono

Music, lyrics: Frank Loesser; musical direction: Jay Blackton

Cast: Vivian Blaine, Marlon Brando, Danny Dayton, Stubby Kaye,
       Renee Renor, Johnny Silver, Jean Simmons, Frank Sinatra

Songs: Overture: Guys and Dolls, A Woman in Love (chorus)
       Fugue for Tinhorns (Kaye, Silver, Dayton)
       Follow the Fold (Simmons, chorus)
       The Oldest Established (Sinatra, Kaye, Silver, men)
       I'll Know (Brando, Simmons)
       Pet Me, Papa (Blaine, chorus)
       Adelaide's Lament (Blaine)
       Guys and Dolls (Sinatra, Kaye, Silver)
       Adelaide (Sinatra, chorus)
---   Dance Sequence (orchestra, trio, Renor)
       If I Were A Bell (Simmons)
       A Woman in Love (Brando, Simmons)
       Take Back Your Mink (Blaine, chorus)
       Luck Be A Lady (orchestra)
       Luck Be A Lady (Brando, chorus)
       Sue Me (Blaine, Sinatra)
       Sit Down You're Rockin' the Boat (Kaye)
       Finale (Kaye, company)

GUYS AND DOLLS (Goldwyn, 1955)

Decca (45/EP) ED 2332 (soundtrack) mono reissued: Stet DS 25001

Songs: A Woman in Love (Brando, Simmons)
       I'll Know (Brando, Simmons)
       Luck Be A Lady (Brando, chorus)
       If I Were A Bell (Simmons)

GYPSY (Warner Bros, 1962)

Warner Bros BS 1480 (soundtrack) stereo

Music: Jule Styne; lyrics: Stephen Sondheim; musical direction:
Frank Perkins

Cast: Roxanne Arlen, Betty Bruce, Suzanne Cupito, Faith Dane,
        Ann Jilliann, Lisa Kirk (for Rosalind Russell), Karl
        Malden, Diane Pace, Paul Wallace, Natalie Wood (with Marni
                                                          Nixon)
Songs: Overture (orchestra)
       Small World (Kirk)
       Some People (Kirk)
       Baby June and Her Newsboys (Cupito, Pace, boys)
       Mr. Goldstone, I Love You (Kirk, chorus)
       Little Lamb (Wood / Nixon)
       You'll Never Get Away from Me (Kirk, Malden)
       Dainty June and Her Farmboys (Jilliann, boys)
       If Mama Was Married (Wood / Nixon, Jilliann)
---   All I Need Is the Girl (Wallace)
       Everything's Coming Up Roses (Kirk)
       Together Wherever We Go (Kirk)
       You Gotta Have A Gimmick (Arlen, Dane, Bruce)
       Let Me Entertain You (Wood / Nixon)
       Rose's Turn (Kirk)
       Finale (orchestra)

Note: The voice of Rosalind Russell can be heard in occasional
        spoken lines and possibly singing a few phrases.

HAIR (United Artists, 1979)

RCA CBL 2 3274 (two records - soundtrack) stereo CD

Music: Galt MacDermot; lyrics: Gerome Ragni, James Rado; musical
direction: Galt MacDermot

Cast: Cheryl Barnes, Laurie Beechman, Charlie Brown, Betty
        Buckley, Vincent Carrella, Nell Carter, Suzette Charles,
        Don Dacus, Beverly D'Angelo, Debi Dye, Ron Dyson, Fred
        Ferrarra, Ellen Foley, Leata Galloway, Annie Golden,
        Carl Hall, David Lassley, Edward Love, John Maestro,
        Melba Moore, Alex Paez, Trudy Perkins, Howard Porter,
        Charlotte Rae, John D Robertas, Jim Rosica, John Savage,
        Toney Watkins, Treat Williams, Victor Willis, Charlaine
        Woodard, Ren Woods, Dorsey Wright, Kurt Yaghjian, Ron Young

Songs: Aquarius (Woods, chorus)
       Sodomy (Dacus, chorus)
       Donna / Hashish (Williams, chorus)
       Colored Spade (Wright, Love, Hall, Porter, Watkins)

       Manchester (Williams, Savage, chorus)
       Abie Boy / Fourscore (Carter, Woodard, Perkins, chorus)
       I'm Black (Wright, Dacus, Williams, Savage)
       Ain't Got No (Carter, Watkins, Yaghjian, chorus)
       Air (Golden, chorus)
--- Party Music (orchestra)
       My Conviction (Rae)
       I Got Life (Williams, chorus)
       Frank Mills (Charles)
       Hair (Dacus, Williams, Wright, chorus)
       L.B.J. (Initials) (chorus)
       Electric Blues / Old Fashioned Melody (Galloway, Dye,
          Willis, Young)
       Hare Krishna (Carter, chorus)
--- Where Do I Go? (Savage, chorus)
       Black Boys (Foley, Beechman, Dye, Carrella, Maestro,
          Rosica, Ferrarra)
       White Boys (Carter, Woodard, Perkins, chorus)
       Walking in Space / My Body (Buckley, chorus)
       Easy to Be Hard (Barnes)
       3-5-0-0 (Moore, Dyson, chorus)
--- Good Morning Sunshine (D'Angelo, chorus)
       What A Piece of Work Is Man (Lassley, Paez)
       Somebody to Love (Brown, chorus)
       Don't Put It Down (orchestra)
       Flesh Failures / Let the Sunshine In (Robertas, Williams,
          chorus)

HALF A SIXPENCE (Paramount, 1967)

RCA LSO 1146 (soundtrack) stereo

Music, lyrics: David Heneker; musical direction: Irwin Kostal

Cast: Tommy Steele, Marti Webb (for Julia Foster)

Songs: Overture (chorus)
       All in the Cause of Economy (Steele, apprentices)
       Half A Sixpence (Steele, Webb)
       Money to Burn (Steele, chorus)
       I Don't Believe A Word of It (Webb, girls)   sung
       I'm Not Talking to You (Steele, apprentices) contrapuntally
       A Proper Gentleman (chorus)
       She's Too Far Above Me (Steele)
--- If the Rain's Got to Fall (Steele, children, chorus)
       Lady Botting's Boating Regatta Cup Racing Song (The Race)
          (Steele, chorus)
       Entr'Acte (Half A Sixpence) (reprise) (chorus)
       Flash, Bang Wallop (Steele, chorus)
       I Know What I Am (Webb)
       This Is My World (Steele)
       Half A Sixpence (reprise) (Steele, Webb, chorus)

Flash, Bang Wallop (reprise) (Steele, Webb, chorus)

HANS CHRISTIAN ANDERSEN (Goldwyn, 1952)

Decca DL 5433 mono reissued: MCA 148

Music, lyrics: Frank Loesser; musical direction: Gordon Jenkins

Cast: Danny Daye, Jane Wyman (not in film)

Songs: I'm Hans Christian Andersen (Kaye)
       Anywhere I Wander (Kaye, chorus)
       The Ugly Duckling (Kaye)
       Inchworm (Kaye, chorus)
---   Thumbalina (Kaye, chorus)
       No Two People (Kaye, Wyman)
       The King's New Clothes (Kaye, chorus)
       Wonderful Copenhagen (Kaye, chorus)

THE HAPPIEST MILLIONAIRE (Disney, 1967)

Buena Vista 5001 (soundtrack) stereo

Music, lyrics: Richard M Sherman, Robert B Sherman; musical
direction: Jack Elliott

Cast: Joyce Bulifant, Gladys Cooper, John Davidson, Eddie
       Hodges, Fred MacMurray, Geraldine Page, Paul Petersen.
       Tommy Steele, Lesley Ann Warren

Songs: Overture (orchestra)
       Fortuosity (Steele)
       What's Wrong with That (MacMurray, Warren)
       Watch Your Footwork (Hodges, Petersen)
       Valentine Candy (Warren)
       Strengthen the Dwelling (MacMurray, chorus)
       I'll Always Be Irish (Steele, MacMurray, Warren)
       Bye-Yum Pum Pum (Bulifant, Warren)
---   Are We Dancing (Davidson, Warren)
       I Believe in This Country (reprise: What's Wrong with
          That) (MacMurray, men)
       Detroit (Davidson, Warren)
       When A Man Has A Daughter (reprise: What's Wrong with
          That) (MacMurray)
       There Are Those (Page, Cooper, Steele)
       Let's Have A Drink on It (Steele, men)
       Finale: Let's Have A Drink on It (Steele, men)

HAPPINESS AHEAD (First National, 1934)

Columbia C2L 44 mono 'Dick Powell in Hollywood'

Music: Allie Wrubel, others;   lyrics: Mort Dixon, others

Cast: Dick Powell

Songs: Pop! Goes Your Heart (Powell)
       Happiness Ahead (Powell)
       Beauty Must Be Loved (Powell) music: Sammy Fain; lyrics:
           Irving Kahal

HAPPY LANDING (Twentieth Century-Fox, 1938)

Encore ST 101 (soundtrack) mono 'Merman in the Movies: 1930-38'

Music: Samuel Pokrass, others; lyrics: Jack Yellen, others;
musical direction: Louis Silvers

Cast: Ethel Merman

Songs: Hot and Happy (Merman)
       You Are the Music to the Words in My Heart (Merman) not
           in film
       You Appeal to Me (Merman) music: Harold Spina; lyrics:
           Walter Bullock

HARD COUNTRY (Universal, 1981)

Epic SE 37367 (soundtrack) stereo

Music, lyrics: Michael Murphey, others

cast: Joe Ely, Jerry Lee Lewis, Kate Moffatt, Michael Murphey,
       Tanya Tucker

Songs: Hard Country (Murphey, Moffatt)
       Hard Partyin' Country Darling (Murphey)
       Texas (When I Die) (Tucker, chorus) music, lyrics: E Bruce,
           B Borchers, P Bruce
       Cowboy Cadillac (Murphey, chorus)
       Break My Mind (Murphey, chorus) music, lyrics: J D
           Loudermilk
---   Take It As It Comes (Murphey, Moffatt)
       Somebody Must Have Loved You Last Night (Tucker) music,
           lyrics: K Bell
       Gonna Love You Anyway (Tucker) music, lyrics: L Martine, Jr
       I Love You So Much It Hurts (Lewis) music, lyrics: F
           Tillman
       West Texas Waltz (Ely, chorus) music, lyrics: B Hancock

A HARD DAY'S NIGHT (United Artists, 1964)

Capitol SW 11921 (soundtrack) stereo   CD

Music, lyrics: John Lennon, Paul McCartney; musical direction:
George Martin

Cast: The Beatles: George Hamilton, John Lennon, Paul McCartney,
        Ringo Starr

Songs: A Hard Day's Night (The Beatles)
        Tell Me Why (The Beatles)
        I'll Cry Instead (The Beatles)
        I Should Have Known Better (orchestra)
        I'm Happy Just to Dance with You (The Beatles)
        And I Love Her (orchestra)
---   I Should Have Known Better (reprise) (The Beatles)
        If I Fell (The Beatles)
        And I Love Her (reprise) (The Beatles)
        Ringo's Theme (This Boy) (orchestra)
        Can't Buy Me Love (The Beatles)
        A Hard Day's Night (reprise) (orchestra)

HARUM SCARUM (MGM, 1965)

RCA LSP 3468 (soundtrack) stereo   reissued: AYL 1-3734

Music: Florence Kaye, others; lyrics: Bill Giant, Bernie Baum,
others

Cast: Elvis Presley

Songs: Harem Holiday (Presley) music: Vince Poncia, Jr; lyrics:
            Peter Andreoli
        My Desert Serenade (Presley) music, lyrics: Stanley J
            Gelber
        Go East   Young Man (Presley)
        Mirage (Presley)
        Kismet (Presley) music: Roy C Bennett; lyrics: Sid Tepper
        Shake That Tamborine (Presley)
---   Hey Little Girl (Presley) music, lyrics: Joy Byers
        Golden Coins (Presley)
        So Close - Yet So Far (Presley) music, lyrics: Joy Byers

THE HARVEY GIRLS (MGM, 1946)

Decca DL 8498 mono   reissued: AEI 3101

Music: Harry Warren; lyrics: Johnny Mercer; musical direction:
Lennie Hayton

Cast: Kenny Baker, Judy Garland, Betty Russell (not in film),
        Virginia O'Brien

Songs: On the Atchison, Topeka and the Santa Fe (Garland, chorus)
        In the Valley (Where the Evening Sun Goes Down) (Garland,
            Chorus)
        Wait and See (Baker)
        Swing Your Partner Round and Round (Garland, chorus)
        It's A Great Big World (Garland, O'Brien, Russell)
        The Wild, Wild West (O'Brien)

Note: Two additional studio recordings were later issued on
        MCA 907 'Judy Garland - from the Decca Vaults':

        March of the Doagies (Garland, Baker) cut from film
        On the Atchison...(Garland, chorus) different version

THE HARVEY GIRLS (MGM, 1946)

Hollywood Soundstage 5002 (soundtrack) mono

Cast: Kenny Baker, Ray Bolger, Ben Carter, Marion Doenges (for
        Cyd Charisse), Edward Earle, Judy Garland, John Hodiak,
        Marjorie Main, Paul Newlan, Virginia O'Brien, Virginia
        Reese (for Angela Lansbury), Selena Royle

Songs: Overture (orchestra)
        In the Valley (Garland)
        Wait and See (Reese)
        On the Atchison, Topeka and the Santa Fe (Carter, Main,
            O'Brien, Bolger, Garland, chorus)
        The Harvey Girls (Earle, Royle, girls, Garland, Newlan)
        Hayride (Bolger, Garland, chorus) cut from film
        Oh, You Kid (Reese)
        It's A Great Big World (Garland, O'Brien, Doenges)
---   The Wild, Wild West (O'Brien)
        My Intuition (Garland, Hodiak) cut from film
        Wait and See (reprise) (Baker, Doenges)
        On the Atchinson...(reprise) (orchestra)
        Swing Your Partner Round and Round (Garland, Main, chorus)
        March of the Doagies (Garland, men) cut from film
        Finale (On the Atchison...) (chorus)

Note: The above recording includes spoken dialog. 'Hayride'
        is the same tune as 'House of Bamboo' (Pagan Love Song).

HAVING A WILD WEEKEND (Warner Bros, 1965)

Epic BN 26162 (soundtrack) stereo

Music, lyrics: Dave Clark

Cast: The Dave Clark Five

Songs: Having A Wild Weekend (Dave Clark Five)
       New Kind of Love (Dave Clark Five)
       Dum-Dee-Dee-Dum (Dave Clark Five)
       I Said I Was Sorry (Dave Clark Five)
       No Stopping (Dave Clark Five)
       Don't Be Taken In (Dave Clark Five)
---   Catch Us If You Can (Dave Clark Five)
       When I'm Alone (Dave Clark Five)
       If You Come Back (Dave Clark Five)
       Sweet memories (Dave Clark Five)
       Don't You Realize (Dave Clark Five)
       On the Move (Dave Clark Five)

HEAD (Columbia, 1968)

Colgems COSO 5008 (soundtrack) stereo reissued: Rhino RNLP 145

Music, lyrics: various; background score, musical direction:
Ken Thorne

Cast: The Monkees

Songs: Opening Ceremony (orchestra)
       Porpoise Song (The Monkees) music, lyrics: Gerry Goffin,
          Carole King
       Ditty Diego (orchestra)
       Circle sky (The Monkees) music, lyrics: Michael Nesmith
       Supplicio (orchestra)
       Can You Dig It? (The Monkees) music, lyrics: Peter Tonk
       Gravy (orchestra)
---   Superstitious (orchestra)
       As We Go Along (The Monkees) music, lyrics: Carole King,
          Toni Stern
       Dandruff (orchestra)
       Daddy's Song (The Monkees) music, lyrics: Nilsson
       Pole (orchestra)
       Long Title: Do I Have to Do This All Over Again?
          (The Monkees) music, lyrics: Peter Tonk
       Swami - Plus Strings (orchestra)

HEAD OVER HEELS (Gaumont, 1937)

Decca Eclipse (British) ECM 2168 mono 'Over My Shoulder'

Music: Harry Revel; lyrics: Mack Gordon

Cast: Jessie Matthews

Songs: There's That Look in Your Eyes (Matthews)

>   Head Over Heels in Love (Matthews)
>   Looking Around Corners for You (Matthews)
>   May I Have the Next Romance with You (Matthews)

THE HEART OF A MAN (Rank, 1959)

Philips (British 45/EP) BBE 12247

Music, lyrics: Frankie Vaughan, Lionel Bart, others; musical direction: Wally Scott

Cast: Frankie Vaughan

Songs: My Boy Flat Top (Vaughan)
       Sometime, Somewhere (Vaughan)
---   Walkin' Tall (Vaughan)
       The Heart of A Man (Vaughan) music, lyrics: Peggy
          Cochrane, Paddy Roberts

HEARTS OF FIRE (Lorimar, 1987)

Columbia SC 40870 (soundtrack) stereo CD

Music, lyrics: various

Cast: Bob Dylan, Rupert Everett, Fiona

Songs: Hearts of Fire (Fiona) music, lyrics: Fiona Flanagan,
          Beau Hill
       The Usual (Dylan) music, lyrics: John Hiatt
       I'm in It for Love (Fiona, chorus) music, lyrics: Andy
          Goldmark, Patricia Henderson
       Tainted Love (Everett, chorus) music, lyrics: Edward C Cobb
       Hair of the Dog (That Bit You) (Fiona, chorus) music,
          lyrics: Sam Bryant
---   Night After Night (Dylan) music, lyrics; Bob Dylan
       In My Heart (Everett, chorus) music, lyrics: Bruce Woolley,
          Simon Darlow
       The Nights We Spent on Earth (Fiona, chorus) music, lyrics:
          Sue Sheridan, Steve Diamond
       Had A Dream About You, Baby (Dylan) music, lyrics:
          Bob Dylan
       Let the Good Times Roll (Fiona, chorus) music, lyrics:
          John Dexter, Paul Hackman

THE HELEN MORGAN STORY (Warner Bros, 1957)

RCA LOC 1030 (soundtrack) mono

Music, lyrics: various; musical direction: Ray Heindorf

Cast: Gogi Grant (for Ann Blyth)

Songs: Why Was I Born (Grant) music: Jerome Kern; lyrics: Oscar
            Hammerstein II
        I Can't Give You Anything but Love (Grant) music: Jimmy
            McHugh; lyrics: Dorothy Fields
        If You Were the Only Girl in the World (Grant) music:
            Nat D Ayer; lyrics: Clifford Grey
        Avalon (Grant, chorus) music: Vincent Rose; lyrics:
            Buddy DeSylva, Al Jolson
        Do Do Do (Grant) music: George Gershwin; lyrics: Ira
            Gershwin
        Breezin' Along with the Breeze (Grant) music: Richard
            Whiting; lyrics: Seymour Simons, Haven Gillespie
        Love Nest (Grant) music: Louis A Hirsch; lyrics: Otto
            Harbach
        Someone to Watch Over me (Grant) music: George Gershwin;
            lyrics: Ira Gershwin
        The One I Love Belongs to Somebody Else (Grant) music:
            Isham Jones; lyrics: Gus Kahn
        Body and Soul (Grant) music: Johnny Green; lyrics: Ed
            Heyman, Robert Sauer, Frank Eyton
        April in Paris (Grant) music: Vernon Duke; lyrics: E Y
            Harburg
        Parlez-moi d'Amour (Grant) music, lyrics: Jean Lenoir
        More Than You Know (Grant) music: Vincent Youmans;
            lyrics: Billy Rose, Edward Eliscu
---   On the Sunny Side of the Street (Grant) music: Jimmy
            McHugh; lyrics: Dorothy Fields
        The Man I Love (Grant) music: George Gershwin; lyrics:
            Ira Gershwin
        Just A Memory (Grant) music: Ray Henderson; lyrics: Buddy
            DeSylva, Lew Brown
        Deep Night (Grant) music: Charlie Henderson; lyrics: Rudy
            Vallee
        Don't Ever Leave Me (Grant) music: Jerome Kern; lyrics:
            Oscar Hammerstein II
        I've Got A Crush on You (Grant) music: George Gershwin;
            lyrics: Ira Gershwin
        I'll Get By (Grant) music: Fred Ahlert; lyrics: Roy Turk
        Something to Remember You By (Grant) music: Arthur
            Schwartz; lyrics: Howard Dietz
        My Melancoly Baby (Grant) music: Ernie Burnett; lyrics:
            George A Norton
        Bill (Grant) music: Jerome Kern; lyrics: P G Wodehouse
        Can't Help Lovin' Dat Man (Grant) music: Jerome Kern;
            lyrics: Oscar Hammerstein II

Note: From liner notes: 'In addition to the actual soundtrack,
        included in this album as an integral part of the
        presentation is special material (not a part of the
        picture) which Helen Morgan had sung.'

HELLO, DOLLY! (Twentieth Century-Fox, 1969)

Fox DTCS 5103 (soundtrack) stereo   reissued: T-102

Music, lyrics: Jerry Herman; musical direction: Lennie Hayton,
Lionel Newman

Cast: Louis Armstrong, Michael Crawford, Danny Locklin,
        Marianne McAndrew, Walter Matthau, E J Pecker, Barbra
        Streisand

Songs: Just Leave Everything to Me (Streisand)
        It Takes A Woman (Matthau, Crawford, Locklin, men)
        It Takes A Woman (reprise) (Streisand)
        Put On Your Sunday Clothes (Crawford, Locklin, Streisand,
            chorus)
        Ribbons Down My Back (McAndrew)
        Dancing (Streisand, Crawford, Locklin, chorus)
        Before the Parade Passes By (Streisand, chorus)
---   Elegance (Crawford, McAndrew, Locklin, Pecker)
        Love Is Only Love (Streisand)
        Hello, Dolly (Streisand, chorus, Armstrong)
        It Only Takes A Moment (Crawford, chorus, McAndrew)
        So Long Dearie (Streisand)
        Finale: Hello, Dolly (Matthau, Streisand)
                Put On Your Sunday Clothes (chorus)
                Dancing (chorus)
                It Only Takes A Moment (Crawford, chorus)
                It Takes A Woman (Matthau, chorus)
                Hello, Dolly (chorus, Streisand)

HELLO, FRISCO, HELLO (Twentieth Century-Fox, 1943)

Hollywood Soundstage 5005 (soundtrack) mono

Music, lyrics: various; musical direction: Charles Henderson,
Emil Newman

Cast: Alice Faye, Kirby Grant, June Havoc, Jack Oakie, John
        Payne

Songs: Overture (chorus, orchestra)
        Medley (Faye, Oakie, Havoc, chorus):
            San Francisco (music: Bronislau Kaper, Walter Jurmann;
                lyrics: Gus Kahn)
            On San Francisco Bay (music: Max Hoffman; lyrics:
                Vincent Bryan)
            A Bird In A Gilded Cage (music: Harry Von Tilzer;
                lyrics: Arthur J Lamb)
            Hello, My Baby (music, lyrics: Joe Howard)
            Lindy (music, lyrics: Irving Berlin)

Hello, Frisco, Hello (Oakie, Payne, Faye, Havoc) music:
    Louis A Hirsch; lyrics: Gene Buck
You'll Never Know (Faye) music: Harry Warren; lyrics:
    Mack Gordon
Ragtime Cowboy Joe (Faye, Oakie, Havoc) music: Lewis
    Muir, Maurice Abraham; lyrics: Grant Clark
Sweet Cider Time (Faye) music: Percy Wenrich; lyrics:
    Joseph McCarthy
The Dance of the Grizzly Bear (Oakie, Faye, Havoc, chorus)
    music: George Botsford; lyrics: Irving Berlin
It's Tulip Time in Holland (Grant, chorus) music: Richard
    Whiting; lyrics: Dave Radford
When You Wore A Tulip (orchestra) music: Percy Wenrich
Why Do They Always Pick on Me (Faye) music: Harry Von
    Tilzer; lyrics: Stanley Murphy
---   Bedelia (Faye, chorus) music: Jean Schwartz; lyrics:
    William Jerome
Has Anybody Here Seen Kelly? (Faye, Oakie, chorus) music:
    C W Murphy, Will Letters; lyrics: William J McKenna
By the Light of the Silvery Moon (Faye, chorus) music:
    Gus Edwards; lyrics: Edward Madden
I Gotta Have You (Havoc) music: Harry Warren; lyrics:
    Mack Gordon (cut from film)
Gee, But It's Great to Meet A Friend from Your Home Town
    (Oakie, Havoc) music: James McGavisk; lyrics: William
    Tracey
You'll Never Know (reprise) (Faye)
Strike Up the Band Here Comes A Sailor (Havoc, chorus)
    music: Charles B Ward; lyrics: Andrew B Sterling
I've Got A Gal in Every Port (Oakie, Havoc, girls) anon
Hello, Frisco, Hello (reprise) (Faye, Payne)
You'll Never Know (reprise) (Faye, Payne, chorus)
End Titles (orchestra)

Note: The above recording includes spoken dialog.

HELP! (United Artists, 1965)

Capitol SMAS 2386 (soundtrack) stereo CD

Music, lyrics: John Lennon, Paul McCartney, others; musical
direction: Ken Thorne

Cast: The Beatles: George Harrison, John Lennon, Paul McCartney,
        Ringo Starr

Songs: Help! (The Beatles)
       The Night Before (The Beatles)
       From Me to You Fantasy (orchestra)
       You've Got to Hide Your Love Away (The Beatles)
       I Need You (The Beatles) music: George Harrison

> In the Tyrol (orchestra) music: Ken Thorne (introducing
> Wagner's Overture to Act III of 'Lohengrin')
> --- Another Girl (The Beatles)
> Another Hard Day's Night (orchestra)
> Ticket to Ride (The Beatles)
> The Bitter End (orchestra) music: Ken Thorne
> You Can't Do That (orchestra)
> You're Going to Lose That Girl (The Beatles)
> The Chase (orchestra) music: Ken Thorne

Note: Additional recording:

Capitol (45rpm) 5407 Yes It Is (The Beatles)

HERE COME THE WAVES (Paramount, 1944)

Decca DL 4258 mono 'Bing's Hollywood - Accentuate the Positive'

Music: Harold Arlen; lyrics: Johnny Mercer; musical direction:
John Scott Trotter, others

Cast: The Andrews Sisters (not in film), Bing Crosby

Songs: Ac-cent-tchu-ate the Positive (Crosby, The Andrews Sisters)
       musical direction: Vic Schoen
       Let's Take the Long Way Home (Crosby)
       There's A Fellow Waiting in Poughkeepsie (Crosby, The
       Andrews Sisters) musical direction: Vic Schoen
       I Promise You (Crosby)

HERE COMES THE GROOM (Paramount, 1951)

Decca DL 4262 mono 'Bing's Hollywood - Cool of the Evening'

Music: Jay Livingston, others; lyrics: Ray Evans, others;
musical direction: John Scott Trotter, others

Cast: Bing Crosby, Jane Wyman

Songs: In the Cool, Cool, Cool of the Evening (Crosby, Wyman,
       chorus) music: Hoagy Carmichael; lyrics: Johnny
       Mercer; musical direction: Matty Matlock
       Your Own Little House (Crosby)
       Misto Cristofo Columbo (Crosby, Wyman, chorus) musical
       direction: Matty Matlock
       Bonne Nuit (Bonwee) (Crosby)

HERE IS MY HEART (Paramount, 1934)

Decca DL 4250 mono 'Bing's Hollywood - Easy to Remember'

Music: Ralph Rainger, others; lyrics: Leo Robin; musical
direction: Georgie Stoll

Cast: Bing Crosby

Songs: Love Is Just Around the Corner (Crosby) music: Lewis E
          Gensler
        June in January (Crosby)
        With Every Breath I Take (Crosby)

HEY BOY! HEY GIRL! (Columbia, 1959)

Capitol T 1160 (soundtrack) mono

Music, lyrics: various; musical direction: Louis Prima, Nelson
Riddle

Cast: Sam Butera, Louis Prima, Keely Smith

Songs: Hey Boy! Hey Girl! (Smith, Prima, chorus) music, lyrics:
          J Thomas, Oscar McLollie
        A Banana Split for My Baby (Prima, chorus) music, lyrics:
          Louis Prima, Stan Irwin
        You Are My Love (Smith) music, lyrics: Joe Saulter
        Fever (Butera, chorus) music, lyrics: John Davenport,
          Eddie Cooley
        Oh Marie (Prima, chorus) music, lyrics: Eduardo di Capua
---   Lazy River (Prima, chorus) music, lyrics: Hoagy Carmichael,
          Sidney Arodin
        Nitey-Nite (Smith) music, lyrics: Louis Prima, Keely
          Smith, Barbara Belle
        When the Saints Go Marching In (Prima, chorus) trad
        Autumn Leaves (Smith, chorus) music: Joseph Kosma; lyrics:
          Jacques Prevert; English lyrics: Johnny Mercer
        Hey Boy! Hey Girl! (reprise) (Smith, Prima, chorus)

HEY, LET'S TWIST! (Paramount, 1962)

Roulette SR 25168 (soundtrack) stereo

Music: Henry Glover, others; lyrics: Joey Dee, Morris Levy,
others

Cast: Kay Armen, Jo-Ann Campbell, Dave, Joey Dee, Teddy Randazzo,
        The Starlighters

Songs: Hey, Let's Twist! (Dee, Starlighters)
        Roly Poly (Dee)
        I Wanna Twist (Armen)

          Peppermint Twist, Part I (Dee, Starlighters)
          Keelee's Twist (orchestra)
          It's A Pity to Say Goodnight (Randazzo) music, lyrics:
              Billy Reid
---   Mother Goose Twist (Randazzo) music, lyrics: Teddy
              Randazzo, Weinstein, Barberis
          Joey's Blues (Dave, Starlighters)
          Let Me Do My Twist (Campbell)
          Blue Twister (orchestra)
          Shout (Dee, Starlighters) music, lyrics: Isley Brothers
          Na Voce, 'Na Chitarra e ' o Poco 'e Luna (Armen) music,
              lyrics: Stillman, Rossi, Calise

HIGH ANXIETY (Twentieth Century-Fox, 1978)

Asylum 5E-501 (soundtrack) stereo

Music, lyrics for songs: Mel Brooks; musical score, direction:
John Morris

Cast: Mel Brooks

Songs: Main Title (orchestra)
       High Anxiety (Brooks)
       Anxious Theme (orchestra)
       If You Love Me Baby, Tell Me Loud (Brooks)
       End Title: High Anxiety (chorus)

HIGH SOCIETY (MGM, 1956)

Capitol W 750 (soundtrack) mono

Music, lyrics: Cole Porter; musical direction: Johnny Green

Cast: Louis Armstrong, Bing Crosby, Celeste Holm, Grace Kelly,
       Frank Sinatra

Songs: High Society Overture (orchestra)
       High Society Calypso (Armstrong, chorus)
       Little One (Crosby)
       Who Wants to Be A Millionaire (Sinatra, Holm)
       True Love (Crosby, Kelly)
---   You're Sensational (Sinatra)
       I Love You, Samantha (Crosby)
       Now You Has Jazz (Crosby, Armstrong)
       Well Did You Evah? (Crosby, Sinatra)
       Mind If I Make Love to You (Sinatra)

HIGHER AND HIGHER (RKO, 1943)

Hollywood Soundstage 411 (soundtrack) mono

Music: Jimmy McHugh, others; lyrics: Harold Adamson, others;
musical direction: Constantin Bakeleinikoff

Cast: Victor Borge, Leon Errol, Barbara Hale, Jack Haley, Paul
        and Grace Hartman, Marcy McGuire, Michele Morgan, Elizabeth
        Risdon, Frank Sinatra, Mel Torme, Mary Wickes, Dooley Wilson

Songs: Main Titles (orchestra)
        It's A Most Important Affair (cast)
        I'm A Debutante (Morgan, Haley, cast)
        Disgustingly Rich (cast) music: Richard Rodgers; lyrics:
            Lorenz Hart
        I Couldn't Sleep A Wink Last Night (Sinatra)
        The Music Stopped (Sinatra)
        I Saw You First (McGuire, Sinatra)
___   A Lovely Way to Spend An Evening (Sinatra)
        Incidental Music (Sinatra, Morgan) spoken
        A Lovely Way to Spend An Evening (reprise) (Sinatra)
        You're On Your Own (Wilson, Torme, McGuire. Sinatra, cast)
        You're On Your Own (reprise) (Sinatra)
        I Couldn't Sleep A Wink Last Night (reprise) (Sinatra)
        Minuet in Boogie (McGuire, Torme, cast)
        Finale:
            I Saw You First (McGuire, Hale)
            A Lovely Way to Spend An Evening (reprise) (Sinatra)
            Dialog (Haley, Sinatra, cast) spoken
            The Music Stopped (reprise) (Sinatra, chorus)

Note: Studio recordings by Frank Sinatra (all on Columbia LP:
        CL 2913, 'Frank Sinatra in Hollywood 1943-49'):

        I Couldn't Sleep A Wink Last Night
        The Music Stopped
        A Lovely Way to Spend An Evening

HIS BUTLER'S SISTER (Universal, 1943)

Decca DL 75289 (soundtrack) mono 'Deanna Durbin'

Music: Walter Jurman, others; lyrics: Bernie Grossman, others;
musical direction: Hans Salter

Cast: Deanna Durbin

Songs: In the Spirit of the Moment (Durbin)
        When You're Away (Durbin) music: Victor Herbert; lyrics:
            Henry Blossom
        Russian Medley (Durbin, chorus) arr: Max Rabinowitsh
        Turandot: The Prince (Durbin) music: Giacomo Puccini;
            lyrics: Sam Lerner

HIT THE DECK (MGM, 1955)

MGM 3163 (soundtrack) mono reissued: MCA 25033 CD

Music: Vincent Youmans, others; lyrics: Leo Robin, others; musical direction: George Stoll

Cast: Kay Armen, Vic Damone, Tony Martin, Ann Miller, Jane
        Powell, Debbie Reynolds, Russ Tamblyn

Songs: Join the Navy! (Reynolds, boys) co-lyricist: Clifford Grey
        Loo-Loo (Reynolds, boys) co-lyricist: Clifford Grey
        Sometimes I'm Happy (Powell, Damone) lyrics: Irving Caesar
        Keepin' Myself for You (girls, Martin) lyrics: Sidney
          Claire
        Why, Oh, Why? (Martin, Damone, Tamblyn, Powell, Reynolds,
          Miller) co-lyricist: Clifford Grey
        Lucky Bird (Powell) co-lyricist: Clifford Grey
        Chiribiribee (Ciribiribin) (Armen, Powell, Martin,
          Reynolds, Damone, Tamblyn) music, lyrics: H Johnson,
          Pestalazza
---   I Know That You Know (Powell, Damone) lyrics: Anne Caldwell
        A Kiss or Two (Reynolds, boys)
        More Than You Know (Martin) lyrics: William Rose, Edward
          Eliscu
        Lady from the Bayou (Miller)
        Sometimes I'm Happy (reprise) (Powell)
        Hallelujah! (Martin, Damone, Tamblyn, chorus) co-lyricist:
          Clifford Grey

HOLD ON! (MGM, 1966)

MGM SE 4342 ST (soundtrack) stereo

Music, lyrics: Fred Karger, Sid Wayne, Ben Wiseman, others

Cast: Shelley Fabares, Herman's Hermits

Songs: Hold On! (Herman's Hermits) music, lyrics: P F Sloan,
          Steve Barri
        The George and the Dragon (Herman's Hermits)
        Got A Feeling (Herman's Hermits)
        Wild Love (Herman's Hermits)
        Leaning On A Lamp Post (Herman's Hermits) music, lyrics:
          Noel Gay
---   Where Were You When I Needed You? (Herman's Hermits)
          music, lyrics: P F Sloan, Steve Barri
        All the Things I Do for You, Baby (Herman's Hermits)
          music, lyrics: P F Sloan, Steve Barri
        Gotta Get Away (Herman's Hermits)
        Make Me Happy (Fabares, Herman's Hermits)

A Must to Avoid (Herman's Hermits) music, lyrics: P F
    Sloan, Steve Barri

HOLIDAY IN MEXICO (MGM, 1946)

Columbia (78rpm) X 271 mono

Music, lyrics: various; musical direction: Carmen Dragon

Cast: Jane Powell

Columbia (78rpm) 4352-M Ave Maria (Powell) music: Franz Schubert
                       Les Filles de Cadiz (Powell) music:
                          Leo Delibes
Columbia (78rpm) 4353-M I Think of You (Powell) music: Don
                          Marcotte (adapted from Rachmaninoff);
                          lyrics: Jack Elliot
                       Italian Street Song (Powell) music:
                          Victor Herbert; lyrics: Rida Johnson
                          Young, Gus Kahn

Note: Soundtrack selection included on Curtain Calls LP: CC 100/4
       'Jane Powell'

       I Think of You (Powell, Jose Iturbi, piano)

       Additional studio recordings by Xavier Cugat Orchestra:

Columbia (78rpm) 36902 Walter Winchell Rhumba
                       Oye Negra
Columbia (78rpm) 37090 You, So It's You

HOLIDAY INN (Paramount, 1942)

Decca DL 4256 mono 'Bing's Hollywood - Holiday Inn' reissued:
MCA 25205 CD

Music, lyrics: Irving Berlin; musical direction: John Scott
Trotter, others

Cast: Fred Astaire, Bing Crosby, Margaret Lenhart (not in film)

Songs: Happy Holiday (Crosby, chorus)
       Be Careful, It's My Heart (Crosby)
       Abraham (Crosby, chorus)
       Easter Parade (Crosby)
       Song of Freedom (Crosby, chorus)
       I Can't Tell A Lie (Astaire) musical direction: Bob Crosby
---   Lazy (Crosby) musical direction: Bob Crosby
       I'll Capture Your Heart (Crosby, Astaire, Lenhart)

        musical direction: Bob Crosby
     I've Got Plenty to Be Thankful For (Crosby) musical
       direction: Bob Crosby
     You're Easy to Dance With (Astaire) musical direction:
       Bob Crosby
     White Christmas (Crosby, chorus)
     Let's Start the New Year Right (Crosby) musical direction:
       Bob Crosby

HOLIDAY INN (Paramount, 1942)

Sountrak 112 (soundtrack) mono

Musical direction: Robert Emmett Dolan

Cast: Fred Astaire, Bing Crosby, Virginia Dale, Martha Mears
       (for Marjorie Reynolds)

Songs: Overture (chorus)
     I'll Capture Your Heart (Crosby, Astaire, Dale)
     Lazy (Crosby) orchestra incorporates 'Oh, How I Hate to
       Get Up in the Morning'
     You're Easy to Dance With (Astaire, chorus)
     White Christmas (Crosby, Mears)
     Happy Holiday (Crosby, Mears, chorus)
     Holiday Inn (Crosby, Mears)
     Let's Start the New Year Right (Crosby)
---   Be Careful, It's My Heart (Crosby)
     I Can't Tell A Lie (Astaire)
     Easter Parade (Crosby)
     Let's Say It with Firecrackers (chorus)
     Song of Freedom (Crosby, chorus)
     Firecracker Dance (orchestra)
     I've Got Plenty to Be Thankful For (Crosby)
     White Christmas (reprise) (chorus, Mears, Crosby)
     I'll Capture Your Heart (reprise) (Astaire, Crosby,
      Mears, chorus)
     Closing Credits (orchestra)

Note: The above recording includes spoken dialog.

HOLLYWOOD CANTEEN (Warner Bros, 1944)

Curtain Calls 100/11-12 (soundtrack) mono

Music, lyrics: various

Cast: The Andrews Sisters, Jack Benny, Joe E Brown, Eddie Cantor,
       Kitty Carlisle, Jack Carson, Carmen Cavallaro Orchestra,
       Bette Davis, Jimmy Dorsey Orchestra, John Garfield, The
       Golden Gate Quartet, Joan Leslie, Nora Martin, Dennis
       Morgan, Roy Rogers, The Sons of the Pioneers, Joseph

Szigeti, Jane Wyman

Songs: Hollywood Canteen (The Andrews Sisters) music: Ray
           Heindorf, M K Jerome; lyrics: Ted Koehler
       One O'Clock Jump (Jimmy Dorsey Orchestra) music: Count
           Basie
       What Are You Doing the Rest of Your Life? (Carson, Wyman)
           music: Burton Lane; lyrics: Ted Koehler
       The General Jumped at Dawn (The Golden Gate Quartet)
           music: Jimmy Mundy; lyrics: Larry Neal
       We're Having A Baby (Cantor, Martin) music: Vernon Duke;
           lyrics: Harold Adamson
       Tumblin' Tumbleweeds (Sons of the Pioneers) music, lyrics:
           Bob Nolan
       Don't Fence Me In (Rogers, Sons of the Pioneers) music,
           lyrics: Cole Porter
       Corns for My Country (The Andrews Sisters) music: Dick
           Charles; lyrics: Jean Barry
       Don't Fence Me In (reprise) (The Andrews Sisters)
       You Can Always Tell A Yank (Morgan, Brown, chorus) music:
           Burton Lane; lyrics: E Y Harburg
---   John Garfield, Bette Davis scene (spoken)
       Sweet Dreams Sweetheart (Leslie, chorus) music: M K Jerome;
           lyrics: Ted Koehler
       Ballet in Jive (orchestra) music: Ray Heindorf
       The Bee (Szigeti, violin) music: Franz Schubert
       Souvenir (Szigeti, Benny) primarily spoken
       Voodoo Moon (Carmen Cavallero Orchestra) music: Marion
           Sunshine, Julio Blanco, Obdulio Morales
       Sweet Dreams Sweetheart (reprise) Carlisle
       Finale (Joan Leslie, Robert Hutton, Bette Davis) spoken

Note: Studio recordings by cast members:

Decca (78rpm) 18628 Corns for My Country (The Andrews Sisters)
Decca (78rpm) 23359 Sweet Dreams, Sweetheart (Carlisle)
Decca (78rpm) 23364 Don't Fence Me In (The Andrews Sisters)
RCA (78rpm) 20-3073 Don't Fence Me In (Rogers)

HOLLYWOOD HOTEL (Warner Bros, 1937)

Hollywood Soundstage H S 5004 (soundtrack) mono

Music: Richard Whiting, others; lyrics: Johnny Mercer, others;
musical direction: Leo F Forbstein

Cast: Jerry Cooper, Johnny 'Scat' Davis, The Benny Goodman
       Orchestra, Ted Healy, Harry James, Gene Krupa, Rosemary
       Lane, Frances Langford, The Raymond Paige Orchestra, Dick
       Powell, Mabel Todd

Hollywood Hotel Exploitation Record:

> Sing, You Son of A Gun (Powell)
> Let That Be A Lesson to You (Langford)
> Silhouetted in the Moonlight (Lane)
> I've Hitched My Wagon to A Star (Powell)

Songs: Opening Titles (orchestra)
   Hooray for Hollywood (Davis, Langford, James, Krupa,
    chorus)
   I'm Like A Fish Out of Water (Powell, Lane)
   Silhouetted in the Moonlight (Powell, Lane)
   Let That Be A Lesson to You (Davis, Powell, Lane, Todd,
    Healy, chorus)
---   Sing, Sing, Sing (Goodman Orchestra) music: Louis Prima
   I've Got A Heartful of Music (Goodman Quintet)
   I've Hitched My Wagon to A Star (Powell)
   I've Got A Heartful of Music (Goodman Orchestra) cut
    from film
   House Hop (Goodman Orchestra) cut from film
   Silhouetted in the Moonlight (reprise) (Cooper, Langford)
   Dark Eyes (Paige Orchestra) trad
   I've Hitched My Wagon to A Star (reprise) (Powell)
   Sing, You Son of A Gun (Powell, cast)
   Hooray for Hollywood (reprise) (Davis, cast)
   Closing Music (orchestra)

Note: The above recording includes spoken dialog. Dick Powell
   studio recordings:

Decca (78rpm) 1557 I've Hitched My Wagon to A Star
        I'm Like A Fish Out of Water

HOLLYWOOD OR BUST (Paramount, 1956)

Capitol (45/EP) EAP 1-806 mono

Music: Sammy Fain; lyrics: Paul Francis Webster

Cast: Dean Martin

Songs: It Looks Like Love (Martin)
   Let's Be Friendly (Martin)
   A Day in the Country (Martin)
   Hollywood or Bust (Martin)

HONEYSUCKLE ROSE (Warner Bros, 1980)

Columbia S2 36752 (two records - soundtrack) stereo CD

Music, lyrics: Willie Nelson, others

Cast: Dyan Cannon, Hank Cochran, Johnny Gimble, Emmylou Harris,
        Amy Irving, Willie Nelson, Jody Payne, Jeannie Seely,
        Kenneth Threadgill

Songs: On the Road Again (Nelson, chorus)
        Pick Up the Tempo (Nelson)
        Heaven or Hell (Nelson)
        Fiddlin' Around (Gimble, chorus) music, lyrics: Johnny
            Gimble
        Blue Eyes Crying in the Rain (Nelson) music, lyrics:
            F Rose
        Working Man Blues (Payne) music, lyrics: Merle Haggard
---   Jumpin' Cotton Eyed Joe (Gimble, chorus) arr: Johnny Gimble
        Whiskey River (Nelson) music, lyrics: J B Shinn III
        Bloody Mary Morning (Nelson)
        Loving You Was Easier (Than Anything I'll Ever Do Again)
            (Nelson, Cannon) music, lyrics: Kris Kristofferson
        I Don't Do Windows (Cochran) music, lyrics: Hank Cochran
        Coming Back to Texas (Threadgill) arr: Kenneth Threadgill,
            C Joyce, J Paul
---   If You Want Me to Love You (Irving)
        It's Not Supposed to Be That Way (Nelson)
        You Show Me Yours (and I'll Show You Mine) (Nelson,
            Irving, chorus) music, lyrics: Kris Kristofferson
        If You Could Touch Her At All (Nelson) music, lyrics:
            L Clayton
        Angel Flying Too Close to the Ground (Nelson)
        I Guess I've Come to Live Here in Your Eyes (Nelson)
---   Angel Eyes (Nelson, Harris) music, lyrics: R Crowell
        So You Think You're A Cowboy (Harris) music, lyrics:
            Hank Cochran, Willie Nelson
        Make the World Go Away (Cochran, Seely) music, lyrics:
            Hank Cochran
        Two Sides to Every Story (Cannon, chorus)
        A Song for You (Nelson) music, lyrics: L Russell
        Uncloudy Day (Nelson, Cannon, chorus) arr: Willie Nelson

HONKY TONK (Warner Bros, 1929)

Take Two TT 104 (soundtrack) mono 'Legends of the Musical Stage'

Music: Milton Ager, others; lyrics: Jack Yellen, others

Cast: Sophie Tucker

Songs: Some of These Days (Tucker) music, lyrics: Shelton Brooks
        I'm the Last of the Red Hot Mammas (Tucker)
        Feathering A Nest (Tucker, chorus)
        Feathering A Nest (reprise) (orchestra)

HONKY TONK (Warner Bros, 1929)

Take Two TT 110 (soundtrack) mono 'Lost Films - Trailers from the
First Years of Sound'

Songs: I'm the Last of the Red Hot Mammas (Tucker, Ted Shapiro,
        piano)
        I'm Doin' What I'm Doin' for Love (Tucker, Ted Shapiro,
        piano)

Note: Studio recordings by Sophie Tucker:

Victor (78rpm) 21993 I'm Doin' What I'm Doin' for Love
                     I'm Feathering A Nest
Victor (78rpm) 21994 I'm the Last of the Red Hot Mammas (LP:
                     RCA LCT 1112)
                     He's A Good Man to Have Around (LP: RCA
                     LPV 538)

HONKYTONK MAN (Warner Bros, 1982)

Warner Bros 237391 (soundtrack) stereo

Music, lyrics: various; musical direction: Steve Dorff

Cast: John Anderson, Clint Eastwood, David Frizzell, Johnny
        Gimble Texas Swing Band, Linda Hopkins, Ray Prince, Marty
        Robbins, Porter Wagoner, Shelly West

Songs: San Antonio Rose (Price, chorus) music, lyrics: Bob Wills
        Turn the Pencil Over (Wagoner, chorus) music, lyrics:
        DeWayne Blackwell
        Please Surrender (Fizzell, West, chorus) music, lyrics:
        John Durrill, Cliff Crofford, Snuff Garrett
        When I Sing About You (Eastwood, chorus) music, lyrics:
        DeWayne Blackwell
        Ricochet Rag (Gimble Texas Swing Band) music: Herb
        Remington
        Honkytonk Man (Robbins, chorus) music, lyrics: DeWayne
        Blackwell
---   One Fiddle, Two Fiddle (Price, chorus) music, lyrics:
        Cliff Crofford, John Durrill, Snuff Garrett
        In the Jailhouse Now (Robbins, Anderson, Frizzell, Eastwood)
        music, lyrics: Jimmie Rogers
        No Sweeter Cheater than You (Eastwood) music, lyrics:
        Mitch Torok, R Redd
        These Cotton Patch Blues (Anderson) music, lyrics: Cliff
        Crofford
        Texas Moonbeam Waltz (Gimble Texas Swing Band) music:
        Cliff Crofford, Steve Dorff, Snuff Garrett
        When the Blues Come Around This Evening (Hopkins) music:

lyrics: Cliff Crofford, John Durrill

HOOTENANNY HOOT (MGM, 1963)

MGM SE 4172 ST (soundtrack) stereo

Music, lyrics: various

Cast: Chris Crosby, The Gateway Trio, Joe & Eddie, Cathie
        Taylor, Sheb Wooley

Songs: Hootenanny Hoot (Wooley, chorus) music, lyrics: Sheb
          Wooley, Fred Karger
       I'm Just A Country Boy (Mark Dinning) not from film
       Puttin' on the Style (The Gateway Trio) arr, adpt:
          Regis, Reynolds
       Sweet, Sweet Love (Crosby, chorus) music, lyrics:
          Lampert, Farrow, Turnbill
       Frozen Logger (Taylor) arr: Cathie Taylor, Fascineto
       There's A Meetin' Here Tonight (Joe & Eddie) music,
          lyrics: Gibson
---   Foolish Questions (The Gateway Trio) music, lyrics:
          Walter
       Black Is the Color of My True Love's Hair (Mark Dinning)
          not from film
       Buildin' A Railroad (Wooley, chorus) music, lyrics:
          Sheb Wooley
       Lost Highway (Mark Dinning) not from film
       Papa's Old Fiddle (Wooley) not from film
       That's My Pa (Wooley) not from film

HOUND-DOG MAN (Twentieth Century-Fox, 1960)

Chancellor CHLA 303 stereo

Music, lyrics: Ken Darby, others

Cast: Fabian

Songs: Hound-Dog Man (Fabian) music, lyrics: Doc Pomus, Mort
          Shuman
       Pretty Little Girl (Fabian) music: Pete De Angelis;
          lyrics: Bob Marcucci
       This Friendly World (Fabian)
       Single (Fabian)
       I'm Growin' Up (Fabian) music: Pete De Angelis; lyrics:
          Bob Marcucci

HOW THE WEST WAS WON (MGM, 1962)

MGM 1SE5ST (soundtrack) stereo

Music: Alfred Newman, others; lyrics: Ken Darby, others; musical
direction: Alfred Newman, others

Cast: Dave Guard, Debbie Reynolds

Songs: Overture: I'm Bound for the Promised Land (chorus) trad
                  Shenandoah (chorus) trad
                  Endless Prairie (chorus)
                  The Ox Driver (Guard, men) music, lyrics: Guard,
                     Faeyar, Henske, Wheat
                  I'm Bound for the Promised Land (chorus)
        Main Title: How the West Was Won (orchestra)
        Berevement and Fulfillment (orchestra)
        The River Pirates (orchestra)
        Home in the Meadow (Reynolds) music (adpt): Robert Emmett
           Dolan; lyrics: Sammy Cahn; musical direction: Robert
           Armbruster
        Cleve and the Mule (orchestra)
        Raise A Ruckus (Reynolds, chorus) music (adpt): Robert
           Emmett Dolan; lyrics: Johnny Mercer; musical direction:
           Robert Emmett Dolan
        Come Share My Life (orchestra)
        The Marriage Proposal (Greensleeves) (orchestra)
---   Entr'acte: Home in the Meadow (chorus)
                   900 Miles (Guard, chorus) trad
                   On the Banks of the Sacramento (chorus)
                   When Johnny Comes Marching Home (chorus) music,
                      lyrics: Patrick S Gilmore
                   I'm Bound for the Promised Land (chorus)
                   Battle Hymn of the Republic (chorus) music:
                      William Steffe; lyrics: Julia Ward Howe
        Cheyennes (orchestra)
        He's Linus' Boy (chorus)
        Climb A Higher Hill (orchestra)
        What Was Your Name in the States? (Reynolds) music (adpt):
           Robert Emmett Dolan; lyrics: Johnny Mercer; musical
           direction: Robert Emmett Dolan
        No Goodbye (orchestra)
        Finale: How the West Was Won (chorus)

Note: Studio recording by Debbie Reynolds:

       Dot (45rpm) 16465 A House in the Meadow

HOW TO STUFF A WILD BIKINI (American International, 1965)

Wand 671 (soundtrack) stereo

Music, lyrics: Guy Hemrick, Jerry Styner, others

Cast: Annette Funicello, Brian Donlevy, The Kingsmen, Harvey
        Lembeck, Mickey Rooney, Lou Ann Simms

Songs: How to Stuff A Wild Bikini (cast)
        That's What I Call A Healthy Girl (cast)
        If It's Gonna Happen (Simms)
        How About Us (Rooney, girls)
        The Boy Next Door (Lembeck, cast)
        After the Party (cast)
---   Better Be Ready (Funicello)
        Follow Your Leader (Lembeck, cast)
        The Perfect Boy (Funicello, girls)
        Madison Avenue (Rooney, Donlevy)
        Give Her Lovin' (The Kingsmen)
        How to Stuff A Wild Bikini (reprise) (The Kingsmen)

HOW TO SUCCEED IN BUSINESS WITHOUT REALLY TRYING (United Artists,
1967)

United Artists UAS 5151 (soundtrack) stereo

Music, lyrics: Frank Loesser; musical direction: Nelson Riddle

Cast: Ruth Kobart, Michele Lee, Robert Morse, John Myhers,
        Kay Reynolds, Sammy Smith, Anthony Teague, Rudy Vallee

Songs: Overture (orchestra)
        How to Succeed in Business without Really Trying (Morse)
        Coffee Break (Teague, Reynolds, company)
        The Company Way (Morse, Smith, Teague, company)
        A Secretary Is Not A Toy (Myhers, company)
        The Company Way (reprise - Finch's Frolic) (orchestra)
        Been A Long Day (Morse, Lee, Reynolds, company)
---   Grand Old Ivy (Vallee, Morse)
        Rosemary (Morse)
        I Believe in You (Lee)
        The Company Way (reprise) (orchestra)
        Paris Original (company party) (orchestra)
        Gotta Stop That Man (men)
        I Believe in You (reprise) (Morse)
        Brotherhood of Man (Morse, Vallee, Kobart, company)
        Finale (company)

HUCKLEBERRY FINN (United Artists, 1974)

United Artists UA LA229-F (soundtrack) stereo

Music, lyrics: Richard M Sherman, Robert B Sherman; musical
direction: Fred Werner

Cast: Jeff East, Roberta Flack (not in film), Harvey Korman,

       Gary Merrill, David Wayne, Paul Winfield

Songs: Freedom (Flack)
       Huckleberry Finn (chorus)
       Someday, Honey Darlin' (Winfield)
       Cairo, Illinois (Winfield, cast)
       A Rose in A Bible (chorus)
---   Royalty (Korman, Wayne)
       The Royal Nonesuch (Korman)
       What's Right - What's Wrong? (East)
       Rotten Luck (Merrill)
       Freedom (reprise) (Flack)

I COULD GO ON SINGING (United Artists, 1963)

Capitol SW 1861 (soundtrack) stereo

Music, lyrics for songs: various; musical score, direction:
Mort Lindsey

Cast: Judy Garland

Songs: Main Title (I Could Go On Singing) (Garland) music:
       Harold Arlen; lyrics: E Y Harburg
       Overture (orchestra)
       Hello Bluebird (Garland) music, lyrics: Cliff Friend
       I Am the Monarch of the Sea (Garland, boys) arr: Mort
       Lindsey; from 'H M S Pinafore' by Gilbert and Sullivan
       It Never Was You (Garland) music: Kurt Weill; lyrics:
       Maxwell Anderson
---   By Myself (Garland) music: Arthur Schwartz; lyrics:
       Howard Dietz
       Helicopter Ride (orchestra)
       Interlude: Matt's Dilemma (orchestra)
       I Could Go On Singing (reprise) (Garland)

I DREAM TOO MUCH (RKO, 1935)

Ariel OSH 14 mono 'Opera Stars in Hollywood'

Music: Jerome Kern; lyrics: Dorothy Fields; musical direction:
Andre Kostelanetz, others

Cast: Lily Pons

Songs: I'm the Echo (You're the Song That I Sing) (Pons)
       The Jockey on the Carousel (Pons, chorus) musical
       direction: Maurice Abravanel
       I Dream Too Much (Pons, chorus)

I LOVE MELVIN (MGM, 1953)

MGM E 190 (soundtrack) mono   reissued: MCA 39081   CD

Music: Josef Myrow; lyrics: Mack Gordon; musical direction:
Georgie Stoll

Cast: Noreen Corcoran, Donald O'Connor, Debbie Reynolds

Songs: I Wanna Wander (O'Connor)
        We Have Never Met As Yet (O'Connor, Reynolds)
        Life Has It's Funny Little Ups and Downs (Corcoran)
        Saturday Afternoon Before the Game (chorus)
---   Where Did You Learn to Dance (O'Connor, Reynolds)
        And There You Are (orchestra)
        A Lady Loves (Reynolds, chorus)
        I Wanna Wander (reprise) (orchestra)

IDLE ON PARADE (Warwick/Columbia, 1959)   British

Decca (British 45/EP) DFE 6566 mono

Music, lyrics: Anthony Newley, Joe Henderson, others;
musical direction: Bill Shepherd

Cast: Anthony Newley

Songs: I've Waited So Long (Newley, chorus) music, lyrics: Lauden
        Idle Rock-A-Boogie (Newley, chorus)
---   Idle on Parade (Newley, chorus) music, lyrics; Praverman
        Sat'day Night Rock-A-Boogie (Newley, chorus)

THE IDOLMAKER (United Artists, 1980)

A & M SP 4840 (soundtrack) stereo

Music, lyrics: Jeff Barry

Cast: (the voice of) Colleen Fitzpatrick, Jesse Frederick (for
        Paul Land), Peter Gallagher, (the voice of) Darlene Love,
        Ray Sharkey, (the voices of) The Sweet Inspirations, (the
        sounds of) Nino Tempo

Songs: Here Is My Love (Frederick)
        Ooo-Wee Baby (Love)
        Come and Get It (Tempo)
        Sweet Little Lover (Frederick)
        I Can't Tell (Fitzpatrick)
        However Dark the Night (Gallagher)
---   Baby (Gallagher)
        I Know Where You're Goin' (Tempo)

>   A Boy and A Girl (The Sweet Inspirations)
>   I Believe It Can Be Done (Sharkey)
>   I Believe It Can Be Done (reprise) (instrumental - Tempo)

IF I HAD MY WAY (Universal, 1940)

Decca DL 4254 mono 'Bing's Hollywood - The Road Begins'

Music: James V Monaco, others; lyrics: John Burke, others;
musical direction: John Scott Trotter

Cast: Bing Crosby

Songs: If I Had My Way (Crosby) music: James Kendis; lyrics:
          Lou Klein
       April Played the Fiddle (Crosby)
       I Haven't Time to Be A Millionaire (Crosby)
       Meet the Sun Half-Way (Crosby)
       The Pessimistic Character (with the Crab Apple Face)
          (Crosby)

I'LL CRY TOMORROW (MGM, 1956)

MGM (45/EP) X 1180 (soundtrack) mono reissued: Stet DS 25001

Music, lyrics: various; musical direction: Charles Henderson

Cast: Susan Hayward

Songs: Happiness Is Just A Thing Called Joe (Hayward) music:
          Harold Arlen; lyrics: E Y Harburg
       The Vagabond King Waltz (Waltz Huguette) (Hayward)
          music: Rudolf Friml; lyrics: Brian Hooker
       I'm Sitting on Top of the World (Hayward) music: Ray
          Henderson; lyrics: Sam M Lewis, Joe Young
---   Sing You Sinners (Hayward, chorus) music: W Frank
          Harling; lyrics: Sam Coslow
       When the Red, Red, Robin Comes Bob, Bob, Bobbin' Along
          (Hayward) music, lyrics: Harry Woods

Note: Susan Hayward also recorded the theme song of this film,
       music by Alex North and lyrics by Johnny Mercer, which was
       not sung in the film:

       MGM (45rpm) K 12174 I'll Cry Tomorrow (Hayward)

       The above recordings, plus 'Just One of Those Things'
       are included on the album, Legends 1000/3 'Susan Hayward'

I'LL SEE YOU IN MY DREAMS (Warner Bros, 1951)

Columbia CL 6198 mono   reissued: CBS P19611

Music: Isham Jones, others; lyrics: Gus Kahn, others; musical
direction: Paul Weston

Cast: Doris Day, Danny Thomas

Songs: Ain't We Got Fun (Day, Thomas, chorus) music: Richard
            Whiting; co-lyricist: Raymond B Egan
        The One I Love (Day)
        I Wish I Had A Girl (Day, chorus) music: Grace LeBoy
        It Had to Be You (Day)
---   Nobody's Sweetheart (Day, chorus) music, lyrics: Elmer
            Schoebel, Ernie Erdman, Gus Kahn, Billy Meyers
        My Buddy (Day) music: Walter Donaldson
        Makin' Whoopee! (Day, Thomas) music: Walter Donaldson
        I'll See You in My Dreams (Day, chorus)

I'LL TAKE SWEDEN (United Artists, 1965)

United Artists UAS 5121 (soundtrack) stereo

Music: "By" Dunham, others; lyrics: Bobby Beverly, others

Cast: Frankie Avalon, Bob Hope, Tuesday Weld

Songs: I'll Take Sweden (Avalon) music, lyrics: Diane Lampert,
            Ken Lauber
        They'll Be Rainbows Again (Avalon)
        Kissin' Polka (orchestra)
        Nothing Can Compare with You (Hope)
        Give It to Me (Weld) lyrics: Jimmy Haskell
        The Bells Keep Ringing (orchestra)
---   Watusi Jo (orchestra)
        Nothing Can Compare with You (reprise) (orchestra)
        Would You Like My Last Name (Avalon) music, lyrics:
            Diane Lampert, Ken Lauber
        The Bells Keep Ringing (reprise) (Avalon)
        Tell Me, Tell Me (chorus) lyrics: Jimmy Haskell
        I'll Take Sweden (end titles - orchestra)

I'M NO ANGEL (Paramount, 1933)

Columbia CL 2751 mono 'Merman - Roberti - West'

Music: Harvey Brooks; lyrics: Gladys DuBois, Ben Ellison

Cast: Mae West

Songs: I'm No Angel (West)
       I Found A New Way to Go to Town (West)
       I Want You - I Need You (West)
       They Call Me Sister Honky Tonk (West, chorus)

IN PERSON (RKO, 1935)

Curtain Calls CC 100/21 (soundtrack) mono 'Ginger Rogers'

Music: Oscar Levant; lyrics: Dorothy Fields; musical direction:
Roy Webb

Cast: Ginger Rogers

Songs: Got A New Lease on Life (Rogers)
       Don't Mention Love to Me (Rogers)
       Out of Sight, Out of Mind (Rogers)

Note: Studio recording by Ginger Rogers:

       Decca (78rpm) 638 Don't Mention Love to Me

IN SEARCH OF THE CASTAWAYS (Disney, 1962)

Disneyland ST 3916 (soundtrack) stereo

Music, lyrics: Richard M Sherman, Robert B Sherman; musical
direction: Muir Mathieson

Cast: Maurice Chevalier, Haley Mills

Songs: In Search of the Castaways (orchestra)
       Grimpons (Let's Climb) (Chevalier, children)
       Castaway (Mills)
---   Enjoy It (Chevalier, Mills)

Note: The above recording consists primarily of spoken dialog,
       with a narration by John Mills.

IN THE GOOD OLD SUMMERTIME (MGM, 1949)

MGM 3232 (soundtrack) mono reissued: MCA 39083 CD

Music, lyrics: various; musical direction: George Stoll

Cast: Judy Garland

Songs: I Don't Care (Garland) music: Harry O Sutton; lyrics:
       Jean Lenox

Meet Me Tonight in Dreamland (Garland) music: Leo
    Friedman; lyrics: Beth Slater Whitson
Play That Barbershop Chord (Garland, men) music: Lewis
    Muir; lyrics: William Tracey, Ballard MacDonald
Last Night When We Were Young (Garland) music: Harold
    Arlen; lyrics: E Y Harburg
Put Your Arms Around Me Honey (Garland) music: Albert Von
    Tilzer; lyrics: Junie McCree
Merry Christmas (Garland) music: Fred Spielman; lyrics:
    Janice Torre

INNOCENTS OF PARIS (Paramount, 1929)

RCA VPM 6055 (two records) mono   'This Is Maurice Chevalier'

Music: Richard Whiting, others; lyrics: Leo Robin, others;
musical direction: Leonard Joy, others

Cast: Maurice Chevalier

Songs: Louise (Chevalier)
       Valentine (Chevalier) music, lyrics: Henri Christine
       Les Ananas (Chevalier) music, lyrics: Pearly, Eddy

Note: Additional studio recordings:

Victor (78rpm) 22007 It's A Habit of Mine (Chevalier)
                     On Top of the World, Alone (Chevalier)
Victor (78rpm) 21918 Wait Till You See 'Ma Cherie' (Chevalier)

INTERRUPTED MELODY (MGM, 1955)

MGM E 3185 (soundtrack) mono reissued: E 3984 'The Voice of...'

Music, lyrics: various; musical direction: Walter Ducloux

Cast: Heinz Blankenburg, Eileen Farrell (for Eleanor Parker),
       Charles Gonzales, William Olvis, Rudolf Petrak, Marcella
       Reale

Songs: La Boheme: Musetta's Waltz (Farrell, Blankenburg, Reale,
           Gonzales) music: Puccini
       Carmen: Habanera (Farrell) music: Bizet
       Il Trovatore: Finale Act I (Farrell, Blankenburg, Petrak)
           music: Verdi
       Madame Butterfly: One Fine Day (Farrell) music: Puccini
       Carmen: Seguidilla (Farrell, Olvis) music: Bizet
       Die Gotterdammerung: Immolation Scene (Farrell) music:
           Wagner
---   Samson and Delilah: My Heart At Thy Sweet Voice (Farrell)

        music: Saint Saens
      Over the Rainbow (Farrell) music: Harold Arlen; lyrics:
        E Y Harburg
      The Marriage of Figaro: Voi Che Sapete (Farrell) music:
        Mozart
      Anchors Aweigh (Farrell) music: Alfred Miles; lyrics:
        Charles Zimmerman
      The Marines' Hymn (Farrell) arr: L Z Phillips
      Don't Sit Under the Apple Tree (Farrell, chorus) music:
        Sam H Stept; lyrics: Lew Brown, Charles Tobias
      Waltzing Matilda (Farrell, chorus) trad: arranged: Marie
        Cowan, A B Paterson, Orrie Lee
      Tristan and Isolde: Excerpts from Act I,II,III (Farrell,
        Blackenburg, Petrak) music: Wagner

IT HAPPENED AT THE WORLD'S FAIR (MGM, 1963)

RCA LSP 2694 (soundtrack) stereo   reissued: APL 1-2568

Music: Roy C Bennett, others; lyrics: Sid Tepper, others

Cast: Elvis Presley

Songs: Beyond the Bend (Presley) music: Ben Weisman; lyrics:
        Fred Wise, Dolores Fuller
      Relax (Presley)
      Take Me to the Fair (Presley)
      They Remind Me Too Much of You (Presley) music, lyrics:
        Don Robertson
      One Broken Heart for Sale (Presley) music: Winfield Scott;
        lyrics: Otis Blackwell
\---   I'm Falling in Love Tonight (Presley) music, lyrics:
        Don Robertson
      Cotton Candy Land (Presley) music: Bob Roberts; lyrics:
        Ruth Batchelor
      A World of Our Own (Presley) music: Florence Kaye; lyrics:
        Bill Giant, Bernie Baum
      How Would You Like to Be (Presley) music: Mark Barkan;
        lyrics: Ben Raleigh
      Happy Ending (Presley) music: Ben Weisman; lyrics: Sid
        Wayne

IT HAPPENED IN BROOKLYN (MGM, 1947)

Hollywood Soundstage 5006 (soundtrack) mono

Music: Jule Styne, others; lyrics: Sammy Cahn, others; musical
direction: Johnny Green

Cast: Jimmy Durante, Kathryn Grayson, Peter Lawford, Bobby Long, (the piano of) Andre Previn, Frank Sinatra

Songs: Opening Credits (orchestra)
      Time After Time (Previn, piano)
      Whose Baby Are You (Sinatra)
      The Brooklyn Bridge (Sinatra)
      Bach Invention No. 1 (Grayson, Sinatra, children)
      I Believe (Sinatra, Durante, Long)
      Time After Time (reprise) (Sinatra)
      The Song's Gotta Come from the Heart (Durante, Sinatra)
---   Don Giovanni: La Ci Darem La Mano (Grayson, Sinatra)
        music: Mozart
      It's the Same Old Dream (Sinatra, chorus)
      Time After Time (reprise) (Grayson)
      Whose Baby Are You (reprise) (Lawford)
      Lakme: The Bell Song (Grayson) music: Delibes
      End Credits (orchestra)

Note: The above recording includes spoken dialog. Studio
      recordings by Sinatra (all on Columbia LP: CL2913,
      'Frank Sinatra in Hollywood'):

Columbia (78rpm) 37288 It's the Same Old Dream
                       The Brooklyn Bridge
Columbia (78rpm) 37300 Time After Time
                       I Believe

            musical direction: Axel Stordahl

IT STARTED IN NAPLES (PARAMOUNT, 1960)

Dot 25324 (soundtrack) stereo reissued: Varese Sarabande
STV 81122

Music, lyrics for songs: various; musical score: Alessandro
Cicognini, Carlo Savina

Cast: Paolo Bacilieri, Sophia Loren, Franco Pace

Songs: Prelude (orchestra)
      Stay Here with Me (Bacilieri) music, lyrics: Domenico
        Modugno, Verde, Milt Gabler
      Pizza on the Piazza (orchestra)
      So Innamurta E Te (Pace)
      Off to School (orchestra)
      Tu Vuo fa l'Americano (Loren, Bacilieri) music, lyrics:
        Renato Carosone, Nisa
      The Second Lie (orchestra)
      Friendship Montage (orchestra)
      Tarantella Veneziana (orchestra)
---   It Started in Naples (Pace) music: Alessandro Cicognini,
        Carlo Savina; lyrics: Sylvana Simoni, Milt Gabler

       Carina (Loren, Bacilieri) music, lyrics: Testa, Poes
       Resta Cu Mme (orchestra)
       Tarantella Romana (orchestra)
       Tu Non M'o Dice Maie (Pace) music: Alessandro Cicognini,
          Carlo Savina; lyrics: Sylvana Simoni
       Ice Cream vs Espresso (orchestra)
       Tarantella Caprise (orchestra)
       Finale (orchestra)

IT'S A DATE (Universal, 1940)

Decca (78rpm) 128 mono 'Deanna Durbin Souvenir Album, no 3'

Music, lyrics: various

Cast: Deanna Durbin

Decca (78rpm) 3061 Ave Maria (Durbin) music: Franz Schubert
                  (LP: Ace of Hearts AH 147)
Decca (78rpm) 3062 La Boheme: Musetta's Waltz Song (Durbin)
                  music: Puccini
                  Loch Lomond (Durbin) trad (LP: Ace of
                  Hearts AH 147)
Decca (78rpm) 3063 Love Is All (Durbin) music: Pinky Tomlin;
                  lyrics: Harry Tobias (LP: AH 93)

IT'S ALWAYS FAIR WEATHER (MGM, 1955)

MGM E 3241 (soundtrack) mono   reissued: MCA 25018

Music: Andre Previn, others; lyrics: Betty Comden, Adolph Green,
others; musical direction: Andre Previn

Cast: Dan Dailey, Dolores Gray, Gene Kelly, Michael Kidd,
      Lou Lubin

Songs: March, March (male chorus)
       Once Upon A Time (Dailey, Kelly, Kidd)
       Thanks A Lot, but No Thanks (Gray)
       The Time for Parting (Kelly, Dailey, Kidd)
       Blue Danube (Why Are We Here?) (Kelly, Dailey, Kidd)
         music: Strauss
---   Music Is Better Than Words (Gray) lyrics: Roger Edens
       Situation-Wise (Dailey)
       I Like Myself (Kelly)
       Stillman's Gym (Lubin, chorus)
       Baby You Knock Me Out (chorus)

IT'S LOVE AGAIN (Gaumont-British, 1936)

Decca Eclipse (British) EMC 2168 mono 'Over My Shoulder'

Music, lyrics: Harry M Woods, others; musical direction: Louis Levy

Cast: Jessie Matthews

Songs: It's Love Again (Matthews) music, lyrics: Sam Coslow
        Tony's in Town (Matthews)
        (I Nearly Let Love Go) Slipping Through My Fingers
            (Matthews)
        Got to Dance My Way to Heaven (Matthews) music, lyrics:
            Sam Coslow

JACQUES BREL IS ALIVE AND WELL AND LIVING IN PARIS (AFT, 1974)

Atlantic SD 2-1000 (two records - soundtrack) stereo

Music, lyrics: Jacques Brel, others; musical direction:
Francois Rauber

Cast: Jacques Brel, Shawn Elliot, Judy Lander, Joe Masiell,
        Joseph Neal, Annette Perrone, Mort Shuman, Elly Stone

Songs: Madeleine (Elliot, Lander, Neal, Perrone) music, lyrics:
            Jean Cortinovis, Gerard Jouannest, Jacques Brel
        Marathon (Les Flamandes) (Stone, Shuman, Masiell)
        My Childhood (Mon Enfance) (Stone)
        The Statue (La Statue) (Masiell) music, lyrics: Jacques
            brel, Francois Rauber
        Brussels (Bruxelles) (Stone, Shuman, Masiell) music,
            lyrics: Jacques Brel, Gerard Jouannest
        Jackie (La Chanson de Jacky) (Shuman) music, lyrics:
            Jacques Brel, Gerard Jouannest
---   Timid Frieda (Les Timides) (Stone)
        The Taxicab (Le Gaz) (Shuman) music, lyrics: Jacques
            Brel, Gerard Jouannest
        Old Folks (Les Vieux) (Stone) music, lyrics: Jacques
            Brel, Jean Cortinovis, Gerard Jouannest
        Alone (Seul) (Masiell)
        I Loved (J'aimais) (Stone) music, lyrics: Francois
            Rauber, Jacques Brel, Gerard Jouannest
        Funeral Tango (Tango Funebre) (Shuman) music, lyrics:
            Jacques Brel, Gerard Jouannest
        Bachelor's Dance (La Bouree du Celibataire) (Masiell)
---   Amsterdam (Shuman)
        Ne Me Quitte Pas (Brel)
        The Desperate Ones (Les Desesperes) (Stone, Shuman,
            Masiell) music, lyrics: Jacques Brel, Gerard Jouannest
        Sons of ... (Fils de ...) (Stone) music, lyrics: Jacques
            Brel, Gerard Jouannest
        The Bulls (Les Toros) (Masiell) music, lyrics: Jean

                    Cortinovis, Jacques Brel, Gerard Jouannest
              Marieke (Stone) music, lyrics: Jacques Brel, Gerard
                    Jouannest
              The Last Supper (Le Dernier Repas) (Stone, Shuman,
                    Masiell)
   ---   Mathilde (Shuman) music, lyrics: Jacques Brel, Gerard
                    Jouannest
              Middle Class (Les Bourgeois)(Shuman, Masiell) music,
                    lyrics: Jean Cortinovis, Jacques Brel
              Song for Old Lovers (La Chanson des Vieux Amants) (Stone)
                    music, lyrics: Jacques Brel, Gerard Jouannest
              Next (Au Suivant) (Masiell)
              Carousel (La Valse a Mille Temps) (Stone)
              If We Only Have Love (Quand On N'A Que L'Amour) (Stone,
                    Shuman, Masiell)

JAILHOUSE ROCK (MGM, 1957)

RCA (45/EP) EPA 4114 mono

Music, lyrics: Jerry Leiber, Mike Stoller, others

Cast: Elvis Presley

Songs: Jailhouse Rock (Presley)
       Young and Beautiful (Presley) music, lyrics: Aaron
            Schroeder, Abner Silver
       I Want to Be Free (Presley)
       Don't Leave Me Now (Presley) music, lyrics: Aaron
            Schroeder, Abner Silver
       (You're So Square) Baby, I Don't Care (Presley)

JAM SESSION (Columbia, 1944)

Hollywood Soundstage 5014 (soundtrack) mono

Music, lyrics: various

Cast: Louis Armstrong, Charlie Barnet Orchestra, Jan Garber
       Orchestra, Glen Gray Orchestra, Ann Miller, The Pied
       Pipers, Teddy Powell Orchestra, Alvino Rey Orchestra,
       Nan Wynn

Songs: Opening Credits (orchestra)
       I Can't Give You Anything but Love, Baby (Armstrong)
            music: Jimmy McHugh; lyrics: Dorothy Fields
       I Lost My Sugar in Salt Lake City (Garber Orchestra,
            female vocal) music, lyrics: Leon Rene, Jimmy Lange
       St Louis Blues (Rey Orchestra, male vocal) music, lyrics:
            W C Handy

    Murder He Says (Powell Orchestra, female vocal, chorus)
       music, lyrics: Jimmy McHugh, Frank Loesser
    It Started All Over Again (Pied Pipers) music: Carl
       Fischer; lyrics: Bill Carey
    No Name Jive (Gray Orchestra) music: Glen Gray
    Cherokee (Barnet Orchestra) music: Ray Noble
    Brazil (Wynn) music: Ary Barroso; English lyrics:
       S K Russell
    Vict'ry Polka (Miller, chorus) music: Jule Styne; lyrics:
       Sammy Cahn

Note: The above recording includes spoken dialog. Studio
      recordings by cast members:

Bluebird (78rpm) 10373 Cherokee (Barnet Orchestra)
Decca   (78rpm) 3089 No Name Jive (Gray Orchestra)
Victor   (78rpm) 20-1522 It Started All Over Again (Pied Pipers)

THE JAZZ SINGER (Warner Bros, 1927)

Sountrak ST 102 (two records - soundtrack) mono

Music, lyrics: various; musical direction: Louis Silvers

Cast: Joseph Diskay (for Warner Oland), Al Jolson, Cantor
      Joseph Rosenblatt

Songs: Overture (orchestra)
      Kol Nidre (Diskay) trad
      Dirty Hands, Dirty Face (Jolson) music: James Monaco;
        lyrics: Edgar Leslie, Grant Clarke
      Toot, Toot, Tootsie! (Goo'bye) (Jolson) music, lyrics:
        Ted Fio Rito, Robert A King, Gus Kahn, Ernie Erdman
---   Yahrzeit (Rosenblatt) trad
      Blue Skies (Jolson) music, lyrics: Irving Berlin
---   Incidental Music
---   Mother of Mine, I Still Have You (Jolson) music: Louis
        Silvers; lyrics: Grant Clarke
      Kol Nidre (reprise) (Jolson)
      My Mammy (Jolson) music: Walter Donaldson; lyrics:
        Sam M Lewis, Joe Young

Note: Studio recordings by Al Jolson:

Brunswick (78rpm) 3719 Mother of Mine, I Still Have You
Brunswick (78rpm) 3912 My Mammy (LP: Ace of Hearts AH 3)
                  Dirty Hands, Dirty Face (LP: AH 3)

THE JAZZ SINGER (Warner Bros, 1953)

RCA LPM 3118 mono

Music: Sammy Fain, others; lyrics: Jerry Seelen, others; musical
direction: Frank DeVol

Cast: Danny Thomas

Songs: Hush-A-Bye (Thomas, chorus)
       Oh Moon (Thomas) music, lyrics: Ray Jacobs
       Living the Life I Love (Thomas)
       The Birth of the Blues (Thomas) music: Ray Henderson;
          lyrics: Buddy De Sylva, Lew Brown
---   This Is A Very Special Day (Thomas) music, lyrics:
          Peggy Lee
       I Hear the Music Now (Thomas)
       Kol Nidre (Thomas, choir) trad (arr: Norman Luboff)
       Hashkivenu (Thomas, choir) music, lyrics: Paul Lamkoff

Note: Additional studio recordings by cast member Peggy Lee:

Decca (45/EP) ED 2003 This Is A Very Special Day
                      I Hear the Music Now
                      Lover
                      Just One of Those Things

THE JAZZ SINGER (AFD - Associated Film Distribution, 1980)

Capitol EMI SWAV 12120 stereo CD

Music, lyrics: Neil Diamond, Gilbert Becaud, others; musical
direction: Alan Lindgren, others

Cast: Neil Diamond

Songs: America (Diamond, chorus) music, lyrics: Neil Diamond
       Adon Olom (chorus) trad
       You Baby (Diamond) music, lyrics: Neil Diamond
       Love on the Rocks (Diamond)
       Amazed and Confused (Diamond) music: Neil Diamond, Richard
          Bennett; lyrics: Neil Diamond; musical direction: with
          Tom Hensley
       On the Robert E Lee (Diamond, chorus)
       Summerlove (Diamond) musical direction: Tom Hensley
---   Hello Again (Diamond) music: Neil Diamond, Alan Lindgren;
          lyrics: Neil Diamond
       Acapulco (Diamond) music: Neil Diamond, Doug Rhone;
          lyrics: Neil Diamond
       Hey Louise (Diamond)
       Songs of Life (Diamond)
       Jerusalem (Diamond) music, lyrics: Neil Diamond; musical
          direction: Tom Hensley
       Kol Nidre (Diamond, choir) trad
       My Name Is Yussel (theme) (orchestra) music: Neil Diamond
       America (reprise) (Diamond, chorus)

JESSICA (United Artists, 1962)

United Artists UAS 5096 (soundtrack) stereo

Music for songs: Marguerite Monnot, others; lyrics: Dusty Negulesco; background music: Mario Nascimbene

Cast: Maurice Chevalier

Songs: Jessica (Chevalier, chorus)
        The Vespa Road (orchestra)
        Will You Remember (Chevalier, chorus)
        Fiesta Sul 'Aia (orchestra) music: S Riela
        Will You Remember (reprise) (orchestra)
---   Fantasia (unidentified vocal, chorus) music: S Riela
        The Vespa Song (Chevalier, chorus) music: Mario Nascimbene
        Vespalero (orchestra)
        Will You Remember (reprise) (orchestra)
        It Is Better to Love (Chevalier, chorus)
        Farewell (orchestra) music: Gangi
        The Circle Dance (orchestra)
        Jessica (reprise) (orchestra)

JESUS CHRIST SUPERSTAR (Universal, 1973)

MCA 2-11000 (two records - soundtrack) stereo CD

Music: Andrew Lloyd Webber; lyrics: Tim Rice; musical direction: Andre Previn

Cast: Carl Anderson, Bob Bingham, Barry Dennen, Yvonne Elliman,
        Larry T Marshall, Joshua Mostel, Ted Neeley, Philip
        Toubus, Kurt Yaghjian

Songs: Overture (orchestra)
        Heaven on Their Minds (Anderson)
        What's the Buzz (Neeley, Elliman, chorus)
        Strange Thing Mystifying (Anderson, Neeley, chorus)
        Then We Are Decided (Bingham, Yaghjian)
        Everything's Alright (Elliman, Neeley, Anderson, chorus)
---   This Jesus Must Die (Bingham, Yaghjian, chorus)
        Hosanna (Neeley, Bingham, chorus)
        Simon Zealotes (Marshall, chorus)
        Poor Jerusalem (Neeley)
        Pilate's Dream (Dennen, choir)
        The Temple (Neeley, chorus)
        I Don't Know How to Love Him (Elliman)
        Damned for All Time / Blood Money (Anderson, Bingham,
           Yaghjian, choir)
---   The Last Supper (Neeley, Anderson, choir)
        Gethsemane (I Only Want to Say) (Neeley)

        The Arrest (Neeley, Toubus, Bingham, Yaghjian, chorus)
        Peter's Denial (Toubus, Elliman, chorus)
        Pilate and Christ (Dennen, Neeley, chorus)
        King Herod's Song (Mostel)
        Could We Start Again, Please? (Elliman, Toubus, chorus)
        Judas' Death (Anderson, Bingham, Yaghjian, choir)
        Trial Before Pilate (Dennen, Anderson, Bingham, chorus)
        Superstar (Anderson, chorus)
        The Crucifixion (Neeley, chorus)
        John Nineteen:Forty-One (orchestra)

JOLSON SINGS AGAIN (Columbia, 1949)

Decca 5006 mono

Music, lyrics: various; musical direction: Morris Stoloff, others

Cast: Al Jolson (for Larry Parks)

Songs: Pretty Baby (Jolson) music: Tony Jackson, Egbert Van
      Alstyne; lyrics: Gus Kahn
     I'm Looking Over A Four Leaf Clover (Jolson) music: Harry
      Woods; lyrics: Mort Dixon
     Give My Regards to Broadway (Jolson) music, lyrics: George
      M Cohan
     I'm Just Wild About Harry (Jolson) music: Eubie Blake;
      lyrics: Noble Sissle
     After You've Gone (Jolson, chorus) music: Turner Layton;
      lyrics: Henry Creamer; musical direction: Matty Malneck
     Chinatown, My Chinatown (Jolson, chorus) music: Jean
      Schwartz; lyrics: William Jerome; musical direction:
      Matty Malneck
     I Only Have Eyes for You (Jolson) music: Harry Warren;
      lyrics: Al Dubin
     Is It True What They Say About Dixie? (Jolson) music:
      Gerald Marks; lyrics: Irving Caesar, Sammy Lerner

THE JOLSON STORY (Columbia, 1946)

Decca 5026 mono 'Al Jolson in Songs He Made Famous'

Music, lyrics: various; musical direction: Morris Stoloff, others

Cast: Al Jolson (for Larry Parks)

Songs: April Showers (Jolson) music: Louis Silvers; lyrics:
     Buddy DeSylva; musical direction: Carmen Dragon
     Swanee (Jolson) music: George Gershwin; lyrics: Irving
      Caesar; musical direction: Carmen Dragon
     California, Here I Come (Jolson) music, lyrics: Joseph
      Meyer, Al Jolson, Buddy DeSylva

Rock-A-Bye Your Baby with A Dixie Melody (Jolson) music:
Jean Schwartz; lyrics: Sam M Lewis, Joe Young
--- You Made Me Love You (Jolson) music: James V Monaco;
lyrics: Joseph McCarthy
Ma Blushin' Rosie (Jolson) music: John Stromberg; lyrics:
Edgar Smith
Sonny Boy (Jolson) music: Ray Henderson; lyrics: Buddy
DeSylva, Lew Brown, Al Jolson (not from film)
My Mammy (Jolson) music: Walter Donaldson; lyrics: Sam
M Lewis, Joe Young

Note: Additional studio recording by Al Jolson:

Decca (78rpm) 23714 Avalon
The Anniversary Song

JOURNEY BACK TO OZ (Filmation, 1974)

RFO - 101 (soundtrack) stereo 'The Return to Oz'

Music: James Van Heusen; lyrics: Sammy Cahn; musical direction:
Walter Scharf

Cast: (the voices of) Milton Berle, Herschel Bernardi, Peter
Lawford (not from film), Jack E Leonard, Ethel Merman,
Liza Minnelli, Rise Stevens, Danny Thomas

Songs: Overture (orchestra)
There's A Faraway Land (Minnelli)
Pity the Horse (Who Must Dwell on the Carousel) (Bernardi)
Be A Witch! (Merman)
B-R-A-N-E (Lawford)
H-E-A-R-T (Thomas)
--- N-E-R-V-E (Berle)
Keep the Happy Thought (Minnelli)
Keep A Gloomy Thought (Merman)
An Elephant Never Forgets (Merman)
I Don't Know Where I Am (Leonard)
You Have Only You (Stevens)
Return to the Land of Oz! (Minnelli)
There's A Sad Little Feeling You Feel (Minnelli)

Note: The above recording includes spoken dialog. According to
Alan W Petrucelli's biography of 'Liza' this film (or at
least the soundtrack) was made in 1962, but did not get a
nationwide release until 1974.

JOURNEY TO THE CENTER OF THE EARTH (Twentieth Century-Fox, 1960)

Dot (45/EP) DEP 1091 (soundtrack) mono

Music: James Van Heusen; lyrics: Sammy Cahn, others; musical
direction: Lionel Newman

Cast: Pat Boone

Songs: Twice As Tall (Boone)
---   My Love Is Like A Red, Red Rose (Boone) words: Robert Burns
        The Faithful Heart (Boone)

Note: The recording also includes a new song 'inspired by the
        motion picture'

        To the Center of the Earth (Boone, chorus) musical direction:
           Mort Lindsey

THE JUNGLE BOOK (Disney, 1967)

Disneyland 3948 (soundtrack) stereo

Music, lyrics: Richard M Sherman, Robert B Sherman, others;
musical direction: George Bruns

Cast: (the voices of) Sebastian Cabot, Darlene Carr, Verna
        Felton, Phil Harris, Sterling Holloway, Lord Tim Hudson,
        J Pat O'Malley, Louis Prima, Bruce Reitherman, Chad
        Stuart, Digby Wolfe

Songs: Trust in Me (Holloway)
        Colonel Hathi's March (O'Malley, Felton, chorus)
        Bare Necessities (Harris, Reitherman) music, lyrics:
           Terry Gilkyson
---   I Wan'na Be Like You (Prima)
        I Wan'na Be Like You (reprise) (Prima, Harris)
        Colonel Hathi's March (reprise) (O'Malley,Felton,
           chorus)
        That's What Friends Are For (O'Malley, Stuart, Hudson,
           Wolfe)
        My Own Home (Carr)
        Bare Necessities (reprise) (Harris, Cabot)

Note: The above recording includes spoken dialog and a narration
        by Dal McKennon.

JUST A GIGOLO (United Artists, 1979)

Jambo JAM 1 (soundtrack) stereo

Music, lyrics: various; musical direction: Gunther Fischer, others

Cast: Marlene Dietrich, (the voices of) The Manhattan Transfer,
        Sydne Rome, (the voices of) The Village People

Songs: Just A Gigolo (Dietrich) music: Leonello Casucci; lyrics:
       Irving Caesar
       Salome (orchestra) music: Robert Stolz
       Johnny (The Manhattan Transfer) music: Frederick
           Hollander; lyrics: Jack Fishman
       The Streets of Berlin (orchestra) music: Gunther Fischer
       Charmaine (male vocal) music, lyrics: Lou Pollack, Erno
           Rapee
       Don't Let It Be Too Long (Rome) music: Gunther Fischer;
           lyrics: David Hemmings
       The Ragtime Dance (orchestra) music: Scott Joplin
       Jealous Eyes (The Village People) music, lyrics: Mihaly
           Erdelyi, Jack Fishman
       The Revolutionary Song (chorus) music: David Bowie;
           lyrics: Jack Fishman
       Easy Winners (orchestra) music: Scott Joplin
       I Kiss Your Hand, Madame (The Manhattan Transfer) music:
           Ralph Erwin; lyrics: Sam M Lewis, Joe Young
       Kissing Time (A Kiss in the Dark, Kiss Me Again)
           (orchestra) music, lyrics: Victor Herbert, Gunther
           Fischer, A K Absalom
       Black Bottom (male vocal) music: Ray Henderson; lyrics:
           Buddy De Sylva, Lew Brown
       Jealous Eyes (reprise) (orchestra)
       Just A Gigolo (reprise) (The Village People)
       I Ain't Got Nobody (The Village People) music: Spencer
           Williams; lyrics: Roger Graham

JUST FOR YOU (Paramount, 1952)

Decca DL 4263 mono 'Bing's Hollywood - Zing A Little Zong'

Music: Harry Warren; lyrics: Leo Robin; musical direction:
various

Cast: The Andrews Sisters (not in film), Bing Crosby, Ben
       Lessy (not in film), Jane Wyman

Songs: A Flight of Fancy (Crosby) musical direction: Camarata
       Just for You (Crosby) musical direction: Camarata
       I'll Si-Si Ya in Bahia (Crosby, Andrews Sisters)
           musical direction: John Scott Trotter
       The Live Oak Tree (Crosby, Andrews Sisters) musical
           direction: John Scott Trotter
       Zing A Little Zong (Crosby, Wyman, chorus) musical
           direction: Nathan Van Cleave
       On the 10:10 from Ten-Ten-Tennessee (Crosby, Lessy)
           musical direction: Nathan Van Cleave

KAZABLAN (MGM, 1973) Israel

MGM 1-SE-48 ST (soundtrack) stereo

Music: Dov Seltzer; lyrics: Haim Hefer, Dan Almagor, Amos
Ettinger; English lyrics: David Paulsen; musical direction:
Dov Seltzer

Cast: Aliza Azikri, Yehoram Gaon

Songs: Overture (orchestra)
       Man of Respect (Gaon, chorus)
       We Are All Jews (chorus)
       Chassidic Rock (orchestra)
       There's A Place (Gaon)
       Democracy (chorus)
       Construction Rock Ballet (orchestra)
       Democracy (reprise) (chorus)
       Jaffa (Azikri, chorus)
       Hey, What's Up! (chorus)
       Rosa, Rosa (Gaon, Azikri)
       Kazablan (Get Off My Back) (Gaon)
       Getting Dressed Ballet (orchestra)
       Brith Milah Pageant (chorus)

KID GALAHAD (United Artists, 1963)

RCA (45/EP) EPA 4371 (soundtrack) stereo

Music: Sherman Edwards, others; lyrics: Hal David, others

Cast: Elvis Presley

Songs: King of the Whole Wide World (Presley) music, lyrics:
          Ruth Batchelor, Bob Roberts
       This Is Living (Presley) music: Ben Weisman; lyrics:
          Fred Wise
       Riding the Rainbow (Presley) music: Ben Wiseman; lyrics:
          Fred Wise
       Home Is Where the Heart Is (Presley)
       I Got Lucky (Presley) music, lyrics: Fred Wise, Ben
          Weisman, Dolores Fuller
       A Whistling Tune (Presley)

KID MILLIONS (Goldwyn, 1934)

Classic International Filmusicals 3007 (soundtrack) mono also:
Sandy Hook SH 2039

Music: Walter Donaldson, others; lyrics: Gus Kahn, others;
musical direction: Alfred Newman

Cast: Eddie Cantor, Ethel Merman, George Murphy, The Nicholas
        Brothers, Ann Sothern

Songs: Opening Music (orchestra)
        An Earful of Music (Merman, chorus)
        When My Ship Comes In (Cantor)
        Your Head on My Shoulder (Murphy, Sothern) music: Burton
          Lane; lyrics: Harold Adamson
        Minstrel Show (montage with Merman, Cantor):
          I Want to Be A Minstrel Man (Nicholas Brothers, chorus)
            music: Burton Lane; lyrics: Harold Adamson
          Minstrel Dialog (Cantor, Murphy) spoken
          Mandy (Cantor, Merman, Sothern, chorus) music, lyrics:
            Irving Berlin
          Your Head on My Shoulder (reprise) (Murphy, Sothern,
            chorus)
          Mandy (reprise) (Cantor, Nicholas Brothers, chorus)
        Okay Toots (Cantor, chorus)
        Ice Cream Fantasy (Merman, Cantor, children, chorus)
        When My Ship Comes In (reprise) (Cantor)

Note: Ethel Merman studio recording:

Brunswick (78rpm) 6995 An Earful of Music (LP: Col CL 2751)

        Eddie Cantor studio recordings:

Melotone (78rpm) 13183 Mandy
                       An Earful of Music
Melotone (78rpm) 13184 Okay Toots
                       When My Ship Comes In

THE KING AND I (Twentieth Century-Fox, 1956)

Capitol W 740 (soundtrack) mono   CD

Music: Richard Rodgers; lyrics: Oscar Hammerstein II; musical
direction: Alfred Newman

Cast: Yul Brynner, Reuben Fuentes (for Carlos Rivas), Rita
        Moreno, Marni Nixon (for Deborah Kerr), Terry Saunders,
        Rex Thompson

Songs: Overture (orchestra)
        I Whistle A Happy Tune (Nixon, Thompson, chorus)
        My Lord and Master (Moreno)
        Hello, Young Lovers (Nixon)
        The March of the Siamese Children (orchestra)
        A Puzzlement (Brynner)
---   Getting to Know You (Kerr, chorus)
        We Kiss in A Shadow (Fuentes, Moreno)

        I Have Dreamed (Moreno, Fuentes)
        Shall I Tell You What I Think of You? (Nixon)
        Something Wonderful (Saunders)
        Song of the King (Brynner, Nixon)
        Shall We Dance? (Brynner, Nixon)
        Something Wonderful (reprise) (chorus)

KING CREOLE (Paramount, 1958)

RCA LPM 1884 mono   reissued: AYL 1-3733   CD

Music, lyrics: Jerry Leiber, Mike Stoller, others

Cast: Elvis Presley

Songs: King Creole (Presley)
       As Long As I Have You (Presley) music, lyrics: Fred Wise,
          Ben Wiseman
       Hard Headed Woman (Presley) music, lyrics: Claude De
          Metrius
       Trouble (Presley)
       Dixieland Rock (Presley) music, lyrics: Claude De Metrius,
          Fred Wise
       Don't Ask Me Why (Presley) music, lyrics: Fred Wise, Ben
          Weisman
       Lover Doll (Presley) music, lyrics: Sid Wayne, Abner Silver
       Crawfish (Presley) music, lyrics: Fred Wise, Ben Wiseman
       Young Dreams (Presley) music, lyrics: Aaron Schroeder,
          Martin Kalmanoff
       Steadfast, Loyal and True (Presley)
       New Orleans (Presley) music, lyrics: Sid Tepper, Roy C
          Bennett

KING OF BURLESQUE (Twentieth Century-Fox, 1935)

Columbia CL 3068 mono 'Alice Faye in Hollywood'

Music: Jimmy McHugh; lyrics: Ted Koehler; musical direction:
Cy Feuer

Cast: Alice Faye

Songs: I've Got My Fingers Crossed (Faye)
       I'm Shooting High (Faye)
       Spreadin' Rhythm Around (Faye)

Note: Additional studio recordings by cast members:

Melotone (78rpm) 60309 I Love to Ride the Horses (Faye)
Victor (78rpm)   25211 Spreadin' Rhythm Around (Fats Waller)

Victor (78rpm) 25211 I've Got My Fingers Crossed (Fats Waller)

Soundtrack recordings by Alice Faye on Curtain Calls
CC 100/3 'Alice Faye'

Whose Big Baby Are You?
I Love to Ride the Horses

THE KING OF JAZZ (Universal, 1930)

Columbia C2L 43 mono 'Bing Crosby in Hollywood'

Music: Milton Ager, others; lyrics: Jack Yellen, others; musical
direction: Paul Whiteman

Cast: The Brox Sisters, Bing Crosby, Johnny Fulton, Jeanie
        Lang, The Rhythm Boys (Bing Crosby, Al Rinker, Harry
        Barris), The Paul Whiteman Orchestra

Songs: Happy Feet (The Rhythm Boys, The Paul Whiteman Orchestra)
       A Bench in the Park (The Brox Sisters, The Rhythm Boys,
         The Paul Whiteman Orchestra)
       A Bench in the Park (Paul Whiteman's Rhythm Boys)
       It Happened in Monterey (Fulton, The Paul Whiteman
         Orchestra) music: Mabel Wayne; lyrics: Billy Rose
       I Like to Do Things for You (The Rhythm Boys, The Paul
         Whiteman Orchestra)
       Ragamuffin Romeo (Lang, The Paul Whiteman Orchestra)
         music: Mabel Wayne; lyrics: Harry DeCosta
       So the Bluebirds and the Blackbirds Got Together (Paul
         Whiteman's Rhythm Boys) music, lyrics: Harry Barris,
         Billy Moll
       Song of the Dawn (Bing Crosby, chorus, The Paul
         Whiteman Orchestra)

Note: Studio recording by John Boles:

Victor (78rpm) 22372 It Happened in Monterey (LP: LPV 538)
                     Song of the Dawn

THE KING STEPS OUT (Columbia, 1936)

Decca DL 9593 mono 'Grace Moore Sings'

Music: Fritz Kreisler; lyrics: Dorothy Fields; musical direction:
Josef Pasternack

Cast: Grace Moore

Songs: Stars in My Eyes (Moore)
       The End Begins (Moore)

Learn How to Lose (Moore)
What Shall Remain (Moore)

KING'S RHAPSODY (Lion, 1955)

Parlophone (British 45/EP) GEP 8533 (soundtrack) mono

Music: Ivor Novello; lyrics: Christopher Hassall

Cast: Edmund Hockridge, Anna Neagle, Patrice Wymore

Songs: The Years Together (Neagle)
        A Violin Began to Play (Wymore, Hockridge)
        If This Were Love (Wymore, Hockridge)
        Someday My Heart Will Sing (Wymore)

KISMET (MGM, 1955)

MGM E 3281 (soundtrack) mono reissued: MCA 1424

Music, lyrics: Robert Wright, George Forrest (music adapted from themes of Alexander Borodin); musical direction: Andre Previn

Cast: Ann Blyth, Vic Damone, Dolores Gray, Howard Keel

Songs: Fate (Keel)
        Not Since Ninevah (Gray, chorus)
        Baubles, Bangles and Beads (Blyth, chorus)
        Stranger in Paradise (Blyth, Damone)
---   Gesticulate (Keel, chorus)
        Night of My Nights (Damone, chorus)
        Bored (Gray)
        The Olive Tree (Keel)
        Rahadlakum (Keel, Gray, chorus)
        And This Is My Beloved (Keel, Blyth, Damone)
        Sands of Time (Keel)

Note: The above recording includes spoken dialog.

KISS ME KATE (MGM, 1953)

MGM E 3077 (soundtrack) mono reissued: MCA 25003

Music, lyrics: Cole Porter; musical direction: Andre Previn

Cast: Bob Fosse, Kathryn Grayson, Howard Keel, Ann Miller,
        Tommy Rall, Bobby Van, James Whitmore, Keenan Wynn

Songs: Too Darn Hot (Miller, men)

So In Love (Grayson, Keel)
We Open in Venice (Grayson, Keel, Miller, Rall)
Why Can't You Behave (Miller)
Were Thine That Special Face (Keel)
Tom, Dick or Harry (Miller, Van, Rall, Fosse)
Wunderbar (Grayson, Keel)
Always True to You in My Fashion (Miller, Rall)
I Hate Men (Grayson)
I've Come to Wive It Wealthily in Padua (Keel, chorus)
From This Moment On (Rall, Miller, Van, Fosse)
Where Is the Life That Late I Led? (Keel)
Brush Up Your Shakespeare (Whitmore, Wynn)
Kiss Me Kate (Grayson, Keel, chorus)

KISSIN' COUSINS (MGM, 1964)

RCA LSP 2894 (soundtrack) stereo

Music: Florence Kaye, others; lyrics: Bill Giant, Bernie Baum, others; musical direction: Fred Karger

Cast: Elvis Presley

Songs: Kissin' Cousins (No. 2) (Presley)
Smokey Mountain Boy (Presley) music, lyrics: Lenore Rosenblatt, Victor Millrose
There's Gold in the Mountains (Presley)
One Boy, Two Little Girls (Presley)
Catchin' on Fast (Presley)
Tender Feeling (Presley)
Anyone Could Fall in Love with You (Presley) music, lyrics: Bennie Benjamin, Sol Marcus, A Dejusus
Barefoot Ballad (Presley) music, lyrics: Dolores Fuller, Lee Morris
Kissin' Cousins (Presley) music: Randy Starr; lyrics: Fred Wise
Echoes of Love (Presley) music, lyrics: Robert McMains
(It's A) Long Lonely Highway (Presley)

THE KISSING BANDIT (MGM, 1948)

Motion Picture Tracks M P T - 7 (soundtrack) mono

Music: Nacio Herb Brown; lyrics: Edward Heyman, others; musical direction: Georgie Stoll

Cast: Kathryn Grayson, Sono Osoto, Frank Sinatra

Songs: Opening Credits (orchestra)
Tomorrow Means Romance (Grayson)

       What's Wrong with Me? (Grayson, Sinatra)
       If I Steal A Kiss (Sinatra)
       I Like You (Osoto)
       If You Steal A Kiss (reprise) (Grayson)
       Siesta (chorus, Sinatra)
---   Dance of Fury (orchestra)
       (I Offer You the Moon) Senorita (Sinatra, Grayson)
       Love Is Where You Find It (Grayson) lyrics: Earl Grant
       If You Steal A Kiss (reprise) (Grayson)
       End Credits (orchestra)

Note: The above recording includes spoken dialog. Other
       recordings by cast members:

Columbia (78rpm) 38334 (I Offer You the Moon) Senorita (Sinatra)
                   If I Steal A Kiss (Sinatra)
    both of the above included on Columbia LP: CL 2913

MGM (78rpm) 30133 What's Wrong with Me? (Grayson)
             Love Is Where You Find It (Grayson) LP: DRG
             2-2100

    Additional recording:

MGM (78rpm) 12305 Dance of Fury (David Rose Orchestra) LP: DRG
             2-2100

KNICKERBOCKER HOLIDAY (United Artists, 1944)

Ariel KWH 10 (soundtrack) mono 'Kurt Weill in Hollywood'

Music: Kurt Weill; lyrics: Maxwell Anderson; musical direction:
Jacques Samossud

Cast: Charles Coburn, Ernest Cossart, Nelson Eddy

Songs: The One Indispensable Man (Coburn, Cossart)
      September Song (Coburn)
      There's Nowhere to Go but Up (Eddy)

KNOCK ON WOOD (Paramount, 1954)

Decca DL 5527 mono

Music, lyrics: Sylvia Fine; musical direction: Vic Schoen,
others

Cast: Danny Kaye

Songs: Knock on Wood (Kaye)
      All About You (Kaye)

___   End of Spring (orchestra) musical direction: Victor Young
       (The Drastic, Livid History of) Monahan, O Han (Kaye)

THE LADY AND THE TRAMP (Disney, 1955)

Decca DL 8462 (partial soundtrack) mono

Music: Sonny Burke; lyrics: Peggy Lee; musical direction: Oliver
Wallace (for soundtrack selections)

Cast: (the voices of) Sonny Burke, George Givot, Peggy Lee

Songs: Bella Notte (Lee, chorus)
       Peace on Earth (Lee, chorus)
       Jim Dear (Lee)
       Lady (orchestra) soundtrack
       Old Trusty (Lee, Burke)
___   Singing (Cause He Wants to Sing) (Lee)
       What Is A Baby (Lee)
       La La Lu (Lee)
       The Siamese Cat Song (Lee) soundtrack
       He's A Tramp (Lee, chorus)
       Home Sweet Home (chorus) trad
       That Fellow's A Friend of Man (Lee)
       Bella Notte and Finale (Givot, chorus) soundtrack

LADY BE GOOD (MGM, 1941)

Hollywood Soundstage H S 5010 (soundtrack) mono

Music: George Gershwin, others; lyrics: Ira Gershwin, others;
musical direction: George Stoll

Cast: The Berry Brothers, John Carroll, Virginia O'Brien,
       Connie Russell, Red Skelton, Ann Sothern, Robert Young

Songs: Opening Titles - Lady Be Good (chorus)
       You'll Never Know (Sothern) music, lyrics: Roger Edens
       Your Words and My Music (Young, Sothern) music: Roger
           Edens; lyrics: Arthur Freed
       You Words and My Music (reprise) (Carroll)
       Your Words and My Music (reprise) (O'Brien)
       You'll Never Know (reprise) (The Berry Brothers)
       Lady Be Good (Sothern, Young)
___   Lady Be Good - montage (reprise) (Skelton, Carroll, cast)
       The Last Time I Saw Paris (Sothern) music: Jerome Kern;
           lyrics: Oscar Hammerstein II
       Lady Be Good (reprise) (danced by Eleanor Powell)
       Fascinating Rhythm (Russell, chorus)
       Lady Be Good (finale) (Skelton, O'Brien, Carroll,

            Sothern, chorus)
        End Titles - Your Words and My Music (orchestra)

LADY IN THE DARK (Paramount, 1944)

Curtain Calls CC 100/21 (soundtrack) mono 'Ginger Rogers'

Music: Kurt Weill; lyrics; Ira Gershwin; musical direction:
Robert Emmett Dolan

Cast: Ray Milland, Ginger Rogers

Songs: My Ship (Rogers, chorus)
        Girl of the Moment (chorus)
        The Greatest Show on Earth (orchestra, Milland, chorus)
        The Saga of Jenny (Rogers, chorus)

Note: The above recording includes spoken dialog. An additional
        selection (cut from film) was released on the following
        album:

        Choice Cuts ST 500/1 Suddenly It's Spring (Rogers)
                             music: Jimmy Van Heusen;
                             lyrics: Johnny Burke

THE LADY IS A SQUARE (Associated British, 1959)

Philips (British 45/EP) BBE 12247

Music, lyrics: various; musical direction: Wally Scott

Cast: Frankie Vaughan

Songs: Honey Bunny Baby (Vaughan) music, lyrics: Frank Abie
        That's My Doll (Vaughan) music, lyrics: Dick Glasser, Ann
---   Hall
        The Lady Is A Square (Vaughan) music, lyrics: Raymond
        Dutch, John Franz
        Love Is the Sweetest Thing (Vaughan) music, lyrics:
        Ray Noble

LADY SINGS THE BLUES (Paramount, 1972)

Motown 758-D (two records - soundtrack) stereo

Music, lyrics: various; musical direction: Gil Askey, Michel
Legrand

Cast: Michele Aller, Diana Ross, Blinky Williams

Songs: Lady Sings the Blues (Ross) music, lyrics: Billie
      Holiday, Herbie Nicholas
    'Tain't Nobody's Bizness If I Do (Williams) music,
      lyrics: Porter Grainger, Clarence Williams, Braham
      Prince
    All of Me (Ross) music, lyrics: Seymour Simons, Gerald
      Marks
    The Man I Love (Ross) music: George Gershwin; lyrics:
      Ira Gershwin
    Them There Eyes (Ross) music: Maceo Pinkard; lyrics:
      William Tracy, Doris Tauber
    Had You Been Around (Aller) music, lyrics: Miller, Yuffy,
      Jacques, Vanderberg
---   Love Theme (orchestra) music: Michel Legrand
    Country Tune (orchestra) music: Gil Askey
    I Cried for You (Ross) music: Abe Lyman, Gus Arnheim;
      lyrics: Arthur Freed
    Don't Explain (orchestra) music: Billie Holiday
    Mean to Me (Ross) music: Fred E Ahlert; lyrics: Roy Turk
    Fine and Mellow (Ross) music, lyrics: Billie Holiday
    What A Little Moonlight Will Do (Ross) music, lyrics:
      Harry Woods
    Love Theme (orchestra) music: Michel Legrand
    'Tain't Nobody's Bizness If I Do (reprise) (Ross)
    Our Love Is Here to Stay (Ross) music: George Gershwin;
---   lyrics: Ira Gershwin
    Fine and Mellow (reprise) (Ross)
    Lover Man (Oh, Where Can You Be?) (Ross) music, lyrics:
      Jimmy Davis, Ram Ramirez, Jimmy Sherman
    You've Changed (Ross) music: Carl Fisher; lyrics: Bill
      Carey
    Gimme A Pigfoot and A Bottle of Beer (Ross) music, lyrics:
      Wesley Wilson
    Good Morning Heartache (Ross) music, lyrics: Irene
      Higginbotham, Ervin Drake, Dan Fisher
---   All of Me (reprise) (Ross)
    Love Theme (orchestra) music: Michel Legrand
    My Man (Ross) music: Maurice Yvain; lyrics: Channing Pollock
    Don't Explain (Ross) music: Billie Holiday; lyrics:
      Arthur Herzog, Jr
    I Cried for You (reprise) (Ross)
    Strange Fruit (Ross) music, lyrics: Lewis Allan
    God Bless the Child (Ross) music, lyrics: Billie Holiday,
      Arthur Herzog, Jr
    Closing Theme (orchestra) music: Michel Legrand

Note: Side One and Side Two contain considerable dialog.

LAS VEGAS NIGHTS (Paramount, 1941)

Hollywood Soundstage 5011 (soundtrack) mono

Music: Burton Lane, others; lyrics: Frank Loesser, others;
musical direction: Victor Young

Cast: Lillian Cornell, Virginia Dale, The Tommy Dorsey Orchestra,
         Connie Haines, Hank Ladd, Constance Moore, The Pied Pipers,
         Phil Regan, Frank Sinatra, Bert Wheeler

Songs: Opening Music (orchestra)
       I've Gotta Ride (Regan, chorus)
       Mary, Mary Quite Contrary (Moore, Cornell, Dale, Wheeler)
       Song of India (Dorsey Orchestra) music: Rimsky-Korsakov
       I'll Never Smile Again (Sinatra, Pied Pipers, Dorsey
          Orchestra) music, lyrics: Ruth Lowe
       Ask the Lamp on the Corner (Cornell)
       That's Southern Hospitality (Dale, Wheeler) music, lyrics:
          Sam Coslow
       Old Miami Shore (Cornell, Pied Pipers, Dorsey Orchestra)
          music: Victor Jacobi; lyrics: William LeBaron
       Dolores (Wheeler, Ladd, trio, Dorsey Orchestra) music:
          Louis Alter
       Trombone Man Is the Best Man in the Band (Pied Pipers,
          Haines, Dorsey Orchestra)
       Finale - Old Miami Shore (Regan, Cornell, Moore, Wheeler,
          Dale, Dorsey Orchestra)
       End Credits: Dolores (orchestra)

Note: The above recording includes spoken dialog. Studio
         recordings by Tommy Dorsey Orchestra:

Victor (78rpm) 25523 Song of India
Victor (78rpm) 26628 I'll Never Smile Again (Sinatra)
Victor (78rpm) 27317 Dolores

THE LAST TIME I SAW PARIS (MGM, 1954)

MGM (45/EP) X 1124 mono

Music, lyrics: various; musical direction: Johnny Guarnieri

Cast: Odette

Songs: The Last Time I Saw Paris (Odette) music: Jerome Kern;
          lyrics: Oscar Hammerstein II
       Dream, Dream, Dream (Odette) music: Jimmy McHugh; lyrics:
---   Mitch Parrish
       Danse avec Moi (Odette) music, lyrics: Lopez, Rome, Hornez
       (All of A Sudden) My Heart Sings (Odette) music, lyrics:
          Herpin, Jamplan, Rome

LET'S BE HAPPY (Pathe British, 1957)

RCA (45/EP) EPA 4060 mono

Music: Nicholas Brodszky; lyrics: Paul Francis Webster

Cast: Tony Martin

Songs: The Man from Idaho (Martin)
       The Rose and the Heather (Martin)
       One Is A Lonely Number (Martin)
       Hold On to Love (Martin)

LET'S MAKE LOVE (Twentieth Century-Fox, 1960)

Columbia CS 8327 (soundtrack) stereo reissued: CSP ACS 8327

Music: Jimmy Van Heusen, others; lyrics: Sammy Cahn, others;
musical direction: Lionel Newman

Cast: Marilyn Monroe, Yves Montand, Frankie Vaughan

Songs: Let's Make Love (Monroe, Vaughan)
       Incurably Romantic (Monroe, Montand)
       Latin One (orchestra) music: Gerald Wiggins
       Specialization (Monroe, Vaughan)
       Let's Make Love (reprise) (Montand)
---   My Heart Belongs to Daddy (Monroe, men) music, lyrics:
          Cole Porter
       Hey You with the Crazy Eyes (Vaughan)
       Strip City (orchestra) music: Gerald Wiggins
       Incurably Romantic (reprise) (Monroe, Vaughan)

LIGHT OF DAY (Tri-Star, 1987)

CBS/Blackheart SZ 40654 (soundtrack) stereo CD

Music, lyrics: various

Cast: John Bon Jovi, Dave Edmunds, The Fabulous Thunderbirds,
        Michael J Fox, Ian Hunter, Joan Jett

Songs: Light of Day (Jett, Barbusters) music, lyrics: Bruce
          Springsteen
       This Means War (Jett, Barbusters) music, lyrics: Joan
          Jett, Bob Halligan, Kenny Laguna
       Twist It Off (The Fabulous Thunderbirds) music, lyrics:
          Jimmy L Vaughn, Ken Wilson, Fran Cristina, Preston
          Hubbard
       Cleveland Rocks (Hunter) music, lyrics: Ian Hunter
       Stay with Me Tonight (Edmunds) music: lyrics: Dave Edmunds,
          John David

    Its All Coming Down Tonight (Jett, Barbusters) music,
       lyrics: Frankie Miller, Andy Fraser
    Rude Mood (Jett, Barbusters) music, lyrics: Stevie Ray
       Vaughn
    Only Lonely (Bon Jovi) music, lyrics: John Bon Jovi,
       David Bryan
    Rabbit's Got the Gun (The Hunzz) music, lyrics: Joan
       Jett, Kenny Laguna
    You Got No Place to Go (Fox) music, lyrics: Alan Mark
       Paul, Michael J Fox
    Elergy (instrumental)

LI'L ABNER (Paramount, 1959)

Columbia OS 2021 (soundtrack) stereo

Music: Gene de Paul; lyrics: Johnny Mercer; musical direction:
Nelson Riddle, Joseph J Lilley

Cast: Carmen Alvarez, Billie Hayes, Bern Hoffman, Stubby Kaye,
      Joe E Marks, Peter Palmer, Leslie Parrish, Ted Thurston

Songs: Overture (orchestra)
      A Typical Day (Alvarez, Kaye, Hoffman, Parrish, Marks,
       Hayes, Palmer, chorus)
      If I Had My Druthers (Palmer, male chorus)
      Jubilation T Cornpone (Kaye, chorus)
      Don't That Take the Rag Offen the Bush (Thurston, chorus)
      Room Enuf for Us (chorus)
      Namely You (Palmer, Parrish)
---   The Country's in the Very Best of Hands (Kaye, Palmer,
       chorus)
      Unnecessary Town (Palmer, Parrish, chorus)
      I'm Past My Prime (Parrish, Kaye)
      Otherwise (Palmer, Parrish)
      Put 'em Back (female chorus)
      The Matrimonial Stomp (Kaye, chorus)

LILI (MGM, 1953)

MGM E 187 (soundtrack) mono reissued: MCA 1426

Music: Bronislau Kaper; lyrics: Helen Deutsch; musical
direction: Hans Sommer

Cast: Leslie Caron, Mel Ferrer

Songs: Adoration (orchestra)
      Hi-Lili, Hi-Lo (Carron, Ferrer)
      Lili and the Puppets (orchestra)

LISZTOMANIA (Warner Bros, 1975)

A & M Records SP 4829 (soundtrack) stereo

Music: Franz Liszt, others; lyrics: various; musical direction: Rick Wakeman

Cast: Roger Daltrey, Linda Lewis, Paul Nicholas, David Wilde
        (piano)

Songs: Riezi / Chopsticks Fantasia (Wilde) music: Franz Liszt,
            Richard Wagner
        Love's Dream (Daltrey) lyrics: Roger Daltrey
        Dante Period (orchestra)
        Orpheus Song (Daltrey) lyrics: Jonathan Benson, Roger
            Daltrey
---   Hell (Lewis)
        Hibernation (orchestra) music: Rick Wakeman
        Excelsior Song (Nicholas) lyrics: Ken Russell, Rick Wakeman
        Master Race (orchestra) music: Richard Wagner
        Rape, Pillage & Clap (orchestra) music: Richard Wagner
        Funerailles (Daltrey) lyrics: Jonathan Benson
        Free Song (Hungarian Rhapsody) (orchestra)
        Peace at Last (Daltrey) lyrics: Jonathan Benson, Roger
            Daltrey

LITTLE BOY LOST (Paramount, 1953)

Decca DL 4264 mono 'Bing's Hollywood - Anything Goes'

Music: James Van Heusen, others; lyrics: John Burke, others;
musical direction: John Scott Trotter

Cast: Bing Crosby

Songs: The Magic Window (Crosby)
        Cela M'est Egal - If It's All the Same to You (Crosby)
        A Propos de Rien (Crosby)
        Violets and Violins (Crosby) music: Miarka Laparcerie;
            lyrics: Jack Lawrence

LITTLE MISS BROADWAY (Twentieth Century-Fox, 1938)

Fox 3045 (soundtrack) mono 'More Little Miss Wonderful'

Music: Harold Spina; lyrics: Walter Bullock; musical direction:
Louis Silvers

Cast: George Murphy, Shirley Temple

Songs: We Should Be Together (Murphy, Temple)
      If All the World Were Paper (Temple)
      Swing Me An Old Fashioned Tune (Temple)
      Thank You for the Use of the Hall (Temple)
      Be Optimistic (Temple, girls)

Note: Additional soundtrack selection on Fox 103-2: 'The Complete Shirley Temple Songbook'

      How Can I Thank You? (Temple)

A LITTLE NIGHT MUSIC (New World, 1978)

Columbia JS 35333 (soundtrack) stereo

Music, lyrics: Stephen Sondheim; musical direction: Jonathan Tunick

Cast: Len Cariou, Lesley-Anne Down, Chloe Franks, Christopher Guard, Laurence Guittard, Diana Rigg, Elizabeth Taylor

Songs: Overture (company)
      Night Waltz (Love Takes Time) (company)
      The Glamorous Life (Franks)
      Now / Soon / Later (Cariou, Down, Guard)
      You Must Meet My Wife (Cariou, Taylor)
      Every Day A Little Death (Rigg)
---   Night Waltz (orchestra)
      A Weekend in the Country (company)
      Send in the Clowns (Taylor)
      It Would Have Been Wonderful (Cariou, Guittard)
      Finale: Send in the Clowns (Taylor, Cariou)
              Night Waltz (Taylor, Cariou)

Note: The above recording includes spoken dialog.

THE LITTLE PRINCE (Paramount, 1974)

ABC ABDP 854 (soundtrack) stereo

Music: Frederick Loewe; lyrics: Alan Jay Lerner; musical direction: Douglas Gamley

Cast: Joss Ackland, Bob Fosse, Richard Kiley, Donna McKechnie, Steven Warner, Gene Wilder

Songs: Overture (orchestra)
      It's A Hat (Kiley, chorus)
      I Need Air (Kiley)
      Be Happy (McKechnie)

```
        I'm On Your Side (Kiley)
        You're A Child (Ackland, Warner, men)
---     Little Prince (Kiley)
        I Never Met A Rose (Kiley)
        Why Is the Desert (Kiley, Warner)
        A Snake in the Grass (Fosse)
        Closer and Closer and Closer (Wilder, Warner)
        Finale: Little Prince (chorus)
```

LITTLE SHOP OF HORRORS (Warner Bros, 1986)

Geffin GHS 24125 (soundtrack) stereo   CD

Music: Alan Menken; lyrics: Howard Ashman; musical direction:
Robby Merkin

Cast: Tichina Arnold, Tisha Campbell, Ellen Greene, Steve
        Martin, Rick Moranis, Levi Stubbs (for plant), Michelle
        Weeks

Songs: Prologue (Little Shop of Horrors) (Weeks, Arnold,
           Campbell) narration: Bill Mitchell
        Skid Row (Downtown) (Weeks, Arnold, Campbell, Greene,
           Moranis, chorus)
        Da-Doo (Moranis, Weeks, Arnold, Campbell, chorus)
        Grow for Me (Moranis, Weeks, Arnold, Campbell)
        Somewhere That's Green (Greene)
        Some Fun Now (Weeks, Arnold, Campbell)
---   Dentist! (Martin, Weeks, Arnold, Campbell)
        Feed Me (Git It) (Stubbs, Moranis, Weeks, Arnold, Campbell)
        Suddenly, Seymour (Moranis, Greene, Weeks, Arnold,
           Campbell)
        Suppertime (Stubbs, Weeks, Arnold, Campbell)
        The Meek Shall Inherit (Moranis, Weeks, Arnold, Campbell)
        Mean Green Mother from Outer Space (Stubbs, chorus)
        Finale (Don't Feed the Plants)(chorus)

THE LIVELY SET (Universal, 1964)

Decca DL 79119 stereo

Music, lyrics: Bobby Darin, others; musical direction: Joseph
        Gershenson

Cast: James Darren, Wink Martindale, Joanie Sommers, Ron Wilson

Songs: The Lively Set (Darren)
        Turbine Montage (sound effects, orchestra)
        Look at Me (Martindale) lyrics: Randy Newman
        Bonneville Boss (Boss Barracuda) (orchestra)

        Coffee Perkin' Time (orchestra)
---   The Pomona Drags (The Lively Set) (sound effects, orchestra)
        If You Love Him (Sommers)
        Theme for Eddie (Look at Me) (orchestra)
        Boss Barracuda (reprise) (Wilson, group) lyrics: Terry
          Melcher
        Casey Wake Up (Sommers)
        The Tri-State Race (sound effects, narration)
        End Title (If You Love Him) (orchestra)

LIVING IT UP (Paramount, 1954)

Capitol (45/EP) EAP 1-533 (soundtrack) mono

Music: Jule Styne; lyrics: Bob Hilliard; musical direction:
Walter Scharf

Cast: Jerry Lewis, Dean Martin

Songs: Money Burns A Hole in My Pocket (Martin)
        Champagne and Wedding Cake (Lewis)
        How Do You Speak to An Angel? (Lewis)
---   That's What I Like (Martin)
        How Do You Speak to An Angel?(reprise) (Martin)
        Ev'ry Street's A Boulevard in Old New York (Martin, Lewis)

LOOKING FOR LOVE (MGM, 1964)

MGM SE 4229 stereo

Music: Hank Hunter, others; lyrics: Stan Vincent, others;
musical direction: Claus Ogerman, others

Cast: Connie Francis

Songs: Looking for Love (Francis, chorus)
        Whoever You Are I Love You (Francis) music: Gary Geld;
          lyrics: Richard Udele
        When the Clock Strikes Midnight (Francis)
        Rock Dem Bells (orchestra) music: Claus Ogerman
        This Is My Happiest Moment (Francis) music: Benny Davis;
          lyrics: Ted Murray
        Be My Love (Francis) music: Nicholas Brodszky; lyrics:
---   Sammy Cahn; musical direction: Joe Mazzu
        Looking for Love (reprise) (Francis)
        Let's Have A Party (Francis, chorus)
        I Can't Believe That You're in Love with Me (Francis)
          music: Jimmy McHugh; lyrics: Clarence Gaskill;
          musical direction: Joe Mazzu
        Connie Francis - Lady Valet Theme (orchestra) music:

Claus Ogerman
Whoever You Are I Love You (reprise) (orchestra)
Looking for Love (reprise) (Francis, chorus)

LOST HORIZON (Columbia, 1973)

Bell 1300 (soundtrack) stereo

Music: Burt Bacharach; lyrics: Hal David; musical direction:
Burt Bacharach

Cast: Peter Finch, Olivia Hussey, Sally Kellerman, (the voice
        of) Shawn Phillips, Liv Ullmann, Bobby Van

Songs: Lost Horizon (Phillips)
       Share the Joy (Hussey)
       The World Is A Circle (Ullmann, chorus)
       Living Together, Growing Together (chorus)
       I Might Frighten Her Away (Finch, Ullmann)
___   The Things I Will Not Miss (Kellerman, Hussey)
       If I Could Go Back (Finch)
       Where Knowledge Ends (Faith Begins) (Ullmann)
       Question Me An Answer (Van, chorus)
       I Come to You (Finch, Ullmann)
       Reflections (Kellerman)

LOVE ME OR LEAVE ME (MGM, 1955)

Columbia CL 710 mono reissued: CBS/Sony 32DP913 CD

Music, lyrics: various; musical direction: Percy Faith

Cast: Doris Day

Songs: It All Depends on You (Day) music: Ray Henderson; lyrics:
          Buddy DeSylva, Lew Brown
       You Made Me Love You (Day) music: James V Monaco; lyrics:
          Joseph McCarthy
       Stay On the Right Side, Sister (Day) music: Rube Bloom;
          lyrics: Ted Koehler
       Mean to Me (Day) music: Fred E Ahlert; lyrics: Roy Turk
       Everybody Loves My Baby (Day) music, lyrics: Jack Palmer,
          Spencer Williams
       Sam, the Old Accordian Man (Day, chorus) music, lyrics:
___   Walter Donaldson
       Shaking the Blues Away (Day, chorus) music, lyrics:
          Irving Berlin
       Ten Cents A Dance (Day) music: Richard Rodgers; lyrics:
          Lorenz Hart
       I'll Never Stop Loving You (Day) music: Nicholas Brodszky;

           lyrics: Sammy Cahn
      Never Look Back (Day) music, lyrics: Chilton Price
      At Sundown (Day) music, lyrics: Walter Donaldson
      Love Me or Leave Me (Day) music: Walter Donaldson;
           lyrics: Gus Kahn

LOVE ME TENDER (Twentieth Century-Fox, 1956)

RCA (45/EP) EPA 4006 mono

Music, lyrics: Elvis Presley, Vera Matson

Cast: Elvis Presley

Songs: Love Me Tender (Presley)
       Let Me (Presley)
       Poor Boy (Presley)
       We're Gonna Move (Presley)

LOVE ME TONIGHT (Paramount, 1932)

Ariel CMF 23 (soundtrack) mono

Music: Richard Rodgers; lyrics: Lorenz Hart; musical direction:
Nat W Finston

Cast: Tyler Brooke, Marion Byron, Joseph Cawthorn, Maurice
       Chevalier, George 'Gabby' Hayes, Jeanette MacDonald,
       Bert Roach, Rolf Sedan

Songs: That's the Song of Paree (Chevalier, Byron, Hayes)
       Isn't It Romantic? (Chevalier, Roach, Sedan, Brooke,
         chorus, MacDonald)
       Lover (MacDonald)
       Mimi (Chevalier)
       A Woman Needs Something (MacDonald, Cawthorn)
       The Poor Apache (Chevalier)
       Love Me Tonight (Chevalier, MacDonald)

Note: The above recording includes spoken dialog. Studio
       recordings by cast members:

Victor (78rpm) 24063 Mimi (Chevalier) LP: RCA VPM 6055
               The Poor Apache (Chevalier)
Victor (78rpm) 24067 Love Me Tonight (MacDonald)
               Isn't It Romantic? (MacDonald)

THE LOVE PARADE (Paramount, 1929)

Ariel CMF 23 (partical soundtrack) mono

Music: Victor Schertzinger; lyrics: Clifford Grey; musical
direction: Victor Schertzinger, others

Cast: Maurice Chevalier, Jeanette MacDonald

Songs: Paris, Stay the Same (Chevalier) Victor (78rpm) 22294
        (musical direction: Leonard Joy)
    Dream Lover (MacDonald) Victor (78rpm) 22247 (musical
        direction: Nathaniel Shilkret)
    My Love Parade (Chevalier) Victor (78rpm) 22285 (musical
        direction: Leonard Joy)
    Anything to Please the Queen (MacDonald, Chevalier)
    March of the Grenadiers (MacDonald, chorus)
    Nobody's Using It Now (Chevalier)
    Love Parade (reprise, finale) (Chevalier, MacDonald)

Note: Other studio recordings:

Victor (78rpm) 22247 March of the Grenadiers (MacDonald)
Victor (78rpm) 22285 Nobody's Using It Now (Chevalier)

LOVELY TO LOOK AT (MGM, 1952)

MGM E 150 (soundtrack) mono reissued: MCA 39084 CD

Music: Jerome Kern; lyrics: Otto Harbach, others; musical
direction: Carmen Dragon

Cast: Gower Champion, Marge Champion, Kathryn Grayson, Howard
    Keel, Ann Miller, Red Skelton

Songs: Lafayette (Skelton, Keel, Gower Champion) lyrics: Dorothy
        Fields
    Smoke Gets in Your Eyes (Grayson)
    I Won't Dance (Marge and Gower Champion) lyrics: Oscar
        Hammerstein II, Otto Harbach, Dorothy Fields, Jimmy
        McHugh
    You're Devestating (Grayson, Keel) lyrics: Otto Harbach,
___   Dorothy Fields
    Yesterdays (Grayson)
    Lovely to Look At (Keel, chorus) lyrics: Otto Harbach,
        Dorothy Fields
    The Most Exciting Night (Keel) lyrics: Otto Harbach,
        Dorothy Fields
    I'll Be Hard to Handle (Miller, chorus) lyrics: Bernard
        Dougall, Dorothy Fields
    The Touch of Your Hand (Grayson, Keel, chorus)
    Lovely to Look At (reprise) (chorus)

Note: See also the 1935 film, 'Roberta'

LOVING YOU (Paramount, 1957)

RCA LPM 1515 mono reissued: AFL 1-1515 CD

Music, lyrics: Jerry Leiber, Mike Stoller, others

Cast: Elvis Presley

Songs: Mean Woman Blues (Presley) music, lyrics: Claude DeMetrius
       (Let Me Be Your) Teddy Bear (Presley) music, lyrics:
         Kal Mann, Bernie Lowe
       Loving You (Presley)
       Got A Lot O' Livin' to Do! (Presley) music, lyrics:
         Aaron Schroeder, Ben Weisman
       Lonesome Cowboy (Presley) music, lyrics: Sid Tepper,
         Roy C Bennett
       Hot Dog (Presley)
       Party (Prsley) music, lyrics: Don Robertson

LUCKY LADY (Twentieth Century-Fox, 1976)

Arista AL 4069 (soundtrack) stereo

Music for new songs: John Kander; lyrics for new songs: Fred Ebb;
background music, musical direction: Ralph Burns

Cast: Vangle Charmichael, Liza Minnelli, Burt Reynolds, (the
       voice of) Bessie Smith

Songs: Too Much Mustard (orchestra) music: Cecil Maskin
       While the Getting Is Good (Minnelli)
       Christy McTeague (orchestra)
       Young Woman Blues (Smith) music, lyrics: Bessie Smith
       The Guymas Connection (orchestra)
       Dizzy Fingers (orchestra) music: Zez Confrey
---   Lucky Lady Montage (Minnelli)
       If I Had A Talking Picture of You (Charmichael) music:
         Ray Henderson; lyrics: Buddy DeSylva, Lew Brown
       All I Do Is Dream of You (Charmichael) music: Nacio Herb
         Brown; lyrics: Arthur Freed
       Ain't Misbehavin' (Reynolds) music: Fats Waller; lyrics:
         Andy Razaf
       Hot Time in the Old Town Tonight (Smith) music: Joe
         Hayden; lyrics: Theo A Metz
       Portobello Waltzes (orchestra)
       Saints Go Marching In (orchestra) arranged: Ralph Burns
       Lucky Lady (Minnelli)

Note: Bessie Smith vocals taken from:

Columbia (78rpm) 14179-D Young Woman Blues
Columbia (78rpm) 14219-D Hot Time in the Old Town Tonight

LULLABY OF BROADWAY (Warner Bros, 1951)

Columbia CL 6168 mono reissued: Columbia CSP P 18421

Music, lyrics, musical direction: various

Cast: Doris Day

Songs: Lullaby of Broadway (Day, chorus) music: Harry Warren;
          lyrics: Al Dubin; musical direction: Buddy Cole
       Fine and Dandy (Day, chorus) music: Kay Swift; lyrics:
          Paul James; musical direction: Buddy Cole
       In A Shanty in Old Shanty Town (Day, chorus) music: Jack
          Little, John Siras; lyrics: Joe Young; musical
          direction: Buddy Cole
       Somebody Loves Me (Day) music: George Gershwin; lyrics:
          Ballard MacDonald, Buddy DeSylva; musical direction:
---   Frank Comstock
       Just One of Those Things (Day) music, lyrics: Cole Porter;
          musical direction: Frank Comstock
       You're Getting to Be A Habit with Me (Day) music: Harry
          Warren; lyrics: Al Dubin; musical direction: Frank
          Comstock
       I Love the Way You Say Goodnight (Day, chorus) music:
          Eddie Pola; lyrics: George Wyle; musical direction:
          Buddy Cole
       Please Don't Talk About Me When I'm Gone (Day) music:
          Sammy Stept; lyrics: Sidney Clare; musical direction:
          Frank Comstock

LULU BELLE (Columbia, 1948)

Coast (78rpm) C 10 mono

Music, lyrics: various; musical direction: Henry Russell

Cast: Dorothy Lamour

Coast (78rpm) 8053 Lulu Belle (Lamour) music: Henry Russell;
                     lyrics: Edgar DeLange
                   Ace in the Hole (Lamour) music: Jack Dempsey;
                     lyrics: George Mitchell
Coast (78rpm) 8054 Sweetie Pie (Lamour) music: Henry Russell;
                     lyrics: John Lehman
                   I Can't Tell Why I Love You (Lamour) music:

Gus Edwards; lyrics: Will D Cobb

THE MAGIC OF LASSIE (International Picture Show, 1978)

Peter Pan 155 (soundtrack) stereo

Music, lyrics: Richard M Sherman, Robert B Sherman; musical
direction: Irwin Kostal

Cast: (the voice of) Debby Boone, (the voice of) Pat Boone,
        Alice Faye, Mickey Rooney, James Stewart

Songs: When You're Loved (D Boone)
       Nobody's Property (chorus)
       Travelin' Music (Rooney)
       There'll Be Other Friday Nights (D Boone)
       A Rose Is Not A Rose (P Boone)
---   Banjo Song (chorus)
       Nobody's Property (reprise) (orchestra)
       A Rose Is Not A Rose (reprise) (Faye)
       That Hometown Feeling (Stewart)
       Brass Rings and Daydreams (D Boone, chorus)
       Thanksgiving Prayer (Stewart) spoken
       I Can't Say Goodbye (chorus)
       When You're Loved (reprise) (D Boone)

MAKE MINE MUSIC (Disney, 1946)

Columbia (78rpm) MM 640 mono 'The Whale Who Wanted to Sing
at the Met'

Original music: Ken Darby; musical direction: Robert Armbruster

Cast: Nelson Eddy

Columbia (78rpm) 4345   This album consists of a narration and
Columbia (78rpm) 4346   vocal selections from Rossini, Donizetti,
Columbia (78rpm) 4347   Wagner, Boito, and Flowtow, as well as
                        'Shortnin' Bread'

Note: Additional studio recordings by cast members:

Columbia (78rpm) 36967 All the Cats Join In (Benny Goodman)
Columbia (78rpm) 36781 After You've Gone (Benny Goodman Sextet)
Capitol (78rpm)   234 Without You (Andy Russell)
Capitol (78rpm)   249 Casey (Jerry Colonna)
Decca   (78rpm) 23474 Johnny Fedora (The Andrews Sisters)

MAME (Warner Bros, 1974)

Warner Bros 2773 (soundtrack) stereo

Music, lyrics: Jerry Herman; musical direction: Fred Werner

Cast: Beatrice Arthur, Lucille Ball, Jane Connell, Bruce
        Davison, Kirby Furlong, Robert Preston

Songs: Main Title (orchestra)
       St Bridget (Connell)
       Main Title (continues) (orchestra)
       It's Today (Ball, chorus)
       Open A New Window (Ball, Furlong, chorus)
       The Man in the Moon (Arthur, chorus)
       My Best Girl (Ball, Furlong)
       We Need A Little Christmas (Ball, cast)
---   Mame (Preston, chorus)
       Loving You (Preston)
       The Letter (Furlong, Davison)
       Bosom Buddies (Ball, Arthur)
       Gooch's Song (Connell)
       If He Walked into My Life (Ball)
       Finale: Open A New Window (Ball)
               Mame (chorus)
               It's Today (orchestra)

MAMMY (Warner Bros, 1930)

A-Jay 3749 (soundtrack) mono 'Al Jolson - The Vitaphone Years'

Music, lyrics: Irving Berlin, others

Cast: Al Jolson

Songs: Who Paid the Rent for Mrs. Rip Van Winkle? (Jolson)
          music: Fred Fisher; lyrics: Alfred Bryan
       Let Me Sing and I'm Happy (Jolson)
       Why Do They All Take the Night Boat to Albany? (Jolson)
          Music: Jean Schwartz; lyrics: Sam M Lewis, Joe Young

Note: Jolson studio recordings:

Brunswick (78rpm) 4721 Let Me Sing and I'm Happy
                       Looking at You Across the Breakfast
                           Table (LP: Decca DEA 7-1)
Brunswick (78rpm) 4722 To My Mammy

A MAN CALLED ADAM (Embassy, 1966)

Reprise 6180 (soundtrack) stereo

Music, lyrics for songs: various; musical score, direction:
Benny Carter

Cast: Louis Armstrong, Sammy Davis, Jr, Mel Torme

Songs: Main Title: All That Jazz (orchestra)
       I Want to Be Wanted (David)
       Go Now (orchestra)
       Someday Sweetheart (Armstrong)
       Ain't I (orchestra)
       Soft Touch (orchestra)
       Claudia (orchestra)
---   All That Jazz (Torme)
       Back of Town Blues (Armstrong)
       Night Walk (orchestra)
       Whisper to Me (Davis)
       Claudia (orchestra)
       Crack Up (Playboy Theme) (orchestra)
       All That Jazz (reprise) (Torme)

MAN OF LA MANCHA (United Artists, 1972)

UA UAS 9906 (soundtrack) stereo

Music: Mitch Leigh; lyrics: Joe Darion; musical direction:
Laurence Rosenthal

Cast: Harry Andrews, James Coco, Gino Conforti, Rosalie
        Crutchley, Simon Gilbert (for Peter O'Toole), Julia
        Gregg, Sophia Loren, Peter O'Toole, Ian Richardson

Songs: Overture (orchestra)
       Man of La Mancha (I, Don Quixote) (Gilbert, Coco)
       It's All the Same (Loren, men)
       Dulcinea (Gilbert, men)
       I'm Only Thinking of Him (Gregg, Crutchley, Richardson)
       I Really Like Him (Coco)
       Barber's Song (Conforti)
---   Golden Helmet of Mambrino (Gilbert, Coco, Conforti)
       Little Bird, Little Bird (men)
       The Impossible Dream (The Quest) (Gilbert)
       The Dubbing (Gilbert, Andrews, Loren, Coco)
       Life As It Really Is (Soliloquy) (O'Toole) spoken
       Man of La Mancha (I, Don Quixote) (reprise) (Gilbert)
       Aldonza (Loren, Gilbert)
       A Little Gossip (Coco)
       Dulcinea (reprise) (Loren)
       The Impossible Dream (reprise) (Loren, O'Toole)
       Man of La Mancha (I, Don Quixote) (reprise) (Gilbert,

Coco)
The Psalm (Richardson)
Finale: The Impossible Dream (Loren, Richardson, Gregg,
    chorus)

MARDI GRAS (Twentieth Century-Fox, 1958)

Dot (45/EP) DEP 1075 mono

Music: Sammy Fain; lyrics: Paul Francis Webster; musical
direction: Billy Vaughn

Cast: Steve Allen (not in film), Pat Boone

Songs: Bourbon Street Blues (Boone)
___   Loyalty (Boone, Allen)
       Bigger Than Texas (Boone)
       A Fiddle, A Rifle, An Axe, and A Bible (Boone)

MARILYN (Twentieth Century-Fox, 1963)

Fox FXG 5000 (soundtrack) mono

Music, lyrics, musical direction: various

Cast: (narration by) Rock Hudson, Marilyn Monroe, Eileen
       Wilson (not in film)

Note: This album consists of soundtrack excerpts from the
       following three films (check under individual titles
       for contents):

       Gentlemen Prefer Blondes (Twentieth Century-Fox, 1953)
       River of No Return (Twentieth Century-Fox, 1954)
       There's No Business Like Show Business (Twentieth
          Century-Fox, 1955)

MARY POPPINS (Disney, 1964)

Buena Vista 4026 (soundtrack) stereo

Music, lyrics: Richard M Sherman, Robert B Sherman; musical
direction: Irwin Kostal

Cast: Julie Andrews, Karen Dotrice, Matthew Garber, Glynis
       Johns, David Tomlinson, Dick Van Dyke, Ed Wynn

Songs: Overture (orchestra)

        The Perfect Nanny (Dotrice, Garber)
        Sister Suffragette (Johns, women)
        The Life I Lead (Tomlinson)
        A Spoonful of Sugar (Andrews)
        Pavement Artist (Chim Chim Cheree) (Van Dyke)
        Jolly Holiday (Van Dyke, Andrews)
        Super-cali-fragil-istic-expi-ali-docious (Andrews, Van
            Dyke, chorus)
---   Stay Awake (Andrews)
        I Love to Laugh (Wynn, Andrews, Van Dyke)
        A British Bank (The Life I Lead) (Tomlinson, Andrews)
        Feed the Birds (Tuppence A Bag) (Andrews, chorus)
        Fidelity Fiduciary Bank (Van Dyke, Tomlinson, men)
        Chim Chim Cheree (Van Dyke, Andrews, Dotrice, Garber)
        Step in Time (Van Dyke, chorus)
        A Man Has Dreams (The Life I Lead; A Spoonful of Sugar)
            (Tomlinson, Van Dyke)
        Let's Go Fly A Kite (Tomlinson, Van Dyke, chorus)

MEET ME IN LAS VEGAS (MGM, 1956)

MGM (45/EP) X 1264 mono

Music: Nicholas Brodszky, others; lyrics: Sammy Cahn, others;
musical direction: LeRoy Holmes

Cast: Dan Dailey

Songs: My Lucky Charm (Dailey)
       The Gal in the Yaller Shoes (Dailey)
       Frankie and Johnny (Dailey) arr: Johnny Green

Note: Other cast recordings:

       It's Fun to Be in Love (Dailey, George Chakiris, Betty
           Lynn) cut from film LP: Choice Cuts ST 500/1
       I Refuse to Rock and Roll (Cara Williams) LP: Legends
           1000/2 'Ladies of Burlesque'
       If You Can Dream (The Four Aces) LP: Decca DL 8312
           'She Loves the Movies'

MEET ME IN ST LOUIS (MGM, 1944)

Decca DL 8498 mono reissued: AEI 3101

Music, lyrics: Hugh Martin, Ralph Blane, others; musical
direction: Georgie Stoll

Cast: Judy Garland

Songs: Meet Me in St Louis, Louis (Garland, chorus) music:
      Kerry Mills; lyrics: Andrew B Sterling
      Skip to My Lou (Garland, chorus) trad
      The Trolley Song (Garland, chorus)
      Boys and Girls Like You (Garland) music: Richard Rodgers;
       lyrics: Oscar Hammerstein II (not from film)
      Have Yourself A Merry Little Christmas (Garland)
      The Boy Next Door (Garland)

MEET ME IN ST LOUIS (MGM, 1944)

Hollywood Soundstage HS 5007 (soundtrack) mono

Cast: Lucille Bremer, Joan Carroll, Henry H Daniels, Jr, Harry
      Davenport, Tom Drake, Arthur Freed (for Leon Ames),
      Judy Garland, D Markas (for Mary Astor), Margaret O'Brien

Songs: Opening Music (orchestra)
      Meet Me in St Louis,   Louis (Davenport, Carroll, chorus)
      The Boy Next Door (Garland)
      Meet Me in St Louis,   Louis (reprise) (Garland, Bremer)
      Skip to My Lou (Garland, Bremer, Daniels, Drake, chorus)
      Under the Bamboo Tree (Garland, O'Brien) music, lyrics:
       J Rosamond Johnson, Bob Cole
---   Over the Bannister (Garland) trad
      The Trolley Song (Garland, chorus)
      You and I (Markas, Freed) music: Nacio Herb Brown; lyrics:
       Arthur Freed
      Have Yourself A Merry Little Christmas (Garland)
      Finale

Note: Additional soundtrack recordings:

      The Trolley Song (Garland, chorus) LP: MGM E 4005P
      The Boy Next Door (Garland) LP: MGM E 4005P
      (The Judy Garland Story, vol 2: The Hollywood Years)
      Under the Bamboo Tree (Garland, O'Brien) LP: MCA
      2-11002 (That's Entertainment)

MELBA (United Artists, 1953)

RCA LM 7012 (soundtrack) mono reissued: Ariel TWS 20

Music, lyrics: various; musical direction: Muir Mathieson

Cast: Patrice Munsel, others

Songs: Romeo and Juliet: Waltz Song (Munsel) music: Gounod
      Tosca: Vissi d'arte (Munsel) music: Puccini
      Marriage of Figaro: Voi che sapete (Munsel) music:
      Mozart

       Barber of Seville: Una voce poco fa (Munsel) music: Rossini
       Daughter of the Regiment: Chancun le sait (Munsel)
         music: Donizetti
       La Traviata: Brindisi (Munsel) music: Verdi
       Lucia di Lammermoor: Mad Scene (Munsel) music: Donizetti
       Ave Maria (Munsel) music: Bach-Gounod
       Home Sweet Home (Munsel) words: John Howard Payne
       On Wings of Song (Munsel) music: Mendelssohn

Note: The above recording includes other unidentified soloists
       and chorus. Additional recordings by Munsel:

RCA (45rpm) 47-5360 music: Mischa Spoliansky; lyrics: N Newell
       The Melba Waltz (musical direction: Henri Rene)
       Is This the Beginning of Love?

MERRY ANDREW (MGM, 1958)

Capitol T 1016 (soundtrack)

Music: Saul Chaplin; lyrics: Johnny Mercer; musical direction:
       Nelson Riddle

Cast: Pier Angeli, Baccaloni, Robert Coote, Rex Evans, Danny
       Kaye, Betty Wand (for Pier Angeli)

Songs: The Pipes of Pan (Kaye, boys)
       Chin Up, Stout Fellow (Kaye, Coote, Evans)
       Everything Is Ticketty-Boo (Kaye, chorus)
       You Can't Always Have What You Want (Kaye, Angeli/Wand,
         boys)
       The Square of the Hypotenuse (Kaye, boys)
       Salud (Kaye, Baccaloni, chorus)

THE MERRY WIDOW (MGM, 1934)

Hollywood Soundstage 5015 (soundtrack) mono

Music: Franz Lehar; lyrics: Lorenz Hart, others; musical
direction: Herbert Stothart

Cast: Maurice Chevalier, Jeanette MacDonald

Songs: Overture (orchestra)
       Girls, Girls, Girls! (men, Chevalier)
       Garden Scene (humming chorus, Bella Loblov, violin)
       Vilia (MacDonald, unidentified tenor, chorus)
       Tonight Will Teach Me How to Forget (MacDonald) lyrics:
         Gus Kahn
       Melody of Laughter (MacDonald, chorus)

Maxim's (Chevalier)
Melody of Laughter (reprise) (MacDonald, chorus)
Maxim's (reprise) (Chevalier, MacDonald, chorus)
Can-Can (orchestra)
Girls, Girls, Girls! (reprise) (Chevalier)
(I Love You So) The Merry Widow Waltz (MacDonald)
Maxim's (reprise) (MacDonald)
If Widows Are Rich (MacDonald, chorus)
Russian Dance (orchestra)
The Merry Widow Waltz (reprise) (chorus)
Melody of Laughter (reprise) (MacDonald, men)
Finale (The Merry Widow Waltz) (orchestra)

Note: The above recording includes spoken dialog. Jeanette
        MacDonald studio recordings:

Victor (78rpm) 24754 (I Love You So) The Merry Widow Waltz
                     Vilia

THE MERRY WIDOW (MGM, 1952)

MGM E 157 (soundtrack) mono

Music: Franz Lehar; lyrics: Paul Francis Webster; musical
direction: Jay Blackton

Cast: Trudy Erwin (for Lana Turner), Richard Haydn, Fernando
        Lamas

Songs: Maxim's (Lamas, Haydn)
       Vilia (Lamas, chorus)
       Girls, Girls, Girls! (Lamas, chorus)
       The Merry Widow Waltz (Lamas, Erwin)
 ---   Night (Lamas)
       Gypsy Music (orchestra)
       Can-Can (orchestra, girls)
       The Merry Widow Waltz (reprise) (chorus)

MISS SADIE THOMPSON (Columbia, 1954)

Mercury MG 25181 (soundtrack) mono

Music, lyrics: Lester Lee, Ned Washington, others; musical
direction: Morris Stoloff

Cast: Jose Ferrer, Jo Ann Greer (for Rita Hayworth)

Songs: Sadie Thompson's Song (orchestra) Leo Diamond, harmonica
       A Marine, A Marine, A Marine (men) lyrics: Allan Roberts

Sadie Thompson's Song (The Blue Pacific Blues) (Greer)
Native Dance (chorus)
___ The Heat Is On (Greer)
Hear No Evil, See No Evil (Greer)
Dialog (Hayworth, Ferrer) spoken
The 23rd Psalm (Ferrer) spoken
Sadie Thompson's Song (reprise) (orchestra)

MISSISSIPPI (Paramount, 1935)

Decca DL 4250 mono 'Bing's Hollywood - Easy to Remember'

Music: Richard Rodgers; lyrics: Lorenz Hart, others; musical
direction: Georgie Stoll

Cast: Bing Crosby

Songs: It's Easy to Remember (Crosby, chorus)
        Soon (Crosby)
        Swanee River (Old Folks at Home) (Crosby, choir) music,
           lyrics: Stephen Collins Foster
        Down by the River (Crosby)

MR. IMPERIUM (MGM, 1951)

RCA LM 61 mono

Music: Harold Arlen, others; lyrics: Dorothy Fields, others;
musical direction: Johnny Green, others

Cast: The Guadalajara Trio, Fran Warren (not in film),
        Ezio Pinza

Songs: Andiamo (Pinza, Warren)
       My Love and My Mule (Pinza, Warren)
       Let Me Look at You (Pinza)
       You Belong to My Heart (Pinza, The Guadalajara Trio)
          music: Augustin Lara; English lyrics: Ray Gilbert

MR. MUSIC (Paramount, 1950)

Decca DL 4262 mono 'Bing's Hollywood - Cool of the Evening'

Music: James Van Heusen; lyrics: John Burke; musical direction:
Victor Young, others

Cast: The Andrews Sisters (not in film), Bing Crosby, Dorothy
        Kirsten

Songs: Accidents Will Happen (Crosby)
       Life Is So Peculiar (Crosby, The Andrews Sisters) musical
          direction: Vic Schoen
       And You'll Be Home (Crosby, chorus)
       Milady (Crosby, Kirsten) musical direction: Jay Blackton
       Wouldn't It Be Funny (Crosby)
\-\-\-   Once More the Blue and White (Crosby, chorus)
       Accidents Will Happen (Crosby, Kirsten) musical direction:
          Jay Blackton
       High on the List (Crosby, The Andrews Sisters) musical
          direction: Vic Schoen

MOTHER WORE TIGHTS (Twentieth Century-Fox, 1947)

Classic International Filmusicals CIF 3008 (soundtrack) mono

Music: Josef Myrow, others; lyrics: Mack Gordon, others; musical
direction: Alfred Newman

Cast: Chick Chandler, Dan Dailey, Mona Freeman, Betty Grable,
      Lee Patrick

Songs: Overture (chorus) narration: Anne Baxter
       Burlington Bertie from Bow (Dailey) music, lyrics: William
          Hargreaves
       You Do (Dailey, chorus)
       Burlington Berie from Bow (reprise) (Grable)
       This Is My Favorite City (Grable, Dailey)
       You Do (reprise) (Grable, chorus)
       Kokomo, Indiana (Grable, Dailey)
       Tra-La-La (Grable, Dailey, Freeman) music: Harry Warren
       Swinging Down the Lane (Freeman, chorus) music: Isham
          Jones; lyrics: Gus Kahn
       Stumbling (Freeman, Patrick, Chandler) music, lyrics:
          Zez Confrey
       There's Nothing Like A Song (Grable, Dailey)
       Kokomo, Indiana (reprise) (Grable, Dailey)
       Rolling Down to Bowling Green (Grable, Dailey)
       Fare-Thee-Well Dear Alma Mater (chorus)
\-\-\-   You Do (reprise) (Freeman, chorus)
       Finale (orchestra)

Note: The above recording includes spoken dialog.

MOULIN ROUGE (Twentieth Century, 1934)

Golden Legends 2000/1 (soundtrack) mono 'Films of Russ Columbo'

Music: Harry Warren; lyrics: Al Dubin; musical direction:

Alfred Newman

Cast: Constance Bennett, Tullio Carminati, The Boswell Sisters,
        Russ Columbo

Songs: Main Title (orchestra)
        Coffee in the Morning and Kisses in the Night (Bennett,
            Columbo, The Boswell Sisters)
        Song of Surrender (Carminati, The Boswell Sisters)
        Boulevard of Broken Dreams (Bennett, chorus)
        End Titles (orchestra)

Note: The above recording includes spoken dialog. Studio
        recordings by the Boswell Sisters:

Brunswick (78rpm) 6733 Song of Surrender
                       Coffee in the Morning, Kisses in the Night

THE MUPPET MOVIE (Associated Film, 1979)

Atlantic SD 16001 (soundtrack) stereo

Music, lyrics: Paul Williams, Kenny Ascher; musical direction:
Ian Freebairn-Smith

Cast: (the voices of) Dave Goelz, Jim Henson, Richard Hunt,
        Kathryn Mullen, Jerry Nelson, Frank Oz, Steve Whitmire

Songs: Rainbow Connection (Henson)
        Movin' Right Along (Henson, Oz)
        Never Before, Never Again (Oz)
        Never Before, Never Again (reprise) (orchestra)
___   I Hope That Something Better Comes Along (Henson)
        Can You Picture That (Henson, Goelz, Nelson, Hunt, Oz)
        I Hope That Something Better Comes Along (reprise)
           (orchestra)
        I'm Going Back There Someday (Goelz)
        America (Oz, Henson) trad
        Finale: The Magic Store (Henson, Oz, Hunt, Goelz,
           Nelson, Mullen, Whitmire)

Note: The above recording includes spoken dialog.

THE MUPPETS TAKE MANHATTAN (Tri-Star, 1984)

Warner Bros 1-25114 (soundtrack) stereo

Music, lyrics: Jeff Moss; musical score, direction: Ralph Burns

Cast: Dave Goelz, Jim Henson, Richard Hunt, Jerry Nelson, Karen
        Prell, Frank Oz, Steve Whitmire

Songs: Together Again (Henson, Oz, chorus)
        You Can't Take No for An Answer (Henson, chorus)
        Saying Goodbye (Henson, Oz, Goelz, Hunt, Nelson)
        Rat Scat (Something Cookin') (Whitmire)
        Together Again (Carriage Ride) (reprise) (Henson, Oz, Hunt)
        I'm Gonna Always Love You (Henson, Oz, Goelz, Hunt)
        William Tell Overture (Goelz, Nelson, chorus) music:
            Rossini
        Looking for Kermit (orchestra)
        Right Where I Belong (Henson, Oz, Goelz, Hunt, chorus)
        Somebody's Getting Married (Henson, Oz, Goelz, Hunt,
            Nelson, Prell, chorus)
        Waiting for the Wedding (Henson, Oz, Nelson, chorus)
        He'll Make Me Happy (Henson, Oz, chorus)
        The Ceremony (Henson, Oz)
        Closing Medley (Final Credits):
            Together Again (reprise) (orchestra)
            Saying Goodbye (reprise) (cast)

Note: The above recording includes spoken dialog.

MUSCLE BEACH PARTY (American International, 1964)

United Artists UAL 3371

Music, lyrics: Gary Usher, Roger Christian, B Wilson, others

Cast: Frankie Avalon

Songs: Muscle Beach Party (Avalon)
        Surfer's Holiday (Avalon)
        A Boy Needs A Girl (Avalon) music, lyrics: Guy Hemric, Jerry
        Beach Party (Avalon)   Styner
        Don't Stop Now (Avalon)
        Runnin' Wild (Avalon)

MUSCLE BEACH PARTY (American International, 1964)

Vista STER 3314 stereo

Cast: Annette Funicello

Songs: Muscle Beach Party (Funicello)
        A Girl Needs A Boy (Funicello)
        A Surfer's Holiday (Funicello)
        Muscle Bustle (Funicello)

THE MUSIC MAN (Warner Bros, 1962)

Warner Bros BS 1459 (soundtrack) stereo CD

Music, lyrics: Meredith Willson; musical direction: Ray Heindorf

Cast: The Buffalo Bills, Hermione Gingold, Buddy Hackett, Ronnie
        Howard, Shirley Jones, Pert Kelton, Robert Preston

Songs: Main Title (orchestra)
        Rock Island (men)
        Iowa Stubborn (chorus)
        Ya Got Trouble (Preston, chorus)
        Piano Lesson (If You Don't Mind My Saying So) (Jones, Kelton)
        Goodnight My Someone (Jones)
        Ya Got Trouble (reprise) (Preston)
        Seventy Six Trombones (Preston, chorus)
        Sincere (The Buffalo Bills)
        The Sadder but Wiser Girl (Preston)
        Pick-A-Little, Talk-A-Little (Gingold, women)
___   Good night Ladies (men)
        Marion the Librarian (Preston)
        Being in Love (Jones)
        Gary, Indiana (Preston, Kelton)
        The Wells Fargo Wagon (chorus)
        Lida Rose (The Buffalo Bills)
        Will I Ever Tell You? (Jones) sung contrapuntally with
           'Lida Rose'
        Gary, Indiana (reprise) (Howard, Kelton, Jones)
        Shipoopi (Hackett, chorus)
        Till There Was You (Jones)
        Seventy Six Trombones (reprise) (Preston, Jones)
        Goodnight My Someone (reprise) (Jones, Preston) sung
           contrapuntally with 'Seventy Six Trombones'
        Seventy Six Trombones (reprise) (chorus)

Note: The above recording includes spoken dialog.

MY FAIR LADY (Warner Bros, 1964)

Columbia KOS 2600 (soundtrack) stereo

Music: Frederick Loewe; lyrics: Alan Jay Lerner; musical
direction: Andre Previn

Cast: John Alderson, Rex Harrison, Stanley Holloway, Wilfrid
        Hyde-White, John McLiam, Marni Nixon (for Audrey Hepburn),
        Bill Shirley (for Jeremy Brett), Mona Washbourne

Songs: Overture (orchestra)

Why Can't the English? (Harrison, Nixon, Hyde-White)
Wouldn't It Be Loverly (Nixon, chorus)
I'm Just An Ordinary Man (Harrison)
With A Little Bit of Luck (Holloway, Alderson, McLiam,
    chorus)
Just You Wait (Nixon)
The Rain in Spain (Harrison, Nixon, Hyde-White)
I Could Have Danced All Night (Nixon, Washbourne, girls)
Ascot Gavotte (chorus)
On the Street Where You Live (Shirley)
You Did It (Harrison, Hyde-White, Washbourne)
Show Me (Nixon, Shirley)
Get Me to the Church on Time (Holloway, chorus)
A Hymn to Him (Harrison, Hyde-White)
Without You (Nixon, Harrison)
I've Grown Accustomed to Her Face (Harrison)

MY GAL SAL (Twentieth Century-Fox, 1942)

Curtain Calls CC 100/22 (soundtrack) mono 'Rita Hayworth'

Music: Ralph Rainger, others; lyrics: Leo Robin, others;
musical direction: Alfred Newman

Cast: Victor Mature, Nan Wynn (for Rita Hayworth)

Songs: On the Gay White Way (Wynn, chorus)
      Come Tell Me What's Your Answer - Yes or No (Wynn, men)
      Oh, the Pity of It All (Wynn, Mature)
      Here You Are (Wynn, Mature)
      My Gal Sal (Wynn, chorus) music, lyrics: Paul Dresser

MY WILD IRISH ROSE (Warner Bros, 1947)

Columbia ML 4272 mono

Music, lyrics: various; musical direction: Charles Hirt

Cast: Dennis Morgan

Songs: My Wild Irish Rose (Morgan, chorus) music, lyrics:
      Chauncey Olcott
      Hush-A-Bye (Wee Rose of Killarney) (Morgan, chorus)
      music: M K Jerome; lyrics: Ted Koehler
      Shine On Harvest Moon (Morgan) music, lyrics: Nora Bayes,
      Jack Norworth
      By the Light of the Silv'ry Moon (Morgan) music: Gus
      Edwards; lyrics: Edward Madden
      The Whiffenpoof Song (Baa! Baa! Baa!) (Morgan, chorus)

music, lyrics: Meade Minnigerode, George S Pomeroy
Alma Mater Medley (Morgan, chorus) Winter Song/Far Above
   Cayuga's Waters/Alma Mater/Varsity
One Sunday Afternoon (Morgan, chorus) music, lyrics:
   Ralph Blane (from 1948 film of that title)
Wait 'Till the Sun Shines, Nellie (Morgan, chorus)
   music: Harry Von Tilzer; lyrics: Andrew B Sterling
One Little, Sweet Little Girl (Morgan) music, lyrics:
   Dan Sullivan

NACHTS IM GRUNEN KAKADU (Real, 1958)

Austroton (German 45/EP) EPA 1158 (soundtrack) mono

Music, lyrics: Michael Jary, others

Cast: Marika Rökk

Songs: Nachts im Grunen Kakadu (chorus)
       Ich hab' so ein Gefuhl (Rökk, chorus)
___   Es traumen zwei Herzen von Liebe (Rökk)
       Manina (Rökk, chorus)
       Eine Schwache Stunde (Rökk)
       Gitarren-Boogie (Troubadour) (Rökk)
       Finale - Nachts im Grunen Kakadu (Rökk, chorus)

NANCY GOES TO RIO (MGM, 1950)

MGM E 508 (soundtrack) mono reissued: MCA 39079 CD

Music, lyrics: various; musical direction: Georgie Stoll

Cast: Bando Da Lua, Carmen Miranda, Jane Powell, Danny Scholl,
       Ann Sothern

Songs: Love Is Like This (Powell, chorus) music, lyrics: Ray Gilbert,
          J DeBarro
       Time and Time Again (Sothern, Scholl, chorus) music: Fred
          Spielman; lyrics: Earl Grant
       Yipsee-I-O (Miranda, Bando Da Lua) music, lyrics: Ray
          Gilbert
___   Magic Is the Moonlight (Powell, Sothern) music: Maria
          Grever; lyrics: Charles Pasquale
       Ca-Room' Pa-Pa (Miranda, Bando Da Lua) music, lyrics:
          Ray Gilbert
       La Boheme: Musetta's Waltz (Powell) music: Puccini

NASHVILLE (ABC, 1975)

ABC Records ABCD 893 (soundtrack) stereo

Music, lyrics: various; musical direction: Richard Baskin

Cast: Karen Black, Ronee Blakely, Timothy Brown, Keith Carradine,
         Henry Gibson, Barbara Harris

Songs: It Don't Worry Me (Carradine) music, lyrics: Keith
            Carradine
         Bluebird (Brown) music, lyrics: Ronee Blakely
         For the Sake of the Children (Gibson, chorus) music,
            lyrics: Richard Baskin, R Reicheg
         Keep A-Goin' (Gibson) music, lyrics: Richard Baskin,
            Henry Gibson
         Memphis (Black) music, lyrics: Karen Black
         Rolling Stone (Black, chorus) music, lyrics: Karen Black
         200 Years (Gibson, chorus) music, lyrics: Richard Baskin,
            Henry Gibson
---   Tapedeck in his Tractor (Blakely) music, lyrics: Ronee
            Blakely
         Dues (Blakely) music, lyrics: Ronee Blakely
         I'm Easy (Carradine) music, lyrics: Keith Carradine
         One, I Love You (Blakely, Gibson) music, lyrics:
            Richard Baskin
         My Idaho Home (Blakely) music, lyrics: Ronee Blakely
         It Don't Worry Me (reprise) (Harris, chorus) music,
            lyrics: Keith Carradine

NAUGHTY MARIETTA (MGM, 1935)

Hollywood Soundstage 413 (soundtrack) mono

Music: Victor Herbert; lyrics: Rida Johnson Young, Gus Kahn;
musical direction: Herbert Stothart

Cast: (the voice of) Alexander Bokefi, Charles Bruins, (the
         voice of) Countess Sonia, Nelson Eddy, Zarubi Elmassian,
         Delos Jewkes, Jeanette MacDonald, (the voice of)
         William Sabot, (the voice of) M Sankar

Songs: Titles (MacDonald, Eddy, chorus)
         Chansonette (MacDonald, chorus)
         Antoinette and Anatole (Bruins, female chorus)
         Song of Goodbye (Prayer) (MacDonald, Jewkes, chorus)
         Tramp, Tramp, Tramp (Eddy, men)
         The Owl and the Polecat (Eddy, chorus)
         'Neath the Southern Moon (Eddy)
---   Italian Street Song (Elmassian, MacDonald, Eddy, chorus)
         Ship Ahoy (Sankar, Sonia, Bokefi, Sabot,MacDonald)
         I'm Falling in Love with Someone (Eddy)
         Ah, Sweet Mystery of Life (MacDonald, Eddy)

                Tramp, Tramp, Tramp (reprise) (Eddy, chorus)
                Ah, Sweet Mystery of Life (reprise) (MacDonald, Eddy)

Note: The above recording includes spoken dialog. Studio
        recordings by cast members:

Victor (78rpm) 24896 Italian Street Song (MacDonald) LP: LPV-526
                     Ah, Sweet Mystery of Life (MacDonald)
                        LP: LPV-526
Victor (78rpm) 4280 Tramp, Tramp, Tramp (Eddy) LP: LPV-526
                     I'm Falling in Love with Someone (Eddy)
                        LP: LPV-526
Victor (78rpm) 4281 Ah, Sweet Mystery of Life (Eddy, chorus)
                     'Neath the Southern Moon (Eddy) LP: LPV-526

NEW FACES (Twentieth Century-Fox, 1954)

RCA (45/EP) EPA 557 mono

Music, lyrics: various; musical direction: Henri Rene, others

Cast: Eartha Kitt

Songs: C'est Si Bon (Kitt, chorus) music: Henri Betti; lyrics:
            Jerry Seelen
        Monotonous (Kitt) music: Arthur Siegel; lyrics: June
            Carroll; musical direction: Anton Coppola
 ---   Uska Dara - A Turkish Tale (Kitt)
        Santa Baby (Kitt, chorus) music, lyrics: Philip Springer,
            Tony Springer, Joan Javits

Note: Although the above album was issued in connection with
        the film release, all of the recordings were made some
        time earlier.

NEW MOON (MGM, 1930)

Pelican 2020 (soundtrack) mono

Music: Sigmund Romberg, others; lyrics: Oscar Hammerstein II;
musical direction: Herbert Stothart

Cast: Emily Fitzroy, Adolph Menjou, Grace Moore, Gus Shy,
        Lawrence Tibbett, Roland Young

Songs: Overture (gypsy chorus)
        Farmer's Daughter (Tibbett) music: Herbert Stothart
        Dialog (Tibbett, Shy) spoken
        Farmer's Daughter (reprise) (Tibbett, Moore, Young,
            Fitzroy)

```
        Wanting You (Tibbett, Moore)
 ___    Lover Come Back to Me (Tibbett)
        One Kiss (Moore)
        Waltz / Dialog (Tibbett, Moore)
        What Is Your Price Madame? (Menjou, Tibbett) music:
            Herbert Stothart
        Stout-Hearted Men (Tibbett, chorus)
        Soldiers Chorus (chorus)
        Lover Come Back to Me (reprise) (Moore)
        Lover Come Back to Me (Finale) (Tibbett, Moore, Young,
            Menjou)
```

Note: The above recording includes spoken dialog, with Tibbett
       and Moore being the only vocalists. Studio recordings
       by Tibbett:

       Victor (78rpm) 1506 Wanting You
                           Lover Come Back to Me

NEW MOON (MGM, 1940)

Pelican 103 (soundtrack) mono

Music: Sigmund Romberg; lyrics: Oscar Hammerstein II; musical
direction: Herbert Stothart

Cast: Nelson Eddy, Jeanette MacDonald

Songs: Introduction (Wanting You, Lover Come Back to Me)
           (MacDonald, Eddy, chorus)
       Stranger in Paree (MacDonald)
       Shoes / Softly, As in A Morning Sunrise (Eddy)
       Wanting You (MacDonald, Eddy)
       One Kiss (MacDonald)
       Stout-Hearted Men (Eddy, MacDonald)
       Lover Come Back to Me (MacDonald, Eddy)
       Finale (orchestra)

Note: Studio recordings by cast members:

Columbia (78rpm) 4240 Softly, As in A Morning Sunrise (Eddy)
                      Lover Come Back to Me (Eddy)
Columbia (78rpm) 4241 Stout-Hearted Men (Eddy, chorus)
                      Wanting You (Eddy)
Victor   (78rpm) 2048 Lover Come Back to Me (MacDonald)
                       One Kiss (MacDonald)

NEW YORK, NEW YORK (United Artists, 1977)

UA LA 750-L2 (two records - soundtrack) stereo CD

Music: John Kander, others; lyrics: Fred Ebb, others; musical
direction: Ralph Burns

Cast: Diahnne Abbott, Georgie Auld (saxophone), Robert De Niro,
        Larry Kert, Liza Minnelli, Mary Kay Place

Songs: Main Title (orchestra)
        You Brought A New Kind of Love to Me (Minnelli) music,
            lyrics: Sammy Fain, Irving Kahal, Pierre Norman
        Flip the Dip (Auld) music; Georgie Auld
        V J Stomp (orchestra) music; Ralph Burns
        Opus Number One (orchestra) music: Sy Oliver
        Once In A While (Minnelli) music: Michael Edwards;
--- lyrics: Bud Green
        You Are My Lucky Star (Minnelli) music: Nacio Herb Brown;
            lyrics: Arthur Freed
        Game Over (Auld) music: Georgie Auld
        It's A Wonderful World (orchestra) music, lyrics: Jan
            Savitt, Leo Watson, Harold Adamson
        The Man I Love (Minnelli) music: George Gershwin; lyrics:
            Ira Gershwin
        Hazoy (orchestra) music: Ralph Burns
        Just You, Just Me (Minnelli) music: Jesse Greer; lyrics:
--- Raymond Klages
        There Goes the Ballgame (Minnelli)
        Blue Moon (De Niro, Place) music: Richard Rodgers; lyrics:
            Lorenz Hart
        Don't Be That Way (orchestra) music: Edgar Sampson, Benny
            Goodman
--- Happy Ending (Minnelli, Kert, chorus) cut from original film
        But the World Goes 'Round (Minnelli)
        Theme from New York, New York (Auld)
        Honeysuckle Rose (Abbott) music: Fats Waller; lyrics:
            Andy Razaf
        Once Again Right Away (Auld) music: Ralph Burns
        Bobby's Dream (orchestra) music: Ralph Burns
        Theme from New York, New York (reprise) (Minnelli)
        Theme from New York, New York (reprise) (orchestra)

NICE GIRL? (Universal, 1941)

Decca (78rpm) 209 mono 'Deanna Durbin Souvenir Album, No 4'

Music: Walter Jurmann, others; lyrics: Bernie Grossman, others;
musical direction: Charles Previn

Cast: Deanna Durbin

Decca (78rpm) 3653 Beneath the Lights of Home (Durbin) LP: Ace of
                  Hearts 60
Decca (78rpm) 3654 Love At Last (Durbin) music: Jacques Press; lyr:

                        Eddie Cherkose; LP: Ace of Hearts 147
                        Perhaps (Durbin) music: Androsde Sequrola;
                          lyrics: Aldo Franchetti; LP: Ace of
                          Hearts 93
Decca (78rpm) 3655   Thank You America (Durbin) LP: Ace of Hearts
                          147
                        Swanee River - The Old Folks at Home (Durbin)
                          music, lyrics: Stephen Foster; LP: Ace
                          of Hearts 93

NIGHT AND DAY (Warner Bros, 1946)

Motion Picture Tracks MPT 6 (soundtrack) mono

Music, lyrics: Cole Porter, others; musical direction: Ray
Heindorf

Cast: Eve Arden, Cary Grant, Dorothy Malone, Mary Martin,
        Ginny Simms, Carlos Ramirez, Roy Rogers, Monty Woolley,
        Jane Wyman

Songs: Overture (Night and Day, Blow Gabriel Blow) (orchestra)
       I'm In Love Again (Wyman)
       Bulldog (male chorus)
       In the Still of the Night (Malone, Grant, chorus)
       An Old-Fashioned Garden (Grant, cast)
       You've Got That Thing (girls)
       Let's Do It (Wyman)
       You Do Something to Me (Wyman, chorus)
       Night and Day (Grant, unidentified male)
       I'm Unlucky at Gambling (Arden)
       Miss Otis Regrets (Woolley)
       I Wonder What's Become of Sally (Simms) music: Milton
          Agar; lyrics: Jack Yellen
       What Is This Thing Called Love (Simms)
---   I've Got You Under My Skin (Simms)
       Rosalie ('buskers' chorus)
       Just One of Those Things (Simms, chorus)
       Anything Goes (orchestra)
       You're the Top (Simms, Grant)
       I Get A Kick Out of You (Simms, chorus)
       Easy to Love (chorus)
       My Heart Belongs to Daddy (Martin)
       Night and Day (reprise) (orchestra)
       Do I Love You (Simms)
       Don't Fence Me In (Rogers)
       Begin the Beguine (Ramirez, chorus)
       Bulldog (reprise) (male chorus)
       Night and Day (reprise) (male chorus)

Note: The above recording includes spoken dialog. Studio
        recordings by cast members:

SMC (78rpm) 2512 Begin the Beguine (Ramirez)

Royale LP: VLP 6055 'Ginny Simms'

            What Is This Thing Called Love
            You're the Top
            Just One of Those Things
            I Get A Kick Out of You
            I've Got You Under My Skin

THE NIGHT THE LIGHTS WENT OUT IN GEORGIA - see page 359

THE NIGHT THEY RAIDED MINSKY'S (United Artists, 1969)

UA S 5191 (soundtrack) stereo

Music: Charles Strouse; lyrics: Lee Adams; musical direction:
Philip J Lang, others

Cast: Lillian Heyman, Dexter Maitland, Jason Robards, (the
        voice of) Rudy Vallee, Norman Wisdom

Songs: The Night They Raided Minsky's (orchestra) musical
            direction: Leroy Holmes
        Overture (orchestra) introduction: Rudy Vallee
        Take 10 Terrific Girls (but Only 9 Costumes) (Maitland,
            girls)
        (Love theme from) The Night They Raided Minsky's (Wait
            for Me) (orchestra)
        You Rat You (Heyman)
        How I Love Her (orchestra)
        Medley: Perfect Gentlemen (orchestra)
                Take 10 Terrific Girls (reprise) (orchestra)
    ---   Take 10 Terrific Girls (reprise) (Vallee)
        The Night They Raided Minsky's (reprise) (orchestra)
        Perfect Gentlemen (Robards, Wisdom)
        Penny Arcade (orchestra) musical direction: Leroy Holmes
        The Night They Raided Minsky's (reprise) (Vallee)

NO LEAVE, NO LOVE (MGM, 1946)

Cosmo (78rpm) DMR 102 mono

Music, lyrics: various; musical direction: George Stoll

Cast: Pat Kirkwood

Songs: Love On A Greyhound Bus (Kirkwood) music, lyrics: Kay
            Thompson, Ralph Blane, George Stoll

Listen to Me (Kirkwood) not in film
Isn't It Wonderful? (Kirkwood) music, lyrics: Kay Thompson
All the Time (Kirkwood) music: Sammy Fain; lyrics: Ralph
    Freed

Note: Additional studio recording by Guy Lombardo Orchestra:

        Decca (78rpm) 18873 Love On A Greyhound Bus
                            All the Time

NO, NO NANETTE (First National, 1930)

Take Two 110 (soundtrack) mono 'Lost Film Trailers from the
                                    First Years of Sound'
Music: Ed Ward, others; lyrics: Al Bryan, others

Songs: Dancing to Heaven (cast)
       King of the Air (cast)
       Three Cheers for the Red, White and Blue (cast)
       I Want to Be Happy (cast) music: Vincent Youmans; lyrics:
          Irving Caesar

Note: The above recording, taken from the soundtrack of the film
        trailer, includes interviews, but no solo vocals.

NORTHWEST OUTPOST (Republic, 1947)

Columbia (78rpm) MM 690 mono

Music: Rudolf Friml; lyrics: Edward Hayman; musical direction:
Robert Armbruster

Cast: Nelson Eddy

Columbia (78rpm) 7563M One More Mile to Go (Eddy, chorus)
                       Raindrops on A Drum (Eddy)
Columbia (78rpm) 7564M Love Is the Time (Eddy, chorus)
                       Nearer and Nearer (Eddy)
Columbia (78rpm) 7565M Tell Me with Your Eyes (Eddy)
                       Russian Easter Hymn (Eddy, chorus) trad

NORWOOD (Paramount, 1970)

Capitol SW 475 (soundtrack) stereo

Music, lyrics: Mac Davis, others; musical direction: Al DeLory

Cast: Glen Campbell

Songs: Ol' Norwood's Comin' Home (Campbell) music, lyrics:
      Ramona Redd, Mitchell Torok
     Country Girl (orchestra) music: Al DeLory
     Marie (Campbell) music, lyrics: Ramona Redd, Mitchell
      Torok
     The Brass Ensemble of Ralph, Texas (orchestra) music:
      Al DeLory
     The Repo Man (Campbell)
     Hot Wheels (orchestra) music: Al DeLory
  --- I'll Paint You A Song (Campbell)
     Norwood (Me and My Guitar) (Campbell)
     The Fring Thing (orchestra) music: Al DeLory
     Down Home (Campbell)
     Chicken Out (Joann's Theme) (orchestra) music: Al DeLory
     I'll Paint You A Song (reprise) (Campbell)
     A Different Kind of Rock (orchestra) music: Al DeLory
     Everything A Man Could Ever Need (Campbell)

OH, ROSALINDA! (Associated British, 1955)

Mercury MG 20145 (soundtrack) mono

Music: Johann Strauss; lyrics: Dennis Arundell; musical direction:
Aleis Melichar ('Die Fledermaus' brought up to date)

Cast: Sari Barabas (for Ludmilla Tcherina), Walter Berry (for
     Anton Walbrook), Dennis Dowling (for Dennis Price),
     Anthony Quayle, Michael Redgrave, Anneliese Rothenberger,
     Alexander Young (for Mel Ferrer)

Songs: Overture (orchestra)
     Alfred's Serenade (Young)
     Adele's Telephone Call (Rothenberger)
     Now, Darling, Let Me Calm You Down (Barabas, Redgrave)
     "Oh Boy, Oh Boy" (Barabas, Redgrave, Young, Rothenberger)
     "Will Love Stay" (Young, Barabas)
  --- "Tete-A-Tete" (Barabas, Young, Dowling)
     Fireworks Music (chorus)
     Laughing Song (Berry, Rothenberger, Dowling, Redgrave,
      chorus)
     Orlofsky's Song (Chacun a son Gout) (Quayle)
     The Great Waltz (orchestra) dialog: Tcherina, Walbrook,
      Redgrave
     Oh, Gentle Bat (chorus, Redgrave, Berry, Quayle, Rothenberger
      Ferrer, Barabas, Price)
     Champagne Song (Barabas, Redgrave, Ferrer, Dowling, Price,
      Oska Sima, Quayle, Rothenberger)
     Be My Friend (Berry, Dowling, Redgrave, Quayle, Barabas,
      chorus)

Note: Some selections on side two include spoken dialog by non-
        singing cast members.

OH! WHAT A LOVELY WAR (Paramount, 1969)

Paramount PAS 5008 (soundtrack) stereo

Music, lyrics: various; musical direction: Alfred Ralston

Cast: Penny Allen, Maurice Arthur, Joanne Brown, Jean Pierre
        Cassel, Pia Colombo, Richard Howard, Joe Milia, Corin
        Redgrave, Maggie Smith

Songs: Overture: Girls and Boys Come Out to Play (orchestra)
                  Oh! It's A Lovely War (orchestra)
                  Are We Downhearted? No-o-o (orchestra)
                  The Bells of Hell (orchestra)
                  Far, Far from Wipers (orchestra)
        Belgium Put the Kaibosh on the Kaiser (Cassel, chorus)
           music, lyrics: Ellerton
        Medley: We Don't Want to Lose You (Your King and Your
                  Country Need You) (Allen, girls) music,
                  lyrics: Reubens)
                I'll Make A Man of You (Smith, girls) music:
                  Finck; lyrics: Wimperis
        Goodbye-ee (Melia, Redgrave) music: R P Weston; lyrics:
           Bert Lee
        Silent Night (men) music: Franz Gruber
        Oh! It's A Lovely War (chorus) music: J P Long; lyrics:
           Maurice Scott
  ---   Oh! It's A Lovely War (reprise) (Irish Guards Band)
        Hush! Here Comes A Whizzbang (men) music, lyrics:
           Weston, Barnes, Scott
        Adieu la Vie (Colombo) music, lyrics: Sablon
        They Were Only Playing Leapfrog (men)
        When This Lousy War Is Over (Arthur, chorus)
        I Want to Go Home (men)
        The Bells of Hell (men)
        Far, Far from Wipers (Howard) music, lyrics: Bingham,
           Greene)
        Pack Up Your Troubles (men) music; Felix Powell; lyrics:
           George Asaf
        Keep the Home Fires Burning (Brown) music: Ivor Novello;
           lyrics: Lena G Ford
        Over There (men) music, lyrics: George M Cohan
        They Didn't Believe Me (men) music: Jerome Kern; lyrics:
           M E Rourke

OKLAHOMA! (Magna, 1955)

Capitol SAO 595 (soundtrack) stereo CD

Music: Richard Rodgers; lyrics: Oscar Hammerstein II; musical
direction: Jay Blackton

Cast: Jay C Flippin, Gloria Grahame,Charlotte Greenwood, Shirley
        Jones, Gordon MacRae, Gene Nelson, Rod Steiger, James
        Whitmore

Songs: Overture (orchestra)
        Oh, What A Beautiful Mornin' (MacRae)
        The Surry with the Fringe on Top (MacRae, Jones, Greenwood)
        Kansas City (Nelson, Greenwood, men)
        I Cain't Say No (Grahame)
___   Many A New Day (Jones, girls)
        People Will Say We're in Love (MacRae, Jones)
        Poor Jud Is Daid (MacRae, Steiger)
        Out of My Dreams (Jones, girls)
        The Farmer and the Cowman (MacRae, Greenwood, Nelson,
           Flippin, Whitmore, Grahame, chorus)
        All er Nothin' (Grahame, Nelson)
        Oklahoma (MacRae, Greenwood, Nelson, Whitmore, Jones,
           Flippin, chorus)

OLIVER! (Columbia, 1968)

Colgems COSD 5501 (soundtrack) stereo reissued: RCA COSD 5501 CD

Music, lyrics: Lionel Bart; musical direction: John Green

Cast: Mark Lester, Ron Moody, Peggy Mount, Harry Secombe,
        Shani Wallis, Sheila White, Jack Wild

Songs: Overture (orchestra)
        Food, Glorious Food (Lester, boys)
        Oliver! (Secome, Mount, boys)
        Boy for Sale (Secombe)
        Where Is Love? (Lester)
        Pick A Pocket or Two (Moody, boys)
        Consider Yourself (Wild, Lester, chorus)
        I'd Do Anything (Wild, Wallis, White, Lester, Moody,
           boys)
___   Be Back Soon (Moody, boys)
        As Long As He Needs Me (Wallis)
        Who Will Buy? (Lester, chorus)
        It's A Fine Life (Wallis, White, chorus)
        Reviewingthe Situation (Moody)
        Oom-Pah-Pah (Wallis, chorus)

Finale: Where Is Love? (orchestra)
         Consider Yourself (chorus)

ON A CLEAR DAY YOU CAN SEE FOREVER (Paramount, 1969)

Columbia S 30086 (soundtrack) stereo

Music: Burton Lane; lyrics: Alan Jay Lerner; musical direction:
Nelson Riddle

Cast: Yves Montand, Barbra Streisand

Songs: Hurry! It's Lovely Up Here (Streisand)
       Main Title - On A Clear Day (chorus)
       Love with All the Trimmings (Streisand)
       Melinda (Montand)
_ _ _ Go to Sleep (Streisand)
       He Isn't You (Streisand)
       What Did I Have That I Don't Have (Streisand)
       Come Back to Me (Montand)
       On A Clear Day (Montand)
       On A Clear Day (reprise) (Streisand)

Note: Additional soundtrack selections, cut from the final film:

        Who Is There Among Us Who Knows? (Jack Nicholson)
           Out Takes OTF - 1
        Wait Till You're Sixty-Five (Larry Blyden, Streisand)
           SPO (45rpm) 145

ON MOONLIGHT BAY (Warner Bros, 1951)

Columbia CL 6186 mono   reissued: CSP P 17660

Music, lyrics: various; musical direction: Paul Weston

Cast: Doris Day, Jack Smith

Songs: On Moonlight Bay (Day, chorus) music: Percy Wenrich;
          lyrics: Edward Madden
       Till We Meet Again (Day, male vocalist) music: Richard
          Whiting; lyrics: Raymond B Egan
       Love Ya (Day, Smith) music: Peter De Rose; lyrics:
          Charles Tobias
       Christmas Srory (Day, chorus) music, lyrics: Pauline
          Walsh
       I'm Forever Blowing Bubbles (Day, Smith, chorus) music,
          lyrics: Jean Kenbrovin, John W Kellette
       Cuddle Up A Little Closer (Day, male vocalist) music:

      Karl Hoschna; lyrics: Otto Harbach
    Every Little Movement (Day, chorus) music: Karl Hoschna;
      lyrics: Otto Harbach
    Tell Me Why Nights Are Lonely (Day) music: Max Kortlander;
      lyrics: J Will Callahan

ON THE AVENUE (Twentieth Century-Fox, 1937)

Hollywood Soundstage 401 (soundtrack) mono also: Sandy Hook 2083

Music, lyrics: Irving Berlin; musical direction: Arthur Lange

Cast: Madeline Carroll, Alice Faye, Dick Powell, The Ritz
      Brothers

Songs: Overture (orchestra)
      He Ain't Got Rhythm (Faye, The Ritz Brothers, chorus)
      The Girl on the Police Gazette (Powell, chorus)
      You're Laughing at Me (Powell, Carroll)
---   This Year's Kisses (Faye)
      I've Got My Love to Keep Me Warm (Powell, Faye)
      Slumming on Park Avenue (Faye, The Ritz Brothers, chorus)
      You're Laughing at Me (reprise) Ochye Tchornia (Dark
        Eyes) (Powell, The Ritz Brothers)
      This Year's Kisses (reprise) (Faye)
      Finale: Slumming on Park Avenue (chorus)

Note: Studio recordings by cast members:

Brunswick (78rpm) 7825 This Year's Kisses (Faye) LP: CL 3068
                  Slumming on Park Avenue (Faye) LP:
                  CL 3068
Brunswick (78rpm) 7821 I've Got My Love to Keep Me Warm (Faye)
                  LP: CL 3068
Decca (78rpm) 1149 This Year's Kisses (Powell) LP: MCA 1691
               I've Got My Love to Keep Me Warm (Powell)
               LP: MCA 1691
Decca (78rpm) 1150 The Girl on the Police Gazette (Powell)
               LP: MCA 1691
               You're Laughing at Me (Powell) LP: MCA 1691

ON THE TOWN (MGM, 1949)

Show Biz Records 5603 (soundtrack) mono

Music: Leonard Bernstein, others; lyrics: Betty Comden, Adolph
Green; musical direction: Lennie Hayton

Cast: Betty Garrett, Bern Hoffman, Gene Kelly, Ann Miller,

Jules Munshin, Alice Pearce, Frank Sinatra, Vera-Ellen

Songs: Overture (orchestra)
(Opening) I Feel Like I'm Not Out of Bed Yet (Hoffman)
New York, New York (Kelly, Sinatra, Munshin)
Prehistoric Man (Miller, Kelly, Sinatra, Munshin, Garrett)
    music: Roger Edens
___ Come Up to My Place (Garrett, Sinatra)
When You Walk Down Mainstreet with Me (Kelly) music:
    Roger Edens
You're Awful (Sinatra, Garrett) music: Roger Edens
Count on Me (Sinatra, Garrett, Munshin, Miller, Pearce,
    Kelly) music: Roger Edens
On the Town (Sinatra, Kelly, Munshin, Miller, Garrett,
    Vera-Ellen) music: Roger Edens

Note: The above recording includes spoken dialog.

THE ONE AND ONLY GENUINE ORIGINAL FAMILY BAND (Disney, 1968)

Vista 5002 (soundtrack) stereo

Music, lyrics: Richard M Sherman, Robert B Sherman; musical
direction: Jack Elliott

Cast: Janet Blair, Walter Brennan, John Craig, Wally Cox, John
    Davidson, Richard Deacon, Buddy Ebsen, Pamelyn Ferdin,
    Steve Harmon, Goldie Jeanne Hawn, Bobby Riha, Heidi Rook,
    Kurt Russell, Debbie Smith, Jon Walmsley, Lesley Ann
    Warren, Smitty Wordes

Songs: The One and Only, Genuine, Original Family Band (Brennan,
    Ebsen, Warren, Blair, children)
The Happiest Girl Alive (Warren)
Let's Put It Over with Grover (Brennan, Ebsen, Warren,
    Blair, children)
Ten Feet Off the Ground (Ebsen, Warren, Blair, children)
___ Dakota (Davidson, chorus)
'Bout Time (Davidson, Warren)
Drummin' Drummin' Drummin' (Brennan, Walmsley, Ferdin,
    Riha, Wordes, Rook, chorus)
West O' the Wide Missouri (Ebsen, Warren, Blair, Smith,
    Russell, Riha, Hawn, Harmon, chorus)
Oh, Benjamin Harrison (Ebsen, Davidson, Harmon, Cox,
    Deacon, Craig)
'Bout Time (reprise) (Davidson, Warren, chorus)
The One and Only, Genuine, Original Family Band - End
    Title (chorus)

ONE HOUR WITH YOU (Paramount, 1932)

Ariel CMF 23 (soundtrack) mono

Music: Oscar Straus, others; lyrics: Leo Robin; musical direction: Nat W Finston

Cast: Maurice Chevalier, Jeanette MacDonald, Donald Novis,
        Charles Ruggles, Genevieve Tobin

Songs: What A Little Thing Like A Wedding Ring Can Do (Chevalier,
           MacDonald)
        We Will Always Be Sweethearts (MacDonald, Tobin)
        Three Times A Day (Chevalier, Tobin) music: Richard A
           Whiting
        One Hour with You (Novis, Tobin, Chevalier, Ruggles,
---   MacDonald) music: Richard A Whiting
        Oh, That Mitzi (Chevalier)
        It Was Only A Dream (We Will Always Be Sweethearts -
           reprise) (MacDonald, Chevalier)
        What Would You Do? (Chevalier) music: Richard A Whiting
        Finale (Chevalier, MacDonald) spoken
        End Titles (orchestra)

Note: Studio recordings by cast members:

Victor (78rpm) 24013 One Hour with You (MacDonald)
                     We Will Always Be Sweethearts (MacDonald)
Victor (78rpm) 22941 What Would You Do? (Chevalier) LP: CAL 579
                     Oh, That Mitzi (Chevalier) LP: RCA LPV 564

ONE TOUCH OF VENUS (Universal, 1948)

Ariel KWH 10 (soundtrack) mono 'Kurt Weill in Hollywood'

Music: Kurt Weill; lyrics: Ogden Nash, others; musical direction: Leo Arnaud

Cast: Eve Arden, Dick Haymes, Olga San Juan, Robert Walker,
        Eileen Wilson (for Ava Gardner)

Songs: Overture (orchestra)
        The Trouble with Women (chorus)
        Speak Low (Wilson, Haymes)
        That's Him (Wilson, San Juan, Arden)
        Don't Look Now (Haymes, San Juan, Wilson, Walker, chorus)
           lyrics: Ann Ronell
        My Week (Haymes, San Juan) lyrics: Ann Ronell

Note: The melody for 'Don't Look Now' is the same as for

'Foolish Heart', and 'My Week' as for 'West Wind.'
The earlier versions are from the Broadway score.

OPERA DO MALANDRO (Austra, 1985)

Philips (Brazil) 830 120-1 (soundtrack) stereo

Music, lyrics: Chico Buarque; musical direction: Ch. de Moraes

Cast: Edson Celulari, Suely Costa, Ney Latorraca, Claudia
        Ohana, Elba Ramalho

Songs: A Volta do Malandro (chorus)
        Las Muchachas de Copacabana (Ramalho, chorus)
        Tema da Geni (orchestra)
        Hino da Repressao (Latorraca)
        Aquela Mulher (Celulari)
        Viver do Amor (Ohana, chorus)
        Sentimental (Ohana)
___   Desafio do Malandro (Celulari, chorus)
        O Ultimo Blues (Ohana)
        Palavra de Mulher (Ramalho)
        O Meu Amor (Ramalho, Ohana)
        Tango do Covil (men)
        Uma Cancao Desnaturada (Costa)
        Rio 42 (chorus)
        Pedaco de Mim (Ramalho, Celulari)

THE OPTIMISTS (Paramount, 1973)

Paramount PAS 1015 (soundtrack) stereo

Music, lyrics: Lionel Bart, others; musical direction: George
Martin

Cast: Don Crown, Peter Sellers

Songs: Main Titles: Sometimes (Sellers)
                    Sam's Theme (orchestra)
        School's Out (orchestra)
        Mary (Sellers) trad
        Sometimes (orchestra) music: George Martin
        London by Bus (orchestra)
        Dreamland (orchestra)
___   Knick Knack Paddy Wack (Sellers) music, lyrics: Warburton
        Mr Bass Drum Man (Crown) music, lyrics: Don Crown
        Sad Sam (orchestra) music: George Martin
        Dreamland Again (orchestra)
        Here Lies Bella (orchestra)

        The Optimists (orchestra) music: George Martin
        Sam Goes Home (Sellers) spoken

ORCHESTRA WIVES (Twentieth Century-Fox, 1942)

RCA LPT 3065 (soundtrack) mono reissued: Mercury 826 635-1 CD

Music: Harry Warren, others; lyrics: Mack Gordon, others;
musical direction: Glenn Miller

Cast: Tex Beneke, Ray Eberle, Pat Friday (for Lynn Bari),
       Marion Hutton, The Glenn Miller Orchestra, The Modernaires

Songs: American Patrol (orchestra) music: F W Meacham
       Serenade in Blue (Friday, Eberle, The Modernaires)
       That's Sabotage (Hutton)
---   Moonlight Sonata (orchestra) music: Beethoven
       (I've Got A Gal in) Kalamazoo (Beneke, Hutton, The
          Modernaires
       People Like You and Me (Hutton, Beneke, Eberle, The
          Modernaires
       Bugle Call Rag (orchestra) music: J Hubert Blake,
          Carey Morgan

Note: Additional selections on reissue:

       Boom Shot (orchestra)
       You Say the Sweetest Things, Baby (orchestra)
       Moonlight Serenade (orchestra)

OUT OF THIS WORLD (Paramount, 1945)

Decca DL 4259 mono 'Bing's Hollywood - Blue Skies'

Music: Harold Arlen, others; lyrics: Johnny Mercer, others;
musical direction: John Scott Trotter

Cast: Bing Crosby (for Eddie Bracken)

Songs: I'd Rather Be Me (Crosby) music, lyrics: Felix Bernard,
          Eddie Cherkose, Sam Coslow
       Out of This World (Crosby)
       June Comes Around Every Year (Crosby)

PAESANO, A VOICE IN THE NIGHT (Mediterraneo, 1974)

MIR Records 733 (soundtrack) stereo

Music: Ray Sinatra, others; lyrics: Harold Adamson, others;
musical direction: Ray Sinatra

Cast: Alberto Sarno

Songs: Voice in the Night (Sarno, chorus) lyrics: Jack Brooks
       You're the Girl (Sarno, chorus) lyrics: Jack Brooks
       My Song (Sarno, chorus) lyrics: Jack Brooks
       Give Me Your Hand (Sarno, chorus) lyrics: Jack Brooks
       Pagliacci: Vesti La Giubba (Sarno) music: Leoncavallo
---   Filomena (Sarno, chorus)
       Music to Love By (Sarno, chorus)
       I Was Only Pretending (Sarno, chorus)
       If You Were Mine (Sarno, chorus)
       Paesan (Sarno, chorus) lyrics: Johnny Mercer
       Who Am I to Love You (Sarno, chorus)
       In the Springtime of Life (Sarno, chorus)

PAGAN LOVE SONG (MGM, 1950)

MGM E 534 (soundtrack) mono reissued: MCA 39080 CD

Music: Harry Warren, others; lyrics: Arthur Freed; musical
direction: Adolph Deutsch

Cast: Howard Keel, Esther Williams

Songs: Pagan Love Song (Keel, chorus) music: Nacio Herb Brown
       Sea of the Moon (Williams)
---   Why Is Love So Crazy (Keel)
       Tahiti (Keel, chorus)
       Singing in the Sun (Williams, Keel, chorus)
       House of Singing Bamboo (Keel, chorus)

Note: An additional soundtrack selection, cut from the final
       film, was issued on Out Takes OTF 3:

       Music of the Water (Keel)

PAINT YOUR WAGON (Paramount, 1969)

Paramount PMS 1001 (soundtrack) stereo reissued: MCA 37099

Music: Frederick Loewe, others; lyrics: Alan Jay Lerner;
musical direction: Nelson Riddle

Cast: Alan Dexter, Clint Eastwood, Anita Gordon (for Jean
       Seberg), Lee Marvin, The Nitty Gritty Dirt Band,
       Harve Presnell

Songs: Main Title: I'm On My Way (chorus)
       I Still See Elisa (Eastwood)
       The First Thing You Know (Marvin) music: Andre Previn
       Hand Me Down That Can O' Beans (Marvin, The Nitty Gritty
         Dirt Band, chorus)
       They Call the Wind Maria (Presnell, chorus)
       A Million Miles Away Behind the Door (Gordon) music:
         Andre Previn
___   There's A Coach Comin' In (Presnell, chorus)
       Whoop-Ti-Ay! (Shivaree) (chorus)
       I Talk to the Trees (Eastwood)
       The Gospel of No Name City (Dexter) music: Andre Previn
       Best Things (Marvin, Eastwood, chorus) music: Andre
         Previn
       Wand'rin' Star (Marvin, chorus)
       Gold Fever (Eastwood, chorus) music: Andre Previn
       Finale (Presnell, Gordon, chorus)

PAINTING THE CLOUDS WITH SUNSHINE (Warner Bros, 1951)

Capitol L 291 mono

Music, lyrics: various; musical direction: George Greeley

Cast: Dennis Morgan, Lucille Norman

Songs: Painting the Clouds with Sunshine (chorus) music: Joe
        Burke; lyrics: Al Dubin
       We're in the Money (chorus) music: Harry Warren; lyrics:
        Al Dubin
       When Irish Eyes Are Smiling (Morgan) music: Ernest R
        Ball; lyrics: Chauncey Olcott, George Graff, Jr
       Tip Toe Through the Tulips with Me (Morgan, Norman)
        music: Joe Burke; lyrics: Al Dubin
___   Jealousy (Norman) music: Jacob Gade; lyrics: Vera Bloom
       The Birth of the Blues (Norman) music: Ray Henderson;
        lyrics: B G DeSylva, Lew Brown
       You're My Everything (Morgan) music: Harry Warren;
        lyrics: Mort Dixon, Joe Young
       Vienna Dreams (Norman) music: Rudolph Sieczynski; lyrics:
        Irving Caesar
       Man Is A Necessary Evil (female trio) music: Sonny Burke;
        lyrics: Jack Elliott
       With A Song in My Heart (Morgan, Norman, chorus) music:
        Richard Rodgers; lyrics: Lorenz Hart
       Finale: Painting the Clouds with Sunshine (reprise)
        (Morgan, Norman, chorus)

THE PAJAMA GAME (Warner Bros, 1957)

Columbia OL 5210 (soundtrack) mono

Music, lyrics: Richard Adler, Jerry Ross; musical direction:
Ray Heindorf

Cast: Doris Day, Eddie Foy, Jr, Carol Haney, Kenneth LeRoy,
        Buzz Miller, John Raitt, Reta Shaw, Jack Straw

Songs: The Pajama Game (Foy, ensemble)
        Racing with the Clock (Foy, ensemble)
        I'm Not At All in Love (Day, girls)
        I'll Never Be Jealous Again (Foy, Shaw)
        Hey There (Raitt)
        Once-A-Year Day (Day, Raitt, ensemble)
---   Small Talk (Day, Raitt)
        There Once Was A Man (Day, Raitt)
        Steam Heat (Haney, LeRoy, Miller)
        Hernando's Hideaway (Haney, ensemble)
        Seven-and-A-Half Cents (Day, Straw, ensemble)
        Finale: The Pajama Game (ensemble)
                Hernando's Hideaway (orchestra)

PAJAMA PARTY (American International, 1964)

Vista 3325 (soundtrack) stereo

Music, lyrics: Guy Hemric, Jerry Styner

Cast: Annette Funicello, Dorothy Lamour

Songs: Pajama Party (Funicello)
        There Has to Be A Reason (Funicello)
        Beach Ball (orchestra)
        It's That Kind of A Day (Funicello)
        Among the Young (Funicello)
        The Maid and the Martian (Funicello, chorus)
---   Pajama Party (reprise) (orchestra)
        Stuffed Animal (Funicello, chorus)
        Among the Young (reprise) (orchestra)
        Where Did I Go Wrong? (Lamour)
        It's That Kind of A Day (reprise) (orchestra)

PAL JOEY (Columbia, 1957)

Capitol W 912 (soundtrack) mono

Music: Richard Rodgers; lyrics: Lorenz Hart; musical direction:

Morris Stoloff

Cast: Trudi Erwin (for Kim Novak), Jo Ann Greer (for Rita
       Hayworth), Frank Sinatra

Songs: Main Title (orchestra)
       That Terrific Rainbow (Erwin, girls)
       I Didn't Know What Time It Was (Sinatra)
       Do It the Hard Way (orchestra)
       Great Big Town (girls)
       There's A Small Hotel (Sinatra)
       Zip (Greer)
       I Could Write A Book (Sinatra)
___   Bewitched (Greer)
       The Lady Is A Tramp (Sinatra)
       Plant You Now, Dig You Later (orchestra)
       My Funny Valentine (Erwin)
       You Mustn't Kick It Around (orchestra)
       Bewitched (reprise) (Sinatra)
       Strip Number (I Could Write A Book) (orchestra)
       Dream Sequence: What Do I Care for A Dame (Sinatra, men)
                       Bewitched (orchestra)
                       I Could Write A Book (chorus)

Note: An additional soundtrack selection, cut from the film,
       is included on Curtain Calls CC 100/22 'Rita Hayworth'

       My Funny Valentine (Greer)

PALM SPRINGS WEEKEND (Warner Bros, 1963)

Warner Bros WS 1519 (soundtrack) stereo

Music, lyrics for songs: various; background score, musical
direction: Frank Perkins

Cast: Bob Conrad, Troy Donahue, Ty Hardin, Modern Folk Quartet,
       Connie Stevens, Jerry Van Dyke

Songs: Live Young (Donahue, chorus) music: Paul Evans; lyrics:
          Larry Kusik
       Hurricane Twist (orchestra)
       Ox-Driver (Modern Folk Quartet) trad
       Shilly-Shally (chorus)
       What Will I Tell Him (Stevens) music, lyrics: Barry
          DeVorzon, Bodie Chandler
       Palm Canyon Bossa-Nova (orchestra)
___   Hurricane Twist (reprise) (orchestra)

        Go, Go-Devil (chorus)
        Bye Bye Blackbird (Hardin, Van Dyke) music: Ray Henderson;
            lyrics: Mort Dixon
        Palm Springs Scramble (orchestra)
        Prescription for Recovery (orchestra)
        A Little Bit o'Give (Conrad, chorus) music: Bodie Chandler;
            lyrics: Vincent Castle
        Live Young (reprise) (orchestra)

PARADISE, HAWAIIAN STYLE (Paramount, 1966)

RCA LSP 3643 (soundtrack) stereo reissued: AFL 1-3643

Music: Florence Kaye, others; lyrics: Bill Giant, Bernie Baum,
others

Cast: Elvis Presley

Songs: Paradise, Hawaiian Style (Presley)
       This Is My Heaven (Presley)
       Scratch My Back (Then I'll Scratch Yours) (Presley)
       House of Sand (Presley)
---   Stop Where You Are (Presley)
       A Dog's Life (Presley) music: Ben Weisman; lyrics:
          Sid Wayne
       Datin' (Presley) music: Randy Starr; lyrics: Fred Wise
       Queenie Wahine's Papaya (Presley)
       Drums of the Islands (Presley) music: Roy C Bennett;
          lyrics: Sid Tepper
       Sand Castles (Presley) music, lyrics: David Hess, Herb
          Goldberg (not from film)

PARDNERS (Paramount, 1956)

Capitol (45/EP) 1-752 mono

Music: James Van Heusen; lyrics: Sammy Cahn; musical direction:
Dick Stabile

Cast: Jerry Lewis, Dean Martin

Songs: Me 'n' You 'n' the Moon (Martin)
       The Wind, The Wind (Martin)
       Buckskin Beauty (Lewis)
       Pardners (Martin, Lewis)

THE PARENT TRAP (Disney, 1961)

Vista 3309 stereo

Music, lyrics: Richard M Sherman, Robert B Sherman; musical
direction: Tutti Camarata

Cast: (the voice of) Annette Funicello , Hayley Mills, Maureen
        O'Hara, (the voice of) Tommy Sands

Songs: For Now for Always (chorus)
        Let's Get Together (Mills)
        Whistling at the Boys (girls)
        Cobbler Cobbler (Mills) not from film
        For Now for Always (O'Hara)
        The Parent Trap (Sands, Funicello)

PARIS HONEYMOON (Paramount, 1939)

Decca DL 4253 mono 'Bing's Hollywood - East Side of Heaven'

Music: Ralph Rainger, others; lyrics: Leo Robin, others;
musical direction: John Scott Trotter

Cast: Bing Crosby, Woody Herman's Woodchoppers (not in film)

Songs: The Funny Old Hills (Crosby)
        I Have Eyes (Crosby)
___   Joobalai (Crosby)
        You're A Sweet Little Headache (Crosby)
        I Ain't Got Nobody (Crosby, Herman's Woodchoppers) music:
            Spencer Williams; lyrics: Roger Graham

LA PARISIENNE (United Artists, 1958)   French

United Artists (45/EP) UAE 100002 (soundtrack) mono

Music, lyrics: Hubert Rostaing, Andre Hodeir

Cast: Christine Legrand (for Brigette Bardot)

Songs: Paris B B (Legrand)
        Un Peu de Toi (Legrand)
        La Parisienne (Legrand)
        Duo du Balcon (Legrand)

PENNIES FROM HEAVEN (Columbia, 1936)

Decca DL 4251 mono 'Bing's Hollywood - Pennies from Heaven'

Music: Arthur Johnston; lyrics: John Burke; musical direction:
Georgie Stoll

Cast: Bing Crosby

Songs: Pennies from Heaven (Crosby)
       Let's Call A Heart A Heart (Crosby)
       One, Two, Button Your Shoe (Crosby)
       So Do I (Crosby)

Note: Additional studio recordings (Frances Langford not in film):

Decca (78rpm) 949   Skeleton in the Closet (Louis Armstrong)
Decca (78rpm) 15027 Pennies from Heaven (Crosby, Langford,
                        Armstrong)
                    Let's Call A Heart A Heart (Langford)
                    So Do I (Crosby, Langford)
                    Skeletonin the Closet (Armstrong)

PEPE (Columbia, 1960)

Colpix P 507 (soundtrack) stereo

Music: Andre Previn, others; lyrics: Dory Langdon, others;
musical direction: Andre Previn, others

Cast: Cantinflas, Maurice Chevalier, Bing Crosby, Bobby Darin,
       Sammy Davis, Jr, (the voice of) Judy Garland, Shirley
       Jones

Songs: Pepe (Cantinflas, Jones, chorus) music: Hans Wittstatt
       Mimi (Chevalier) music: Richard Rodgers; lyrics: Lorenz
          Hart
       September Song (Chevalier) music: Kurt Weill; lyrics:
          Maxwell Anderson
       Hooray for Hollywood (Davis) music: Richard Whiting;
          lyrics: Johnny Mercer
---   The Rumble (orchestra)
       That's How It Went, All Right (Darin)
       The Far Away Part of Town (Garland)
       Suzy's Theme (orchestra) music: Johnny Green
       Medley: Pennies from Heaven (Crosby) music: Arthur Johnston;
                  lyrics: John Burke
               Let's Fall in Love (Crosby) music: Harold Arlen;
                  lyrics: Ted Koehler
               South of the Border (Crosby, Cantinflas) music:
                  Michael Carr; lyrics: Jimmy Kennedy
       Lovely Day (Jones) music: Maria Teresa Lara

PERILS OF PAULINE (Paramount, 1947)

Capitol 1565501 mono 'Betty Hutton'

Music, lyrics: Frank Loesser; musical direction: Joseph J Lilley

Cast: Betty Hutton

Songs: Poppa Don't Preach to Me (Hutton) Capitol (78rpm) 380
        Rumble, Rumble, Rumble (Hutton) Capitol (78rpm) 380
        I Wish I Didn't Love You So (Hutton) Capitol (78rpm) 409
        The Sewing Machine (Hutton) Capitol (78rpm) 409

PETE KELLY'S BLUES (Warner Bros, 1955)

Decca DL 8166 mono   reissued: Jasmine 1024

Music, lyrics: various; musical direction: Harold Mooney

Cast: Ella Fitzgerald, Peggy Lee

Songs: Oh Didn't He Ramble (Lee, chorus) music, lyrics: Will
            Handy
        Sugar (That Sugar Baby of Mine) (Lee) music, lyrics:
            Maceo Pinkard, Sidney Mitchell, Edna Alexander
        Somebody Loves Me (Lee) music: George Gershwin;
            lyrics: Ballard MacDonald, Buddy DeSylva
        I'm Gonna Meet My Sweetie Now (Lee) music: Jesse Greer;
            lyrics: Benny Davis
        I Never Knew (Lee) music: Ted Fio Rito; lyrics: Gus Kahn
        Bye, Bye, Blackbird (Lee) music: Ray Henderson; lyrics:
---   Mort Dixon
        What Can I Say After I Say I'm Sorry (Lee) music: Walter
            Donaldson; lyrics: Abe Lyman
        Hard Hearted Hannah (The Vamp of Savannah) (Fitzgerald)
            music: Milton Ager; lyrics: Jack Yellen, Bob Bigelow,
            Charles Bates
        Ella Hums the Blues (Fitzgerald) music: Ray Heindorf
        He Needs Me (Lee) music, lyrics: Arthur Hamilton
        Sing A Rainbow (Lee) music, lyrics: Arthur Hamilton
        Pete Kelly's Blues (Fitzgerald) music: Ray Heindorf;
            lyrics: Sammy Cahn

Note: Soundtrack selections included on WB 3XX2736 'Fifty
        Years of Film Music'

        He Needs Me (Lee)
        Sugar (Lee)

PETER PAN (Disney, 1953)

Disneyland 1206 (soundtrack) mono

Music: Sammy Fain, others; lyrics: Sammy Cahn, others; musical
direction: Ed Plumb

Cast: (the voices of) Kathryn Beaumont, Henry Calvin (not from
        film), Candy Candido, Hans Conried, Jimmie Dodd (not
        from film), Bobby Driscoll, Bill Thompson

Songs: Main Title (chorus)
        Second Star to the Right (chorus)
        You Can Fly! You Can Fly! You Can Fly! (Driscoll, Beaumont,
            children)
        A Pirate's Life (Thompson) music, lyrics: Ed Penner,
            Oliver Wallace
        Following the Leader (chorus) music, lyrics: Winston
            Hibler, Ted Sears, Oliver Wallace
___   What Makes the Red Man Red? (Candido, chorus)
        Your Mother and Mine (Beaumont)
        The Elegant Captain Hook (Conried, chorus)
        Finale: You Can Fly! You Can Fly! You Can Fly! (chorus)

Note: Additional non-soundtrack selections included on the
        above album:

        Following the Leader (Dodd, chorus)
        Never Smile At A Crocodile (Calvin) music: Frank Churchill;
            lyrics: Jack Lawrence
        You Can Fly! You Can Fly! You Can Fly! (chorus)
        Your Mother and Mine (Dodd)

PETE'S DRAGON (Disney, 1977)

Capitol EMI SW 11704 (soundtrack) stereo

Music, lyrics: Al Kasha, Joel Hirschhorn; musical direction:
Irwin Kostal

Cast: Red Buttons, Charlie Callas, Jeff Conaway, Jim Dale,
        Sean Marshall, Gary Morgan, Helen Reddy, Mickey Rooney,
        Charles Tyner, Shelley Winters

Songs: Main Title (orchestra)
        Candle on the Water (Reddy)
        I Saw A Dragon (Reddy, Rooney, chorus)
        It's Not Easy (Reddy, Marshall)
        Every Little Piece (Buttons, Dale)
        The Happiest Home in These Hills (Winters, Tyner, Morgan,

___   Conaway)
   Brazzle Dazzle Day (Reddy, Rooney, Marshall)
   Boo Bop Bopbop Bop (I Love You, Too) (Marshall, Callas)
   There's Room for Everyone (Reddy, Marshall, children)
   Passamashloddy (Dale, Buttons, chorus)
   Bill of Sale (Reddy, Winters, Tyner, Morgan, Conaway)
   Candle on the Water (reprise) (Reddy)

THE PHANTOM OF THE OPERA (Universal, 1943)

Sountrak STK 114 (soundtrack - two records) mono

Music: Edward Ward, others; lyrics: George Waggner, others;
musical direction: Edward Ward

Cast: Nelson Eddy, Susanna Foster

Songs: Lullaby of the Bells (Foster, Eddy)

Note: In addition to the above song, which is sung as a solo by
   Miss Foster, as well as with Mr. Eddy, numerous operatic
   sequences are included in this film, including scenes from
   'Martha' (Von Flotow), excerpts from Acts III and IV.
   Other sequences are based on music by Chopin and Tchaikovsky.
   The above recording is the complete film soundtrack, with
   all dialog.

PHANTOM OF THE PARADISE (Twentieth Century-Fox, 1974)

A & M SP 3653 (soundtrack) stereo

Music, lyrics: Paul Williams; musical direction: Paul Williams

Cast: Jeffrey Comanor, Bill Finley, Archie Hahn, Jessica Harper,
   Ray Kennedy, Harold Oblong, Paul Williams

Songs: Goodbye, Eddie, Goodbye (Hahn, group)
   Faust (Finley)
   Upholstery (Comanor, group)
   Special to Me (Phoenix Audition Song) (Harper)
___ Phantom's Theme (Beauty and the Beast) (Williams)
   Somebody Super Like You (Beef Construction Song)
    (Oblong, group)
   Life at Last (Kennedy)
   Old Souls (Harper)
   Faust (reprise) (Williams)
   The Hell of It (Williams)

PIGSKIN PARADE (Twentieth Century-Fox, 1936)

AEI 2108 (soundtrack) mono 'Judy Garland: Born in A Trunk'

Music: Lew Pollack; lyrics: Sidney D Mitchell; musical direction: David Buttolph

Cast: Johnny Downs, Judy Garland, Betty Grable

Songs: It's Love I'm After (Garland)
       Texas Tornado (Garland)
       The Balboa (Garland, Grable, Downs, chorus)

Note: Studio recordings by Tony Martin:

Decca (78rpm) 957 It's Love I'm After
                  You're Slightly Terrific

PINOCCHIO (Disney, 1940)

Disneyland 4002 (soundtrack) mono

Music for songs: Leigh Harline; lyrics: Ned Washington; background score: Paul J Smith; musical direction: Leigh Harline, Paul J Smith

Cast: (the voices of) Walter Cantlett, Cliff Edwards, Dickie Jones

Songs: When You Wish Upon A Star (Edwards, chorus)
       Cricket Theme - Little Wooden Head (orchestra)
       The Blue Fairy Arrives - When You Wish Upon A Star
          (reprise) (orchestra)
---   Give A Little Whistle (Edwards, Jones)
       Pinocchio Goes to School - The Village Awakens (orchestra)
       Hi-Diddle-Dee-Dee (Cantlett)
       I've Got No Strings (Jones, girls)
       Hi-Diddle-Dee-Dee (reprise) (Cantlett)
       The Whale Chase (orchestra)
       Turn On the Old Music Box (orchestra)
       When You Wish Upon A Star (reprise) (Edwards, chorus)

Note: At the time of this film's release, Victor Records issued
        an 'RCA Photophone' album 'made right from the movie
        sound track.' Album P-18:

        Victor (78rpm) 26477 When You Wish Upon A Star
                              Little Wooden Head
        Victor (78rpm) 26478 Give A Little Whistle
                              Hi-Diddle-Dee-Dee

Victor (78rpm) 26479 I've Got No Strings
                      Turn On the Old Music Box

Decca Records also issued an album of songs from this
film with Cliff Edwards (LP: 5151); musical direction:
Victor Young

Decca (78rpm) 3000 I've Got No Strings
                    When You Wish Upon A Star (Edwards)
Decca (78rpm) 3001 Little Wooden Head
                    Turn On the Old Music Box
Decca (78rpm) 3002 Three Cheers for Anything
                    Jimmy Cricket (Edwards)
Decca (78rpm) 3003 Hi-Diddle-Dee-Dee
                    Give A Little Whislte (Edwards)

THE PIRATE (MGM, 1948)

MGM E 21 (soundtrack) mono reissued: MCA 39080 CD

Music, lyrics: Cole Porter; musical direction: Lennie Hayton

Cast: Judy Garland, Gene Kelly

Songs: Mack the Black (Garland, chorus)
       Nina (Kelly)
       Love of My Life (Garland)
       Pirate Ballet (orchestra)
       You Can Do No Wrong (Garland)
       Be A Clown (Garland, Kelly)

Note: An additional soundtrack selection, cut from the final
       film, was issued on Out Takes OTF -1:

       Voodoo (Garland)

THE PIRATE MOVIE (Twentieth Century-Fox, 1982)

Polydor PD 2-9503 (two records - soundtrack) stereo

Music: Arthur Sullivan, others; lyrics: W S Gilbert, others;
musical direction: Peter Sullivan, others

Cast: Christopher Atkins, Peter Cuppies Band, Ted Hamilton,
       Bill Kerr, Kool and the Gang, Garry McDonald, Kristy
       McNichol, Ian Mason

Songs: Victory (men) music, lyrics: Terry Britten

First Love (McNichol, Atkins) music, lyrics: Kit Hain
How Can I Live Without Her (Atkins) music, lyrics: Terry
    Britten, Sue Shifrin
Hold On (McNichol) music, lyrics: Terry Britten, Sue
    Shifrin
--- We Are the Pirates (Mason, men) music, lyrics: Kit Hain
Pumpin' and Blowin' (McNichol, men) music, lyrics: Terry
    Britten, B A Robertson, Sue Shifrin
Stand Up and Sing (Kool and the Gang) music, lyrics:
    Ronald Bell, James Taylor
Happy Endings (Peter Cuppies Band) music, lyrics: Terry
    Britten, B A Robertson, Sue Shifrin
The Chase (orchestra) music: Peter Sullivan
--- (The Pirate Movie) I Am A Pirate King (Hamilton, men)
Happy Ending (reprise) (cast)
The Chinese Battle (orchestra) music: Peter Sullivan,
    Terry Britten
(The Pirate Movie) The Modern Major General's Song
    (Kerr, cast)
We Are the Pirates (reprise) (Hamilton, men)
--- Medley (orchestra) arr: Peter Sullivan
(The Pirate Movie) Tarantara (McDonald, men)
The Duel (orchestra) music: Peter Sullivan, Terry Britten
The Sisters' Song (girls)
Pirates, Police and Pizza (orchestra) music: Peter
    Sullivan, Terry Britten
Come Friends Who Plough the Sea (Hamilton, men)

Note: Modern lyrics to the Gilbert and Sullivan songs by
       Trevor Farrant.

THE PLEASURE SEEKERS (Twentieth Century-Fox, 1965)

RCA LSO 1101 (soundtrack) stereo

Music for songs: James Van Heusen; lyrics: Sammy Cahn; background
score, musical direction: Lionel Newman

Cast: Ann-Margret

Songs: Madrid (orchestra)
       The Pleasure Seekers (Ann-Margret)
       Blue Moon Cha-Cha (orchestra)
       Next Time (Ann-Margret)
       Romantic Bossa Nova (orchestra)
       Tender Moment (orchestra)
       The Pleasure Seekers Bossa Nova (orchestra)
   --- Zig-A-Dig-A-Ding-Boom-Bah (orchestra)
       Adiocita (orchestra)

       Something to Think About (Ann-Margret)
       The Terrace (orchestra)
       Costa del Sol (orchestra)
       Everything Makes Music When You're in Love (Ann-Margret,
          chorus)
       Prado Museum (orchestra)
       End Title (The Pleasure Seekers) (orchestra)

POLLYANNA (Disney, 1960)

Disneyland ST 1906 (soundtrack) stereo

Music, lyrics: various

Cast: Hayley Mills

Songs: Pollyanna's Song (Mills) music: Paul Smith; lyrics:
       David Swift
      America the Beautiful (Mills, chorus) music: Samuel A
       Ward; lyrics: Katharine L Bates
      Pollyanna (The Glad Game) (chorus) music: Paul Smith;
       lyrics: Gil George

Note: The above recording consists primarily of spoken dialog.

POOR LITTLE RICH GIRL (Twentieth Century-Fox, 1936)

Fox 3006, 3045 (soundtrack) mono 'Little Miss Wonderful, vol I
and vol II'

Music: Harry Revel; lyrics: Mack Gordon; musical direction:
Louis Silvers

Cast: Alice Faye, Jack Haley, Shirley Temple

Songs: When I'm with You (Temple)
      Oh, My Goodness (Temple)
      You Gotta Eat Your Spinach, Baby (Faye, Haley, Temple)
      But Definately (Temple, chorus)
      Where There's Life There's Soap (Temple)

Note: Additional soundtrack selection:

       When I'm with You (Alice Faye) LP: Curtain Calls 100/3

POPEYE (Disney / Paramount, 1980)

Boardwalk Records SW 36880 (soundtrack) stereo

Music, lyrics: Harry Nilsson; musical direction: Van Dyke Parks

Cast: Shelley Duvall, Robert Fortier, Paul L Smith, Ray Walston
       Robin Williams

Songs: I Yam What I Yam (Williams, chorus)
       He Needs Me (Duvall)
       Swee'pea's Lullaby (Williams)
       Din'we (Fortier)
       Sweethaven (chorus)
___   Blow Me Down (Williams, chorus)
       Sailin' (Williams, Duvall)
       It's Not Easy Being Me (Walston, Smith)
       He's Large (Duvall, chorus)
       I'm Mean (Smith, chorus)
       Kids (Walston)
       I'm Popeye the Sailor Man (Williams, chorus) music, lyrics:
          Sam Lerner

PORGY AND BESS (Goldwyn, 1959)

Columbia OS 2016 (soundtrack) stereo

Music: George Gershwin; lyrics: DuBose Heyward, Ira Gershwin;
musical direction: Andre Previn

Cast: Adele Addison (for Dorothy Dandridge), Pearl Bailey, Cab
       Calloway (not in film), Robert McFerrin (for Sidney Poitier),
       Inez Matthews (for Ruth Attaway), Loulie Jean Norman (for
       Diahann Carroll), Brock Peters, Leslie Scott, Merritt
       Smith, Helen Thigpen

Songs: Overture (orchestra)
       Summertime (Norman)
       A Woman Is A Sometime Thing (Scott)
       The Wake: Gone, Gone, Gone (chorus)
                 Porgy's Prayer (McFerrin)
       My Man's Gone Now (Matthews)
       I Got Plenty o' Nuttin' (McFerrin, chorus)
       Bess, You Is My Woman Now (McFerrin, Addison)
___   Morning (chorus)
       I Can't Sit Down (Bailey, chorus)
       It Ain't Necessarily So (Calloway, chorus)
       I Ain't Got No Shame (chorus)
       What You Want with Bess? (Addison, Peters)
       Strawberry Woman (Thigpen)
       Crab Man (Smith)

       I Loves You, Porgy (Addison, McFerrin)
       A Red Headed Woman (Peters, chorus)
       Clara, Clara (female chorus)
       There's A Boat That's Leavin' Soon for New York (Calloway)
       Oh, Where's My Bess (McFerrin)
       I'm On My Way (McFerrin, chorus)

Note: Additional albums recorded by cast members:

       Pearl Bailey (Roulette R 25063)
       Sammy Davis, Jr (Decca DL 78854)

PRESENTING LILY MARS (MGM, 1943)

Sountrak STK 117 (two records - soundtrack) mono

Music: Walter Jurmann, others; lyrics: Paul Francis Webster, others; musical direction: George Stoll

Cast: Bob Crosby, Martha Eggerth, Judy Garland, Connie Gilchrist

Songs: Main Titles (orchestra)
       Is It Love (or the Gypsy in Me?) (Eggerth)
       Tom, Tom the Piper's Son (Garland) music: Burton Lane;
          lyrics: E Y Harburg
       Every Little Movement (Gilchrist, Garland) music: Jimmy
          McHugh; lyrics: Karl Hoschna
       Love Is Everywhere (female chorus)
       Think of Me (Crosby, chorus)
       When I Look at You (and reprise) (Garland)
       A Russian Rhapsody (Eggerth, chorus)
       Where There's Music (Garland, chorus) music, lyrics:
          Roger Edens
       Medley: Three O'Clock in the Morning (Garland, chorus)
             music: Julian Robledo; lyrics: Dorothy Terriss
           Broadway Rhythm (Garland, chorus) music: Nacio
             Herb Brown; lyrics: Arthur Freed
       End Credits (orchestra)

Note: The above recording is the complete soundtrack, with all
      the dialog. Additional numbers from the medley which
      were cut from the final film were issued on Out Takes
      OTF - 2:

       St Louis Blues (Garland)
       It's A Long Way to Tipperary (Garland, chorus)
       In the Shade of the Old Apple Tree (Garland)
       Don't Sit Under the Apple Tree (male vocal)

PRINCESS CHARMING (Gaumont-British, 1934)

Music for Pleasure (British) MFP 1162 mono 'The Entrancing
Evelyn Laye'

Music: Ray Noble; lyrics: Max Kester; musical direction: Ray
Noble

Cast: Evelyn Laye

Songs: The Princess's Awakening (Laye)
       Near and Yet So Far (Laye)
       Love Is A Song (Laye)

Note: Additional studio recording:

       HMV (78rpm) B-8136 Brave Hearts (Laye)

PRIVILEGE (Universal, 1967)

Uni 73005 (soundtrack) stereo

Music: Mike Leander; lyrics: Mark London; musical direction:
MIke Leander

Cast: George Bean, Paul Jones

Songs: Privilege (Jones, chorus)
       Stephen (orchestra)
       Vanessa (orchestra)
       Free Me (Jones, chorus)
       It's Overotherness Time (orchestra)
  ___ Free Me (reprise) (Jones, chorus)
       I've Been A Bad, Bad Boy (Jones, chorus)
       Onward Christian Soldiers (Bean, chorus) trad
       I'm Alright Jackboot (orchestra)
       Alvin (orchestra)
       Jerusalem (Bean)
       Birmingham, Oh Birmingham (orchestra)

THE PRODUCERS (Embassy, 1968)

RCA LSP 4008 (soundtrack) stereo

Music: John Morris, others; lyrics: Mel Brooks, others;
musical direction: John Morris

Cast: Michael Davis, Dick Shawn

Songs: Titles (orchestra)
        The Producers (orchestra)
        Love Power (Shawn) music:Norman Blagman; lyrics: Herb
           Hartig
        Springtime for Hitler (Davis, chorus) music, lyrics:
           Mel Brooks
        Prisoners of Love (chorus) music, lyrics: Mel Brooks

Note: This album consists primarily of spoken dialog, with
        Zero Mostel, Gene Wilder, and other members of the cast.

PUFNSTUF (Universal, 1970)

Capitol SW 542 (soundtrack) stereo

Music, lyrics: Charles Fox, Norman Gimbel

Cast: Mama Cass, Billie Hayes, Martha Raye, Jack Wild

Songs: If I Could (Wild)
        Fire in the Castle (orchestra)
        Living Island (Wild, cast)
        Witchiepoo's Lament (orchestra)
        Angel Raid (orchestra)
        A Friend in You (Wild)
        How Lucky I Am (orchestra)
---   Pufnstuf (Wild)
        Charge (orchestra)
        Different (Cass)
        Zap the World (Wild, Hayes, Raye)
        Leaving Living Island (orchestra)
        Rescue Racer to the Rescue (orchestra)
        Finale: If I Could (Wild)
                Living Island (Wild, cast)

PURPLE RAIN (Warner Bros, 1984)

Warner Bros 1-25110 stereo CD

Music, lyrics: Prince

Cast: Apollonia Kotero, Prince (and the Revolution)

Songs: Let's Go Crazy (Prince)
        Take Me with U (Kotero, Prince)
        The Beautiful Ones (Prince)
        Computer Blue (Prince)
        Darling Nikki (Prince)

--- When Doves Cry (Prince)
I Would Die 4 U (Prince)
Baby I'm A Star (Prince)
Purple Rain (Prince)

RACHEL AND THE STRANGER (RKO, 1948)

Decca (78rpm) 695 mono

Music: Roy Webb; lyrics: Waldo Scott

Cast: Gary Gray, Robert Mitchum

Decca (78rpm) 24484 Oh He-Oh Hi-Oh Ho (Mitchum) LP: AH 68
                    Summer Song (Mitchum)
Decca (78rpm) 24485 Just Like Me (Mitchum, Gray)
                    Foolish Pride (Mitchum) LP: COPS 7683/1-2
Decca (78rpm) 24486 (Along Came A) Tall Dark Stranger (Mitchum)
                    Rachel (Mitchum) LP: AH 68

RAGGEDY ANN AND ANDY (Twentieth Century-Fox, 1977)

Columbia 34686 (soundtrack) stereo

Music, lyrics, musical direction: Joe Raposo

Cast: (the voices of) Mark Baker, Marty Brill, Didi Conn, Paul
       Dooley, Niki Flacks, Margery Gray, George S Irving, Joe
       Silver, Lynne Stuart, Fred Stuthman, Alan Sues

Songs: Main Title - Rag Dolly (orchestra)
       Where'd You Go? (Gray, Stuart)
       I Look and What Do I See (Conn, dolls)
       I'm No Girl's Toy (Baker, dolls)
       Rag Dolly (Conn, Baker, dolls)
       Poor Babette (Flacks)
       A Miracle (Irving, parrot)
       The Abduction and Ho-Yo (Irving, parrot, pirates)
       Candy Hearts (Conn, Baker)
---   Blue (Stuthman)
       Camel's Mirage (Stuthman, chorus)
       I Never Get Enough (Silver)
       I Love You (Sues)
       Hail to Our Glorious King (chorus)
       It's Not Easy Being King (Brill)
       Hooray for Me (Flacks, pirates)
       You're My Friend (Irving, parrot)
       The Plot Thickens (Dooley, cast)
       The Tickling (cast)

        The Last Laugh (cast)
        Home (Conn, Baker, Stuthman, cast)

Note: The above recording includes spoken dialog.

RAINBOW 'ROUND MY SHOULDER (Columbia, 1952)

Columbia (45/EP) B 1512 mono

Music, lyrics: various; musical direction: Paul Weston

Cast: Frankie Laine

Songs: Wonderful, Wasn't It? (Laine) music: Don Rodney; lyrics:
            Hal David
        The Girl in the Wood (Laine, chorus) music, lyrics:
            Terry Gilkyson, Neal Stuart
        She's Funny That Way (Laine) music, lyrics: Richard
            Whiting, Neil Moret
        There's A Rainbow 'Round My Shoulder (Laine) music,
            lyrics: Dave Dryer, Billy Rose, Al Jolson

REBECCA OF SUNNYBROOK FARM (Twentieth Century-Fox, 1938)

Fox 103-2 (two records - soundtrack) mono 'The Complete Shirley
Temple Songbook'

Music, lyrics: various; musical direction: Arthur Lange

Cast: Shirley Temple

Songs: Come and Get Your Happiness (Temple) music: Samuel
            Pokrass; lyrics: Jack Yellen
        An Old Straw Hat (Temple) music: Harry Revel; lyrics:
            Mack Gordon
        Happy Ending (Temple) music: Lew Pollock; lyrics: Sidney
            Mitchell

RED AND BLUE (United Artists, 1967)

UA (British) SULP 1184 stereo

Music: Cyrus Bassiak; English lyrics: Julian More; musical
direction: Stanley Black

Cast: Vanessa Redgrave

Songs: Red and Blue (Redgrave)
        Nothing Words (Redgrave)

Evening Star (Redgrave) not from film
Our Night Ferry (Redgrave)
My Life Is Over (Redgrave)
Jo le Rouge (Redgrave) not from film
We Dreamed On (Redgrave) not from film
Once I Had A Friend (Redgrave)
Pink Angora (Redgrave)
Paris-Orly (Redgrave)

RED GARTERS (Paramount, 1954)

Columbia CL 6282 mono

Music, lyrics: Jay Livingston, Ray Evans; musical direction:
Joseph J Lilley, others

Cast: Rosemary Clooney, Joanne Gilbert, Guy Mitchell

Songs: Red Garters (Clooney, chorus)
       A Dime and A Dozen (Mitchell, chorus) musical direction:
          Mitch Miller
       Brave Man (Clooney, chorus) musical direction: Percy Faith
       This Is Greater Than I Thought (Gilbert)
       Good Intentions (Clooney) musical direction: Percy Faith
       Meet A Happy Guy (Mitchell) musical direction: Mitch
          Miller
       Bad News (Clooney)
       Man and Woman (Clooney, Mitchell)

RED, HOT AND BLUE (Paramount, 1949)

Vedette 8702 mono 'Hutton in Hollywood' also: AEI 2120

Music, lyrics: Frank Loesser

Cast: Betty Hutton

Songs: That's Loyalty (Hutton)
       Hamlet (Hutton)
       I Wake Up in the Morning Feeling Fine (Hutton)
       (Where Are You) Now That I Need You (Hutton. chorus)

THE RESCUERS (Disney, 1977)

Disney 3816 (soundtrack) stereo

Music, lyrics: Carol Connors, Ayn Robbins, others; musical
direction: Artie Butler

Cast: (the voice of) Shelby Flint

Songs: The Journey (Flint)
      Rescue Aid Society (Flint)
      Tomorrow Is Another Day (Flint)
      Someone's Waiting for You (Flint) music, lyrics:
        Sammy Fain, Carol Connor, Ayn Robbins
      The U S Air Force

REVEILLE WITH BEVERLY (Columbia, 1943)

Hollywood Soundstage 5014 (soundtrack) mono

Music, lyrics: various; musical direction: Morris Stoloff

Cast: Count Basie Orchestra, Bob Crosby, Duke Ellington
       Orchestra, Ann Miller, The Mills Brothers, Ella Mae
       Morse, The Radio Rogues, Frank Sinatra, Freddie Slack
       Orchestra

Songs: Opening Credits (orchestra)
      One O'Clock Jump (Basie Orchestra) music: Count Basie
      Big Noise from Winnetka (Crosby) music, lyrics: Bob Crosby,
        Gil Rodin, Ray Bauduc, Bob Haggart
      Take the 'A' Train (Ellington Orchestra, female vocal,
        chorus) music, lyrics: Billy Strayhorn
      Night and Day (Sinatra) music, lyrics: Cole Porter
      Cow-Cow Boogie (Morse, Slack Orchestra) music: Gene
        de Paul; lyrics: Don Raye
      Sweet Lucy Brown (The Mills Brothers)
      Comedy and Impressions (Radio Rogues)
      V for Victory (Miller, chorus)

Note: The above recording includes spoken dialog. Studio
      recordings by cast members:

Decca (78rpm) 1363 One O'Clock Jump (Basie Orchestra)
Decca (78rpm) 2208 Big Noise from Winnetka (Crosby Orchestra)
Victor (78rpm) 27380 Take the 'A' Train (Ellington Orchestra)
Capitol (78rpm) 102 Cow-Cow Boogie (Morse, Slack Orchestra)
Bluebird (78rpm) 11463 Night and Day (Sinatra)

RHAPSODY IN BLUE (Warner Bros, 1945)

Warner Bros 3XX 2736 (soundtrack) mono 'Fifty Years of Film Music'

Music: George Gershwin; lyrics: Ira Gershwin, others; musical
direction: Ray Heindorf

Cast: Al Jolson, Oscar Levant (piano), Hazel Scott, Paul
        Whiteman Orchestra

Songs: Swanee (Jolson) lyrics: Irving Caesar

Note: An additional soundtrack selection was issued on:

V-Disc (78rpm) 517A Gershwin Piano Concerto (First and Third
                    Movements) (Levant, Whiteman Orchestra)

        Studio recordings by Hazel Scott:

        Decca (78rpm) 23429 The Man I Love
                            Fascinating Rhythm

RHINESTONE (Twentieth Century-Fox, 1984)

RCA ABL 1-5082 (partial soundtrack) stereo   CD

Music, lyrics: Dolly Parton, others; musical direction:
Mike Post

Cast: Rusty Buchanan, Dolly Parton, Floyd Parton, Randy Parton,
        Stella Parton, Sylvester Stallone, Kin Vassy

Songs: Tennessee Homesick Blues (Dolly Parton, chorus)
        Too Much Water (Randy Parton, chorus)
        The Day My Baby Died (Buchanan) music: Mike Post;
            lyrics: Phil Alden Robinson
        One Emotion After Another (Dolly Parton, chorus)
        Goin' Back to Heaven (Stella Parton, Vassy)
        What A Heartache (Dolly Parton, chorus)
 ___   Stay Out of My Bedroom (Stallone, Dolly Parton)
        Woke Up in Love (Dolly Parton, Stallone)
        God Won't Get You (Dolly Parton, chorus)
        Drinkin'stein (Stallone)
        Sweet Lovin' Friends (Dolly Parton, Stallone)
        Waltz Me to Heaven (Floyd Parton, chorus)
        Butterflies (Dolly Parton, chorus)
        Be There (Dolly Parton, Stallone, chorus)

RHYTHM ON THE RANGE (Paramount, 1936)

Decca DL 4251 mono 'Bing's Hollywood - Pennies from Heaven'

Music, lyrics: various; musical direction: Victor Young, others

Cast: Bing Crosby

Songs: Empty Saddles (Crosby) music, lyrics: Billy Hill
        I'm An Old Cowhand (from the Rio Grande) (Crosby) music,
            lyrics: Johnny Mercer; musical direction: Jimmy Dorsey
        Roundup Lullaby (Crosby) music: Gertrude Ross; lyrics:
---   Badger Clark
        I Can't Escape from You (Crosby) music: Richard A Whiting;
            lyrics: Leo Robin; musical direction: Jimmy Dorsey
        The House Jack Built for Jill (Crosby) music: Frederick
            Hollander; lyrics: Leo Robin; musical direction:
            Jimmy Dorsey

Note: Additional soundtrack selections:

        The House Jack Built for Jill (Crosby, Frances Farmer) LP:
            Out-Takes OTF-2
        (If You Can't Sing It) You'll Have to Swing It (Martha
            Raye) LP: Legends 1000/5-6 'Martha Raye'

RHYTHM ON THE RIVER (Paramount, 1940)

Decca DL 4255 mono 'Bing's Hollywood - Only Forever'

Music: James V Monaco; lyrics: John Burke; musical direction:
John Scott Trotter

Cast: Bing Crosby

Songs: Only Forever (Crosby)
        That's for Me (Crosby)
        Rhythm on the River (Crosby)
        When the Moon Comes Over Madison Square (or The Love
            Lament of A Western Gent) (Crosby)

Note: Studio recordings by Mary Martin:

Decca (78rpm) 23164 Ain't It A Shame About Mame
                    I Don't Want to Cry Anymore

RICH, YOUNG AND PRETTY (MGM, 1951)

MGM E 86 (soundtrack) mono   reissued: MCA 39079 CD

Music: Nicholas Brodszky, others; lyrics: Sammy Cahn, others;
musical direction: David Rose

Cast: Vic Damone, Danielle Darrieux, Fernando Lamas, Jane
        Powell

Songs: Wonder Why (Powell)
        L'Amour Toujours (Darrieux)

Dark Is the Night (C'est Fini) (Powell)
Paris (Lamas)
——— I Can See You (Powell)
We Never Talk Much (Darrieux, Lamas)
My Little Nest of Heavenly Blue (Powell) music: Franz
    Lehar; lyrics: Sigmund Spaeth
There's Danger in Your Eyes, Cherie (Darrieux) music,
    lyrics: Pete Wendling, Harry Richman, Jack Meskill

Note: Additional soundtrack recordings (both on Curtain Calls
       LP: CC 100/4 'Jane Powell'):

       The Old Piano Roll Blues (Powell, Damone)
       How Do You Like Your Eggs in the Morning? (Powell,
           Damone, chorus)

       Studio recordings by cast members:

Mercury (78rpm) 5669 Wonder Why (Damone)
                     I Can See You (Damone)
Mercury (78rpm) 5670 How D'Ya Like Your Eggs in the Morning?
                        (Damone)
MGM (45rpm) K 30383 We Never Talk Much (Powell, chorus)
                     L'Amour Toujours (Powell)

RIDING HIGH (Paramount, 1943)

Legends 1000/4 (soundtrack) mono 'Dorothy Lamour'

Music: Ralph Rainger, others; lyrics: Leo Robin; musical
direction: Victor Young

Cast: Cass Daley, Dorothy Lamour

Songs: Get Your Man (Lamour)
       Injun Gal Heap Hep (Lamour, chorus) additional music:
           Joseph J Lilley
       I'm the Secretary to the Sultan (Lamour)
       Whistling in the Light (Lamour, Daley)

RIDING HIGH (Paramount, 1950)

Decca DL 4261 mono 'Bing's Hollywood - Sunshine Cake'

Music: James Van Heusen; lyrics: John Burke; musical direction:
Victor Young

Cast: Bing Crosby, Carole Richards (not in film)

Songs: Sunshine Cake (Crosby, Richards, chorus)

> (We've Got) A Sure Thing (Crosby, chorus)
> The Horse Told Me (Crosby, chorus)
> Someplace on Anywhere Road (Crosby, chorus)

RIVER OF NO RETURN (Twentieth Century-Fox, 1954)

Fox FXG 5000 (soundtrack) mono 'Marilyn'

Music: Lionel Newman; lyrics: Ken Darby; musical direction: Lionel Newman

Cast: Marilyn Monroe

Songs: One Silver Dollar (Monroe)
       I'm Gonna File My Claim (Monroe)
       River of No Return (Monroe, chorus)

Note: The above recording includes a narration by Rock Hudson. Additional soundtrack recording:

       Down in the Meadow (Monroe) LP: Legends 1000/1 'Marilyn Monroe'

       Studio recordings by Marilyn Monroe:

       RCA (45rpm) 47-5745 River of No Return
                           I'm Gonna File My Claim

ROAD TO BALI (Paramount, 1953)

Decca DL 4263 mono 'Bing's Hollywood - Zing A Little Zong'

Music: James Van Heusen; lyrics: John Burke; musical direction: various

Cast: Bing Crosby, Bob Hope, Peggy Lee (not in film)

Songs: The Road to Bali (Crosby, Hope, chorus) musical direction: Sonny Burke
       Chicago Style (Crosby, Hope) musical direction: Joseph Lilley
       Hoot Mon (Crosby, Hope, chorus) musical direction: Joseph Lilley
       Merry-Go-Run-Around (Crosby, Lee, Hope) musical direction: Sonny Burke
       To See You (Crosby) musical direction: Axel Stordahl
       Moonflowers (Lee) musical direction: Axel Stordahl

THE ROAD TO HONG KONG (United Artists, 1961)

Liberty 17002 (soundtrack) stereo

Music for songs: James Van Heusen; lyrics for songs: Sammy Cahn;
musical score, direction: Robert Farnon

Cast: Joan Collins, Bing Crosby, Bob Hope, Dorothy Lamour

Songs: Overture (orchestra)
        Let's Not Be Sensible (Crosby, Collins)
        Moon Over Hong Kong (orchestra)
        Team Work (Crosby, Hope)
        The Only Way to Travel (orchestra)
        The Chase (orchestra)
___   Road to Hong Kong (Crosby, Hope)
        Let's Not Be Sensible Blues (orchestra)
        Reluctant Astronauts (orchestra)
        Warmer Than A Whisper (Lamour)
        Lamasery Chant (orchestra)

ROAD TO MOROCCO (Paramount, 1942)

Decca DL 4257 mono 'Bing's Hollywood - Swinging On A Star'

Music: James Van Heusen; lyrics: John Burke; musical direction:
Vic Schoen, others

Cast: Bing Crosby, Bob Hope

Songs: Road to Morocco (Crosby, Hope)
        Moonlight Becomes You (Crosby) musical direction: John
            Scott Trotter
        Ain't Got A Dime to My Name (Ho Ho Ho Ho Hum) (Crosby)
        Constantly (Crosby) musical direction: John Scott Trotter

ROAD TO RIO (Paramount, 1948)

Decca DL 4260 mono 'Bing's Hollywood - But Beautiful'

Music: James Van Heusen; lyrics: John Burke; musical direction:
Vic Schoen

Cast: The Andrews Sisters, Bing Crosby, Nan Wynn (not in film)

Songs: Experience (Crosby, Wynn) musical direction: Victor Young
        Apalachicola, Fla (Crosby, The Andrews Sisters)
        But Beautiful (Crosby) musical direction: Victor Young
        You Don't Have to Know the Language (Crosby, The Andrews
            Sisters)

ROAD TO SINGAPORE (Paramount, 1940)

Decca DL 4254 mono 'Bing's Hollywood - The Road Begins'

Music: James V Monaco, others; lyrics: John Burke; musical direction: John Scott Trotter

Cast: Bing Crosby

Songs: Too Romantic (Crosby)
        Sweet Potato Piper (Crosby, chorus)
        The Moon and the Willow Tree (Crosby) music: Victor
            Schertzinger

Note: Additional studio recordings by Dorothy Lamour:

        Bluebird (78rpm) 10608 Too Romantic
                                The Moon and the Willow

        Bluebird (78rpm) 10651 Sweet Potato Piper

ROAD TO UTOPIA (Paramount, 1946)

Decca DL 4258 mono 'Bing's Hollywood - Accentuate the Positive'

Music: James Van Heusen; lyrics: John Burke; musical direction: John Scott Trotter, others

Cast: Bing Crosby, Bob Hope

Songs: Put It There, Pal (Crosby, Hope) musical direction:
            Vic Schoen
        Would You? (Crosby)
        It's Anybody's Spring (Crosby)
        Welcome to My Dream (Crosby)
        Personality (Crosby) musical direction: Eddie Condon

ROAD TO ZANZIBAR (Paramount, 1941)

Decca DL 4255 mono 'Bing's Hollywood - Only Forever'

Music: James Van Heusen; lyrics:John Burke; musical direction: John Scott Trotter

Cast: Bing Crosby

Songs: Birds of A Feather (Crosby)
        You're Dangerous (Crosby)
        It's Always You (Crosby)
        You Lucky People You (Crosby)

ROBERTA (RKO, 1935)

Classic International Filmusicals C I F 3011 (soundtrack) mono
also: Sandy Hook SH 2061

Music: Jerome Kern; lyrics: Otto Harbach, Dorothy Fields,
others; musical direction: Max Steiner

Cast: Fred Astaire, Candy Candido, Irene Dunne, Ginger Rogers,
       Gene Sheldon

Songs: Main Titles(orchestra):
          Smoke Gets in Your Eyes
          Lovely to Look At
          I Won't Dance
       Back Home Again in Indiana (chorus) music: James F
          Hanley; lyrics: Ballard MacDonald
       Let's Begin (Astaire, Candido, Sheldon) lyrics: Harbach
       Song of Russia (Dunne) trad
       I'll Be Hard to Handle (Rogers, Astaire) lyrics: Bernard
          Dougall
       Yesterdays (Dunne) lyrics: Harbach
       I Won't Dance (Rogers, Astaire) lyrics: Fields, Oscar
          Hammerstein II
       Smoke Gets in Your Eyes (Dunne) lyrics: Harbach (dialog
          with Dunne, Randolph Scott)
       Fashion Show (Astaire) lyrics: Fields
       Lovely to Look At (Dunne, chorus, Astaire, Rogers)
          lyrics: Fields
       Smoke Gets in Your Eyes (reprise) (orchestra)
       Finale: I Won't Dance (orchestra)

Note: The above recording includes spoken dialog. Studio
       recording by Irene Dunne:

Brunswick (78rpm) 7420   Lovely to Look At (LP: Epic SN 6059)

ROBIN AND THE SEVEN HOODS (Warner Bros, 1964)

Reprise 2021 stereo

Music: James Van Heusen; lyrics: Sammy Cahn; musical direction:
Nelson Riddle

Cast: Bing Crosby, Sammy Davis, Jr, Peter Falk, Dean Martin,
       Frank Sinatra

Songs: Overture: Robin and the Seven Hoods (orchestra)
       My Kind of Town (Sinatra)
       All for One and One for All (Falk, chorus)
       Don't Be A Do-Badder (Crosby, children)

--- Any Man Who Loves His Mother (Martin, male quartet)
Style (Crosby, Sinatra, Martin)
Mister Booze (Crosby, Sinatra, Martin, Davis, chorus)
I Like to Lead When I Dance (Sinatra)
Bang! Bang! (Davis)
Charlotte Couldn't Charleston (female chorus)
Give Praise! Give Praise! Give Praise! (chorus)
Don't Be A Do-Badder (finale) (Crosby, Sinatra, Martin, Davis)

ROCK 'N' ROLL HIGH SCHOOL (New World, 1979)

Sire SRK 6070 (soundtrack) stereo

Music, lyrics: various

Cast: (the sounds of) Chuck Berry, Brownsville Station, Alice Cooper, Devo, Eddie and the Hot Rods, Eno, Nick Lowe, The Paley Brothers. Todd Rundgren; (on screen) The Ramones, P J Soles

Songs: Rock 'n' Roll High School (The Ramones)
I Want You Around (The Ramones)
C'mon Let's Go (Paley Brothers, The Ramones)
Medley (The Ramones):
    Blitzkrieg Bop
    Teenage Lobotomy
    California Sun
    Pinhead
    She's the One
So It Goes (Lowe)
Energy Fools the Magician (Eno)
--- Rock 'n' Roll High School (reprise) (Soles)
Come Back Jonee (Davo)
Teenage Depression (Eddie and the Hot Rods)
Smoking in the Boy's Room (Brownsville Station)
School Days (Berry)
A Dream Goes on Forever (Rundgren)
School's Out (Cooper)

ROCK, PRETTY BABY (Universal, 1957)

Decca DL 8429 (soundtrack) mono reissued: Jasmine JASM 1028

Music: Henry Mancini, others; lyrics: various; musical direction: Joseph Gershenson

Cast: (the voice of) Alan Copeland, Hal Dickinson, The Ding-A-Lings, Rod McKuen

Songs: Rock, Pretty Baby (Copeland) music, lyrics: Sonny Burke
       Dark Blue (orchestra)
       Free and Easy (orchestra)
       What's It Gonna Be (Ding-A-Lings) lyrics: Bill Carey
       Rockin' the Boogie (orchestra)
       Rockabye Lullaby Blues (Dickinson, Ding-A-Lings) music,
           lyrics: Bobby Troup
       Teen Age Bop (orchestra)
___   The Most (orchestra)
       Can I Steal A Little Love (Ding-A-Lings) music, lyrics:
           Phil Tuminello
       Juke Box Rock (orchestra)
       The Saints Rock 'n' Roll (orchestra) arr: Bill Haley,
           Milt Gabler
       Picnic by the Sea (McKuen, Ding-A-Lings) music, lyrics:
           Rod McKuen, Bobby Troup
       Young Love (orchestra)
       Happy Is A Boy Named Me (McKuen) music, lyrics: Rod McKuen
       Hot Rod (orchestra)
       Big Band Rock and Roll (orchestra)

ROCK, ROCK, ROCK (Distributors Corp of America, 1956)

Chess 1425 (soundtrack) mono reissued: Chess/MCA 9254 CD

Music, lyrics: various

Cast: Chuck Berry, The Flamingos, The Moonglows

Songs: I Knew from the Start (The Moonglows)
       Would I Be Crying (The Flamingos)
       Mabellene (Berry)
       Sincerely (The Moonglows)
       Thirty Days (Berry)
___   The Vow (The Flamingos)
       You Can't Catch Me (Berry)
       Over and Over Again (The Moonglows)
       Roll Over Beethoven (Berry)
       I'll Be Home (The Flamingos)
       See Saw (The Moonglows)
       A Kiss from Your Lips (The Flamingos)

THE ROCKY HORROR PICTURE SHOW (Twentieth Century-Fox, 1975)

Ode OSV 21653 (soundtrack) stereo   CD

Music, lyrics: Richard O'Brien; musical direction: Richard Hartley

Cast: Jonathan Adams, Barry Bostwick, Tim Curry, Charles Gray,
       Peter Hinwood, Little Nell, Meatloaf, Richard O'Brien,

      Patricia Quinn, Susan Sarandon

Songs: Science Fiction / Double Feature (O'Brien, chorus)
      Dammit Janet (Bostwick, Sarandon,chorus)
      Over at the Frankenstein Place (Bostwick, Sarandon,
        O'Brien, chorus)
      The Time Warp (O'Brien, Little Nell, Quinn, Gray, Chorus)
      Sweet Transvestite (Curry, chorus) dialog: Bostwick,
        Sarandon
      I Can Make You A Man (Curry, chorus)
      Hot Patootie - Bless My Soul (Meatloaf, chorus)
---   I Can Make You A Man (reprise) (Curry, chorus)
      Touch-A, Touch-A, Touch Me (Sarandon, chorus)
      Eddie (Adams, chorus)
      Rose Tint My World:
        Floor Show (Bostwick, Sarandon, Little Nell, Hinwood)
        Fanfare / Don't Dream It (Curry, chorus)
        Wild and Untamed Thing (Curry, O'Brien, chorus)
      I'm Going Home (Curry, chorus)
      Super Heroes (Bostwick, Sarandon, chorus)
      Science Fiction / Double Feature (reprise) (O'Brien)

THE ROGUE SONG (MGM, 1930)

Pelican LP 2019 (soundtrack) mono

Music: Herbert Stothart, others; lyrics: Clifford Grey; musical
direction: Herbert Stothart

Cast: Oliver Hardy, Ullrich Haupt, Stan Laurel, Catherine
      Dale Owen, Lawrence Tibbett, Judith Vosselli

Songs: Overture (orchestra)
      The Rogue Song (Tibbett, chorus)
      Love Comes Like A Bird on the Wing (Owen, Tibbett,
        Vosselli, chorus) music: Franz Lehar
      Hardy Mounts His Horse (Laurel, Hardy) spoken
      The Narrative (Tibbett)
      The White Dove (Tibbett, Owen) music: Franz Lehar
      Ballet Music (orchestra) music: Dimitri Tiomkin
---   Once in the Georgian Hills (Tibbett)
      Pursuit (orchestra)
      Death of Sergei (Haupt, Tibbett) spoken
      Flight to the Mountains (orchestra)
      When I'm Looking at You (Tibbett)
      Shaving Scene (Laurel, Hardy) spoken
      Cave Scene (Laurel, Hardy) spoken
      Whipping Scene (Tibbett, Owen)
        The Lash
        When I'm Looking at You (reprise)
        The Narrative (reprise)

Death of Yegor (Laurel, Hardy) spoken
Farewell (Tibbett, Owen)
    When I'm Looking at You (reprise)
Finale: The Rogue Song (reprise) (Laurel, Hardy, Tibbett,
            chorus)
Closing Titles (orchestra)

Note: The above recording contains spoken dialog, with Tibbett
        being the only singing cast member. Tibbett also made
        studio recordings of songs from this score:

        Victrola (78rpm) 1446 The Rogue Song (LP: Ariel OSH 14)
                              The Narrative
        Victrola (78rpm) 1447 The White Dove
                              When I'm Looking at You (LP:
                                  Ariel OSH 14)

ROMAN SCANDALS (Goldwyn, 1933)

Classic International Filmusicals C I F 3007 (soundtrack) mono
also: Sandy Hook SH 2039

Music: Harry Warren; lyrics: Al Dubin; musical direction:
Alfred Newman

Cast: Eddie Cantor, Ruth Etting

Songs: Opening Titles (orchestra)
        Build A Little Home (Cantor, chorus)
        No More Love (Etting, chorus)
        Keep Young and Beautiful (Cantor, chorus)
        Don't Put A Tax on Love (Cantor)
        Build A Little Home (reprise) (Cantor, chorus)

Note: Studio recordings by Ruth Etting:

        Brunswick (78rpm) 6697 No More Love
                               Build A Little Home

THE ROSE (Twentieth Century-Fox, 1979)

Atlantic ATC 16010 (soundtrack) stereo   CD

Music, lyrics: various; musical arrangements: Paul A Rothchild

Cast: Bette Midler

Songs: Whose Side Are You On (Midler, chorus) music, lyrics:
            Kenny Hopkins, Charley Williams
        Midnight in Memphis (Midler, group) music, lyrics:
            Tony Johnson

    Concert Monologue (Midler) spoken
    When A Man Loves A Woman (Midler, group) music, lyrics:
       Calvin Lewis, Andrew Wright
    Sold My Soul to Rock 'n' Roll (Midler, group) music,
       lyrics: Gene Pistilli
    Keep on Rockin' (Midler, group) music, lyrics: Sam Hagar,
       John Carter
---   Love Me with A Feeling (Midler, group) music, lyrics:
       Hudson Whittaker
    Camellia (band) music: Stephen Hunter
    Homecoming Monologue (Midler) spoken
    Stay with Me (Midler, group) music, lyrics: Jerry
       Ragavoy, George Weiss
    Let Me Call You Sweetheart (Midler) music: Leo Friedman;
       lyrics: Beth Slater Whitson
    The Rose (Midler, group) music, lyrics: Amanda McBroom

Note: Live recordings in concert.

ROSE MARIE (MGM, 1936)

Hollywood Soundstage 414 (soundtrack) mono

Music: Rudolf Friml, others; lyrics: Otto Harbach, Oscar
Hammerstein II, others; musical direction: Herbert Stothart

Cast: Nelson Eddy, Gilda Gray, Allan Jones, Jeanette MacDonald

Songs: Title Music (MacDonald, chorus)
      Romeo et Juliette (medley) music: Gounod
        Capulet's Ball (chorus)
        Recitative (Jones)
        Waltz (MacDonald)
        Finale Montage (chorus)
        Duels
        Potion Scene
        Finale Duet (MacDonald, Jones)
      Pardon Me, Madame (MacDonald, chorus) music: Herbert
        Stothart; lyrics: Gus Kahn
      The Mounties (Eddy, chorus)
      Dinah (MacDonald) music, lyrics: Harry Akst, Sam Lewis,
        Joe Young
      Some of These Days (MacDonald, Gray) music, lyrics:
        Shelton Brooks
---   Rose Marie (Eddy, MacDonald)
      Totem Tom-Tom (chorus)
      Rose Marie (reprise) (Eddy)
      Just for You (Eddy)
      Three Blind Mice (MacDonald) anon
      Indian Love Call (MacDonald, Eddy)
      Indian Love Call (reprise) (MacDonald)

       Tosca: Act IV, Finale (MacDonald, Jones) music: Puccini
       Indian Love Call (reprise) (MacDonald, Eddy)
       Finale (orchestra)

Note: The above recording includes spoken dialog. Studio
       recordings by cast members (all on LP: RCA LPV 526):

Victor (78rpm) 4323 Indian Love Call (MacDonald, Eddy)
Victor (78rpm) 4305 The Mounties (Eddy, chorus)
                    Rose Marie (Eddy, chorus)

ROSE MARIE (MGM, 1954)

MGM E 229 (soundtrack) mono reissued: MCA 25009 CD

Music: Rudolf Friml. others; lyrics: Otto A Harbach, Oscar
Hammerstein II, others; musical direction: George Stoll

Cast: Ann Blyth, Howard Keel, Bert Lahr, Fernando Lamas,
       Marjorie Main

Songs: The Right Place for A Girl (Keel) lyrics: Paul Francis
          Webster
       Free to Be Free (Blyth) lyrics: Paul Francis Webster
       Love and Kisses (Lahr, Main) lyrics: Paul Francis Webster
 ___   Indian Love Call (Blyth, Lamas)
       Rose Marie (Keel)
       I'm A Mountie Who Never Got His Man (Lahr) music: George
          Stoll; lyrics: Baker
       I Have the Love (Blyth, Lamas) lyrics: Paul Francis
          Webster
       The Mounties (Keel)

Note: The above recording includes spoken dialog.

ROSE OF WASHINGTON SQUARE (Twentieth Century-Fox, 1939)

Sandy Hook SH 2074 (soundtrack) mono

Music, lyrics: various; musical direction: Louis Silvers

Cast; Alice Faye, Al Jolson

Songs: Pretty Baby (Jolson) music: Tony Jackson, Egbert Van
          Alstyne; lyrics: Gus Kahn
       I'm Sorry I Made You Cry (Faye) music, lyrics: N J Clesi
       Vamp (Faye, chorus) music, lyrics: Byron Gay
       Rock-A-Bye Your Baby with A Dixie Melody (Jolson) music:
          Jean Schwartz; lyrics: Sam M Lewis, Joe Young

Toot Toot Tootsie (Jolson) music, lyrics: Ted Fio Rito,
    Robert A King, Gus Kahn, Ernie Erdman
I'm Just Wild About Harry (Faye) music: Eubie Blake;
    lyrics: Noble Sissle
California, Here I Come (Jolson) music, lyrics: Joseph
    Meyer, Al Jolson, Buddy De Sylva
I Never Knew Heaven Could Speak (Faye) music: Harry
    Revel; lyrics: Mack Gordon
Rose of Washington Square (Faye, chorus) music: James
    F Hanley; lyrics: Ballard MacDonald
My Mammy (Jolson) music: Walter Donaldson; lyrics: Sam
    M Lewis, Joe Young
My Man (Faye) music: Maurice Yvain; lyrics: Channing Pollock

Note: Additional soundtrack recording, cut from final film:

         I'll See You In My Dreams (Faye) LP: Out Takes OTF-3

ROUSTABOUT (Paramount, 1964)

RCA LSP 2999 (soundtrack) stereo   reissued: AFL 1-2999

Music: Roy C Bennett, others; lyrics: Sid Tepper, others

Cast: Elvis Presley

Songs: Roustabout (Presley) music: Florence Kaye; lyrics:
            Bill Giant, Bernie Baum
        Little Egypt (Presley) music, lyrics: Jerry Leiber,
            Mike Stoller
        Poison Ivy League (Presley) music: Florence Kaye;
            lyrics: Bill Giant, Bernie Baum
        Hard Knocks (Presley) music, lyrics: Joy Byers
        It's A Wonderful World (Presley)
        Big Love Big Heartache (Presley) music: James Hendrix;
___   lyrics: Dolores Fuller, Lee Morris
        One Track Heart (Presley) music: Florence Kaye; lyrics:
            Bill Giant, Bernie Baum
        It's Carnival Time (Presley) music: Ben Wiseman; lyrics:
            Sid Wayne
        Carny Town (Presley) music: Randy Starr; lyrics: Fred
            Wise
        There's A Brand New Day on the Horizon (Presley) music,
            lyrics: Joy Byers
        Wheels on My Heels (Presley)

A ROYAL AFFAIR (Le Roi) (Discina, 1949) France

Decca (78rpm) DU 758 mono

Music, lyrics: Fred Freed, Maurice Chevalier, others; musical
direction: Raymond Legrand

Cast: Maurice Chevalier

Decca (78rpm) 40158 Bouquet de Paris (Chevalier) music, lyrics:
                    Henri Bourtayre, Maurice Chevalier,
                    Maurice Vandair
                    La Barbe (Chevalier)
Decca (78rpm) 40159 C'est Fini (Chevalier)
                    La Cachucha (Chevalier) music, lyrics: Henri
                    Bourtayre, Maurice Chevalier, Maurice
                    Vandair

ROYAL WEDDING (MGM, 1951)

MGM E 543 (soundtrack) mono   reissued: MCAD 5952 (CD)

Music: Burton Lane; lyrics: Alan Jay Lerner; musical direction:
Johnny Green

Cast: Fred Astaire, Jane Powell

Songs: Too Late Now (Powell)
       Every Night at Seven (Astaire)
       Happiest Day of My Life (Powell)
 ___   I Left My Hat in Haiti (Astaire)
       Open Your Eyes (Powell)
       Sunday Jumps (orchestra)
       You're All the World to Me (Astaire)
       How Could You Believe Me When I Said I Love You When You
           Know I've Been A Liar All My Life (Astaire, Powell)

SALUDOS AMIGOS (Disney, 1942)

Decca (78rpm) 369 mono   also: Disneyland LP: WDL 3039 (soundtrack)

Music, lyrics: Charles Wolcott, Aloysio Oliveira, others; musical
direction: Charles Wolcott

Cast: Aloysio Oliveira, Kenneth Rundquist (not in film)

Note: The contents of this album are untraced. Some of the songs
        from this film include:

        Saludos Amigos (music: Charles Wolcott; lyrics: Ned
           Washington)
        Tico Tico (music: Zaquinta Abreu; lyrics: Ervin Drake)
        Brazil (music: Ary Barroso; lyrics: Bob Russell)

ST LOUIS BLUES (Paramount, 1958)

Roulette 25037 stereo

Music: W C Handy; lyrics: W C Handy, others; musical direction:
Don Redman

Cast: Pearl Bailey

Songs: St Louis Blues (Bailey)
       Hesitatin' Blues (Bailey) not from film
       Shine Like A Mornin' Star (Bailey) new lyrics: Mack David
       Aunt Hagar's Blues (Bailey) not from film
       I'll Turn Back No More (Bailey) not from film
      Ole Miss (Bailey) not from film
---   Long Gone (Bailey) not from film
       Friendless Blues (Bailey) lyrics: Mercedes Gilbert
       Careless Love (Bailey) lyrics: Martha Koenig, Spencer
          Williams
       Way Down South Where the Blues Began (Bailey) not from
          film
       I've Heard of A City Called Heaven (Bailey) not from film
       Beale Street Blues (Bailey)

ST LOUIS BLUES (Paramount, 1958)

Capitol SW 993 stereo

Musical direction: Nelson Riddle

Cast: Nat Cole

Songs: Overture (introducing 'Love Theme' and 'Hesitating Blues')
          (orchestra)
       Harlem Blues (Cole)
       Chantez les Bas (Cole)
       Friendless Blues (Cole)
       Stay (Cole)
---   Joe Turner's Blues (Cole) not from film
       Beale Street Blues (Cole)
       Careless Blues (Cole)
       Morning Blues (Cole)
       Memphis Blues (Cole) not from film
       Yellow Dog Blues (Cole)
       St Louis Blues (Cole)

ST LOUIS BLUES (Paramount, 1958)

RCA SLP 1661 stereo

Musical direction: Shorty Rogers

Cast: Eartha Kitt

Songs: St Louis Blues (Kitt)
       Beale Street Blues (Kitt)
       Chantez-les Bas (Sing 'em Low) (Kitt)
       Hesitating Blues (Kitt) not from film
       Steal Away (Kitt)
___   Careless Love (Kitt)
       Atlanta Blues (Make Me One Pallet on Your Floor) (Kitt)
       Long Gone (Kitt)
       Hist the Window, Noah (Kitt)
       Yellow Dog Blues (Kitt)
       Friendless Blues (Kitt)
       The Memphis Blues (Kitt) not from film

SAN FRANCISCO (MGM, 1936)

Sunbeam P 514 (soundtrack) mono 'Jeanette MacDonald Sings!'

Music, lyrics: various; musical direction: Herbert Stothart

Cast: Jeanette MacDonald

Songs: Would You? (MacDonald) music: Nacio Herb Brown; lyrics:
           Arthur Freed
       Faust: Jewel Song (MacDonald) music: Gounod
       San Francisco (MacDonald, chorus) music: Bronislaw Kaper,
           Walter Jurmann; lyrics: Gus Kahn

Note: The above recording includes spoken dialog and a radio
       narration.

SANDERS OF THE RIVER (Korda UA, 1935)

HMV (British 45/EP) 7EG 8185 mono

Music: Mischa Spoliansky; lyrics: Arthur Wimperis; musical
direction: Muir Mathieson

Cast: Paul Robeson

Songs: Canoe Song (Robeson, chorus)
       Love Song (Robeson, chorus)
       Congo Lullaby (Robeson, chorus)
       The Killing Song (Robeson, chorus)

SAY IT WITH SONGS (Warner Bros, 1929)

Take Two TT 104 (soundtrack) mono

Music, lyrics: Al Jolson, Billy Rose, Dave Dreyer, others;
musical direction: Louis Silvers

Cast: Al Jolson

Songs: Back in Your Own Back Yard (Jolson)
       I'm Ka-razy for You (Jolson)
       Used to You (Jolson) music, lyrics: Al Jolson, Buddy
         DeSylva, Lew Brown, Ray Henderson

Note: The above recording also includes the song, 'Sonny Boy'
       which is not from this film. Studio recordings by
       Al Jolson:

Brunswick (78rpm) 4400 I'm in Seventh Heaven (LP: AH 33)
                       Little Pal (LP: AH 33)
Brunswick (78rpm) 4401 Used to You (LP: AH 87)
                       Why Can't You?
Brunswick (78rpm) 4402 One Sweet Kiss (LP: AH 87)

       Additional soundtrack selection:

       I'm in Seventh Heaven (Jolson) LP: A-Jay 3749 'The Vita-
         graph Years'

SAY ONE FOR ME (Twentieth Century-Fox, 1959)

Columbia CS 8147 (soundtrack) stereo

Music: James Van Heusen; lyrics: Sammy Cahn; musical direction:
Lionel Newman, others

Cast: Bing Crosby, Judy Harriet, Debbie Reynolds, Robert Wagner

Songs: Main Title (orchestra)
       Say One for Me (Crosby, Reynolds)
       Say One for Me (reprise) (orchestra)
       You Can't Love 'em All (Reynolds, Wagner)
       Say One for Me (reprise) (orchestra)
       The Girl Most Likely to Succeed (Reynolds, Wagner)
  --- You Can't Love 'em All (reprise) (orchestra)
       The Night That Rock and Roll Died (Almost) (orchestra)
       I Couldn't Care Less (Crosby) musical direction: Buddy
         Cole
       I Couldn't Care Less (reprise) (orchestra)
       The Night That Rock and Roll Died (Almost) (reprise)
         (Harriet)
       Say One for Me (reprise) (Crosby)
       Chico's Choo-Choo (Reynolds, Wagner, chorus)
       The Secret of Christmas (Crosby, chorus)

SCROOGE (National General, 1970)

Columbia S 30258 (soundtrack) stereo

Music, lyrics: Leslie Bricusse; musical direction: Ian Fraser

Cast: Richard Beaumont, David Collings, Albert Finney, Alec
        Guinness, Kenneth More, Laurence Naismith, Suzanne Neve,
        Anton Rodgers, Karen Scargill

Songs: Overture (orchestra)
        A Christmas Carol (choir)
        Christmas Children (Collings, Beaumont, Scargill)
        I Hate People (Finney)
        Father Christmas (children)
        See the Phantoms (Guinness, chorus)
        December the 25th (Naismith, chorus)
        Happiness (Neve)
        You .. You (Finney)
        I Like Life (More, Finney)
        The Beautiful Day (Beaumont)
        Happiness (reprise) (Neve, Finney)
        Thank You Very Much (Rodgers, Finney, chorus)
        I'll Begin Again (Finney)
        I Like Life (reprise) (Finney)
        Father Christmas (reprise) (children)
        Thank You Very Much (reprise) (Finney, children)
        A Christmas Carol (reprise) (Finney, choir)

SEARCH FOR PARADISE (Cinerama, 1957)

RCA (45/EP) EPA 4117 mono

Music: Dimitri Tiomkin; lyrics: Ned Washington, Lowell Thomas;
musical direction: David Terry

Cast: (the voice of) Robert Merrill

Songs: Kashmir (Merrill)
        Happy Land of Hunza (Merrill)
        Search for Paradise (Merrill)
        Shalimar (Merrill)

Note: Soundtrack versions of these four songs are included on
        RCA LOC 1034, along with other orchestral selections.
        Musical direction is by Dimitri Tiomkin.

SEASIDE SWINGERS (EVERY DAY'S A HOLIDAY) (Avco Embassy, 1965)

Mercury 61031 stereo British

Music, lyrics: Clive Westlake, Kenny Lynch, others

Cast: Grazina Frame, Freddie and the Dreamers, John Leyton, Mike Sarne

Songs: What's Cooking (Freddie and the Dreamers) music: Tony Osborne; lyrics: Jackie Rae
Every Day's A Holiday (Leyton, Sarne, Frame) music, lyrics: Mort Shuman, Clive Westlake
All I Want Is You (Leyton)
Love Me Please (Sarne)
--- A Boy Needs A Girl (Leyton, Frame)
Don't Do That to Me (Freddie and the Dreamers) music, lyrics: Freddie Garrity
Say You Do (Leyton, Sarne, Frame) music, lyrics: Tony Osborne, Gary Osborne
Indubitably Me (Sarne) music, lyrics: Kenny Lynch
Second Time Shy (Frame) music, lyrics: Clive Westlake
Crazy Horse Saloon (Leyton) music: Tony Osborne; lyrics: Jackie Rae

Note: A second soundtrack album was issued by British Decca under the British title of this film. See:

EVERY DAY'S A HOLIDAY (Grand National, 1964)

SECOND CHORUS (Paramount, 1940)

Hollywood Soundstage 404 (soundtrack) mono

Music: Artie Shaw, others; lyrics: Johnny Mercer, others; musical direction: Artie Shaw

Cast: Fred Astaire, Paulette Goddard, Artie Shaw (clarinet)

Songs: Second Chorus (Main Title) (orchestra)
Sugar (orchestra) music: Maceo Pinkard, Sidney Mitchell, Edna Alexander
Everything's Jumpin' (orchestra)
I Ain't Hep to That Step but I'll Dig It (Astaire, Goddard, chorus) music: Hal Borne
Ivy Shuffle (orchestra)
Sweet Sue (orchestra) music: Victor Young
Love of My Life (Astaire)
I'm Yours (orchestra) music: Johnny Green
--- Double Mellow (orchestra)
The New Moon Is Shining (orchestra)
Love of My Life (Russian reprise) (Astaire)
Hoe Down the Bayou (Poor Mr Chisholm) (Astaire) music: Bernie Hanighen
Poor Mr Chisholm (Astaire) music: Bernie Hanighen

Concerto for Clarinet (Swing Concerto) (Shaw, orchestra)
Poor Mr Chisholm (reprise) (orchestra)
Love of My Life (finale) (Astaire)
End Titles (orchestra)

Note: The above recording includes spoken dialog. Studio
recordings:

Columbia (78rpm) 35852 Dig It (Astaire)
                       Poor Mr Chisholm (Astaire)
Columbia (78rpm) 35815 Love of My Life (Astaire)
Victor   (78rpm) 36383 Concerto for Clarinet (Shaw)
Victor   (78rpm) 26790 Love of My Life (Shaw)

SERENADE (Warner Bros, 1956)

RCA LM 1996 (soundtrack) mono

Music: Nicholas Brodszky, others; lyrics: Sammy Cahn, others;
musical direction: Ray Heindorf

Cast: Licia Albanese, Jean Fenn, Mario Lanza

Songs: Serenade (Lanza)
       La Danza (Lanza) music: Rossini
       Torna a Surriento (Lanza) music: de Curtis
       La Boheme: O Soave fanciulla (Lanza, Fenn) music: Puccini
       Der Rosenkavalier: Di rigori armato (Lanza) music:
           Richard Strauss
       Il Trovatore: Di Quella pira (Lanza) music: Verdi
       L'Africana: O Paradiso (Lanza) music: Meyerbeer
       Otello: Dio ti giocondi (Lanza, Albanese) music: Verdi
       Ave Maria (Lanza) music: Schubert
       L'Arlesiana: Lamento di Federico (Lanza) music: Cilea
       Turandot: Nessun dorma (Lanza) music: Puccini
       My Destiny (Lanza)

SGT PEPPER'S LONELY HEARTS CLUB BAND (Universal, 1978)

RSO 2-4100 (two records - soundtrack) stereo

Music, lyrics: John Lennon, Paul McCartney, others; musical
direction: George Martin

Cast: Aerosmith, The Bee Gees, George Burns, Alice Cooper, Earth,
       Wind & Fire, Sandy Farina, Peter Frampton, Barry Gibb,
       Maurice Gibb, Robin Gibb, Frankie Howerd, Jay MacIntosh,
       Steve Martin, Paul Nicholas, Donald Pleasence, Billy
       Preston, Stargard, Dianne Steinberg, John Wheeler

Songs: Sgt Pepper's Lonely Hearts Club Band (The Bee Gees,
      Nicholas)
      With A Little Help from My Friends (The Bee Gees, Frampton)
      Here Comes the Sun (Farina) music, lyrics: George Harrison
      Getting Better (Frampton, The Bee Gees)
      Lucy in the Sky with Diamonds (Steinberg, Stargard)
      I Want You (She's So Heavy) (The Bee Gees, Steinberg,
---   Nicholas, Pleasence, Stargard)
      Good Morning, Good Morning (Nicholas, Frampton, The Bee
      Gees)
      She's Leaving Home (The Bee Gees, MacIntosh, Wheeler)
      You Never Give Me Your Money (Nicholas, Steinberg)
      Oh! Darling (Robin Gibb)
      Maxwell's Silver Hammer (Martin, chorus)
      Polythene Pam (The Bee Gees)
      She Came In Through the Bathroom Window (Frampton, The
      Bee Gees)
      Nowhere Man (The Bee Gees)
      Sgt Pepper's Lonely Hearts Club Band (reprise) (Frampton,
---   The Bee Gees)
      Got to Get You into My Life (Earth, Wind & Fire)
      Strawberry Fields Forever (Farina)
      When I'm Sixty-Four (Howerd, Farina)
      Mean Mr Mustard (Howerd)
      Fixing A Hole (Burns)
      Because (Cooper, The Bee Gees)
      Golden Slumbers (Frampton)
---   Carry That Weight (The Bee Gees)
      Come Together (Aerosmith)
      Being for the Benefit of Mr Kite (Maurice Gibb, Frampton,
      Burns, The Bee Gees)
      The Long and Winding Road (Frampton)
      A Day in the Life (Barry Gibb, The Bee Gees)
      Get Back (Preston)
      Sgt Pepper's Lonely Hearts Club Band (finale) (cast)

SERIOUS CHARGE (Eros, 1959)

Columbia (British 45/EP) SEG 7895 mono

Music, lyrics: Lionel Bart, others

Cast: Cliff Richard

Songs: Living Doll (Richard)
      No Turning Back (Richard)
      Mad About You (Richard)
      Chinchilla - The Drifters (Richard) music, lyrics: Starr,
      Wolf

SEVEN BRIDES FOR SEVEN BROTHERS (MGM, 1954)

MGM E 244 (soundtrack) mono reissued: MCA 25021   CD

Music: Gene dePaul; lyrics: Johnny Mercer; musical direction:
Adolph Deutsch

Cast: Virginia Gibson, Howard Keel, Bill Lee (for Matt Mattox),
        Jane Powell

Songs: Bless Yore Beautiful Hide (Keel)
        Wonderful, Wonderful Day (Powell)
        Lament (Lee, men)
___   Goin' Co'tin' (Powell, men)
        Sobbin' Women (Keel, men)
        June Bride (Gibson, girls)
        Spring, Spring, Spring (chorus)
        When You're in Love (Powell, Keel)

SEVEN HILLS OF ROME (MGM, 1958)

RCA LM 2211 (soundtrack) mono

Music, lyrics: various; musical direction: George Stoll

Cast: Mario Lanza

Songs: Seven Hills of Rome (Lanza) music: Victor Young; lyrics:
            Harold Adamson
        Italiano Calypso (Lanza, chorus) music: George Stoll
        Lolita (Lanza) music, lyrics: Buzzi-Peccia
        Rigoletto: Questa O Quella (Lanza) music: Verdi
        Arrividerci Roma (Lanza, girl) music: Renato Rascal;
            lyrics: Carl Sigman
        Imitation Sequence (Lanza, chorus):
            Temptation (music: Nacio Herb Brown; lyrics: Arthur
                Freed)
            Jezebel (music, lyrics: Wayne Shanklin)
            Memories Are Made of This (music, lyrics: Terry Gilkyson,
                Richard Dehr, Frank Miller)
            When the Saints Go Marching In (trad)
        Come Dance with Me (Lanza, chorus) music: Richard Leibert;
            lyrics: George Blake

Note: The young girl is uncredited on this recording, but the
        film credits list Luisa Di Meo as the 'street singer.'

THE SEVEN LITTLE FOYS (Paramount, 1955)

RCA LPM 3275 mono

Music, lyrics: various; musical direction: Joseph A Lilley

Cast: James Cagney, Bob Hope, Veola Vonn (not in film)

Songs: I'm the Greatest Father of Them All (Hope, children)
           music, lyrics: William Jerome, Eddie Foy; arr:
           Joseph A Lilley
       Comedy Ballet (Hope) spoken
       Nobody (Hope, Vonn) music: Bert Williams; lyrics: Alex
           Rogers
       Love Scene (Hope, Vonn) spoken
       I'm Tired (Hope) music: Jean Schwartz; lyrics: William
   ___   Jerome
       Mary's A Grand Old Name (Cagney) music, lyrics: George
           M Cohan
       Yankee Doodle Dandy (Cagney, Hope) music, lyrics:
           George M Cohan
       Row, Row, Row (Hope, children) music: James V Monaco;
           lyrics: William Jerome
       Chinatown, My Chinatown (Hope, children) music: Jean
           Schwartz; lyrics: William Jerome
       Finale: I'm the Greatest Father of Them All (Hope,
           children)

Note: The above recording includes a narration by Bob Hope.

1776 (Columbia, 1972)

Columbia S 31741 (soundtrack) stereo

Music, lyrics: Sherman Edwards; musical direction: Ray Heindorf

Cast: John Cullum, William Daniels, Blythe Danner, Howard
        Da Silva, William Duell, David Ford, Ralston Hill,
        Ronald Holgate, Ken Howard, Mark Montgomery, John Myhers,
        Stephen Nathan, Rex Robbins, Virginia Vestoff

Songs: Overture (orchestra)
       Sit Down, John (Daniels, company)
       Piddle, Twiddle and Resolve (Daniels)
       Till Then (Daniels, Vestoff)
       The Lees of Old Virginia (Holgate, Da Silva, Daniels)
       But, Mr Adams (Daniels, Da Silva, Howard, Robbins, Myhers)
   ___ Yours, Yours, Yours (Daniels, Vestoff)
       He Plays the Violin (Danner, Da Silva, Daniels)
       Momma Look Sharp (Nathan, Duell, Montgomery)
       The Egg (Da Silva, Daniels, Howard)
       Molasses to Rum (Cullum)
       Is Anybody There? (Daniels)
       Finale (Ford, Hill)

SHALL WE DANCE (RKO, 1937)

EMI (British) EMTC 102 (soundtrack) mono also: Sandy Hook
SH 2028

Music: George Gershwin; lyrics: Ira Gershwin; musical
direction: Nathaniel Shilkret

Cast: Fred Astaire, Ginger Rogers

Songs: Overture (orchestra)
       Slap That Bass (Astaire, chorus)
       (I've Got) Beginner's Luck (Astaire)
       They All Laughed (Rogers)
       Let's Call the Whole Thing Off (Astaire, Rogers)
       They Can't Take That Away from Me (Astaire)
       Shall We Dance - Finale (Astaire, Rogers)

Note: Studio recordings by Astaire (all on LP: Col SG 32472):

       Brunswick (78rpm) 7856 Slap That Bass
                              They All Laughed
       Brunswick (78rpm) 7857 Let's Call the Whole Thing Off
                              Shall We Dance?
       Brunswick (78rpm) 7855 I've Got Beginner's Luck
                              They Can't Take That Away from Me

SHE LOVES ME NOT (Paramount, 1934)

Columbia C2L 43 (two records) mono 'Bing Crosby in Hollywood'

Music: Harry Revel, others; lyrics: Mack Gordon, others;
musical direction: Irving Aaronson

Cast· Bing Crosby

Songs: I'm Hummin' - I'm Whistlin' - I'm Singin' (Crosby)
       Love in Bloom (Crosby) music: Ralph Rainger; lyrics:
          Leo Robin
       Straight from the Shoulder (Right from the Heart) (Crosby)

Note: Additional soundtrack recording:

       Put A Little Rhythm in Everything You Do (Miriam Hopkins)
          LP: Legends 1000/2 'Ladies of Burlesque'

SHIP AHOY (MGM, 1942)

Hollywood Soundstage H S 5011 (soundtrack) mono

Music: Burton Lane, others; lyrics: E Y Harburg, others; musical
direction: Tommy Dorsey

Cast: Tommy Dorsey Orchestra, Bert Lahr, Virginia O'Brien,
       The Pied Pipers, Eleanor Powell, Frank Sinatra, Red
       Skelton

Songs: Opening Music (Dorsey Orchestra):
            Last Call for Love
            I'll Take Tallulah
            I'm Getting Sentimental Over You (music: George Bassman)
            Hawaiian War Chant (music: Leleiohako)
       Last Call for Love (Sinatra, Pied Pipers, Dorsey Orchestra)
       I'll Take Tallulah (Lahr, Skelton, Powell, Dorsey Orchestra)
       Poor You (Sinatra, Skelton, O'Brien, Dorsey Orchestra)
       Processional and Cape Dance (orchestra) music: Walter
            Ruick
       On Moonlight Bay (Sinatra, Pied Pipers) music: Percy
            Weinrich; lyrics: Edward Madden
       Last Call for Love (reprise) (cast, Dorsey Orchestra)
       Closing Music (Poor You) (orchestra)

Note: The above recording includes spoken dialog. Studio
       recordings:

Victor (78rpm) 27849 Poor You (Sinatra, Dorsey Orchestra)
                     Last Call for Love (Sinatra, Dorsey Orchestra)
Victor (78rpm) 27869 I'll Take Tallulah (Dorsey Orchestra)

SHIPYARD SALLY (Twentieth Century-Fox, 1939)

World SH 170 (British - soundtrack) mono reissued: EMI GX 41 25301

Music, lyrics: various

Cast: Gracie Fields

Songs: Danny Boy (Fields) trad (adapted by Fred E Weatherly)
       Grandfather's Bagpipes (intro: Annie Laurie) (Fields,
            chorus) music, lyrics: Harper, Haines
       Wish Me Luck As You Wave Me Goodbye (Fields) music:
            Phil Park; lyrics: Harry Parr-Davies

Note: An additional selection:

Regal Zonophone (78rpm) MR 3119 I've Got the Jitterbugs (Fields)

THE SHOCKING MISS PILGRIM (Twentieth Century-Fox, 1947)

Classic International Filmusicals C I F 3008 (soundtrack) mono

Music: George Gershwin; lyrics: Ira Gershwin; musical direction:
Alfred Newman

Cast: Betty Grable, Dick Haymes, Allyn Joslyn, Charles Kemper

Songs: Opening Music (orchestra)
       Sweet Packard (chorus)
       Changing My Tune (Grable)
       Stand Up and Fight (chorus)
       Aren't You Kind of Glad We Did? (Grable, Haymes)
       Changing My Tune (reprise) (Grable)
       Back Bay Polka (But Not in Boston) (Grable, Joslyn,
          Kemper)
       One, Two, Three (Haymes, chorus)
       Waltzing Is Better Sitting Down (Haymes, Grable)
       For You, For Me, For Evermore (Haymes, Grable)
       For You, For Me, For Evermore (reprise) (Haymes)
       Aren't You Kind of Glad We Did? (reprise) (Haymes, Grable)
       Finale (orchestra)

Note: The above recording includes spoken dialog. Studio
       recordings by Dick Haymes:

Decca (78rpm) 23687 For You, For Me, For Evermore (with Judy
                       Garland) LP: DRG SL 5187
                    Aren't You Kind of Glad We Did? (with
                       Judy Garland) LP: DRG SL 5187

SHOW BOAT (Universal, 1936)

Xeno 251 (soundtrack) mono

Music: Jerome Kern, others; lyrics: Oscar Hammerstein II, others;
musical direction: Victor Baravalle

Cast: Irene Dunne, Allan Jones, Hattie McDaniel, Helen Morgan,
       Paul Robeson, Queenie Smith, Sammy White

Songs: Introduction (Ol' Man River, Cotton Blossom) (chorus)
       Where's the Mate for Me? (Jones)
       Make Believe (Dunne, Jones)
       Ol' Man River (Robeson, chorus)
       Can't Help Lovin' Dat Man (Morgan, McDaniel, Robeson,
          chorus)
 ---   I Have the Room Above (Jones, Dunne)
       Gallavantin' Around (Dunne, chorus)
       You Are Love (Jones, Dunne)
       Ol' Man River (reprise) (Robeson)
       Ah Still Suits Me (Robeson, McDaniel)
       Make Believe (reprise) (Jones)
       Bill (Morgan) lyrics: P G Wodehouse

          Can't Help Lovin' Dat Man (reprise) (Dunne)
          Goodbye My Lady Love (White, Smith) music, lyrics:
             Joe Howard
          Cakewalk (orchestra)
          After the Ball (Dunne, chorus) music, lyrics: Charles
             K Harris
          You Are Love (reprise) (Dunne, Jones)
          Finale: Ol' Man River (Robeson)

Note: The above recording includes spoken dialog. An additional
        soundtrack recording, cut from the final film:

        Why Do I Love You? (Dunne, Jones) LP: Out Takes OTF - 3

SHOW BOAT (MGM, 1951)

MGM E 559 (soundtrack) mono reissued: MCA 1439

Musical direction: Adolph Deutsch

Cast: Gower Champion, Marge Champion, Ava Gardner, Kathryn
        Grayson, Howard Keel, William Warfield

Songs: Make Believe (Grayson, Keel)
        Bill (Gardner) lyrics: P G Wodehouse
        Life Upon the Wicked Stage (Marge and Gower Champion, girls)
___   You Are Love (Grayson, Keel)
        Can't Help Lovin' Dat Man (Gardner)
        I Might Fall Back on You (Marge and Gower Champion)
        Why Do I Love You (Grayson, Keel)
        Ol' Man River (Warfield)

Note: Annette Warren dubbed for the voice of Ava Gardner on the
        film soundtrack, but Miss Gardner's voice is used on the
        above recording. An additional soundtrack recording:

        Cotton Blossom (chorus) LP: MCA 2-11002 That's Entertainment

THE SILENCERS (Columbia, 1966)

Reprise R 6211 stereo

Music, lyrics: various; musical direction: Ernie Freeman, Gene
Page

Cast: Dean Martin

Songs: The Glory of Love (Martin) music, lyrics: Billy Hill
        Empty Saddles in the Old Corral (Martin) music: Billy
           Hill; lyrics: J Keirn Brennan
        Lovely Kravezit (orchestra) music, lyrics: H Greenfield,

                J Keller
        The Last Round-Up (Martin) music, lyrics: Billy Hill
        Anniversary Song (orchestra) music, lyrics: Al Jolson,
            Saul Chaplin
---   Side by Side (Martin) music, lyrics: Harry Woods
        South of the Border (Martin) music: Michael Carr; lyrics:
            Jimmy Kennedy
        Red Sails in the Sunset (Martin) music: Hugh Williams;
            lyrics: Jimmy Kennedy
        Lord, You Made the Night Too Long (orchestra) music:
            Sam M Lewis; lyrics: Joe Young
        If You Knew Susie (Martin) music: Joseph Meyer; lyrics:
            Buddy DeSylva
        On the Sunny Side of the Street (Martin) music: Jimmy
            McHugh; lyrics: Dorothy Fields
        The Silencers (orchestra) music: Elmer Bernstein; lyrics:
            Hal David

SILK STOCKINGS (MGM, 1957)

MGM E 3542 ST (soundtrack) mono reissued: MCA 39074 CD

Music, lyrics: Cole Porter; musical direction: Andre Previn

Cast: Fred Astaire, Joseph Buloff, Cyd Charisse, Peter Lorre,
        Jules Munshin, Janis Paige, Carol Richards (for Cyd
        Charisse)

Songs: Too Bad (Astaire, Lorre, Buloff, Munshin)
        Paris Loves Lovers (Astaire, Charisse, Richards)
        Stereophonic Sound (Astaire, Paige)
        It's A Chemical Reaction, That's All (Charisse,Richards)
        All of You (Astaire)
        Satin and Silk (Paige)
---   Silk Stockings (orchestra)
        Without Love (Astaire, Charisse, Richards)
        Fated to Be Mated (Astaire, Charisse)
        Josephine (Paige)
        Siberia (Lorre, Buloff, Munshin)
        Red Blues (chorus)
        The Ritz Rock and Roll (Astaire)
        Too Bad (reprise) (Charisse, Lorre, Buloff, Munshin)

Note: The above recording includes spoken dialog.

SING BOY SING (Twentieth Century-Fox, 1957)

Capitol T 929 (soundtrack) mono

Music, lyrics: various; musical direction: Lionel Newman

Cast: Tommy Sands

Songs: I'm Gonna Walk and Talk with My Lord (Sands) music,
            lyrics: Martha Carson
        Who Baby (Sands) music, lyrics: Billy Olofson, Jeanne
            Carroll
        A Bundle of Dreams (Sands) music, lyrics: Billy Strange,
            Homer Escamilla
        Just A Little Bit More (Sands) music, lyrics: Charles
            Singleton, Rose Marie McCoy
        People in Love (Sands) music: Lionel Newman; lyrics:
            Leven
        Crazy 'Cause I Love You (Sands) music, lyrics: Spade
            Cooley
        Your Daddy Wants to Do Right (Sands) music, lyrics:
            Tommy Sands
        That's All I Want from You (Sands) music: Rotha (Fritz
            Rotter)
        Soda-Pop Pop (Sands) music, lyrics: Betty and Darla Daret
        Would I Love You (Sands) music, lyrics: Harold Spina,
            Bob Russell
        Rock of Ages (Sands) anon
        Sing Boy Sing (Sands) music, lyrics: Tommy Sands, Rod
            McKuen

SING YOU SINNERS (Paramount, 1938)

Decca DL 4252 mono 'Bing's Hollywood - Pocket Full of Dreams'

Music: James V Monaco, others; lyrics: John Burke, others;
musical direction: John Scott Trotter, others

Cast: Bing Crosby, Johnny Mercer (not in film)

Songs: I've Got A Pocketful of Dreams (Crosby)
        Small Fry (Crosby, Mercer) music: Hoagy Carmichael;
            lyrics: Frank Loesser; musical direction: Victor Young
        Laugh and Call It Love (Crosby)
        Don't Let That Moon Get Away (Crosby)

SINGIN' IN THE RAIN (MGM, 1952)

MGM E 113 (soundtrack) mono reissued: MCA 39044 CD

Music: Nacio Herb Brown, others; lyrics: Arthur Freed, others;
musical direction: Lennie Hayton

Cast: Gene Kelly, Donald O'Connor, Debbie Reynolds

Songs: Singin' in the Rain (Kelly)

Make 'em Laugh (O'Connor)
You Were Meant for Me (Kelly)
All I Do Is Dream of You (Reynolds, girly chorus)
Fit As A Fiddle (Kelly, O'Connor) music: Al Hoffman,
    Al Goodhart
Moses (Kelly, O'Connor) music: Roger Edens; lyrics:
    Betty Comden, Adolph Green
All I Do Is Dream of You (Kelly)
Good Morning (Kelly, O'Connor, Reynolds)
You Are My Lucky Star (Kelly, Reynolds)

Note: An additional soundtrack selection, later included with
        the above album:

MGM (45rpm) X1026 Broadway Ballet (The Broadway Melody, Broadway
                Rhythm) (Kelly, chorus)

        An additional selection, cut from the final film:

        You Are My Lucky Star (Reynolds) LP: Out Takes OTF - 1

THE SINGING FOOL (Warner Bros, 1928)

Take Two TT 106 (soundtrack) mono

Music: Ray Henderson, others; lyrics: Lew Brown, Buddy DeSylva,
others

Cast: Al Jolson

Songs: Title Music (orchestra)
        Background music at Blackie Joe's (orchestra)
        It All Depends on You (Jolson)
        I'm Sitting on Top of the World (Jolson) lyrics:
            Sam M Lewis, Joe Young
        The Spaniard That Blighted My Life (Jolson) music,
            lyrics: Billy Merson
        There's A Rainbow 'Round My Shoulder (Jolson) music,
            lyrics: Dave Dreyer, Billy Rose, Al Jolson
        Golden Gate (Jolson) music: Joseph Meyer, Al Jolson;
___   lyrics: Dave Dreyer, Billy Rose
        Sonny Boy (Jolson) additional lyrics: Al Jolson
        New Year's Eve Party background music (orchestra)
        Keep Smiling at Trouble (Jolson) music, lyrics: Lewis
            Gensler, Buddy DeSylva, Al Jolson
        Sonny Boy (reprise) (Jolson)
        Sonny Boy (reprise) (Jolson)
        Closing Theme (orchestra)

Note: The above recording includes spoken dialog. Studio
        recordings by Jolson (both on LP: Ace of Hearts AH 33):

        Brunswick (78rpm) 4033 Sonny Boy
                        There's A Rainbow 'Round My Shoulder

THE SINGING MARINE (Warner Bros, 1937)

MCA 1511 mono 'Dick Powell'

Music: Harry Warren; lyrics: Al Dubin; musical direction:
Lou Forbes

Cast: Dick Powell

Songs: I Know Now (Powell)
       You Can't Run Away from Love Tonight (Powell)
       'Cause My Baby Says It's So (Powell)

Note: Additional studio recording:

       Decca (78rpm) 1311 Song of the Marines (Powell)

THE SINGING NUN (MGM, 1966)

MGM S1E-7 (soundtrack) stereo reissued: MCA 25090

Music, lyrics: Soeur Sourire, Randy Sparks; musical direction:
Harry Sukman

Cast: Debbie Reynolds

Songs: Dominique (Reynolds, female chorus)
       Sister Adele (Reynolds)
       Avec Toi (Reynolds)
       Alleluia (Reynolds)
       Brother John (Reynolds, chorus)
       Beyond the Stars (Reynolds, female chorus)
___   Lovely (Harry Sukman, piano)
       It's A Miracle (Reynolds)
       Je Voudrais (Reynolds)
       Raindrops (Reynolds)
       A Pied Piper's Song (Reynolds, children)
       Mets Ton Joli Jupon (Reynolds)
       Dibwe Diambula Kabanda (native chorus)
       Kyrie (native chorus)

Note: Final two selections are from the soundtrack of the film,
       'Missa Luba.'

THE SKY'S THE LIMIT (RKO, 1943)

Curtain Calls CC 100/19 (soundtrack) mono

Music: Harold Arlen; lyrics: Johnny Mercer; musical direction:
Leigh Harline

Cast: Fred Astaire, Robert Benchley, Sally Sweetland (for
       Joan Leslie)

Songs: Main Title (orchestra)
       My Shining Hour (Sweetland, chorus)
       My Shining Hour (reprise) (Astaire, Sweetland)
       A Lot in Common with You (Sweetland, Astaire)
       Dinner Speech (Benchley) spoken
       One for My Baby (and One More for the Road) (Astaire)

THE SLEEPING BEAUTY (Disney, 1959)

Buena Vista STER 4036 (soundtrack) stereo

Music for songs: Sammy Fain; lyrics: Jack Lawrence, others;
music adapted by George Bruns from the Tchaikovsky ballet;
musical direction: George Bruns

Cast: (the voices of) Mary Costa, Bill Shirley

Songs: Main Title (Once Upon A Dream) (chorus)
       Hail to the Princess Aurora (chorus) music: Bruns;
          lyrics: Tom Adair
       The Gifts of Beauty and Song (chorus) music: Bruns
       Maleficent Appears (orchestra)
       True Love Conquers All (chorus) music: Bruns
       Bluebird (Costa) music: Bruns
       I Wonder (Costa) music, lyrics: Winston Hibler, Ted
          Sears, George Bruns
       Woodland Symphony (orchestra)
       Once Upon A Dream (reprise) (Costa, Shirley, chorus)
       Sing A Smiling Song (orchestra) music: Bruns; lyrics:
          Tom Adair
---   Skumps (chorus) music, lyrics: Tom Adair, Endman Penner,
          George Bruns
       Maleficent's Evil Spell (orchestra)
       Sleeping Beauty Song (chorus) music: George Bruns;
          lyrics: Tom Adair
       Fairies to the Rescue (orchestra)
       Bacchanal (orchestra)
       The Prince Dreams of Sleeping Beauty (Love Theme) (orchestra)
       Battle with the Forces of Evil (orchestra)
       Awakening (Love Theme) (orchestra)
       Finale (Once Upon A Dream) (chorus)

THE SLIPPER AND THE ROSE (Universal, 1976)

MCA 2097 (soundtrack) stereo

Music, lyrics: Richard M Sherman, Robert B Sherman; musical
direction: Angela Morley

Cast: Richard Chamberlain, Gemma Craven, Annette Crosbie,
        Christopher Gable, Peter Graves, Michael Hordern,
        Kenneth More, Julian Orchard, John Turner

Songs: Main Title (Secret Kingdom, Once I Was Loved) (orchestra)
        Why Can't I Be Two People? (Chamberlain)
        Once I Was Loved (Craven)
        What A Comforting Thing to Know (Chamberlain, Gable)
        Protocoligorically Correct (Hordern, More, Graves, chorus)
        A Bride Finding Ball (Chamberlain, Orchard)
---   Suddenly It Happens (Crosbie, Craven, chorus)
        The Slipper and the Rose Waltz (orchestra)
        Secret Kingdom (Chamberlain, Craven)
        He Danced with Me - She Danced with Me (The Slipper and
            the Rose Waltz) (Craven, Chamberlain)
        Position and Positioning (Gable, Turner, chorus)
        Tell Him Anything (But Not That I Love Him) (Craven)
        Secret Kingdom (reprise) (Chamberlain, Craven)

SMASHING TIME (Paramount, 1967)

ABC S OC 6 (soundtrack) stereo

Music: John Addison; lyrics: George Melly, John Addison;
musical direction: John Addison

Cast: Lynn Redgrave, Rita Tushingham

Songs: Main Title: Smashing Time (Tushingham, Redgrave)
        Carnaby Street (Tushingham, Redgrave)
        Waiting for My Friend (Tushingham)
        Aerosol Knock-About (orchestra)
        New Clothes (Tushingham)
        It's Always Your Fault (Tushingham, Redgrave)
        While I'm Still Young (Redgrave)
---   Day Out (Tushingham, Redgrave)
        Trouble (Tushingham)
        The Morning After (Tushingham, Redgrave)
        Jabberwock March (orchestra)
        Baby Don't Go (Redgrave)
        Can't Help Laughing (orchestra)
        Swinging Thru London (Tushingham, Redgrave)
        Pie Fight (orchestra)
        End Title: Smashing Time (Tushingham, Redgrave)

SMILIN' THROUGH (MGM, 1941)

RCA (78rpm) M 847 mono

Music, lyrics: various; musical direction: Herbert Stothart

Cast: Jeanette MacDonald

Victor (78rpm) 18315 Smilin' Through (MacDonald) music, lyrics:
                      Arthur A Penn (LP: Camden CAL 325)
                      A Little Love, A Little Kiss (MacDonald)
                      music: Adrian Ross; lyrics: Lao Silesu
Victor (78rpm) 18316 Kerry Dance (MacDonald) music, lyrics:
                      J L Molloy
                      Ouvre ton coeur (MacDonald) music: Bizet
Victor (78rpm) 18317 Land of Hope and Glory (MacDonald) music:
                      Sir Edward Elgar; lyrics: A C Blason
                      Drink to Me Only with Thine Eyes (MacDonald)
                      music: anon; lyrics: Ben Jonson (LP:
                      Camden CAL 325)

SNOOPY, COME HOME (National General, 1972)

Columbia S 31541 (soundtrack) stereo

Music, lyrics: Richard M Sherman, Robert B Sherman; musical
direction: Don Ralke

Cast: (the voices of) Linda Ercoli, Shelby Flint, Guy Pohlman,
      Ray Pohlman, Don Ralke, Thurl Ravenscroft

Songs: Snoopy, Come Home (chorus)
       Lila's Theme (Do You Remember Me) (Flint)
       At the Beach (chorus)
       No Dogs Allowed! (Ravenscroft)
       The Best of Buddies (Ralke, R Pohlman)
       Fundamental-Friend-Dependability (Ercoli)
       Woodstock's Samba (Woodstock, orchestra)
---   Charlie Brown's Caliope (orchestra)
       Snoopy, Come Home (sad reprise) (Peppermint Patty, Lucy,
         Linus, Charlie Brown)
       Gettin' It Together (Ralke, R Pohlman)
       It Changes (G Pohlman)
       The Best of Buddies (reprise) (Ralke, R Pohlman, chorus)
       Lila's Theme (reprise) (orchestra)
       Snoopy, Come Home (reprise) (chorus)

SNOW WHITE AND THE SEVEN DWARFS (Disney, 1937)

Disneyland DQ 1201 (soundtrack) mono   CD

Music: Frank Churchill; lyrics: Larry Morey; background score:
Leigh Harline, Paul J Smith; musical direction: Frank Churchill,
Paul J Smith, Leigh Harline

Cast: (the voices of) Roy Atwell, Adriana Caselotti, Pinto Colvig,
         Billy Gilbert, Otis Harlan, Harry Stockwell, Scotty Mattraw

Songs: Overture (orchestra)
       I'm Wishing (Caselotti)
       One Song (Stockwell)
       With A Smile and A Song (Caselotti)
       Whistle While You Work (Caselotti)
       Heigh-Ho (Atwell, Colvig, Harlan, Gilbert, Mattraw)
---   Bluddle-Uddle-um-Dum (The Washing Song) (Atwell, Colvig,
           Harlan, Gilbert, Mattraw)
       A Silly Song (Atwell, Colvig, Harlan, Gilbert, Mattraw)
       Some Day My Prince Will Come (Caselotti)
       Finale: One Song (Stockwell, chorus)
               Some Day My Prince Will Come (chorus)

Note: The Disney Organization also released the complete soundtrack
         of this film in a box set on the Vista label. At the time
         of the film's original release, Victor issued a 78rpm album
         of the songs taken from the film soundtrack (now on CD):

         Victor (78rpm) 25735 Heigh-Ho
                              With A Smile and A Song
         Victor (78rpm) 25736 Whistle While You Work
                              One Song
         Victor (78rpm) 25737 Dwarf's Yodel Song
                              Someday My Prince Will Come

SO DEAR TO MY HEART (Disney, 1948)

Capitol (78rpm) DD 109 mono

Music, lyrics: various; musical direction: Billy May

Cast: (the voices of) John Beal, Ken Carson, others

Capitol (78rpm) 25050 The contents of this album are untraced.
                      Some of the songs from this film include:
Capitol (78rpm) 25251 It's What You Do With What You've Got
                      Ol' Dan Patch
Capitol (78rpm) 25252 Stick-to-it-ivity
                      Country Fair
Capitol (78rpm) 25253 So Dear to My Heart

Note: Other recordings by cast members:

Decca (78rpm) 24547 Lavender Blue (Burl Ives)

Billy Boy (Burl Ives)

SO THIS IS LOVE (Warner Bros, 1953)

RCA LOC 3000 (soundtrack) mono

Music, lyrics: various; musical direction: Ray Heindorf

Cast: Kathryn Grayson

Songs: Remember (Grayson, chorus) music, lyrics: Irving Berlin
       La Boheme: Act I: Mi Chiamano Mini (Grayson) music: Puccini
       Time on My Hands (Grayson, chorus) music: Vincent Youmans;
           lyrics: Harold Adamson, Mack Gordon
---   Ciribiribin (Grayson) music: Pestalozza
       Romeo and Juliet: Act I: Waltz Song (Grayson) music: Gounod
       The Marriage of Figaro: Act II: Voi Che Sapete (Grayson)
           music: Mozart
       Everybody Ought to Know How to Do the Tickle Toe (Grayson)
           music: Louis Hirsch; lyrics: Otto Harbach
       Faust: Act III: Jewel Song (Grayson) music: Gounod
       Oh Me, Oh My (Grayson, chorus) music: Vincent Youmans;
           lyrics: Ira Gershwin
       I Wish I Could Shimmy Like My Sister Kate (Grayson)
           music, lyrics: Armand Piron
       The Kiss Waltz (Grayson) music: Joe Burke; lyrics: Al Dubin

SO THIS IS PARIS (Universal, 1955)

Decca DL 5553 (soundtrack) mono

Music, lyrics: Pony Sherrill, Phil Moody; musical direction:
Joseph Gershenson

Cast: Gloria De Haven, Tony Curtis, Paul Gilbert, Gene Nelson

Songs: So This Is Paris (chorus)
       The Two of Us (Curtis, De Haven)
       A Dame's A Dame (Curtis, Nelson, Gilbert)
       So This Is Paris (reprise) (chorus)
---   If You Were There (Nelson, De Haven)
       Looking for Someone to Love (Nelson)
       Wait 'Til Paris Sees Us (Curtis, Nelson, Gilbert)

SOME LIKE IT HOT (United Artists, 1959)

United Artists UAS 4030 (soundtrack) stereo reissued: UA LA-272

Music, lyrics: various; musical direction: Matty Malneck, others

Cast: Marilyn Monroe

Songs: Runnin' Wild (Monroe) music: A Harrington Gibbs; lyrics:
          Joe Grey, Leo Wood
       Sugar Blues (orchestra) music: Clarence Williams
       Runnin' Wild (reprise) (orchestra) musical direction:
          Adolph Deutsch
       Down Around the Sheltering Palms (chorus) music: Abe
          Olman; lyrics: James Brockman
       Randolph Street Rag (orchestra) music: Adolph Deutsch
       I Wanna Be Loved by You (Monroe) music: Harry Ruby,
          Herbert Stothart; lyrics: Bert Kalmar
       Park Avenue Fantasy (orchestra) music: Matty Malneck
       Down Around the Sheltering Palms (reprise) (orchestra)
       La Cumprasita (orchestra)
       I Wanna Be Loved by You (reprise) (orchestra) musical
          direction: Adolph Deutsch
---   I'm Through with Love (Monroe) music, lyrics: Matty
          Malneck, Fud Livingston, Gus Kahn
       Sugar Blues (reprise) (orchestra)
       Tell the whole Darn World (orchestra) music: Adolph
          Deutsch
       Play It Again Charlie (orchestra) music: Adolph Deutsch
       Sweet Georgia Brown (orchestra) music, lyrics: Ben Bernie,
          Maceo Packard, Kenneth Casey
       By the Beautiful Sea (chorus) music: Harry Carroll;
          lyrics: Harold Atteridge
       Park Avenue Fantasy (reprise) (orchestra)
       Some Like It Hot (orchestra)

Note: Additional soundtrack selection, cut from final film:

        Some Like It Hot (Monroe) LP: Legends 1000/1

SOMEBODY LOVES ME (Paramount, 1952)

RCA LPM 3097 mono

Music, lyrics: Jay Livingston, Ray Evans, others; musical
direction: Emil Newman

Cast: Betty Hutton, Pat Morgan (for Ralph Meeker)

Songs: Somebody Loves Me (Hutton) music: George Gershwin; lyrics:
          Ballard MacDonald, Buddy DeSylva
       Dixie Dreams (Hutton, chorus) music: Arthur Johnson, George
          Meyer; lyrics: Roy Turk, Grant Clarke
       Jealous (Hutton, Morgan) music: Jack Little; lyrics:
          Tommie Malie, Dick Finch

'Way Down Yonder in New Orleans (Hutton, chorus) music:
    Turner Layton; lyrics: Henry Creamer
--- That Teasin' Rag (Hutton) music, lyrics: Joe Jordan
Toddling the Todalo (Hutton) music: A Baldwin Sloane;
    lyrics: E Ray Goetz
Love Him (Hutton)
Mister Banjo Man (Hutton, chorus)
Rose Room (Hutton, chorus) music: Art Hickman; lyrics:
    Harry Williams

SOMEBODY LOVES ME (Paramount, 1952)

Motion Picture Tracks M P T - 5 (soundtrack) mono

Cast: Jack Benny, Betty Hutton, Adele Jergens, Pat Morgan (for
      Ralph Meeker), Henry Slate, Sid Tomack

Songs: Overture (orchestra)
      That Teasin' Rag (Hutton)
      I Can't Tell Why I Love You (Hutton) music: Gus Edwards;
        lyrics: Will D Cobb
      Honey, Oh, My Honey (Jergens)
      Toddling the Todalo (Jergens)
      Toddling the Todalo (reprise) (Hutton)
      June (Hutton) music: A Baldwin Sloane; lyrics: E Ray Goetz
      On San Francisco Bay (Hutton) music: Gertrude Hoffman;
        lyrics: Vincent Bryan
      Smiles (Hutton, chorus) music: Lee M Roberts; lyrics:
        J Will Callahan
      I Cried for You (Morgan) music: Gus Arnheim, Abe Lyman;
        lyrics: Arthur Freed
      Almost Time for the Show (Hutton, cast)
      Rose Room (Hutton, Morgan)
      'Way Down Yonder in New Orleans (Hutton, chorus)
      Wang Wang Blues (Slate, Tomack)   music: Gus Mueller,
        Buster Johnson, Henry Busse; lyrics: Leo Wood
--- Somebody Loves Me (Morgan)
      Jealous (Hutton, Morgan)
      Love Him (Hutton) introduction: Jack Benny
      Mister Banjo Man (Hutton, chorus)
      Dixie Dreams (Hutton, chorus)
      Routine Number (Love Him - reprise) (Hutton, Morgan)
      June (reprise) (Morgan, chorus)
      Thanks to You (Morgan) music: Pete Wendling; lyrics:
        Grant Clarke
      Somebody Loves Me (reprise) (Hutton, Morgan, chorus)
      End Credits (orchestra)

Note: The above recording includes spoken dialog.

SOMETHING IN THE WIND (Universal, 1947)

Decca (78rpm) 601 mono

Music: John Green; lyrics: Leo Robin; musical direction: John Green

Cast: Deanna Durbin

Decca (78rpm) 24167 Something in the Wind (Durbin)
                   It's Only Love (Durbin)
Decca (78rpm) 24166 You Wanna Keep Your Baby Lookin' Right (Durbin)
                   The Turntable Song (Durbin)

Note: The first three songs listed above are included on British
        Ace of Hearts albums (AH 60 and AH 93). The last selection
        is included on the Decca LP 8785.

A SONG IS BORN (Goldwyn, 1948)

Capitol (78rpm) CC 106 mono

Music: Gene de Paul, others; lyrics: Don Raye

Cast: Louis Armstrong, Charlie Barnet, The Brazilians, The Page
        Cavanaugh Trio, Tommy Dorsey, The Golden Gate Quartet,
        Benny Goodman, Mel Powell, Jeri Sullivan (for Virginia
        Mayo)

Capitol (78rpm) 10172 A Song Is Born (part I and II) (The Golden
                      Gate Quartet, Sullivan, The Brazilians,
                      Goodman, Dorsey, Barnet, Armstrong,
                      Powell)
Capitol (78rpm) 10173 Muskrat Ramble (Powell) music: Kid Ory
                      Stealin' Apples (Goodman) music: Fats
                      Waller
Capitol (78rpm) 10174 The Redskin Rhumba (Barnet) music: Dale
                      Bennett
                      Daddy-O (I'm Gonna Teach You Some Blues)
                      (Sullivan, Cavanaugh)

SONG OF FREEDOM (British Lion, 1936)

HMV (45/EP) 7EG 8431 mono

Music: Eric Ansell; lyrics: Henrik Ege; musical direction:
Eric Ansell

Cast: Paul Robeson, Elisabeth Welch

Songs: Sleepy River (Robeson, Welch, chorus)
       Lonely Road (Robeson, chorus)
       Song of Freedom (Robeson, chorus)
       The Black Emperor (Robeson, chorus)

SONG OF NORWAY (ABC, 1970)

ABC S-OC-14 (soundtrack) stereo

Music: Edvard Grieg, arranged by Robert Wright, George Forrest;
lyrics: Robert Wright, George Forrest, others; musical direction:
Roland Shaw

Cast: Florence Henderson, Elizabeth Larner, Toralv Maurstad,
        Frank Porretta, Christina Schollin, Harry Secombe

Songs: Opening - Piano Concerto (orchestra)
       Life of A Wife of A Sailor (chorus)
       John Heggerstrom (Maurstad, Schollin)
       Freddy and his Fiddle (children, chorus)
       Strange Music (Maurstad)
       The Song of Norway (Porretta)
       A Rhyme and A Reason (Henderson, children)
       When We Wed (chorus)
       The Little House (Henderson)
       Hill of Dreams (Henderson, Porretta, Maurstad)
  --- I Love You (Henderson)
       Hymn of Betrothal (chorus)
       Be A Boy Again (Poretta)
       Midsummer's Eve - Hand in Hand (chorus)
       Three There Were (Porretta)
       The Solitary Wanderer (Henderson)
       At Christmastime (Secombe, Larner, Maurstad, Henderson,
          chorus)
       A Welcome Toast (Secombe)
       Ribbons and Wrappings (Secombe, Henderson, Larner,
          Maurstad, chorus)
       Wrong to Dream (Henderson)
       Solvejg's Song - Norwegian National Anthem (chorus)
          music, lyrics: B Bjorson, R Nordraak
       Finale - Piano Concerto (chorus, orchestra)

SONG OF SCHEHERAZADE (Universal, 1947)

Columbia (78rpm) X 272 mono

Music: Nicolai Rimsky-Korsakov, arranged by Miklos Rozsa;
lyrics: Jack Brooks; musical direction: Julius Burger

Cast: Charles Kullman

Columbia (78rpm) 4459 Sadko: Song of India (Kullman)
                         Le Coq d'Or: Hymn to the Sun (Kullman)
Columbia (78rpm) 4355 Gypsy Song (Kullman)
                         Capriccio Espagnole: Fandango (Kullman)

SONG OF THE OPEN ROAD (United Artists, 1944)

Curtain Calls CC 100/4 (soundtrack) mono   'Jane Powell'

Music: Walter Kent; lyrics: Kim Gannon

Cast: Edgar Bergen, Jane Powell

Songs: Rolling Down the Road (Powell, chorus)
        I'm Having Fun in the Sun (Powell)
        Here It Is Monday (Bergen, Powell, chorus)

SONG OF THE SOUTH (Disney, 1946)

Disneyland DQ 1205 (soundtrack) mono   'Uncle Remus'

Music: Allie Wrubel, others; lyrics: Ray Gilbert, others;
musical direction: Daniele Amfitheatrof, Paul J Smith

Cast: James Baskett, Bobby Driscoll, (the voice of) Johnny
        Lee, Hattie McDaniel, Luana Patten, (the voice of)
        Nicodemus Stewart

Songs: Song of the South (chorus) music: Arthur Johnson; lyrics:
            Sam Coslow
        Uncle Remus (chorus) music, lyrics: Johnny Lange, Hy
            Heath, Eliot Danial
        Zip-A-Dee-Doo-Dah (Baskett, chorus)
        Who Wants to Live Like That (Baskett) music: Foster
            Carling; lyrics: Ken Darby
        Let the Rain Pour Down (chorus) music: Foster Carling;
            lyrics: Ken Darby
---   How Do You Do (Baskett, Lee, chorus) music, lyrics:
            Robert MacGimsey
        Sooner or Later (McDaniel) music: Charles Wolcott
        Everybody Has A Laughing Place (Lee, Stewart)
        All I Want (chorus) trad; lyrics: Ken Darby
        Finale: Zip-A-Dee-Doo-Dah (Patten, Driscoll, Baskett,
                chorus)
                Song of the South (chorus)

Note: An earlier 78rpm album was issued (Capitol CC-40) with
        the additional voices of Johnny Mercer and the Pied
        Pipers (LP: Capitol J 3265).

THE SOUND OF MUSIC (Twentieth Century-Fox, 1965)

RCA LSOD 2005 (soundtrack) stereo   CD

Music: Richard Rodgers; lyrics: Oscar Hammerstein II, others;
musical direction: Irwin Kostal

Cast: Julie Andrews, Charmain Carr, Bill Lee (for Christopher
        Plummer), Margery McKay (for Peggy Wood), Don Truhitte

Songs: Prelude (orchestra)
        The Sound of Music (Andrews)
        Overture (orchestra)
        Preludium (Dixit Dominus) (Nuns chorus)
        Morning Hymn / Alleluia (Nuns chorus)
        Maria (Nuns chorus)
        I Have Confidence (Andrews) lyrics: Richard Rodgers
        Sixteen Going on Seventeen (Truhitte, Carr)
        My Favorite Things (Andrews)
        Climb Ev'ry Mountain (McKay)
---   The Lonely Goatherd (Andrews, children)
        The Sound of Music (reprise) (Lee, children)
        Do-Re-Mi (Andrews, children)
        Something Good (Andrews, Lee) lyrics: Richard Rodgers
        Porcessional / Maria (reprise) (Nuns chorus)
        Edelweiss (Lee, Andrews, children, chorus)
        So Long, Farewell (children)
        Climb Ev'ry Mountain (reprise) (chorus)

SOUTH PACIFIC (Twentieth Century-Fox, 1958)

RCA LOCD 2000 (soundtrack) mono   CD

Music: Richard Rodgers; lyrics: Oscar Hammerstein II; musical
direction: Alfred Newman

Cast: Mitzi Gaynor, Marie Greene (for Candace Lee), Bill Lee
        (for John Kerr), Muriel Smith (for Juanita Hall), Giorgio
        Tozzi (for Rosanno Brazzi), Betty Wand (for Warren Hsieh)

Songs: Overture (orchestra)
        Dites-moi (Greene, Wand)
        Cockeyed Optimist (Gaynor)
        Twin Soliloquies (Gaynor, Tozzi)
        Some Enchanted Evening (Tozzi)
        Bloody Mary (chorus)
        My Girl Back Home (Lee)
        There Is Nothing Like A Dame (chorus)
        Bali Ha'i (Smith)
---   I'm Gonna Wash That Man Right Outa My Hair (Gaynor, chorus)
        I'm in Love with A Wonderful Guy (Gaynor, chorus)

        Younger than Springtime (Lee)
        Happy Talk (Smith)
        Honey Bun (Gaynor)
        Carefully Taught (Lee)
        This Nearly Was Mine (Tozzi)
        Finale: Twin Soliloquies (Gaynor, Tozzi)
                Some Enchanted Evening (Tozzi, Gaynor)

SPEEDWAY (MGM, 1968)

RCA LSP 3989 (soundtrack) stereo

Music: Roy C Bennett, others; lyrics: Sid Tepper, others

Cast: Elvis Presley, Nancy Sinatra

Songs: Speedway (Presley) music, lyrics: Tom Glazer, Schlaks
       There Ain't Nothing Like A Song (Presley, Sinatra)
         music, lyrics: Joy Byers, Johnston
       Your Time Hasn't Come Yet, Baby (Presley) music, lyrics:
         Joel Hirschhorn, Al Kasha
       Who Are You (Who Am I) (Presley) music, lyrics: Sid Wayne,
         Ben Weisman
       He's Your Uncle, Not Your Dad (Presley) music, lyrics:
         Sid Wayne, Ben Weisman
       Let Yourself Go (Presley) music, lyrics: Joy Byers
---   Your Groovy Self (Sinatra) music, lyrics: Lee Hazelwood
       Five Sleepy Heads (Presley)
       Western Union (Presley)
       Mine (Presley)
       Goin' Home (Presley) music, lyrics: Joy Byers
       Suppose (Presley) music, lyrics: Dee, Goehring

SPINOUT (MGM, 1966)

RCA LSP 3702 (soundtrack) stereo reissued: AYL 1-3684

Music: Roy C Bennett, others; lyrics: Sid Tepper, others

Cast: Elvis Presley

Songs: Stop, Look and Listen (Presley) music, lyrics: Joy Byers
       Adam and Evil (Presley) music: Randy Starr; lyrics: Fred
        Wise
       All That I Am (Presley)
       Never Say Yes (Presley) music: Mort Shuman; lyrics:
        Doc Pomus
       Am I Ready (Presley)
       Beach Shack (Presley) music: Florence Kaye; lyrics: Bill
        Giant, Bernie Baum

---   Spinout (Presley) music: Ben Weisman; lyrics: Dolores
      Fuller, Sid Wayne
   Smorgasbord (Presley)
   I'll Be Back (Presley) music: Ben Weisman; lyrics: Sid
      Wayne
   Tomorrow Is A Long Time (Presley) music, lyrics: Bob Dylan
   Down in the Alley (Presley) music, lyrics: Jesse Stone
      and the Clovers
   I'll Remember You (Presley) music, lyrics: Kuiokalani Lee

SPRING PARADE (Universal, 1940)

Decca (78rpm) 209 mono 'Deanna Durbin Souvenir Album, No 4'

Music: Robert Stolz; lyrics: Gus Kahn; musical direction:
Charles Previn

Cast: Deanna Durbin

Decca (78rpm) 3414 Waltzing in the Clouds (Durbin) LP: AH 60
               When April Sings (Durbin) LP: Decca DL 8785
Decca (78rpm) 3653 It's Foolish But It's Fun (Durbin) LP: AH 147

Note: Additional recordings:

      Blue Danube Dream (Durbin) music: Johann Strauss
        LP: Decca DL 8785
   When April Sings (Durbin) LP: RCA LPV 579

SPRINGTIME IN THE ROCKIES (Twentieth Century-Fox, 1942)

Hollywood Soundstage 5013 (soundtrack) mono also: Sandy Hook
SH 2090

Music: Harry Warren, others; lyrics: Mack Gordon, others;
musical direction: Alfred Newman

Cast: Bando Da Lua, Helen Forrest, Betty Grable, Charlotte
      Greenwood, Harry James Orchestra, Carmen Miranda, John
      Payne

Songs: Opening Music (orchestra)
      Run, Little Raindrop, Run (Grable, Payne, chorus)
      Chiribiribin (Harry James Orchestra) music: Pestalozza
      I Had the Craziest Dream (Forrest, Harry James Orchestra)
      You Made Me Love You (Harry James Orchestra) music:
         James V Monaco
      Run, Little Raindrop, Run (reprise) (Harry James Orchestra)
      Chattanooga Choo Choo (Miranda, Bando Da Lua)
      A Poem Set to Music (Harry James Orchestra)

       I Had the Craziest Dream (reprise) (Greenwood) spoken
       Tic-Tac Do Meu Coracao (Miranda, Bando Da Lua) music,
          lyrics: Alcyr Peres Vermelho, Walfrido Silva
       Pan Americana Jubilee (Grable, Payne, Miranda, chorus,
          Harry James Orchestra)

Note: The above soundtrack recording is followed by a studio
       recording

       TCF 157, 158 (78rpm) A Poem Set to Music (Harry James
                        Orchestra, Johnny McAfee, vocal)

       Additional studio recordings:

       Decca (78rpm) 23265 Chattanooga Choo Choo (Miranda)
                     Tic Tac do Meu Coracao (Miranda)
       Col   (78rpm) 36649 A Poem Set to Music (James Orchestra)
                     I Had the Craziest Dream (James Orch)

STAGE DOOR CANTEEN (United Artists, 1943)

Curtain Calls CC 100/11-12 (soundtrack) mono   also: Sandy Hook
SH 2093

Music: James V Monaco, others; lyrics: Al Dubin, others

Cast: Harry Babbitt, Kenny Baker, Tallulah Bankhead, Count
      Basie Orchestra, Edgar Bergen, Ray Bolger, Julie Conway,
      Jane Cowl, Xavier Cugat Orchestra, Trudy Erwin, Gracie
      Fields, Benny Goodman Orchestra, Katharine Hepburn,
      Allen Jenkins, Kay Kyser Orchestra, Gypsy Rose Lee,
      Peggy Lee, Guy Lombardo Orchestra, Jack Martin, Freddy
      Martin Orchestra, Harpo Marx, Sully Mason, Yehudi Menuhin,
      Ethel Merman, Lina Romay, Lanny Ross, Ned Sparks, Ethel
      Waters

Songs: Main Title (orchestra)
      Comedy Routine (Bergen) spoken
      The Machine Gun Song (Fields)
      The Lord's Prayer (Fields) music: Albert Hay Malotte
      A Rookie and his Rhythm (Kay Kyser Orchestra, Conway,
         Mason, Babbitt, Erwin, Jack Martin)
      The Girl I Love to Leave Behind (Bolger) music: Richard
         Rodgers; lyrics: Lorenz Hart
      Marching Through Berlin (Merman) music, lyrics: Bob
         Reed, Harry Miller
      She's A Bombshell from Brooklyn (Xavier Cugat Orchestra,
         Romay, chorus)
      Hungarian Rhapsody (Marx) harp solo
      Dialog (Bankhead) spoken
      Sleep, Baby, Sleep in Your Jeep (Guy Lombardo Orchestra)

---   Goodnight Sweetheart (Baker) music, lyrics: Ray Noble,
          James Campbell, Reg Connelly
        Quicksands (Waters, Count Basie Orchestra)
        I Can't Strip to Brahms (Gypsy Rose Lee) introduction:
          Allen Jenkins
        Dialog (Sparks) spoken
        Don't Worry Island (Freddy Martin Orchestra, vocal with
          chorus)
        Why Don't You Do Right? (Lee, Benny Goodman Orchestra)
        Bugle Call Rag (Benny Goodman Orchestra) music: J Hubert
          Blake, Carey Morgan
        We Mustn't Say Goodbye (Ross)
        Ave Maria (Menuhin) violin solo; music: Gounod; introduction:
          Jane Cowl
        Flight of the Bumble Bee (Menuhin) violin solo; music:
          Rimsky-Korsakov
        Dialog (Hepburn) spoken
        Finale (orchestra)

Note: The above recording includes spoken dialog. Studio
        recordings by cast members:

Victor (78rpm) 20-1521 Marching Through Berlin (Merman)
Columbia (78rpm) 36652 Why Don't You Do Right? (Lee, Benny
                       Goodman Orchestra)

STAR! (Twentieth Century-Fox, 1968)

Fox DTCS 5102 (soundtrack) stereo

Music, lyrics: Noel Coward, others; musical direction: Lennie
Hayton

Cast: Julie Andrews, Bruce Forsyth, Garrett Lewis, Daniel
        Massey, Beryl Reid

Songs: Overture (orchestra)
        Star! (Andrews) music: James Van Heusen; lyrics: Sammy
          Cahn
        Piccadilly (Andrews, Forsyth, Reid) music, lyrics:
          Walter Williams, Bruce Seiver, Paul Morande
        In My Garden of Joy (chorus) music, lyrics: Saul Chaplin
        Oh, It's A Lovely War (Andrews, chorus) music: J P Long;
          lyrics: Maurice Scott
        'N' Everything (Lewis) music, lyrics: Buddy DeSylva, Gus
          Kahn, Al Jolson
        Burlington Bertie from Bow (Andrews) music, lyrics:
          William Hargreaves
        Parisian Pierrot (Andrews)
        Limehouse Blues (Andrews, chorus) music: Philip Braham;
          lyrics: Douglas Furber

---   Someone to Watch Over Me (Andrews) music: George Gershwin;
       lyrics: Ira Gershwin
     Do, Do, Do (Andrews) music: George Gershwin; lyrics: Ira
       Gershwin
     Dear Little Boy (Dear Little Girl) (Andrews, Massey)
       music: George Gershwin; lyrics: Ira Gershwin
     Has Anybody Seen Our Ship? (Andrews, Massey)
     Someday I'll Find You (Andrews)
     The Physician (Andrews, chorus) music, lyrics: Cole Porter
     My Ship (Andrews) music: Kurt Weill; lyrics: Ira Gershwin
     Jenny (Andrews, chorus) music: Kurt Weill; lyrics:
       Ira Gershwin

A STAR IS BORN (Warner Bros, 1954)

Columbia BL 1201 (soundtrack) mono   reissued: CSP ACS 8740   CD

Music: Harold Arlen, others; lyrics: Ira Gershwin, others;
musical direction: Ray Heindorf

Cast: Judy Garland

Songs: Gotta Have Me Go with You (Garland, male group)
      The Man That Got Away (Garland)
      Born in a Truck (Garland) music, lyrics: Leonard Gershe
        incorporates:
        I'll Get By (Garland) music: Fred E Ahlert; lyrics:
          Roy Turk
        You Took Advantage of Me (Garland) music: Richard
          Rodgers; lyrics: Lorenz Hart
        Black Bottom (girlie chorus) music; Ray Henderson;
          lyrics: Buddy De Sylva, Lew Brown
        Peanut Vendor (Garland) music: Moises Simons; lyrics:
          L Wolfe Gilbert, Marion Sunshine
        My Melancoly Baby (Garland) music: Ernie Burnett;
          lyrics: George A Norton
        Swanee (Garland, chorus) music: George Gershwin;
          lyrics: Irving Caesar
---   Here's What I'm Here For (Garland, chorus)
      It's A New World (Garland)
      Someone At Last (Garland, chorus)
      Lose That Long Face (Garland)

Note: An additional soundtrack selection, deleted from the
      original film, was issued on Out Takes OTF - 3:

      When My Sugar Walks Down the Street (Garland) music,
       lyrics: Jimmy McHugh, Gene Austin, Irving Mills

A STAR IS BORN (Warner Bros, 1976)

Columbia JS 34403 (soundtrack) stereo

Music, lyrics: Paul Williams, Kenny Ascher, others; musical
direction: Paul Williams

Cast: Vanetta Fields, Clydie King, Kris Kristofferson, Barbra
       Streisand

Songs: Watch Closely Now (Kristofferson)
       Queen Bee (Streisand, Fields, King) music, lyrics:
          Rupert Holmes
       Everything (Streisand, chorus) music, lyrics: Rupert
          Holmes, Paul Williams
       Lost Inside of You (Streisand, Kristofferson, chorus)
          music, lyrics: Barbra Streisand, Leon Russell
       Hellacious Acres (Kristofferson)
       Evergreen (Love Theme from 'A Star Is Born') (Streisand)
          music, lyrics: Barbra Streisand, Paul Williams
---   The Woman in the Moon (Streisand, chorus)
       I Believe in Love (Streisand, chorus) music: Kenny
          Loggins; lyrics: Alan and Marilyn Bergman
       Crippled Crow (Kristofferson) music, lyrics: Donna Weiss
       Finale:
          With One More Look at You (Streisand)
          Watch Closely Now (reprise) (Streisand, chorus)
          Evergreen (reprise) (Streisand, Kristofferson, chorus)

THE STAR MAKER (Paramount, 1939)

Decca DL 4254 mono 'Bing's Hollywood - The Road Begins'

Music: Gus Edwards, others; lyrics: Will D Cobb, others;
musical direction: John Scott Trotter

Cast: Connie Boswell (not in film), Bing Crosby

Songs: An Apple for the Teacher (Crosby, Boswell) music: James
          V Monaco; lyrics: John Burke
       In My Merry Oldsmobile (Crosby, chorus) lyrics: Vincent
          Bryan
       A Man and His Dream (Crosby) music: James V Monaco;
          lyrics: John Burke
       Gus Edwards Medley:
          School Days (chorus)
          Sunbonnet Sue (Crosby)
          Jimmy Valentine (Crosby) lyrics: Edward Madden
          If I Was A Millionaire (Crosby)
       Still the Bluebird Sings (Crosby) music: James V Monaco;
          lyrics: John Burke

        Go Fly A Kite (Crosby) music: James V Monaco; lyrics:
        John Burke

STAR SPANGLED RHYTHM (Paramount, 1942)

Curtain Calls 100/20 (soundtrack) mono also: Sandy Hook SH 2045

Music: Harold Arlen, others; lyrics: Johnny Mercer; musical
direction: Robert Emmett Dolan

Cast: Eddie 'Rochester' Anderson, William Bendix, Walter Catlett,
       Chester Clute, Jerry Colonna, Bing Crosby, Donna Drake,
       Katherine Dunham, Paulette Goddard, The Golden Gate
       Quartet, Susan Hayward, Sterling Holloway, Bob Hope, Betty
       Hutton, Johnnie Johnston, Dorothy Lamour, Fred MacMurray,
       Marion Martin, Mary Martin, Martha Mears (for Veronica
       Lake), Ray Milland, Lynne Overman, Dick Powell, Marjorie
       Reynolds, Betty Rhodes, Slim and Slam, Franchot Tone,
       Arthur Treacher, Ernest Truex

Songs: Main Title (orchestra)
       Hit the Road to Dreamland (Powell, Mary Martin, The Golden
         Gate Quartet)
       On the Swing Shift (Reynolds, Rhodes, Drake)
       I'm Doing It for Defense (Hutton)
       A Sweater, A Sarong and A Peek-A-Boo Bang (Goddard,
         Lamour, Mears, Catlett, Treacher, Holloway)
       Priorities (Hayward, Truex) spoken
       That Old Black Magic (Johnston)
---   If Men Played Cards as Women Do (Milland, MacMurray,
         Tone, Overman) spoken
       Sharp as A Tack (Anderson, Dunham, Slim and Slam)
       Wife, Husband and Wolf (Hope, Bendix, Clute, Marion
         Martin) spoken (introduction: Colonna)
       Old Glory (Crosby, chorus)

THE STARS ARE SINGING (Paramount, 1953)

Columbia (45/EP) B 1618 mono

Music, lyrics: Jay Livingston, Ray Evans, others; musical
direction: Paul Weston, others

Cast: Rosemary Clooney

Songs: I Do! I Do! I Do! (Clooney)
       Haven't Got A Worry (Clooney)
       Lovely Weather for Ducks (Clooney)
       Come On-A My House (Clooney) music: Ross Bagdasarian;
         lyrics: William Saroyan; musical direction: Stan Freeman

Note: An additional studio recording:

MGM (45rpm) K 30470 Pagliacci: Vesti la Giubba (Lauritz Melchior)
                music: Leoncavallo

STATE FAIR (Twentieth Century-Fox, 1945)

Decca (78rpm) A 412 mono

Music: Richard Rodgers; lyrics: Oscar Hammerstein II; musical
direction: Victor Young, others

Cast: Dick Haymes

Decca (78rpm) 18706 That's for Me (Haymes)
                    It Might As Well Be Spring (Haymes)
Decca (78rpm) 18710 Isn't It Kinda Fun (Haymes)
                    The Lord's Been Good to Me (Haymes) music,
                      lyrics: Sam H Stept (not from film)
Decca (78rpm) 18740 It's A Grand Night for Singing (Haymes,
                      chorus) musical direction: Earle Hagen;
                      LP: Ace of Hearts AH 68
                    All I Owe Ioway (Haymes, chorus) musical
                      direction: Earle Hagen

STATE FAIR (Twentieth Century-Fox, 1945)

Classic International Filmusicals C I F (soundtrack) mono

Musical direction: Alfred Newman, Charles Henderson

Cast: Dana Andrews, Fay Bainter, Vivian Blaine, Dick Haymes,
        Louanna Hogan (for Jeanne Crain), Percy Kilbride,
        William Marshall, Donald Meek, Charles Winninger

Songs: Opening Music (orchestra)
        Our State Fair (Kilbride, Winninger, Bainter, chorus)
        It Might As Well Be Spring (Hogan) two reprises
        That's for Me (Blaine)
        It's A Grand Night for Singing (Marshall, Haymes, Hogan,
          Andrews, chorus)
        That's for Me (reprise) (Hogan, Haymes)
        It's A Grand Night for Singing (reprise) (Blaine, Marshall,
          chorus)
        Isn't It Kinda Fun (Blaine, Haymes)
        All I Owe Ioway (Marshall, Blaine, Winninger, Bainter,
          Meek, chorus)
        It's A Grand Night for Singing (reprise) (Haymes, cast)

STATE FAIR (Twentieth Century-Fox, 1962)

Dot DLP 29011 (soundtrack) stereo

Musical direction: Alfred Newman

Cast: Ann-Margret, Pat Boone, Bobby Darin, Tom Ewell, Alice Faye,
       Anita Gordon (for Pamela Tiffin), Bob Smart, David Street

Songs: Overture /Main Title (orchestra)
       Our State Fair (Boone, Faye, Ewell, chorus)
       It Might As Well Be Spring (Gordon)
       That's for Me (Boone)
       More Than Just A Friend (Ewell) lyrics: Richard Rodgers
       Isn't It Kinda Fun (Ann-Margret, Street)
---   Willing and Eager (Boone, Ann-Margret) lyrics: Richard
          Rodgers
       Never Say No to A Man (Faye) lyrics: Richard Rodgers
       It's A Grand Night for Singing (Boone, Darin, Gordon,
          Smart, chorus)
       This Isn't Heaven (Darin) lyrics: Richard Rodgers
       The Little Things in Texas (Ewell, Faye, children)
          lyrics: Richard Rodgers
       Our State Fair Finale (chorus)

STEP LIVELY (RKO, 1944)

Hollywood Soundstage 412 (soundtrack) mono

Music: Jule Styne; lyrics: Sammy Cahn; musical direction:
Constantin Bakaleinikoff

Cast: Anne Jeffreys, Gloria De Haven, George Murphy, Frank Sinatra

Songs: Opening Music (orchestra)
       Where Does Love Begin (De Haven, Murphy, chorus)
       Come Out, Come Out, Wherever You Are (De Haven, Sinatra,
          chorus)
       As Long As There's Music (Sinatra)
       Where Does Love Begin (Jeffreys, Sinatra)
---   Some Other Time (Sinatra, De Haven, chorus)
       Why Must There Be An Opening Song (Jeffreys)
       Ask the Madam (Murphy, De Haven, chorus)
       Finale:
          As Long As There's Music (reprise) (Sinatra, chorus)
          Some Other Time (reprise) (De Haven, Sinatra, chorus)
          As Long As There's Music (reprise) (Sinatra)
          Where Does Love Begin (reprise) (chorus)

THE STOOGE (Paramount, 1952)

Capitol H 401 mono

Music, lyrics: various; musical direction: Dick Stabile

Cast: Dean Martin

Songs: I Feel A Song Coming On (Martin) music: Jimmy McHugh;
            lyrics: Dorothy Fields, George Oppenheim
        A Girl Named Mary and A Boy Named Bill (Martin) music,
            lyrics: Mack David, Jerry Livingston
        Just One More Chance (Martin) music: Arthur Johnston;
            lyrics: Sam Coslow
        Who's Your Little Who-zis! (Martin) music, lyrics: Al
            Goering, Ben Bernie, Walter Hirsch
        I'm Yours (Martin) music: Johnny Green; lyrics: E Y
            Harburg
        I Feel Like A Feather in the Breeze (Martin) music:
            Harry Revel; lyrics: Mack Gordon
        With My Eyes Wide Open I'm Dreaming (Martin) music:
            Harry Revel; lyrics: Mack Gordon
        Louise (Martin) music: Richard Whiting; lyrics: Leo Robin

STOP THE WORLD I WANT TO GET OFF! (Warner Bros, 1966)

Warner Bros B 1643 (soundtrack) stereo

Music, lyrics: Anthony Newley, Leslie Bricusse, others; musical
direction: Al Ham

Cast: Millicent Martin, Tony Tanner

Songs: Overture (orchestra)
        I Wanna Be Rich (Tanner, chorus)
        Typically English (Martin, Tanner)
        Lumbered (Tanner, Martin)
        Gonna Build A Mountain (Tanner)
        Glorious Russian (Martin)
        Malinki Meilchick (Tanner, Martin)
---   Family Fugue and Nag Nag Nag (Tanner, Martin, chorus)
        Typically Japanese (Martin)
        The New York Scene and All American (Martin)
        Mumbo Jumbo (Tanner)
        Once in A Life Time (Tanner)
        Someone Nice Like You (Tanner, Martin)
        What Kind of Fool Am I (Tanner)
        I Believed It All (chorus) music, lyrics: Al Ham

STORMY WEATHER (Twentieth Century-Fox, 1943)

Sountrak STK 103 (soundtrack) mono also: Sandy Hook SH 2037

Music, lyrics: various

Cast: Cab Calloway, Lena Horne, Bill 'Bojangles' Robinson,
        Zutty Singleton Orchestra, Fats Waller

Songs: Stormy Weather (Horne, chorus) music: Harold Arlen;
            lyrics: Ted Koehler
        I Can't Give You Anything But Love, Baby (Horne, Calloway)
            music: Jimmy McHugh; lyrics: Dorothy Fields
        Ain't That Something? (Robinson) music, lyrics: Pinky
            Tomlin, Harry Tobias
        Jumpin' Jive (Calloway) music, lyrics: Cab Calloway,
            Frank Froeba, Jack Palmer
---   Sunday in Savannah (Calloway) music, lyrics: Willard
            Robison
        Lonesome Blues (Calloway) music, lyrics: Perry Bradford
        Good for Nothin' Joe (Horne) music, lyrics: Rube Bloom
        Ain't Misbehavin' (Waller) music: Fats Waller, Harry
            Brooks; lyrics: Andy Razaf
        Moppin' and Boppin' (Zutty Singleton Orchestra) music,
            lyrics: Fats Waller, B Carter, Ed Kirkeby
        Diga Diga Do (Horne) music: Jimmy McHugh; lyrics:
            Dorothy Fields

Note: Additional cast recordings:

V-Disc (78rpm) 126 Lena Horne with the Cab Calloway Orchestra:
                   Diga Diga Do
                   There's No Two Ways About Love
                   Good for Nothin' Joe

THE STORY OF ROBIN HOOD (Disney, 1952)

Disneyland DQ 1249 (soundtrack) mono

Music, lyrics: Laurence Edward Watkin, Elton Hayes, others

Cast: Elton Hayes, James Hayter

Songs: Riddle de Diddle de Day (Hayes) music, lyrics: Pola, Whyle
        Come Sing Low, Come Sing High (Hayter)
---   Ballad of Robin Hood (Hayes)
        Riddle de Diddle de Day (reprise) (Hayes)

Note: The above recording consists primarily of spoken dialog,
        with a narration by Dal McKennon. Studio recordings by
        Elton Hayes:

Parlophone (British 78rpm) R-3509 Whistle My Love
                                 Riddle de Diddle de Day

STRIKE UP THE BAND (MGM, 1940)

Curtain Calls CC 100/9-10 (soundtrack) mono

Music, lyrics: various; musical direction: George Stoll

Cast: Margaret Early, Judy Garland, Larry Nunn, June Preisser,
       Mickey Rooney, Six Hits and A Miss, William Tracy,
       Paul Whiteman Orchestra

Songs: Main Title (orchestra)
       Our Love Affair (Garland, Rooney) music: Roger Edens;
          lyrics: Arthur Freed
       Do the Conga (Garland, Rooney, Six Hits and A Miss)
          music, lyrics: Roger Edens
       Nobody (Garland) music, lyrics: Roger Edens
       The Gay Ninties Revue (Part I) (Rooney, Garland, Preisser,
          Early, Tracy, Nunn, chorus)
---   The Gay Ninties Revue (Part II)
       When Day Is Done (Paul Whiteman Orchestra) music: Robert
          Katscher; lyrics: Buddy DeSylva
       Drummer Boy (Six Hits and A Miss) music, lyrics: Roger
          Edens
       Band Contest Montage (orchestra)
       Finale: Strike Up the Band (Garland, Rooney, Six Hits and
          A Miss, chorus) music: George Gershwin; lyrics: Ira
          Gershwin

Note: Studio recordings by cast members:

Decca (78rpm) 3953 Our Love Affair (Garland) LP: MCA 4003
Victor (78rpm) 35828 When Day Is Done (Whiteman Orchestra)

THE STUDENT PRINCE (MGM, 1954)

RCA LM 1837 mono   reissued: RCA 1188

Music: Sigmund Romberg, others; lyrics: Dorothy Donnelly, others;
musical direction: Constantine Callinicos

Cast: Elizabeth Doubleday (not in film), Mario Lanza (for
       Edmund Purdom)

Songs: Introduction (orchestra)
       Serenade (Lanza, chorus)
       Golden Days (Lanza)
       Drink, Drink, Drink (Lanza, chorus)
       Summertime in Heidelberg (Lanza, Doubleday) music:
          Nicholas Brodszky; lyrics: Paul Francis Webster
       Beloved (Lanza) music: Nicholas Brodszky; lyrics:
          Paul Francis Webster

>Gaudeamus Igitur (Lanza, chorus) trad
>Deep in My Heart, Dear (Lanza, Doubleday)
>I'll Walk with God (Lanza, chorus) music: Nicholas Brodszky

Note: Additional recordings by cast members:

MGM (45rpm) K30853 Deep in My Heart, Dear (Ann Blyth)
                   The Students' Marching Song (Blyth, chorus)

SUMMER HOLIDAY (MGM, 1948)

Four Jays HW 602 (soundtrack) mono

Music: Harry Warren; lyrics: Ralph Blane; musical direction:
Lennie Hayton

Cast: Gloria De Haven, Walter Huston, Butch Jenkins, Shirley
        Johns, Michael Kirby, Marilyn Maxwell, Agnes Moorehead,
        Frank Morgan, Emory Parnell, Mickey Rooney, Selena Royle

Songs: Overture (orchestra)
        Our Home Town (Huston, Royle, Jenkins, Johns, Kirby,
           Morgan, Moorehead, De Haven, Rooney)
        Never Again (Morgan) cut from film
        Afraid to Fall in Love (Rooney, De Haven)
        Danville High (De Haven, chorus)
        The Stanley Steamer (De Haven, Royle, Rooney, Huston)
        Independence Day (chorus)
---   Omar and the Princess (Rooney, De Haven) cut from film
        Wish I Had A Braver Heart (De Haven) cut from film
        Barroom Sequence:
            The Weary Blues (Maxwell, Rooney, Parnell)
            You're the Sweetest Kid I've Ever Known (Maxwell,
               Rooney)
        Spring Isn't Everything (Huston) cut from film

Note: The above recording includes spoken dialog

SUMMER HOLIDAY (American International, 1963) British

Epic BN 26063 (soundtrack) stereo   reissued: MFP 6021   CD

Music, lyrics: Peter Myers, Ronald Cass

Cast: Cliff Richard, The Shadows

Songs: Summer Holiday (Richard, Shadows)
        Bachelor Boy (Richard, Shadows)
        The Next Time (Richard, Shadows)
        Dancing Shoes (Richard, Shadows)

SUMMER LOVE (Universal, 1958)

Decca DL 8714 (soundtrack) mono

Music: Henry Mancini, Rod McKuen, Malvina Reynolds, Milton Rosen;
lyrics: Bill Carey, Everett Carter, Malvina Reynolds, Rod McKuen;
musical direction: Joseph Gershenson

Cast: Molly Bee, Jimmy Daley, The Ding-A-Lings, Rod McKuen,
        Kip Tyler

Songs: Main Title: Summer Love (Tyler, Daley, The Ding-A-Lings)
        Beatin' on the Bongos (Bee, Daley, The Ding-A-Lings)
        Sox Hop (Daley, The Ding-A-Lings)
        Love Is Something (Bee, Daley, The Ding-A-Lings)
        Walkin' the Rock (Daley, The Ding-A-Lings)
        Ding-A-Ling (Daley, The Ding-A-Lings)
        Night Walk (Daley)
        To Know You Is to Love You (McKuen, Bee)
        Boppin' at the Bash (Daley)
---   To Know You Is to Love You (reprise) (Daley)
        Calypso Rock (McKuen, Daley)
        Joannie (Daley)
        The Rock Talks (Daley)
        Theme for A Crazy Chick (Daley, The Ding-A-Lings)
        Soft Touch (Daley, The Ding-A-Lings)
        Sad Sax (Daley, The Ding-A-Lings)
        Kool Breeze (orchestra)
        So, Good Night (Daley, The Ding A Lings)

SUMMER MAGIC (Disney, 1962)

Vista 4025 stereo

Music, lyrics: Richard M Sherman, Robert B Sherman; musical
direction: Tutti Camarata

Cast: Eddie Hodges, Marilyn Hooven (for Dorothy Maguire), Burl
        Ives, Hayley Mills, Wendy Turner, Deborah Walley

Songs: Overture (orchestra)
        Railroad Rag (orchestra)
        Flitterin' (Mills, Hodges, chorus)
        Beautiful Beulah (Mills, Hodges, chorus)
        Ugly Bug Ball (Ives)
        Pink of Perfection (Mills, Hodges)
---   Summer Magic (Hooven)
        Beautiful Beulah (reprise) (Mills, Hodges)
        Femininity (Mills, Walley, Turner) Flitterin' (reprise)
        On the Front Porch (Ives, chorus)
        Finale (chorus)

SUMMER STOCK (MGM, 1950)

MGM E 519 (soundtrack) mono reissued: MCA 39084 CD

Music: Harry Warren, others; lyrics: Mack Gordon, others;
musical direction: Johnny Green

Cast: Gloria De Haven, Judy Garland, Gene Kelly, Pete Roberts
        (for Hans Conried), Phil Silvers

Songs: (Howdy Neighbor) Happy Harvest (Garland, chorus)
        You Wonderful You (Kelly)
        Friendly Star (Garland)
        Heavenly Music (Kelly, Silvers) music, lyrics: Saul
          Chaplin
---   If You Feel Like Singing, Sing (Garland)
        Mem'ry Island (De Haven, Roberts, chorus)
        Get Happy (Garland, chorus) music: Harold Arlen; lyrics:
          Ted Koehler
        Dig-Dig-Dig Dig for Your Supper (Kelly, Silvers, chorus)

SUN VALLEY SERENADE (Twentieth Century-Fox, 1941)

RCA LPT 3064 (soundtrack) mono reissued: Mercury 826 635-1 CD

Music: Harry Warren, others; lyrics: Mack Gordon; musical
direction: Glenn Miller

Cast: Tex Beneke, Dorothy Dandridge, Pat Friday (for Lynn
        Bari), Paula Kelly, The Glenn Miller Orchestra, The
        Modernaires, The Nicholas Brothers, John Payne

Songs: It Happened in Sun Valley (chorus, Modernaires)
        In the Mood (orchestra) music: Joe Garland
        At Last (Friday, Payne)
        Chattanooga Choo Choo (Beneke, Kelly, Modernaires,
          The Nicholas Brothers, Dorothy Dandridge)
---   I Know Why (Friday, Modernaires, Payne)
        Sun Valley Jump (orchestra) music: Jerry Grey
        Measure for Measure (orchestra) music: Arletta May
        The Spirit is Willing (orchestra) music: Jerry Grey

Note: Glenn Miller studio recordings:

Bluebird (78rpm) 11263 It Happened in Sun Valley
                       The Kiss Polka
Bluebird (78rpm) 11230 I Know Why
                       Chattanooga Choo Choo

11263 is included on 'The Complete Glenn Miller' vol 7 (RCA
LP: AXM 2-5570);11230 is on vol 6 (AXM 2-5569).

SUNNY SIDE OF THE STREET (Columbia, 1951)

Mercury MG 25100 mono

Music, lyrics: various

Cast: Vic Damone (not in film), Billy Daniels, Tony Fontaine
       (not in film), Frankie Laine

Songs: I May Be Wrong (Laine) music: Henry Sullivan; lyrics:
          Harry Ruskin
       On the Sunny Side of the Street (Laine) music: Jimmy
          McHugh; lyrics: Dorothy Fields
       I'm Gonna Live Till I Die (Laine) music, lyrics: Al
          Hoffman, Walter Kent, Mann Curtis
       Too Marvelous for Words (Daniels) music: Richard Whiting;
          lyrics: Johnny Mercer
       I Get A Kick Out of You (Daniels) music, lyrics: Cole
          Porter
       I Hadn't Anyone Till You (Damone) music, lyrics: Ray
          Noble
       The Love of A Gypsy (Fontaine) music: Morris Stoloff;
          Fred Karger

SWEET CHARITY (Universal, 1968)

Decca DL 71502 (soundtrack) stereo

Music: Cy Coleman; lyrics: Dorothy Fields; musical direction:
Joseph Gershenson

Cast: Sammy Davis, Stubby Kaye, Paula Kelly, Shirley MacLaine,
       John McMartin, Chita Rivera

Songs: Overture (Big Spender, It's A Nice Face, Sweet Charity,
          Where Am I Going, I'm A Brass Band) (orchestra)
       My Personal Property (MacLaine)
       Big Spender (girls)
       The Pompeii Club (Rich Man's Frug) (orchestra)
       If My Friends Could See Me Now (MacLaine)
       There's Gotta Be Something Better than This (MacLaine,
          Rivera, Kelly)
       It's A Nice Face (MacLaine)
---   Rhythm of Life (Davis, ensemble)
       Sweet Charity (McMartin)
       I'm A Brass Band (MacLaine)
       I Love to Cry at Weddings (Kaye, ensemble)
       Where Am I Going? (MacLaine)
       Finale: Sweet Charity (rebirth) (orchestra)

SWEET DREAMS (Tri-Star, 1985)

MCA 6149 (soundtrack) stereo CD

Music, lyrics: various

Cast: Patsy Cline (for Jessica Lange)

Songs: San Antonio Rose (Cline) music, lyrics: Bob Wills
        Seven Lonely Days (Cline) music, lyrics: Earl Schuman,
            Alden Schuman, Marshall Brown
        Your Cheatin' Heart (Cline) music, lyrics: Hank Williams
        Lovesick Blues (Cline) music, lyrics: Irving Mills, Cliff
            Friend
        Walking After Midnight (Cline) music, lyrics: Don Hecht,
            Alan Block
        Foolin' Around (Cline) music, lyrics: Harlan Howard,
            Buck Owens
        Half As Much (Cline) music, lyrics: Curley Williams
        I Fall to Pieces (Cline) music, lyrics: Hank Cochran,
            Harland Howard
        Crazy (Cline) music, lyrics: Willie Nelson
        Blue Moon of Kentucky (Cline) music, lyrics: Bill Monroe
        She's Got You (Cline) music, lyrics: Hank Cochran
        Sweet Dreams (Cline) music, lyrics: Don Gibson

SWEET ROSIE O'GRADY (Twentieth Century-Fox, 1943)

Sandy Hook SH 2090 (soundtrack) mono

Music: Harry Warren, others; lyrics: Mack Gordon, others; musical
direction: Alfred Newman, Charles Henderson

Cast: Betty Grable, Adolphe Menjou, Frank Orth, Phil Regan,
        Robert Young

Songs: Overture (orchestra)
        Waitin' at the Church (Grable, chorus)
        My Heart Tells Me (Regan, Grable)
        Sweet Rosie O'Grady (Young) music, lyrics: Maude Nugent
        The Wishing Waltz (Regan, chorus)
        My Heart Tells Me (reprise) (Grable)
        Two Little Girls in Blue (Grable, Young) music, lyrics:
            Charles Graham
        Little Annie Rooney (Grable, Young, Orth) music, lyrics:
            Michael Nolan
        Sweet Rosie O'Grady (reprise) (Grable, Young, Menjou,
            chorus)
        Get Your Police Gazette (chorus)
        Sweet Rosie O'Grady (reprise) (Grable)
        Going to the Country Fair (Grable)

My Sam (Grable)
Finale

SWING TIME (RKO, 1936)

EMI (British) EMTC 101 (soundtrack) mono also: Sandy Hook SH 2028

Music: Jerome Kern; lyrics: Dorothy Fields; musical direction:
Nathaniel Shilkret

Cast: Fred Astaire, Helen Broderick, George Metaxa, Victor
       Moore, Ginger Rogers

Songs: Overture (chorus)
       Pick Yourself Up (Astaire, Rogers)
       The Way You Look Tonight (Astaire)
       The Waltz in Swing Time (orchestra)
       A Fine Romance (Astaire, Rogers)
       Bojangles of Harlem (chorus)
       Never Gonna Dance (Astaire)
       Finale (Astaire, Rogers, Metaxa, Moore, Broderick)

Note: Studio recordings by Astaire, all on Columbia LP: SG 32472:

Brunswick (78rpm) 7716 A Fine Romance
                       The Waltz in Swing Time (orchestra only)
Brunswick (78rpm) 7717 Pick Yourself Up
                       The Way You Look Tonight
Brunswick (78rpm) 7718 Bojangles of Harlem
                       Never Gonna Dance

THE SWINGER (Paramount, 1966)

RCA LSP 3710 stereo

Music: Marty Paich, others; lyrics: various; musical direction:
Marty Paich

Cast: Ann-Margret

Songs: The Swinger (Ann-Margret) music: Andre Previn; lyrics:
          Dory Previn
       Swinger's Holiday (orchestra)
       I Wanna Be Loved (Ann-Margret) music: Johnny Green;
          lyrics: Ed Heyman, Billy Rose
       Kelly's Dance (orchestra)
       That Old Black Magic (Ann-Margret) music: Harold Arlen;
          lyrics: Johnny Mercer

Note: The above recording contains other selections not from
          the film.

THE SWORD IN THE STONE (Disney, 1963)

Disney 4901 (soundtrack) stereo

Music, lyrics: Richard M Sherman, Robert B Sherman

Cast: Vocals uncredited

Songs: A Most Befuddling Thing
        Blue Oak Tree
        Mad Madam Mim
        That's What Makes the World Go Round
        Higitus Figitus
        The Legend of the Sword in the Stone

TAKE ME OUT TO THE BALL GAME (MGM, 1949)

Curtain Calls 100/18 (soundtrack) mono

Music: Roger Edens, others; lyrics: Betty Comden, Adolph Green,
others; musical direction: Adolph Deutsch

Cast: Betty Garrett, Gene Kelly, Jules Munshin, Frank Sinatra,
        Esther Williams

Songs: Titles (orchestra)
        Take Me Out to the Ball Game (Kelly, Sinatra) music:
            Albert Von Tilzer; lyrics: Jack Norwood
        Yes Indeedy (Kelly, Sinatra, Munshin, chorus)
        O'Brien to Ryan to Goldberg (Kelly, Sinatra, Munshin)
        She's the Right Girl for Me (Sinatra)
        Boys and Girls Like You (Sinatra) music: Richard Rodgers;
            lyrics: Oscar Hammerstein II (cut from film)
---   It's Fate, Baby, It's Fate (Sinatra, Garrett)
        Baby Doll (Kelly) music: Harry Warren; lyrics: Johnny
            Mercer (cut from film)
        Strictly USA (Munshin, Garrett, Sinatra, Williams, Kelly,
            chorus)
        The Hat My Father Wore Upon St Patrick's Day (Kelly,
            chorus)
        Strictly USA (reprise) (cast)

Note: Additional recordings by cast members:

Columbia (78rpm) 38456 The Right Girl for Me (Sinatra)
                    LP: Columbia CL 2913
MGM (78rpm) 30193 Take Me Out to the Ball Game (Kelly, Garrett)
                    LP: Lion L 70089; Stet DS 15010
                Yes Indeedy (Kelly, Garrett)
MGM (78rpm) 30190 It's Fate, Baby, It's Fate (Garrett)

TEA FOR TWO (Warner Bros, 1950)

Columbia CL 6149 mono   reissued: Columbia CSP P 17660

Music: Vincent Youmans, others; lyrics: Irving Caesar, others;
musical direction: Axel Stordahl

Cast: The Page Cavanaugh Trio (not in film), Doris Day, Gene
        Nelson

Songs: Crazy Rhythm (Day, Nelson, Cavanaugh Trio) music: Roger
            Wolfe Kahn, Joseph Meyer
        Here in My Arms (Day, chorus) music: Richard Rodgers;
            lyrics: Lorenz Hart
        I Know That You Know (Day, Nelson, Cavanaugh Trio)
            lyrics: Ann Caldwell
        I Want to Be Happy (Day, Cavanaugh Trio)
---   Do Do Do (Day, male quartet) music: George Gershwin;
            lyrics: Ira Gershwin
        I Only Have Eyes for You (Day, chorus) music: Harry
            Warren; lyrics: Al Dubin
        Oh Me! Oh My! (Day, Nelson, Cavanaugh Trio) lyrics:
            Ira Gershwin (as 'Arthur Francis')
        Tea for Two (Day, chorus)

TELL ME LIES (Mira / Walter Reade, 1968)

GRE-GAR GGS 5000 (soundtrack) stereo

Music: Richard Peaslee; lyrics: Adrian Mitchell; musical
direction: Tony Russell

Cast: John Hussey, Glenda Jackson, Mark Jones, Margie Lawrence,
        Leon Lissek, Robert Lloyd, Ursula Mohan, Pauline Munro,
        Barry Stanton, Hugh Sullivan, Michael Williams

Songs: Tell Me Lies (Jones, Lloyd)
        Road Number One (Jackson, Lawrence, Munro, Mohan, chorus)
        Make and Break (Jackson, Williams, Stanton, chorus)
        Barry Bondhus (Lloyd, chorus)
        God Is Flame (Hussey, Lawrence, chorus)
---   Escalation (chorus)
        The Leeches (Sullivan, Lissek, Jackson, chorus)
        When Dreams Collide (Sullivan, Williams, Lloyd, Jackson)
        Rose of Saigon (Williams, Lawrence, chorus)
        Tell Me Lies (reprise) (Jones, Lloyd)
        Any Complaints (Lawrence, chorus)
        Icarus (chorus)

'10' (Orion, 1979)

Warner Bros BSK 3399 (soundtrack) stereo

Music: Henry Mancini, others; lyrics: Robert Wells, others; musical direction: Henry Mancini

Cast: Julie Andrews, Dudley Moore, Max Showalter

Songs: Main Theme (Don't Call It Love) (orchestra; piano
            soloist: Henry Mancini)
        He Pleases Me (Andrews)
        Keyboard Harmony (orchestra)
        It's Easy to Say (chorus)
        Something for Jenny (orchestra)
        Don't Call It Love (chorus) lyrics: Carole Bayer Sager
---   Get It On (chorus)
        It's Easy to Say (reprise) (Andrews, Moore)
        The Hot Sand Mexican Band (orchestra)
        I Have An Ear for Love (Showalter)
        It's Easy to Say (reprise) (piano soloist: Dudley Moore)
        Bolero (orchestra) music: Ravel

TEN THOUSAND BEDROOMS (MGM, 1957)

Capitol (45/EP) 1-840 mono

Music: Nicholas Brodszky; lyrics: Sammy Cahn

Cast: Dean Martin

Songs: Money Is A Problem (Martin)
        Ten Thousand Bedrooms (Martin)
        I Only Trust Your Heart (Martin)
        You I Love (Martin)

Note: An additional selection:

Capitol (45rpm) 3648 The Man Who Plays the Mandolino (Martin)

TEVYE AND HIS 7 DAUGHTERS (Israel, 1968)

CBS (Israeli 7" LP) 6430   stereo

Music: Dov Seltzer; lyrics: Haim Hefer; musical direction: Dov Seltzer

Cast: Chava Alberstein, Yehoram Gaon

Songs: Tevye's Village (Gaon)

```
        The Young Lover's Dance (orchestra)
---     My Love Has Gone (Alberstein)
        Dance of the Peasants (orchestra)
```

THANK GOD IT'S FRIDAY (Columbia, 1978)

Casablanca 2-7099 (two records - soundtrack) stereo

Music, lyrics: various

Cast: The Commadores, Paul Jabara, Donna Sumner, (and the
       sounds and voices of) Pattie Brooks, Cameo, Santa
       Esmeralda, Thelma Houston, Love and Kisses, D C LaRue,
       Marathon, Natural Juices, Diana Ross, Sunshine, The
       Wright Bros Flying Machine

Songs: Thank God It's Friday (Love and Kisses) music, lyrics:
          Alec R Costandinos
       After Dark (Brooks) music, lyrics: Simon and Sabrina
          Soussan
       With Your Love (Sumner) music, lyrics: Donna Sumner,
          George Moroder, Pete Bellotte
       Last Dance (Sumner) music, lyrics: Paul Jabara
---   Disco Queen (Jabara) music, lyrics: Paul Jabara
       Find My Way (Cameo) music, lyrics: Johnny Melfi
       Too Hot Ta Trot (The Commadores) music, lyrics: T McClary,
          M Williams, W Orange, L Ritchie, R LaPread, W King
       Leatherman's Theme (Wright Bros Flying Machine) music,
          lyrics: Arthur Wright
       I Wanna Dance (Marathon) music, lyrics: Pete Bellotte
---   Take It to the Zoo (Sunshine) music, lyrics: Donna Sumner,
          Bruce Sudano, Joe Esposito
       Seville Nights (Santa Esmeralda) music, lyrics: N Skorsky,
          J M de Scarano, J C Petit
       You're the Most Precious Thing in My Life (Love and
          Kisses) music, lyrics: Alec R Costandinos
---   Do You Want the Real Thing (LaRue) music, lyrics: D C
          LaRue, Bob Esty
       Trapped in A Stairway (Jabara) music, lyrics: Paul Jabara,
          Bob Esty
       Floyd's Theme (Natural Juices) music, lyrics: Dick St
          Nicklaus
       Lovin' Livin' and Givin' (Ross) music, lyrics: Kenneth
          Stover, Pam Davis
       Love Masterpiece (Houston) music, lyrics: Hal Davis, Josef
          Powell, Art Posey
       Last Dance (reprise) (Sumner)

Note: Included with the above album was a special bonus 12"
       single:

Je T'Aime (Moi Non Plus) (Sumner) music, lyrics: Serge
    Gainsbourg

THANK YOUR LUCKY STARS (Warner Bros, 1943)

Curtain Calls 100/8 (soundtrack) mono also: Sandy Hook SH 2012

Music: Arthur Schwartz, others; lyrics: Frank Loesser, others;
musical direction: Ray Heindorf

Cast: Willie Best, Jesse Lee Brooks, Eddie Cantor, Jack Carson,
        Rita Christina, Bette Davis, Olivia de Havilland, Errol
        Flynn, John Garfield, Alan Hale, Spike Jones and his
        City Slickers, Joan Leslie, Ida Lupino, Hattie McDaniel,
        Dennis Morgan, Joyce Reynolds, Ann Sheridan, Dinah Shore,
        George Tobias

Songs: Overture (orchestra)
        Thank Your Lucky Stars (Shore)
        Blues in the Night (Garfield) music: Harold Arlen; lyrics:
            Johnny Mercer
        Hotcha Cornia (The Volga Boatman) (Jones)
        Ridin' for A Fall (Morgan, Leslie, Jones, chorus)
        We're Staying Home Tonight (Cantor)
        Goin' North (Carson, Hale)
        Love Isn't Born, It's Made (Reynolds, Sheridan, girls)
        No You, No Me (Morgan, Leslie)
        The Dreamer (Shore)
---   Ice Cold Katie (MaDaniel, Best, Brooks, Christina, chorus)
        How Sweet You Are (Shore, chorus)
        That's What You Jolly Well Get (Flynn, chorus)
        They're Either Too Young or Too Old (Davis)
        The Dreamer (reprise) (deHavilland, Lupino, Tobias)
        Good Night, Good Neighbor (Morgan, chorus)
        Finale: How Sweet you Are (chorus)
                Goin' North (Carson, Hale)
                The Dreamer (Shore, de Havilland, Lupino, Tobias)
                Ridin' for A Fall (Morgan, Leslie, chorus)
                Love Isn't Born, It's Made (Sheridan)
                That's What You Jolly Well Get (Flynn, chorus)
                Good Night, Good Neighbor (Morgan, chorus)
                They're Either Too Young or Too Old (Davis)
                Ice Cold Katie (Cantor, McDaniel)
                Thank Your Lucky Stars (chorus)

Note: Studio recording by Spike Jones and his City Slickers:

        Bluebird (78rpm) 30 0818 Hotcha Cornia

THAT MIDNIGHT KISS (MGM, 1949)

RCA LM 86 mono   reissued: RCA LM 2422

Music, lyrics: various; musical direction: Constantine Callinicos,
others

Cast: Mario Lanza

Songs: La Boheme: Act I: Che Gelida Manina (Lanza) music: Puccini
       Mamma mia che vo' sape? (Lanza) music: Nutile; lyrics:
          F Russo
       I Know, I Know, I Know (Lanza) music: Bronislaw Kaper;
          lyrics: Bob Russell; musical direction: Ray Sinatra
       They Didn't Believe Me (Lanza) music: Jerome Kern;
          lyrics: M E Rourke; musical direction: Ray Sinatra
       Core 'ngrato (Lanza) music: Cardillo; lyrics: Ricardo
          Cordiferro
       Aida: Act I: Celeste Aida (Lanza) music: Verdi

Note: Additional recording:

       MGM (78rpm) 30210 They Didn't Believe Me (Kathryn Grayson)

THAT NIGHT IN RIO (Twentieth Century-Fox, 1941)

Curtain Calls CC 100/14 (soundtrack) mono

Music: Harry Warren, others; lyrics: Mack Gordon, others;
musical direction: Alfred Newman

Cast: Don Ameche, Bando Da Lua, Alice Faye, Carmen Miranda

Songs: Main Title (orchestra)
       Chica Chica Boom Chic (Miranda, Ameche, Bando Da Lua,
          chorus)
       The Baron Is in Conference (chorus)
       Boi Noite (Ameche, chorus)
       They Met in Rio (Faye, Ameche, chorus)
       Cae Cae (Miranda, Bando Da Lua) music, lyrics: Roberto
          Martins
       I Yi, Yi, Yi, Yi (Miranda, Bando Da Lua)
       Chica Chica Boom Chic (Faye, Ameche) cut from film
       Boa Noite (reprise) (Faye)
       Finale:
          Chica Chica Boom Chic (Miranda, Bando Da Lua)
          They Met in Rio (Ameche, chorus)
          I Yi, Yi, Yi, Yi (Miranda, chorus)
          Boa Noite (Faye, Ameche, Chorus)

Note: Studio recordings by Carmen Miranda:

      Decca (78rpm) 23209 I Yi, Yi, Yi,Yi (LP: AH 99)
      Decca (78rpm) 23210 Chica Chica Boom Chic (LP: AH 99)
      Decca (78rpm) 23211 Cae Cae (LP: CDLM 8092)

THAT'S DANCING! (MGM, 1985)

EMI America SJ-17149 (soundtrack) stereo

Music, lyrics: various; musical direction: Henry Mancini, others

Cast: As listed

Songs: That's Dancing! (Chorus) music: Henry Mancini; lyrics:
      Larry Grossman, Ellen Fitzhugh
     Invitation to the Dance (Kim Carnes) music, lyrics:
      K Carnes, M Page, B Fairweather, D Ellington
     42nd Street (Ruby Keeler, chorus) from '42nd Street'
      music: Harry Warren; lyrics: Al Dubin
     Lullaby of Broadway (Wini Shaw, Dick Powell, chorus)
      from 'Gold Diggers of 1935' music: Harry Warren; lyrics:
      Al Dubin
     Pick Yourself Up (Fred Astaire, Ginger Rogers) from
      'Swing Time' music: Jerome Kern; lyrics: Dorothy Fields
     If I Only Had A Brain (Ray Bolger, Judy Garland) from
      'The Wizard of Oz' music: Harold Arlen; lyrics:
      E Y Harburg
     Moses (Gene Kelly, Donald O'Connor) from 'Singin' in the
      Rain' music: Roger Edens; lyrics: Betty Comden,
      Adolph Green
     Tom, Dick or Harry (Ann Miller, Bobby Van, Tommy Rall,
      Bob Fosse) from 'Kiss Me Kate' music, lyrics:
      Cole Porter
     You Should Be Dancing (The Bee Gees) from 'Saturday
      Night Fever' music, lyrics: B R and M Gibb
     Fame (Irene Cara) from 'Fame' music: Michael Gore;
      lyrics: Dean Pitchford

THAT'S ENTERTAINMENT (MGM, 1974)

MCA 2-11002 (two records - soundtrack) stereo

Music, lyrics: various; musical direction: Henry Mancini, others

Cast: As listed

Songs: Overture (orchestra - Mancini)
     Singin' in the Rain (Cliff Edwards) from 'Hollywood
      Revue of 1929'; (Jimmy Durante) from 'Speak Easy';
      (Judy Garland) from 'Little Nellie Kelly'; (Gene
      Kelly, Debbie Reynolds, Donald O'Connor) from 'Singin'

in the Rain'; music: Nacio Herb Brown; lyrics: Arthur
Freed
That's Entertainment (orchestra - Mancini) music: Arthur
Schwartz; lyrics: Howard Dietz
Broadway Melody (Charles King) from 'Broadway Melody of
1929'; music: Nacio Herb Brown; lyrics: Arthur Freed
Going Hollywood (Bing Crosby, chorus) from 'Going Hollywood'
music: Nacio Herb Brown; lyrics: Arthur Freed
Rosalie (chorus) from 'Rosalie'; music, lyrics: Cole Porter
A Pretty Girl Is Like A Melody (Allan Jones, chorus) from
'The Great Ziegfeld'; music, lyrics: Irving Berlin
I've Got A Feeling for You (Joan Crawford, chorus) from
'Hollywood Revue of 1929' (introduction by Conrad
Nagel); music: Louis Alter; lyrics: Jo Trent
Reckless (Jean Harlow, chorus) from 'Reckless'; music:
Jerome Kern; lyrics: Oscar Hammerstein II
Did I Remember (Cary Grant) from 'Suzy'; music: Walter
Donaldson; lyrics: Harold Adamson
Easy to Love (James Stewart, Eleanor Powell) from 'Born to
Dance';   music, lyrics: Cole Porter
Putting on the Ritz (Clark Gable, girls) from 'Idiot's
Delight'; music, lyrics: Irving Berlin
Heigh Ho, The Gang's All Here (Fred Astaire, Joan Crawford,
chorus) from 'Dancing Lady'; music: Burton Lane;
lyrics: Harold Adamson
By Myself (Fred Astaire) from 'The Band Wagon'; music:
Arthur Schwartz; lyrics: Howard Dietz
I Guess I'll Have to Change My Plan (Fred Astaire, Jack
Buchanan) from 'The Band Wagon'; music: Arthur Schwartz;
lyrics: Howard Dietz
They Can't Take That Away from Me (Fred Astaire) from
'The Barkleys of Broadway'; music: George Gershwin;
lyrics: Ira Gershwin
(Dear Mr Gable) You Made Me Love You (Judy Garland) from
'Broadway Melody of 1938'; music: James Monaco; lyrics:
Joseph McCarthy, Roger Edens
Wizard of Oz Medley (Judy Garland, Bert Lahr, Jack Haley,
Ray Bolger, chorus) from 'The Wizard of Oz'; music:
Harold Arlen; lyrics: E Y Harburg
Over the Rainbow (Judy Garland) from 'The Wizard of Oz'
music: Harold Arlen; lyrics: E Y Harburg
Babes in Arms (Mickey Rooney, Judy Garland, Douglas
McPhail, chorus) from 'Babes in Arms'; music: Richard
Rodgers; lyrics: Lorenz Hart
Waiting for the Robert E Lee / Babes on Broadway (Mickey
Rooney, Judy Garland, chorus) from 'Babes on Broadway'
music: Lewis F Muir; lyrics: L Wolfe Gilbert / music:
Burton Lane; lyrics: Ralph Freed
Strike up the Band (Mickey Rooney, Judy Garland, chorus)
from 'Strike Up the Band'; music: George Gershwin;
lyrics: Ira Gershwin
Under the Bamboo Tree (Judy Garland, Margaret O'Brien)

from 'Meet Me in St Louis'; music: J Rosamond Johnson;
    lyrics: Bob Cole
Get Happy (Judy Garland, chorus) from 'Summer Stock';
    music: Harold Arlen; lyrics: Ted Koehler
--- Aba Daba Honeymoon (Debbie Reynolds, Carlton Carpenter,
    chorus) from 'Two Weeks with Love'; music: Walter
    Donaldson; lyrics: Arthur Fields
It's A Most Unusual Day (Jane Powell, chorus) from 'A Date
    with Judy'; music: Gene de Paul; lyrics: Don Raye
Thou Swell (June Allyson, The Blackburn Twins) from
    'Words and Music'; music: Richard Rodgers; lyrics:
    Lorenz Hart
Varsity Drag (June Allyson, Peter Lawford, chorus) from
    'Good News'; music: Ray Henderson; lyrics: B G DeSylva,
    Lew Brown
The Song's Gotta Come from the Heart (Jimmy Durante, Frank
    Sinatra) from 'It Happened in Brooklyn'; music: Jule
    Styne; lyrics: Sammy Cahn
Honeysuckle Rose (Lena Horne) from 'Thousands Cheer'
    music: Fats Waller; lyrics: Andy Razaf
Be My Love (Kathryn Grayson, Mario Lanza) from 'The
    Toast of New Orleans'; music: Nicholas Brodszky; lyrics:
    Sammy Cahn
On the Atchison, Topeka and the Santa Fe (Judy Garland,
    chorus) from 'The Harvey Girls'; music: Harry Warren;
    lyrics: Johnny Mercer
--- Cotton Blossom (chorus) from 'Show Boat' (1951) music:
    Jerome Kern; lyrics: Oscar Hammerstein II
Make Believe (Kathryn Grayson, Howard Keel) from 'Show
    Boat' (1951) music: Jerome Kern; lyrics; Oscar
    Hammerstein II
Ol' Man River (William Warfield, chorus) from 'Show Boat'
    (1951) music: Jerome Kern; lyrics: Oscar Hammerstein II
Make 'Em Laugh (Donald O'Connor) from 'Singin' in the
    Rain'; music: Nacio Herb Brown; lyrics: Arthur Freed
Singin' in the Rain (Gene Kelly) from 'Singin' in the
    Rain'; music: Nacio Herb Brown; lyrics: Arthur Freed
Broadway Melody / Broadway Ballet (Gene Kelly, chorus)
    from 'Singin' in the Rain'; music: Nacio Herb Brown;
    lyrics: Arthur Freed
Hallelujah (Tony Martin, Vic Damone, Debbie Reynolds, Jane
    Powell, Ann Miller, Kay Armen, chorus) from 'Hit the
    Deck'; music: Vincent Youmans; lyrics: Leo Robin,
    Clifford Grey
Gigi (Louis Jourdan) from 'Gigi'; music: Frederick Loewe;
    lyrics: Alan Jay Lerner
Thank Heaven for Little Girls (Maurice Chevalier, chorus)
    from 'Gigi'; music: Frederick Loewe; lyrics: Alan Jay
    Lerner
An American in Paris Ballet (orchestra) from 'An American
    in Paris'; music: George Gershwin

That's Entertainment (Fred Astaire, Jack Buchanan, Nanette
    Fabray, India Adams, Oscar Levant, chorus) from 'The
    Band Wagon'; music: Arthur Schwartz; lyrics: Howard Dietz

THAT'S ENTERTAINMENT , PART 2 (MGM, 1976)

MGM 1-5301 (soundtrack) stereo   reissued: MCA 1655

Music, lyrics: various; musical direction: Nelson Riddle, others

Cast: As listed

Songs: Overture (orchestra - Riddle):
           That's Entertainment
           Temptation
           Hi-Lili, Hi-Lo
           Be A Clown
           Broadway Rhythm
           Have Yourself A Merry Little Christmas
       That's Entertainment (Fred Astaire, Gene Kelly, Nanette
           Fabray, Jack Buchanan, Oscar Levant) Astaire and last
           three from 'The Band Wagon'; music: Arthur Schwartz;
           lyrics: Howard Dietz
       For Me and My Gal (Judy Garland, Gene Kelly) from 'For
           Me and My Gal'; music: George W Meyer; lyrics: Edgar
           Leslie, E Ray Goetz
       I've Got A Feelin' You're Foolin' (Robert Taylor, June
           Knight, chorus) from 'Broadway Melody of 1936'; music:
           Nacio Herb Brown; lyrics: Arthur Freed
       Hi-Lili, Hi-Lo (Leslie Caron, Mel Ferrer) from 'Lili';
           music: Bronislaw Kaper; lyrics: Helen Deutsch
       All of You (Fred Astaire) from 'Silk Stockings'; music,
           lyrics: Cole Porter
       The Lady Is A Tramp (Lena Horne) from 'Words and Music';
           music: Richard Rodgers; lyrics: Lorenz Hart
       Smoke Gets in Your Eyes (Kathryn Grayson) from 'Lovely
           to Look At'; music: Jerome Kern; lyrics: Dorothy Fields
       Temptation (Bing Crosby) from 'Going Hollywood'; music:
           Nacio Herb Brown; lyrics: Arthur Freed
       Takin' A Chance on Love (Ethel Waters) from 'Cabin in the
           Sky'; music: Vernon Duke; lyrics: John Latouche, Ted
           Fetter
       Inka Dinka Doo (Jimmy Durante, Harry James Orchestra) from
           'Two Girls and A Sailor'; music: Jimmy Durante; lyrics:
           Ben Ryan
       Easter Parade (Fred Astaire, Judy Garland, chorus) from
           'Easter Parade'; music, lyrics: Irving Berlin
 ---   Good Morning (Debbie Reynolds, Gene Kelly, Donald O'Connor)
           from 'Singin' in the Rain'; music: Nacio Herb Brown;
           lyrics: Arthur Freed
       Triplets (Fred Astaire, Nanette Fabray, Jack Buchanan)

                    from 'The Band Wagon'; music: Arthur Schwartz; lyrics:
                    Howard Dietz
          The Last Time I Saw Paris (Dinah Shore) from 'Till the
                    Clouds Roll By'; music: Jerome Kern; lyrics: Oscar
                    Hammerstein II
          I'll Build A Stairway to Paradise (Georges Guetary) from
                    'An American in Paris'; music: George Gershwin; lyrics:
                    Ira Gershwin, B G DeSylva
          A Couple of Swells (Judy Garland, Fred Astaire) from
                    'Easter Parade'; music, lyrics: Irving Berlin
          There's No Business Like Show Business (Howard Keel,
                    Betty Hutton, Keenan Wynn, Louis Calhern, chorus) from
                    'Annie Get Your Gun'; music, lyrics: Irving Berlin
          Have Yourself A Merry Little Christmas (Judy Garland) from
                    'Meet Me in St Louis'; music, lyrics: Hugh Martin,
                    Ralph Blane
          I Got Rhythm (Gene Kelly, children) from 'An American
                    in Paris'; music: George Gershwin; lyrics: Ira Gershwin
          I Remember It Well (Maurice Chevalier, Hermione Gingold)
                    from 'Gigi'; music: Frederick Loewe; lyrics: Alan
                    Jay Lerner
          That's Entertainment (Finale) (Fred Astaire, Gene Kelly,
                    Nanette Fabray, Jack Buchanan, Oscar Levant) Astaire
                    and last three from 'The Band Wagon'; music: Arthur
                    Schwartz; lyrics: Howard Dietz

THERE'S NO BUSINESS LIKE SHOW BUSINESS (Twentieth Century-Fox, 1954)

Decca DL 8091 (soundtrack) mono

Music, lyrics: Irving Berlin; musical direction: Alfred Newman,
Lionel Newman

Cast: Dan Dailey, Mitzi Gaynor, Dolores Gray (not in film),
       Ethel Merman, Donald O'Connor, Johnnie Ray

Songs: There's No Business Like Show Business (Merman)
       When the Midnight Choo-Choo (Merman, Dailey)
       Play A Simple Melody (Merman, Dailey) orchestral reprise
       After What You Get What You Want, You Don't Want It (Gray)
       If You Believe (Ray, chorus)
       A Man Chases A Girl (Until She Catches Him) (O'Connor,
           chorus)
       Lazy (Gray)
---   Heat Wave (Gray, chorus)
       A Sailor's Not A Sailor (Merman, Gaynor)
       Alexander's Ragtime Band (Merman, Dailey, O'Connor,
           Gaynor, Ray, chorus)
       There's No Business Like Show Business - Finale
           Alexander's Ragtime Band (cast)
           There's No Business Like Show Business (cast, chorus)

Note: Recordings by Marilyn Monroe:

RCA (45/EP) EPA 593 (soundtrack) mono   reissued: DRG DS 15005

Songs: You'd Be Suprised (Monroe)
       Heat Wave (Monroe, chorus)
---   Lazy (Monroe)
       After You Get What You Want (You Don't Want It) (Monroe)

THIS COULD BE THE NIGHT (MGM, 1957)

MGM E3530 (soundtrack) mono   reissued: MCA 39085

Music, lyrics: various; musical direction: Ray Anthony

Cast: Neile Adams, Ray Anthony Orchestra, Julie Wilson

Songs: This Could Be the Night (orchestra) music: Nicholas
           Brodszky
       Trumpet Boogie (orchestra) music: Ray Anthony
       I Got It Bad and That and That Ain't Good (Wilson) music:
           Duke Ellington; lyrics: Paul Francis Webster
       Mambo Cambo (orchestra) music: Pete Rugolo
       Hustlin' Newsgal (Adams) music, lyrics: George Stoll
       Blue Moon (orchestra) music: Richard Rodgers
       Dream Dancing (orchestra) music: Ray Anthony
       I'm Gonna Live Till I Die (Wilson) music, lyrics: Al
           Hoffman, Walter Kent, Mann Curtis
       The Tender Trap (orchestra) music: James Van Heusen
---   When the Saints Go Marching in (orchestra) music
           arranged by Ray Anthony
       Just You, Just Me (orchestra) music: Jesse Greer
       Sadie Green, the Vamp of New Orleans (Wilson)
       Club Tonic Blues (orchestra)
       Taking A Chance on Love (Wilson) music: Vernon Duke;
           lyrics: Ted Fetter, John Latouche
       I've Got You Under My Skin (orchestra) music: Cole Porter
       This Could Be the Night (reprise) (Wilson) music:
           Nicholas Brodszky; lyrics: Sammy Cahn
       Bunny Hop (orchestra) music: Ray Anthony

THIS IS THE ARMY (Warner Bros, 1943)

Hollywood Soundstage HSS 408 (soundtrack) mono   also: Sandy Hook
SH 2035

Music, lyrics: Irving Berlin; musical direction: Leo F Forbstein

Cast: Irving Berlin, Dick Bernie, James Burell, James Cross,
        Alan Hale, Henry Jones, Frances Langford, James MacColl,

Ralph Magelssen, Alan Manson, George Murphy, Gertrude
Niesen, Jules Oshins, Earl Oxford, Tileston Perry, Sidney
Robin, William Roerich, Robert Shanley, Kate Smith, Ezra
Stone, George Tobias, Philip Truex

Songs: Overture (orchestra, chorus)
      Your Country and My Country (Niesen, chorus)
      My Sweetie (Murphy)
      Poor Little Me, I'm on K P (Tobias, chorus)
      We're on Our Way to France (Murphy, Tobias, Hale, chorus)
      God Bless America (Smith)
      What Does He Look Like (Langford, chorus)
      This Is the Army, Mr. Jones (Robin, Roerich, Jones,
        chorus)
      Hunting Story (Bernie, Manson) spoken
      I'm Getting Tired So I Can Sleep (Burell, chorus)
      Mandy (Magelssen, chorus)
      The Army's Made A Man Out of Me (Stone, Oshins, Truex,
        chorus)
---   Ladies of the Chorus (Hale, chorus)
      That's What the Well-Dressed Man in Harlem Will Wear
        (Cross, chorus)
      How About A Cheer for the Navy (chorus)
      Stage Door Canteen Scene (Manson, Perry, MacColl)
      I Left My Heart at the Stage Door Canteen (Oxford, chorus)
      With My Head in the Clouds (Shanley, chorus)
      American Eagles (Shanley, chorus)
      Oh How I Hate to Get Up in the Morning (Berlin, chorus)
      This Time Is the Last Time (Shanley, chorus)

Note: The above recording includes spoken dialog.

THIS WEEK OF GRACE (Real Art-Radio, 1933) British

World (British) SH 170 mono reissued: EMI GX 41 2530 1

Music, lyrics: Harry Parr-Davies, others

Cast: Gracie Fields

Songs: Happy Ending (Fields)
      My Lucky Day (Fields)
      Heaven Will Protect An Honest Girl (Fields)

Note: An additional recording:

      HMV (78rpm) B 4471 Mary Rose (Fields)

THIS'LL MAKE YOU WHISTLE (Wilcox, 1936) British

Ace of Clubs (British) ACL 1140 mono 'London Screen Scene'

Music, lyrics: Maurice Sigler, Al Goodhart, Al Hoffman

Cast: Jack Buchanan, Elsie Randolph

Songs: I'm in A Dancing Mood (Buchanan, Randolph)
       Without Rhythm (Buchanan)
       This'll Make You Whistle (Buchanan, Randolph)
       There Isn't Any Limit to My Love (Buchanan)

Note: Additional recordings:

Brunswick (78rpm) 02349 My Red-Letter Day (Randolph)
                        You've Got the Wrong Rhumba (Randolph)

THOROUGHLY MODERN MILLIE (Universal, 1967)

Decca DL 71500 (soundtrack) stereo

Music: James Van Heusen, others; lyrics: Sammy Cahn, others;
musical direction: Andre Previn

Cast: Julie Andrews, Carol Channing, Ann Dee, James Fox

Songs: Prelude: Thoroughly Modern Millie (Andrews)
       Overture (orchestra)
           Baby Face (music: Harry Akst)
           Do It Again (music: George Gershwin)
           Poor Butterfly (music: Raymond Hubbell)
           Stumbling (music: Zez Confrey)
           Japanese Sandman (music: Richard Whiting)
       Jimmy (Andrews) music, lyrics: Jay Thompson
       The Tapioca (Fox)
       Jazz Baby (Channing) music, lyrics: M K Jerome
       Jewish Wedding Song (Trink Le Chaim) (Andrews) music,
           lyrics: Sylvia Neufield
---   Intermission Medley (orchestra)
           Baby Face
           Jimmy
           Jewish Wedding Song
           Thoroughly Modern Millie
       Poor Butterfly (Andrews - with dialog with John Gavin)
           music: Raymond Hubbell; lyrics: John Golden
       Rose of Washington Square (Dee) music: James F Hanley;
           lyrics: Ballard MacDonald
       Baby Face (Andrews, chorus) music: Harry Akst; lyrics:
           Benny Davis
       Do It Again (Channing) music: George Gershwin; lyrics:
           Buddy DeSylva
       Reprise: Thoroughly Modern Millie (Andrews)

        Exit Music (orchestra)
          Jazz Baby
          Jimmy
          Thoroughly Modern Millie

1001 ARABIAN NIGHTS (Columbia, 1959)

Colpix SCP 410 (soundtrack) stereo   reissued: Varese STV 81138

Music: George Duning; lyrics: Ned Washington; musical direction:
Morris Stoloff

Cast: (the voices of) Jim Bachus, The Clark Sisters

Songs: Main Title (orchestra)
          Magoo's Blues (Backus)
          Sultan's Parade (orchestra)
          You Are My Dream (chorus)
          Palanquin Chase (orchestra)
          Wedding Celebration (orchestra)
          Bar Fly Magoo (orchestra)
---   You Are My Dream (reprise) (orchestra)
          Three Little Maids from Damascus (The Clark Sisters)
          Unhappy Magoo (orchestra)
          Dream Ballet (You Are My Dream - reprise) (chorus)
          Crazy Carpet (orchestra)
          End Title (orchestra)

THOUSANDS CHEER (MGM, 1943)

Hollywood Soundstage HSS 409 (soundtrack) mono

Music, lyrics: various

Cast: June Allyson, Georgia Carroll, The Benny Carter Band,
        Bob Crosby Orchestra, Gloria De Haven, Judy Garland,
        Kathryn Grayson, Lena Horne, Jose Iturbi, Gene Kelly,
        Kay Kyser Orchestra, Margaret O'Brien, Virginia O'Brien,
        Donna Reed, Mickey Rooney, Red Skelton

Songs: Overture (orchestra, chorus)
          Caprice Espanol (orchestra) music: Rimsky-Korsakov
          La Traviata: Sempre Libera (Grayson) music: Verdi
          Daybreak (Grayson) music: Ferde Grofe; lyrics: Harold
            Adamson
          Three Letters in the Mailbox (Grayson) music: Walter
            Jurmann; lyrics: Paul Francis Webster
          I Dug A Ditch (vocal group) music: Burton Lane; lyrics:
            Lew Brown, Ralph Freed
          I Dug A Ditch (reprise) (Grayson, chorus)

Let There Be Music (Grayson) music, adapted: Earl Brent;
    lyrics: E Y Harburg
Hungarian Rhapsody No 2 (Iturbi - piano) music: Liszt
Let Me Call You Sweetheart (Kelly) music: Leo Friedman;
    lyrics: Beth Slater Whitson
I Dug A Ditch (reprise) (orchestra) (danced by Kelly)
American Patrol (orchestra) music: F W Meacham
Boogie Woogie Number (orchestra) Rooney introduces Powell
--- In A Little Spanish Town (Virginia O'Brien, Allyson, De
    Haven, Crosby Orchestra) music: Mabel Wayne; lyrics:
    Sam M Lewis, Joe Young
I Dug A Ditch (reprise) (Kyer Orchestra) vocal
Should I (Carroll, chorus, Kyser Orchestra) music: Nacio
    Herb Brown; lyrics: Arthur Freed
I Dug A Ditch (reprise) (vocal group)
South American Fantasy (orchestra)
Skit (Test Pilot) (Rooney) spoken
Honeysuckle Rose (Horne, Carter Band) music: Fats Waller;
    lyrics: Andy Razaf
Comedy Skit (Skelton, Reed, Margaret O'Brien, girls) spoken
The Joint Is Really Jumpin' (Garland, Iturbi - piano)
    music, lyrics: Roger Edens, Ralph Blane, Hugh Martin
The United Nations (Victory Song) (Grayson, chorus)
    music: Dmitri Shostakovich; lyrics: Harold Rome, E Y
    Harburg

Note: The above recording includes spoken dialog.

THREE AMIGOS! (Orion, 1957)

Warner Bros 25558-1 (soundtrack) stereo

Music, lyrics for songs: Randy Newman; background score,
musical direction: Elmer Bernstein

Cast: Fred Asparagus, Chevy Chase, Steve Martin, Randy Newman,
    Martin Short

Songs: The Ballad of the Three Amigos (Martin, Chase, Short)
    Main Title (orchestra)
    The Big Sneak (orchestra) birdcalls: Martin
    My Little Buttercup (Martin, Short, Asparagus)
    Santa Poco (orchestra)
    Fiesta and Flamenco (orchestra) guitar: Chase
    El Guapo (orchestra)
    The Return of the Amigos (orchestra)
--- Blue Shadows on the Trail (Martin, Chase, Short)
    The Singing Bush (Newman)
    Amigos at the Mission (orchestra)
    Capture (Martin, Allonso Arau) spoken
    El Guapo's Birthday (orchestra)

        The Chase (orchestra)
        Amigos, Amigos, Amigos (orchestra)
        Farewell (orchestra)
        End Credits (orchestra)

Note: The above recording includes spoken dialog.

THE THREE CABALLEROS (Disney, 1944)

Decca (78rpm) 373 mono

Music: Augustin Lara, others; lyrics: Ray Gilbert, others;
musical direction: Charles Wolcott

Cast: Nestor Amaral, Ray Gilbert (not in film)

Decca (78rpm) 23341 The Three Caballeros (Gilbert) music: Charles
                        Wolcott
                    Jesusita (orchestra)
Decca (78rpm) 23342 Baia (Gilbert, chorus)
                    The Siren's Song (chorus)
                    Os Quindins de Yaya (Amaral)
Decca (78rpm) 23343 You Belong to My Heart (Gilbert)
                    Mexico (Gilbert)

Note: Soundtrack selections on Ovation 5000:

        The Three Caballeros (Jose Oliveira, Joaquin Garay,
                            Clarence Nash)
        You Belong to My Heart (Dora Luz)

THREE FOR THE SHOW (Columbia, 1955)

Mercury MG 25204 (soundtrack) mono

Music, lyrics: various; musical direction: Morris Stoloff

Cast: Marge Champion, Betty Grable, Jack Lemon

Songs: Overture (orchestra)
        Which One (Grable, Champion) music: Lester Lee; lyrics:
            Ned Washington
        Someone to Watch Over Me (Champion) music: George Gershwin;
            lyrics: Ira Gershwin
        Swan Lake Ballet (orchestra) music: Tchaikovsky
---   I've Got A Crush on You (Grable, Lemmon) music: George
            Gershwin; lyrics: Ira Gershwin
        Down Boy (Grable, chorus) music: Hoagy Charmichael;
            lyrics: Harold Adamson

Someone to Watch Over Me (reprise) (orchestra)
How Come You Do Me Like You Do? (Grable, chorus) music,
    lyrics: Gene Austin, Roy Bergere
Finale - I've Got A Crush on You (Grable, Lemmon)

THREE LITTLE GIRLS IN BLUE (Twentieth Century-Fox, 1946)

Hollywood Soundstage 410 (soundtrack) mono

Music: Josef Myrow, others; lyrics: Mack Gordon, others; musical
direction: Alfred Newman

Cast: Vivian Blaine, Ben Gage (for George Montgomery), June
        Haver, Celeste Holm, Del Porter (for Charlie Smith),
        Carol Stewart (for Vera-Ellen)

Songs: Overture (orchestra)
        Three Little Girls in Blue (chorus)
        A Farmer's Life Is A Very Merry Life (Stewart, Haver,
            Blaine)
        On the Boardwalk (in Atlantic City) (Haver, Blaine,
            Stewart)
        Three Little Girls in Blue (reprise) (Haver, Blaine,
            Stewart)
        Oh My Love (chorus)
        I Like Mike (Stewart)
        Somewhere in the Night (Blaine)
        If You Can't Get A Girl in the Summertime (Gage, Haver)
---   You Make Me Feel So Young (Stewart, Porter, chorus)
        This Is Always (Haver, Gage) music, lyrics: Harry Warren
        Always the Lady (Holm)
        Finale (cast)

THREE LITTLE WORDS (MGM, 1950)

MGM E 516 (soundtrack) mono

Music: Harry Ruby, others; lyrics: Bert Kalmar, others; musical
direction: Andre Previn

Cast: Fred Astaire, Arlene Dahl, Gloria De Haven, Anita Ellis
        (for Vera-Ellen), Helen Kane (for Debbie Reynolds),
        Gale Robbins, Red Skelton

Songs: Nevertheless (I'm in Love with You) (Astaire, Skelton,
            Ellis)
        I Love You So Much (Dahl, chorus)
        All Alone Monday (Robbins)
        Where Did You Get That Girl? (Astaire, Ellis) music:
            Harry Puck

---   Thinking of You (Ellis)
         I Wanna Be Loved by You (Kane) co-composer: Herbert
             Stothart
         Who's Sorry Now? (De Haven) music: Ted Snyder; lyrics:
             Harry Ruby, Bert Kalmar
         My Sunny Tennessee (Astaire, Skelton)
         So Long Oolong (How Long You Gonna Be Gone?) (Astaire,
             Skelton)
         Three Little Words (Astaire)

3 SAILORS AND A GIRL (Warner Bros, 1953)

Capitol L 485 mono

Music: Sammy Fain, others; lyrics: Sammy Cahn; musical direction:
George Greeley

Cast: Gordon MacRae, Jane Powell

Songs: You're But Oh So Right (MacRae, chorus)
         Kiss Me or I'll Scream (Powell)
         Face to Face (MacRae)
         The Lately Song (MacRae, chorus, Powell)
---   There Must Be A Reason (MacRae, Powell)
         When It's Love (Powell, MacRae) music: Strauss
         Show Me A Happy Woman (Powell, chorus)
         My Heart Is A Singing Heart (MacRae, Powell)
         Home Is Where the Heart Is (MacRae, Powell, chorus)

THE THREEPENNY OPERA (Die Dreigroschenoper) (Nero, 1931) Germany

Capitol P 8117 mono   reissued: Telefunken (German) 6.41911 AJ

Music: Kurt Weill; lyrics: Bertolt Brecht; musical direction:
Theo Mackeben

Cast: Kurt Gerron (not in film), Erika Helmke (not in film),
         Lotte Lenya, Erich Ponto (not in film), Willie Trenk-
         Trebitsch (not in film)

Songs: Ouverture (orchestra) narration: Gerron
         Moritat vom Mackie Messer (Gerron)
         Seerauberjenny (Lenya)
         Kanonensong (Trenk-Trebitsch, Gerron, men)
         Liebeslied (Helmke, Trenk-Trebitsch)
         Barbarasong (Lenya)
         Erstes Dreigroschen-Finale (Lenya, Ponto, Helmke)
         Abscheid (Helmke, Trenk-Trebitsch)
         Zuhalterballade (Lenya, Trenk-Trebitsch)
         Ballade vom angenehmen Leben (Trenk-Trebitsch)

Eifersuchtsduett (Lenya, Helmke)
Zweites Dreigroschen-Finale (Trenk-Trebitsch, chorus)
Lied von der Unzulanglichkeit menschlichen Strebens
    (Ponto)
Moritat und Schlusschoral (Lenya, chorus)

Note: The above is a studio recording of this famous score
        made at the time of the film version's release. A
        French language version was also made, with the following
        recordings:

THE THREEPENNY OPERA (L'Opera de Quat'sous)

Telefunken (German) 6.41911 AJ (sung in French)

Cast: Jacques Henley, Margo Lion, Albert Prejean

Songs: Chant des canons (Prejean, Henley)
       Chant d'amour (Prejean)
       Tangoballade (Lion, Prejean)
       Ballade de la vie agreable (Prejean)

THE THREEPENNY OPERA (Die Dreigroschenoper) (Gloria, 1963) Germany

London 76004 (soundtrack) stereo (sung in German)

Music: Kurt Weill; lyrics: Bertolt Brecht; musical direction:
Peter Sandloff

Cast: Gert Frobe, Hilde Hildebrand, Curt Jurgens, Maria Korber
        (for June Ritchie), Kurt Muhlhardt (for Sammy Davis, Jr),
        Hildegard Neff, June Ritchie, Konrad Wagner (for Lino
        Ventura), Marlene Warrlich

Songs: Overture (orchestra, chorus)
       Moritat of Mack the Knife (Muhlhardt)
       Instead of That Song (Frobe, Hildebrand)
       Canon Song (Jurgens, Wagner)
       Love Duet (Ritchie, Jurgens)
       Barbara Song (Korber)
       Ballad of That Pleasant Life (Jurgens)
       Threepenny Finale I (Frobe, Korber, cast)
---   Pirate Jenny (Neff)
       Ballette (orchestra)
       Ballad of the Pimp (Neff, Jurgens)
       Jealousy Duet (Korber, Warrlich)
       Threepenny Finale II (Neff, Frobe, chorus)
       Song About the Inadequacy of Human Ambition (Frobe,
           Muhlhardt)
       Threepenny Finale III (cast)

Note: An English soundtrack version of the above film was also released. Various voices for this recording were not identified.

THE THREEPENNY OPERA (Embassy, 1964)

RCA LSO 1086 (soundtrack) stereo

English lyrics: Marc Blitzstein; musical direction: Samuel Matlovsky

Cast: Sammy Davis, Jr, George S Irving (for Curt Jurgens), Martha Schlamme (for Hildegard Neff), Jo Wilder (for June Ritchie)

Songs: Overture (orchestra)
       The Ballad of Mack the Knife (Davis)
       Morning Anthem ('J J Peachum')
       Instead-Of Song ('J J Peachum', 'Mrs Peachum')
       Love Song (Wilder, Irving)
       Barbara Song (Wilder)
       Melodrama and Polly's Song (Wilder, Irving)
       The World Is Mean (Wilder, 'J J Peachum', 'Mrs Peachum')
 ---   Solomon Song (Davis)
       Pirate Jenny (Schlamme)
       Tango Ballad (Schlamme, Irving)
       Ballad of Dependency ('Mrs Peachum')
       Jealousy Duet (Wilder, 'Lucy')
       Useless Song (chorus, 'J J Peachum', 'Brown')
       Call from the Grave (Irving)
       How to Survive (Davis)
       The Mounted Messenger (chorus, messenger)
       Reprieved (Irving, Wilder, chorus)
       Happy Ending (Davis)

Note: The above recording includes a narration by Sammy Davis, Jr

THRILL OF A ROMANCE (MGM, 1945)

Camden 424 mono 'The Lighter Side of Lauritz Melchior'

Music, lyrics: various

Cast: Lauritz Melchior

Songs: I Love You (Melchior) music: Edvard Grieg
       Lonely Night (Melchior) music: George Stoll; lyrics:
          Richard Connell
       Serenade (Melchior) music: Jack Meskill; lyrics: Earl
          Brent
       Vive l'Amour (Melchior) music, lyrics: Ralph Blane, Kay
          Thompson, George Stoll

Please Don't Say No (Melchior) music: Sammy Fain; lyrics:
    Ralph Freed
I Want What I Want When I Want It (Melchior) music:
    Victor Herbert; lyrics: Henry Blossom

Note: Additional studio recordings by Tommy Dorsey Orchestra:

    RCA (78rpm) 20-1625 Please Don't Say No
                       I Should Care

TICKLE ME (Allied Artists, 1965)

RCA (45/EP) EPA 4383 stereo

Music, lyrics: various

Cast: Elvis Presley

Songs: I Feel That I've Known You Forever (Presley) music:
            Alan Jeffries; lyrics: Doc Pomus
        Slowly but Surely (Presley) music: Ben Weisman; lyrics:
            Sid Wayne
        Night Rider (Presley) music: Mort Shuman; lyrics: Doc
            Pomus
        Put the Blame on Me (Presley) music, lyrics: Fred Wise,
            Norman Blagman, Kay Twomey
        Dirty, Dirty Feeling (Presley) music, lyrics: Jerry
            Leiber, Mike Stoller

TILL THE CLOUDS ROLL BY (MGM, 1946)

MGM E 501 (soundtrack) mono   reissued: MCA 25000

Music: Jerome Kern; lyrics: Oscar Hammerstein II, others;
musical direction: Lennie Hayton

Cast: June Allyson, Judy Garland, Kathryn Grayson, Lena Horne,
        Tony Martin, Virginia O'Brien, Caleb Peterson

Songs: Till the Clouds Roll By (chorus) lyrics: P G Wodehouse
        Look for the Silver Lining (Garland) lyrics: Buddy De
            Sylva
        Can't Help Lovin' Dat Man (Horne)
        Leave It To Jane (Allyson, chorus) lyrics: P G Wodehouse
        Cleopatterer (Allyson) lyrics: P G Wodehouse
  ---   Who Cares If My Boat Goes Upstream (Martin)
        Make Believe (Grayson, Martin)
        Life Upon the Wicked Stage (O'Brien, girls)
        Who (Garland, chorus) lyrics: Oscar Hammerstein II,
            Otto Harbach

     Ol' Man River (Peterson, chorus)

TILL THE CLOUDS ROLL BY (MGM, 1946)

Sountrak STK 115 (two records - soundtrack) mono also: Sandy Hook SH 2080

Cast: June Allyson, Trudy Erwin (for Lucille Bremer), Judy
        Garland, Kathryn Grayson, Lena Horne, Van Johnson, Angela
        Lansbury, Ray MacDonald, Tony Martin, Virginia O'Brien,
        Caleb Peterson, Dinah Shore, Frank Sinatra, The Wilde
        Twins

Songs: Overture: Till the Clouds Roll By (orchestra)
                The Touch of Your Hand (orchestra)
                The Siren's Song (chorus) lyrics: P G Wodehouse
      Ol' Man River (chorus)
      Cotton Blossom (chorus)
      Who Cares If My Boat Goes Upstream (Martin)
      Make Believe (Grayson, Martin)
      Life Upon the Wicked Stage (O'Brien, girls)
      Can't Help Lovin' Dat Man (Horne)
      Ol' Man River (reprise) (Peterson, chorus)
---   Ka-Lu-A (orchestra) dialog: Robert Walker, Van Heflin,
        Joan Wells
      How'd You Like to Spoon with Me? (Lansbury, chorus)
        lyrics: Edward Lasker
      They Didn't Believe Me (Shore) lyrics: Herbert Reynolds
      Till the Clouds Roll By (MacDonald, chorus) lyrics: P G
        Wodehouse
---   Leave It to Jane (Allyson, chorus) lyrics: P G Wodehouse
      Cleopatterer (Allyson, chorus) lyrics: P G Wodehouse
      Look for the Silver Lining (Garland) lyrics: Buddy De
        Sylva
      Sunny (chorus) lyrics: Oscar Hammerstein II; Otto Harbach
      Who (Garland, chorus) lyrics: Oscar Hammerstein II, Otto
        Harbach
      One More Dance (Erwin)
      I Won't Dance (Erwin, Johnson) lyrics: Jimmy McHugh,
        Dorothy Fields
---   She Didn't Say Yes (The Wilde Twins) lyrics: Otto Harbach
      Smoke Gets In Your Eyes (Martin, chorus) lyrics: Otto
        Harbach
      The Last Time I Saw Paris (Shore)
      The Land Where Good Songs Go (Erwin) lyrics: P G Wodehouse
      Yesterdays (chorus) lyrics: Otto Harbach
      Long Ago and Far Away (Grayson) lyrics: Ira Gershwin
      A Fine Romance (O'Brien) lyrics: Dorothy Fields
      All the Things You Are (Martin)
      Why Was I Born? (Horne)
      Ol' Man River (reprise) (Sinatra, chorus)

Note: The above recording includes spoken dialog. Additional
        soundtrack selections, cut from the final film:

        D'Ye Love Me? (Garland) lyrics: Oscar Hammerstein II,
            Otto Harbach LP: Out Takes OTF - 1
        Bill (Horne) lyrics: P G Wodehouse LP: Out Takes OTF -2
        I've Told Ev'ry Little Star (Grayson) Out Takes OTF - 2
        The Song Is You (Grayson, Johnnie Johnston) LP: Out
            Takes OTF - 2

A TIME TO SING (MGM, 1968)

MGM 4540 (soundtrack) stereo   reissued: MCA 1458

Music, lyrics: Hank Williams, Jr, others

Cast: Shelley Fabares, Hank Williams, Jr

Songs: A Time to Sing (Williams) music, lyrics: John Scoggins
        Next Time I Say Goodbye I'm Leaving (Fabares, chorus)
            music, lyrics: Larry Kusik, Edward Snyder
        Old Before My Time (Williams, men) music, lyrics:
            Steve Karliski
        Rock in My Shoe (Williams, men)
        Money Can't Buy Happiness (Williams, men) music, lyrics:
            Steve Karliski
---   A Man on His Own (Williams, chorus)
        There's Gotta Be Much More to Life than You (Williams,
            chorus) music, lyrics: Steve Karliski
        It's All Over but the Crying (Williams, men)
        Give Me the Hummingbird Line (Williams, men)
        A Time to Sing (reprise) (Williams, chorus)

TIN PAN ALLEY (Twentieth Century-Fox, 1940)

Sountrak STK 110 (soundtrack) mono

Music, lyrics: various; musical direction: Alfred Newman

Cast: The Brian Sisters, Alice Faye, Billy Gilbert, Betty
        Grable, John Loder, Jack Oakie, John Payne, The Roberts
        Brothers

Songs: Overture (orchestra, chorus)
        K-K-K-Katy (Dixie Style) (Oakie, Payne) music, lyrics:
            Geoffrey O'Hara
        K-K-K-Katy (Hawaiian Style) (Oakie, Faye, Grable)
        You Say the Sweetest Things (Faye, Payne, Oakie, chorus)
            music: Harry Revel; lyrics: Mack Gordon
        On Moonlight Bay (Faye) music: Percy Wenrich; lyrics:

                Edward Madden
        Honeysuckle Rose (Grable, chorus) music: Fats Waller;
            lyrics: Andy Razaf
        Moonlight and Roses (Grable, chorus) music: Edwin H
            Lemare, Neil Moret; lyrics: Ben Black
---   America, I Love You (Faye, The Roberts Brothers, The
            Brian Sisters, Payne, chorus) music: Archie Gottler;
            lyrics: Edgar Leslie
        Goodbye Broadway, Hello France (Oakie) music: Billy
            Baskette; lyrics: C Francis Reisner, Benny Davis
        Arabian Number (girls, orchestra)
        The Shiek of Araby (Faye, Grable, Gilbert, chorus)
            music: Ted Snyder; lyrics: Harry B Smith, Francis
            Wheeler
        Finale: K-K-K-Katy (Oakie, Faye, Payne, Grable, Loder,
                chorus)
                You Say the Sweetest Things (orchestra)

Note: The above recording includes spoken dialog.

TO BE OR NOT TO BE (Twentieth Century-Fox, 1983)

Antilles 8 Asta 2 (soundtrack) stereo

Music, lyrics for songs: Mel Brooks, Ronny Graham, others;
musical score, direction: John Morris

Cast: Anne Bancroft, Mel Brooks

Songs: Overture (orchestra)
        Sweet Georgia Brown (and the Bronskis backstage) (Bancroft,
            Brooks) music, lyrics: Ben Bernie, Maceo Pinkard,
            Kenneth Casey
        Sidewalks of Warsaw (orchestra)
        A Little Peace (Brooks, men)
        Anna Bronski's Dressing Room (the Rendezvous) spoken
        Ladies (Brooks, chorus)
---   Polish Fliers Chorus (chorus) music: Chopin
        Anna Bronski serenades Professor Siletski:
            You and the Night and the Music (Bancroft) music:
                Arthur Schwartz; lyrics: Howard Dietz
            Sweetheart, Sweetheart, Sweetheart (Bancroft) music:
                Sigmund Romberg; lyrics: Rida Johnson Young
            Heart and Soul (Bancroft) music: Hoagy Carmichael;
                lyrics: Frank Loesser
        Bronski meets Colonel Erhardt - Subterfuge (orchestra)
        Bronski Soliloquy (Brooks) spoken
        Curtain Call Ladies (orchestra)
        To Be or Not to Be (The Hitler Rap) (Brooks) music, lyrics:
            Mel Brooks, Pete Wingfield

Note: The above recording includes spoken dialog.

THE TOAST OF NEW ORLEANS (MGM, 1950)

RCA (45rpm) WDM 1417

Music: Nicholas Brodszky; lyrics: Sammy Cahn; musical direction:
Ray Sinatra

Cast: Mario Lanza

Songs: Toast of New Orleans (Lanza)
        Boom Biddy Boom Boom (Lanza, chorus)
        Tina-Lina (Lanza, chorus)
        The Bayou Lullaby (Lanza, chorus)

Additional selections:

RCA (45rpm) 49-1353 Be My Love (Lanza)
                   I'll Never Love You (Lanza)

MCA 2-11002 (soundtrack) Be My Love (Lanza, Kathryn Grayson)

RCA LM 2422 mono; classical selections with Elaine Malbin (not in
film); musical direction: Constantine Callinicos

Songs: La Traviata: Act I: Brindisi: Libiamo, Libiamo, ne'lieti
            calici (Lanza, Malbin, chorus) music: Verdi
        Madama Butterfly: Act I: Love Duet: Stolta paura, l'amor
            (Lanza, Melbin) music: Puccini
        L'Africana: Act IV: O Paradiso! (Lanza) music: Meyerbeer
        Carmen: Act II: La Fleur que tu m'avais jetee (Lanza)
            music: Bizet
        Martha: Act III: M'appari (Lanza) music: Flotow

TOM SAWYER (United Artists, 1973)

United Artists LA 057 F (soundtrack) stereo

Music, lyrics: Richard M Sherman, Robert B Sherman; musical
direction: John Williams

Cast: Jeff East, Celeste Holm, Susan Joyce, Joshua Hill Lewis,
        (the voice of) Charlie Pride, Johnny Whitaker, Warren Oates

Songs: Overture (orchestra)
        Main Title (orchestra)
        River Song (The Theme from 'Tom Sawyer') (Pride, chorus)
        Tom Sawyer (Holm, Lewis, Joyce)
        Gratifaction (Whitaker, boys)

      A Man's Gotta Be (What He's Born to Be) (Oates, Whitaker,
        East)
      How Come? (Whitaker)
 --- If'n I Was God (Whitaker)
      Freebootin' (Whitaker, East)
      Aunt Polly's Soliloquy (Holm)
      Hannibal Mo-(Zouree)! (cast)
      River Song (reprise) (Pride, cast)
      Finale (orchestra)

TOM THUMB (MGM, 1958)

Lion L 70084 (soundtrack) mono   reissued: MCA 25006

Music: Fred Spielman, others; lyrics: Janice Torre, others;
musical direction: Muir Mathieson

Cast: (the voice of) Stan Freberg, Russ Tamblyn, Ian Wallace,
      Norma Zimmer (for Jessie Matthews)

Songs: After All These Years (Zimmer)
      Tom Thumb's Tune (Tamblyn, chorus) music, lyrics: Peggy Lee
 --- The Talented Shoes (Wallace)
      The Yawning Song (Freberg, chorus) lyrics: Kermit Goell

Note: The above recording consists primarily of spoken dialog,
      with a narration by Dean Jones.

TOMMY (Columbia, 1975)

Polydor PD 2 9502 (two records - soundtrack) stereo

Music, lyrics: Peter Townshend, others

Cast: Ann-Margret, Vicki Brown, Eric Clapton, Roger Daltrey,
      Alison Dowling, Elton John, Keith Moon, Margo Newman,
      Paul Nicholas, Jack Nicholson, Oliver Reed, Peter
      Townshend, Simon Townshend, Tina Turner, The Who

Songs: Prologue - 1945 (orchestra)
      Captain Walker / It's A Boy (P Townshend, Newman, Brown)
      Bernie's Holiday Camp (Ann-Margret, Reed, Dowling)
      1951 - What About the Boy (Ann-Margret, Reed)
      Amazing Journey (P Townshend)
      Christmas (Ann-Margret, Reed, Dowling)
      Eyesight to the Blind (Clapton) music, lyrics: Sonny Boy
        Williamson
 --- Acid Queen (Turner)
      Do You Think It's Alright? (1) (Ann-Margret, Reed)
      Cousin Kevin (Nicholas) music, lyrics: John Entwistle

Do You Think It's Alright? (11) (Ann-Margret, Reed)
Fiddle Around (Moon) music, lyrics: John Entwistle
Do You Think It's Alright? (111) (Ann-Margret, Reed)
Sparks (The Who)
Extra, Extra, Extra (S Townshend)
Pinball Wizard (John)
--- Champagne (Ann-Margret, Daltrey)
There's A Doctor (Ann-Margret, Reed)
Go to the Mirror (Ann-Margret, Reed, Nicholson, Daltrey)
Tommy, Can You Hear Me? (Ann-Margret)
Smash the Mirror (Ann-Margret)
I'm Free (Daltrey)
Mother and Son (Ann-Margret, Daltrey)
Sensation (Daltrey)
--- Miracle Cure (S Townshend)
Sally Simpson (P Townshend, Daltrey)
Welcome (Ann-Margret, Reed, Daltrey)
T V Studio (Ann-Margret, Reed)
Tommy's Holiday Camp (Moon) music, lyrics: Keith Moon
We're Not Gonna Take It (Daltrey, chorus)
Listening to You / See Me, Feel Me (Daltrey, chorus)

THE TOMMY STEELE STORY (Rock Around the World) (Anglo, 1957)

Decca (British) LF 1288 (soundtrack) mono also: London LL 1770

Music, lyrics: Lionel Bart, Michael Pratt, Tommy Steele

Cast: Tommy Steele

Songs: Take Me Back, Baby (Steele)
       Butterfingers (Steele)
       I Like (Steele)
       A Handful of Songs (Steele)
       You Gotta Go (Steele)
       Water, Water (Steele)
       Cannibal Pot (Steele)
--- Will It Be You (Steele)
       Two Eyes (Steele)
       Build Up (Steele)
       Time to Kill (Steele)
       Elevator Rock (Steele)
       Doomsday Rock (Steele)
       Teenage Party (Steele)

TOMMY THE TOREADOR (British Pathe, 1959)

Decca (British 45/EP) DFE 6607 (soundtrack) mono

Music, lyrics: Lionel Bart, Michael Pratt, Jimmy Bennett

musical direction: Stanley Black

Cast: Bernard Cribbins, Sidney James, Tommy Steele

Songs: Tommy the Toreador (Steele)
       Take A Ride (Steele)
       Where's the Birdie (Steele, James, Cribbins)
---   Little White Bull (Steele, chorus)
       Singing Time (Steele, chorus)
       Amanda (Steele)

Note: 'Jimmy Bennett' is a pseudonym for Tommy Steele

TONIGHT WE SING (Twentieth Century-Fox, 1953)

RCA LM 7016 (soundtrack) mono   reissued: Ariel TWS 20

Music, lyrics: various; musical direction: Alfred Newman

Cast: (the voice of) Jan Peerce, Roberta Peters, Ezio Pinza

Songs: Madama Butterfly: Love Duet (Peerce, Peters) music:
           Puccini
       Madama Butterfly: Pinkerton's Farewell (Peerce) music:
           Puccini
       Boris Godounoff: Coronation Scene (Pinza) music:
           Moussorgsky
       Faust: Love Duet, Act III (Peters, Peerce) music:
           Gounod
       Faust: Trio and Finale, Act V (Pinza, Peters, Peerce)
           music: Gounod
---   Faust: Serenade, Act IV (Pinza) music: Gounod
       Kalinka (Pinza) Russian folk song
       Boris Godounoff: Death of Boris (Pinza) music:
           Moussorgsky
       Faust: Jewel Song (Peters) music: Gounod
       La Traviata: Sempre Libera (Peters) music: Verdi

TOO MUCH HARMONY (Paramount, 1933)

Columbia C2L 43 (two records) mono 'Bing Crosby in Hollywood'

Music: Arthur Johnston; lyrics: Sam Coslow; musical direction:
Jimmie Grier

Cast: Bing Crosby

Songs: Thanks (Crosby)
       The Day You Came Along (Crosby)
       I Guess It Had to Be That Way (Crosby) cut from film

Black Moonlight (Crosby)

Note: Additional soundtrack selection:

Cradle Me with A Ha-Cha Lullaby (Grace Bradley) LP: Legends
    1000/2 'Ladies of Burlesque'

TOP HAT (RKO, 1935)

EMI (British) EMTC 102 (soundtrack) mono   also: Sountrak STK 105

Music, lyrics: Irving Berlin; musical direction: Max Steiner

Cast: Fred Astaire, Ginger Rogers

Songs: Overture (orchestra)
        No Strings (Astaire)
        Isn't This A Lovely Day to Be Caught in the Rain (Astaire)
        Top Hat, White Tie and Tails (Astaire)
        Cheek to Cheek (Astaire)
        The Piccolino (Rogers, Astaire)

Note: Studio recordings by Astaire (all on LP: Col SG 32472):

Brunswick (78rpm) 7486 No Strings
                      Cheek to Cheek
Brunswick (78rpm) 7487 Isn't This A Lovely Day
                      Top Hat
Brunswick (78rpm) 7488 The Piccolino

        Studio recordings by Rogers:

Decca (British 78rpm) 5746 No Strings
                      Isn't This A Lovely Day
Decca (British 784pm) 5747 The Piccolino
                      Cheek to Cheek

TOP O' THE MORNING (Paramount, 1949)

Decca DL 4261 mono 'Bing's Hollywood - Sunshine Cake'

Music: James Van Heusen, others; lyrics: John Burke, others;
musical direction: Victor Young, others

Cast: Ann Blyth, Bing Crosby

Songs: You're in Love with Someone (Crosby, chorus)
        The Donovans (Crosby, chorus) music: Alice Adelaide
            Needham; lyrics: Francis A Fahy
---   Top O' the Morning (Crosby, chorus)

Oh, 'Tis Sweet to Think (Crosby, Blyth) music, lyrics:
Thomas Moore; musical direction: Simon Rady

TORCH SONG (MGM, 1953)

MGM E 214 mono

Music, lyrics: various; musical direction: Walter Gross

Cast: India Adams (for Joan Crawford)

Songs: Blue Moon (trio) music: Richard Rodgers; lyrics: Lorenz
          Hart
       You're All the World to Me (trio) music: Burton Lane;
          lyrics: Alan Jay Lerner
       Follow Me (Adams) music, lyrics: Adolph Deutsch
---   Tenderly (trio) music: Walter Gross; lyrics: Jack Lawrence
       You Won't Forget Me (Adams) music: Fred Spielman; lyrics:
          Kermit Goell

Note: The above recording contains other selections not from
        the film.   Additional soundtrack vocals:

Curtain Calls CC 100/23 (soundtrack) mono 'Joan Crawford'

Cast: Joan Crawford, India Adams (for Joan Crawford)

Songs: You Won't Forget Me (Adams)
       Two-Faced Woman (Adams, chorus)   musical direction:
       Tenderly (Adams, Crawford)   Adolph Deutsch

TWO FOR TONIGHT (Paramount, 1935)

Decca DL 4250 mono 'Bing's Hollywood - Easy to Remember'

Music: Harry Revel; lyrics: Mack Gordon; musical direction:
The Dorsey Brothers

Cast: Bing Crosby

Songs: Without A Word of Warning (Crosby)
       Two for Tonight (Crosby)
       From the Top of Your Head (to the Tip of Your Toes)
          (Crosby)
       I Wish I Were Alladin (Crosby)
       Takes Two to Make A Bargain (Crosby)

TWO GIRLS AND A SAILOR (MGM, 1944)

Sound/Stage 2307 (soundtrack) mono

Music, lyrics: various

Cast: Gracie Allen, June Allyson, Xavier Cugat Orchestra,
       Gloria De Haven, Tom Drake, Jimmy Durante, Lena Horne,
       Jose and Amparo Iturbi, Harry James Orchestra, Van
       Johnson, Lina Romay, Frank Sully

Songs: Thrill of A New Romance (Cugat Orchestra) music: Xavier
           Cugat; lyrics: Harold Adamson
        Rhumba, Rhumba (Romay, Cugat Orchestra)
        Thrill of A New Romance (reprise) (Cugat Orchestra)
        Take It Easy (Romay, chorus, Cugat Orchestra) music,
           lyrics: Albert De Bru, Vic Mizzy, Irving Taylor
        My Mother Told Me (De Haven, chorus) music: Jimmy
           McHugh; lyrics: George Stoll
        Ritual Fire Dance (Jose, Amparo Iturbi, pianos) music:
           Manuel de Falla
        Inka-Dinka-Doo (Durante, chorus) music: Jimmy Durante;
           lyrics: Ben Ryan
        My Mother Told Me (reprise) (Johnson, Drake, Sully)
---   Charmaine (James Orchestra) music, lyrics: Erno Rapee,
           Lew Pollack
        Estrellita (James Orchestra) music: Manuel Ponce
        Sweet and Lovely (James Orchestra) music, lyrics:
           Gus Arnheim, Harry Tobias, Jules Lemare
        A Young Man with A Horn (Allyson, chorus, James Orchestra)
           music: George Stoll; lyrics: Ralph Freed
        Concerto for Index Finger (Allen) musical direction:
           Albert Coates
        A-Tisket, A-Tasket (Allyson, De Haven) music, lyrics:
           Al Feldman, Ella Fitzgerald
        Sweet and Lovely (reprise) (Allyson, De Haven)
        Paper Doll (Horne) music, lyrics: Johnny S Black

TWO SISTERS FROM BOSTON (MGM, 1946)

RCA (78rpm) DM 1056 mono

Music, lyrics: various; musical direction; Charles Previn

Cast: Nadine Connor (not in film), Lauritz Melchior

RCA (78rpm) 10-1224 My Country (pt 1) (Melchior) music:
                     Franz Liszt, Charles Previn; lyrics:
                     Ralph Freed
                     Serenade (Melchior) not from film
RCA (78rpm) 10-1225 My Country (pt 2) (Melchior)
                     The House I Live In (Melchior) not from film

RCA (78rpm) 10-1226 Marie Antoinette (pt 1 and 2) (Melchior,
                    Connor) music: Felix Mendelssohn, Charles
                    Previn; lyrics: Earl Brent

Note: Additional recordings by Jimmy Durante:

Majestic (78rpm) 1059 G'wan Home, Your Mudder's Callin (with
                      Eddie Jackson)
                 There Are Two Sides to Every Girl (with
                      Eddie Jackson) music: Sammy Fain;
                      lyrics: Ralph Freed

TWO TICKETS TO BROADWAY (RKO, 1951)

RCA (45/EP) EPA 331 mono

Music: Jule Styne, others; lyrics: Leo Robin, others; musical
direction: Henri Rene

Cast: Tony Martin, Dinah Shore (not in film)

Songs: The Closer You Are (Martin)
        Are You Just A Beautiful Dream? (Martin)
---   Let the Worry Bird Worry for You (Martin)
        Manhattan (Martin, Shore) music: Richard Rodgers;
            lyrics: Lorenz Hart

Note: Additional studio recordings by cast member Gloria De
        Haven:

        Decca (45rpm) 9-27781 The Closer You Are
                              Let the Worry Bird Worry for You

TWO TICKETS TO PARIS (Columbia, 1963)

Roulette 25182 (soundtrack) stereo

Music: Henry Glover, others; lyrics: Joey Dee, Morris Levy,
others; musical direction: Marty Manning

Cast: Gary Crosby, Willie Davis, Joe Dee, Jeri Lynne Fraser,
        Kay Medford, The Starlighters

Songs: What Kind of Love Is This (Dee, chorus) music, lyrics:
            Johnny Nash
        Willy Willy (Davis, Starlighters)
        The Open sea (orchestra)
        Twistin' on A Liner (Dee)
        C'est la Vie (Crosby) music: Mack Wolfson; lyrics:
            Eddie White

Instant Men (Medford) music: Don Gohman; lyrics: Hal
    Hackaday
--- Two Tickets to Paris (chorus) music: Don Gohrman; lyrics:
    Hal Hackaday
Teenage Vamp (Fraser) music, lyrics: Albert Seigal
Left Bank Blues (orchestra)
C'est Si Bon (Dee, chorus) music: Henri Betti; lyrics:
    Jerry Seelen
Everytime (I Think About You) (Dee, Starlighers) music:
    Henry Glover; lyrics: Joey Dee, Sam Taylor
The Boat (Dee, Starlighters)

TWO WEEKS WITH LOVE (MGM, 1950)

MGM E 530 (soundtrack) mono reissued: MCA 39082 CD

Music, lyrics: various; musical direction: Georgie Stoll

Cast: Carleton Carpenter, Jane Powell, Debbie Reynolds

Songs: A Heart That's Free (Powell) music: Alfred G Robyn;
    lyrics: Thomas T Railey
Row, Row, Row (Carpenter, Reynolds) music: James V
    Monaco; lyrics: William Jerome
Oceana Roll (Powell, chorus) music: Lucien Denni; lyrics:
    Roger Lewis
--- By the Light of the Silvery Moon (Powell, chorus) music:
    Gus Edwards; lyrics: Edward Madden
Aba Daba Honeymoon (Reynolds, Carpenter, chorus) music,
    lyrics: Arthur Fields, Walter Donovan
My Hero (Powell, chorus) music: Oscar Straus; lyrics:
    Stanislaus Stange

THE UMBRELLAS OF CHERBOURG (Les Parapluies de Cherbourg)
(Parc-Madeleine-Beta, 1964) French

Philips 840.537 BY (two records - soundtrack) stereo CD

Music: Michel Legrand; lyrics: Jacques Demy; musical direction:
Michel Legrand

Cast: Jose Bartel (for Nino Castelnuovo), Georges Blanes (for
    Marc Michel), Claire Leclerc (for Mireille Perrey),
    Christiane Legrand (for Anne Vernon), Danielle Licari
    (for Catherine Deneuve), Claudine Meunier (for Ellen
    Farner), Harald Wolff

Songs: Generique (orchestra)
    Scene du Garage (Bartel)

        Devant le Magasin (Bartel, Licari)
        Au Dancing (Bartel, Licari)
        Sur le Quai (Bartel, Licari)
        Dans le Magasin de Parapluies (Legrand, Licari)
        Chez Dubourg, Le Joaillier (Wolff, Blanes, Legrand, Licari)
---   Dans le Magasin (Legrand, Licari)
        Arrivee de Cassard (Blanes)
        Duo Genevieve - Guy (Devant le Garage) (Licari, Bartel)
        A l'Appartement (Legrand, Licari)
        Adieux a Elise (Leclerc, Bartel, Licari)
        Le Gare: Guy s'en Va (Licari, Bartel)
        Dans le Magasin (Legrand, Licari)
---   Diner (Blanes, Licari, Legrand)
        Recit de Cassard (Blanes)
        La Lettre de Guy (Bartel)
        Le Carnaval (Legrand, Lecari)
        Le Mariage (organ music)
        Chez Elise (Leclerc, Bartel, Meunier)
---   Le Garage - Dispute (Bartel, men)
        Guy au Cafe (Bartel, men)
        La Boite a Matelots (Bartel, girl)
        Duo Guy - Madeleine (Bartel, Meunier)
        La Terrasse du Cafe (Bartel, Meunier)
        La Station Service (Meunier, Bartel)
        Finale (Licari, Bartel, chorus)

UNCLE TOM'S CABIN (Germany, 1965) released by Hallmark in USA in 1970

Philips PHS 600-272 (soundtrack) stereo

Music: Peter Thomas; lyrics: Aldo von Pinelli; musical direction: Peter Thomas

Cast: George Goodman, Juliette Greco, Eartha Kitt

Songs: Melody of the Southland; Mississippi Blues
       Western Waltz
       Farewell to Mississippi
       Joshua Fit de Battle of Jericho
       Crocodiles in the River
       Happy Journey
       Symphony of the South
       Yearning for the Old Mississippi
       Hours of Happiness
       Dream My Baby Dream (Evangeline's Lullaby)
---   Night Over the Fields
       Could Be in the Morning
       So Much the Worse for Me
       Go Down Moses
       Independence Day

Song of the Negro Children
Revolt of the Slaves
In the Cabins (Song of the Negro)
At the Fair Ground
Flight through the Swamp
And the Old Mississippi Keeps Rolling Along

Note: Vocals are not listed on the above recording.

UNDER THE CHERRY MOON (Warner Bros, 1986)

Warner Bros 1-25395 stereo 'Parade' CD

Music, lyrics: Prince

Cast: Prince (and the Revolution)

Songs: Christopher Tracy's Parade (Prince)
       New Position (Prince)
       I Wonder U (prince)
       Under the Cherry Moon (Prince)
       Girls & Boys (Prince)
       Life Can Be So Nice (Prince)
       Venus de Milo (Prince)
       Mountains (Prince)
       Do U Lie? (Prince)
       Kiss (Prince)
       Anotherloverholenyohead (Prince)
       Sometimes It Snows in April (Prince)

THE UNDERPUP (Universal, 1939)

Decca (78rpm) 125 mono 'Gloria Jean Souvenir Album'

Music, lyrics: various; musical direction: Charles Previn

Cast: Gloria Jean

Decca (78rpm) 3116 Annie Laurie (Jean) anon
                    Penguin Song (Jean, chorus) music: John
                       Philip Sousa; lyrics: Ralph Freed
Decca (78rpm) 15047 I'm Like A Bird (Jean) music arranged by
                    Charles Previn; lyrics: Harold Adamson

THE UNFINISHED DANCE (MGM, 1947)

MGM (78rpm) 4 mono

Music, lyrics: various; musical direction: Herbert Stothart

Cast: Danny Thomas

MGM (78rpm) 30021 Prelude (orchestra) narration of introduction
                 by Walter Pidgeon; music: Saint-Saens,
                 Tschaikowsky
                 The Bartered Bride (orchestra) music: Smetana
MGM (78rpm) 30022 The Faust Fantasy (orchestra) music: Gounod
                 Liebesfreud (orchestra) music: Kreisler
MGM (78rpm) 30023 Holiday for Strings (orchestra) music: Rose
                 Caprice (orchestra) music: Thomas, Chopin
MGM (78rpm) 30024 Merrily-Merrily (Thomas) music, lyrics:
                 Sammy Fain
                 Minor Melody (Thomas) music, lyrics: Ray Jacobs,
                 Danny Thomas

THE UNSINKABLE MOLLY BROWN (MGM, 1964)

MGM SE 4232 ST (soundtrack) stereo reissued: MCA 25011

Music, lyrics: Meredith Willson; musical direction: Robert
Armbruster

Cast: Hermione Baddeley, Ed Begley, Martita Hunt, Jack Kruschen,
       Harve Presnell, Debbie Reynolds

Songs: Overture (orchestra)
       I Ain't Down Yet (Reynolds, chorus)
       I'll Never Say No (Presnell, Reynolds)
       Belly Up to the Bar, Boys (Reynolds, chorus)
       Dolce Far Niente (orchestra)
       I'll Never Say No (reprise) (Presnell)
---   Colorado, My Home (Presnell)
       Up Where the People Are (orchestra)
       I'll Never Say No (reprise) (Reynolds)
       He's My Friend (Presnell, Begley, Kruschen, Hunt, Baddeley,
          cast)
       Leadville Johnny Brown (Soliloquy) (Presnell)
       Colorado, My Home (Finale) (Presnell)

Note: The above recording includes spoken dialog.

UNTAMED (MGM, 1929)

Curtain Calls CC 100/23 (soundtrack) mono 'Joan Crawford'

Music, lyrics: various

Cast: Joan Crawford, George Montgomery

Songs: Chant of the Jungle (Crawford) music: Nacio Herb Brown;
      lyrics: Arthur Freed
      That Wonderful Something Is Love (Montgomery, Crawford)
        music: Louis Alter; lyrics: Joe Goodwin
      Chant of the Jungle (reprise) (Crawford)

UP IN ARMS (Goldwyn, 1944)

Sountrak STK 113 (soundtrack) mono

Music: Harold Arlen, others; lyrics: Ted Koehler, others; musical
direction: Ray Heindorf

Cast: Danny Kaye, Dinah Shore

Songs: Overture (orchestra)
      Comedy Sketch (Kaye, cast) spoken
      The Lobby Number (Kaye, cast) music, lyrics: Sylvia Fine,
        Max Liebman
      Now I Know (Shore)
      All Out for Freedom (orchestra)
      Love Scene (Kaye, Shore, cast) spoken
      Tess's Torch Song (Shore, chorus)
\-\-\-   Melody in 4-F (Kaye, chorus) music, lyrics: Sylvia Fine,
        Max Liebman
      Dream Sequence:
        Melody in 4-F (reprise) (Kaye)
        Tess's Torch Song (reprise) (Kaye, Shore, chorus)
        Greetings, Gates (Kaye, Shore, chorus) music, lyrics:
          Sylvia Fine
      The Capture (Kaye, cast) spoken
      Finale:
      Greetings, Gates (reprise) (Kaye, Shore)
      All Out for Freedom (reprise) (orchestra)

Note: Studio recordings by cast members:

RCA Victor (78rpm) 20-1562 Now I Know (Shore)
Columbia (78rpm)   37854 Tess's Torch Song (Shore)
Decca (LP) DLP   5033 The Lobby Number (Kaye)

THE VAGABOND KING (Paramount, 1956)

RCA LM 2004 mono

Music: Rudolf Friml, others; lyrics: Brian Hooker, others;
musical direction: Henri Rene

Cast: Jean Fenn (not in film), Oreste

Songs: Overture (orchestra)
       Bon Jour (Oreste, chorus) lyrics: Johnny Burke
       Some Day (Fenn)
       The Vagabond King Waltz (Huguette Waltz) (Oreste)
       The Scotch Archers' Song (chorus)
       Only A Rose (Oreste, Fenn)
---   Viva La You (Fenn, chorus) lyrics: Johnny Burke
       Lord, I'm Glad I Know Thee (Oreste, chorus) music: Victor
         Young; lyrics: Johnny Burke
       Love Me Tonight (Oreste, Fenn)
       Drinking Song (chorus)
       This Same Heart (Oreste) lyrics: Johnny Burke
       Song of the Vagabonds (Oreste, chorus)

VALLEY OF THE DOLLS (Twentieth Century-Fox, 1967)

Fox S 4196 (soundtrack) stereo

Music, lyrics for songs: Dory and Andre Previn; musical score,
direction: John Williams

Cast: Tony Scotti, Eileen Wilson (not from film), other
      unidentified vocals

Songs: Theme from 'Valley of the Dolls' (vocal) narration:
       Barbara Perkins
       It's Impossible (vocal)
       Ann at Lawrenceville (orchestra)
       Chance Meeting (orchestra)
       Neely's Career Montage (orchestra)
       Come Live with Me (Scotti)
---   I'll Plant My Own Tree (Wilson)
       The Gillian Girl Commercial (orchestra)
       Jennifer's French Movie (orchestra)
       Give A Little More (vocal)
       Jennifer's Recollection (Scotti)
       Theme from 'Valley of the Dolls' (reprise) (vocal)

Note: Patty Duke recorded an album of songs from this film
      on United Artists UAS 6623.
      Dionne Warwick recorded songs from this film on Scepter
      S-568.
      Judy Garland recorded 'I'll Plant My Own Tree' (unused
      in film). Released on Out Takes OTF-1.

VARSITY SHOW (Warner Bros, 1937)

MCA 1511 mono 'Dick Powell'

Music: Richard Whiting; lyrics: Johnny Mercer; musical direction:

Lou Forbes

Cast: Dick Powell

Songs: Love Is on the Air Tonight (Powell)
       You've Got Something There (Powell)
       Have You Got Any Castles, Baby? (Powell)

Note: Additional recording:

       Decca (78rpm) 1430 Moonlight on the Campus (Powell)

VICTOR / VICTORIA (MGM, 1982)

MGM MG 1-5407 (soundtrack) stereo

Music: Henry Mancini; lyrics: Leslie Bricusse; musical
direction: Henry Mancini

Cast: Julie Andrews, Robert Preston, Lesley Ann Warren

Songs: Main Title (Crazy World) (orchestra)
       You and Me (Andrews, Preston)
       The Shady Lady from Seville (Andrews)
       Alone in Paris (orchestra)
       King's Can-Can (orchestra)
       Le Jazz Hot (Andrews, chorus)
---   Crazy World (Andrews)
       Chicago, Illinois (Warren, chorus)
       Cat and Mouse (orchestra)
       You and Me (reprise) (orchestra)
       Gay Paree (Preston)
       Finale (orchestra):
           The Shady Lady from Seville
           Crazy World
           You and Me
           Le Jazz Hot

VIVA LAS VEGAS (MGM, 1964)

RCA (45/EP) EPA 4382 stereo

Music, lyrics: various

Cast: Elvis Presley

Songs: If You Think I Don't Need You (Presley) music, lyrics:
           Bob 'Red' West, Joe Cooper
       I Need Somebody to Lean On (Presley) music: Mort Shuman;
           lyrics: Doc Pomus

> C'mon Everybody (Presley) music, lyrics: Joy Byers
> Today, Tomorrow and Forever (Presley) music: Florence
>   Kaye; lyrics: Bill Giant, Bernië Baum

VIVA MARIA! (United Artists, 1965) French

United Artists UAS 4135 (soundtrack) stereo

Music: George Delerue; lyrics: Louis Malle, Jean Claude
Carriere; musical direction: George Delerue

Cast: Brigette Bardot, Jeanne Moreau

Songs: Overture (orchestra)
       Viva Maria (orchestra)
       Interieui Roulotte (orchestra)
       Dame Blanche (orchestra)
       Theme Victoire Colline (orchestra)
       Generique (orchestra)
       Les Petites Femmes (orchestra)
---   Paris, Paris, Paris (Bardot, Moreau)
       Cirque (orchestra)
       Musique de Cachot Jeanne Flores (orchestra)
       Les Petites Femmes (Bardot, Moreau)
       Revolution March (orchestra)
       Maria, Maria (Bardot, Moreau)
       Finale (orchestra)

WAIKIKI WEDDING (Paramount, 1937)

Decca DL 4252 mono 'Bing's Hollywood - Pocket Full of Dreams'

Music: Ralph Rainger, others; lyrics: Leo Robin, others;
musical direction: various

Cast: Bing Crosby

Songs: Blue Hawaii (Crosby) musical direction: Lani McIntire
       In A Little Hula Heaven (Crosby) musical direction:
           Jimmy Dorsey
       Sweet Leilani (Crosby) music, lyrics: Harry Owens;
           musical direction: Lani McIntire
       Sweet Is the Word for You (Crosby) musical direction:
           Victor Young

WAKE UP AND DREAM (Universal, 1934)

Golden Legends 2000/1 mono

Music, lyrics: Russ Columbo, Grace Hamilton, Jack Stern;
musical direction: Jimmie Grier

Cast: Russ Columbo

Brunswick (78rpm) 6972 When You're in Love (Columbo)
Epic (LP) L2N6064   Too Beautiful for Words (Columbo)
Brunswick (78rpm) 6972 Let's Pretend There's A Moon (Columbo)

WAKE UP AND LIVE (Twentieth Century-Fox, 1937)

Hollywood Soundstage 403 (soundtrack) mono

Music: Harry Revel, others; lyrics: Mack Gordon, others; musical
direction: Louis Silvers

Cast: Bobby Baker, Ben Bernie, Grace Bradley, The Brewster
       Twins, Buddy Clark (for Jack Haley), Alice Faye, Patsy
       Kelly, Barnett Parker, Leah Ray, Ned Sparks

Songs: Titles (orchestra)
       It's Swell of You (orchestra)
       I'm Bubbling Over (Bradley, The Brewster Twins)
       Wake Up and Live (Faye)
       Red Seal Malt (Bernie, quartet)
       I'm Bubbling Over (reprise) (orchestra)
       Never in A Million Years (Clark)
       Never in A Million Years (reprise) (Baker)
       It's Swell of You (reprise) (Clark)
---   Wake Up and Live (reprise) (Clark)
       De Camptown Races (Parker, chorus) music, lyrics: Stephen
           Foster
       Oh, But I'm Happy (Clark)
       I Love You Too Much, Muchacha (Ray, chorus)
       There's A Lull in My Life (Faye)
       Finale:
           Wake Up and Live (Clark)
           Never in A Million Years (Faye, Clark)
           I'm Bubbling Over (Bradley)
           There's A Lull in My Life (Kelly, Sparks)
           It's Swell of You (Bernie)
           Wake Up and Live (chorus)
       End Credits (orchestra)

Note: The above recording includes spoken dialog. Studio
       recordings by Alice Faye (all on LP: Columbia CL 3068):

       Brunswick (78rpm) 7860 Never in A Million Years
                              It's Swell of You
       Brunswick (78rpm) 7876 There's A Lull in My Life
                              Wake Up and Live

WEEK-END IN HAVANA (Twentieth Century-Fox, 1941)

Decca (78rpm) 295 mono

Music: Harry Warren, others; lyrics: Mack Gordon, others

Cast: The Bando Da Lua, Carmen Miranda

Decca (78rpm) 23239 A Weekend in Havana (Miranda, Bando Da Lua)
                        (LP: Ace of Hearts AH 99)
                    Ella Diz Que Tem (Miranda, Bando Da Lua)
                        (not from film)
Decca (78rpm) 23240 When I Love I Love (Miranda, Bando Da Lua)
                        (LP: Ace of Hearts 99)
                    Rebola A Bola (Miranda, Bando Da Lua) music,
                        lyrics: Aloysio Oliveira, Nestor Amaral,
                        Brant Horta (LP: Ace of Hearts 99)
Decca (78rpm) 23241 The Man with the Lollypop Song (Miranda,
                        Bando Da Lua) (LP: Ace of Hearts 99)
                    Nao te Dou a Chupeta (Miranda, Bando Da
                        Lua) (not from film)

WEEK-END IN HAVANA (Twentieth Century-Fox, 1941)

Curtain Calls CC 100/14 (soundtrack) mono

Musical direction: Alfred Newman

Cast: The Bando Da Lua, Alice Faye, Carmen Miranda, John
        Payne, Cesar Romero

Songs: Main Title (orchestra)
        Weekend in Havana (Miranda, chorus)
        Weekend in Havana (reprise) (chorus)
        Siboney (orchestra) music: Ernesto Lecuona; lyrics:
            Dolly Morse
        Mama Inez (chorus) music: Eliseo Grenet; lyrics: L Wolfe
            Gilbert
        Rebola A Bola (Miranda, Bando Da Lua)
        When I Love I Love (Miranda, Bando Da Lua)
        Tropical Magic (Faye, chorus)
        Romance and Rhumba (Faye, Romero, chorus) lyrics; James
            V Monaco
        The Man with the Lollypop Song (Faye) cut from film
        Tropical Magic (reprise) (Faye, Payne)
        The Nango (Miranda, chorus)
        Weekend in Havana - Finale (Faye, Miranda, Payne,
            Romero, chorus)

Note: The above recording includes spoken dialog.

WELCOME, STRANGER (Paramount, 1947)

Decca DL 4260 mono 'Bing's Hollywood - But Beautiful'

Music: James Van Heusen; lyrics: John Burke; musical direction:
John Scott Trotter

Cast: Bing Crosby

Songs: Smile Right Back at the Sun (Crosby)
       As Long As I'm Dreaming (Crosby)
       My Heart Is A Hobo (Crosby)
       Country Style (Square Dance) (Crosby, chorus)

WELCOME TO L A (United Artists, 1977)

MCA 25040 (soundtrack) stereo

Music, lyrics: Richard Baskin

Cast: Richard Baskin, Keith Carradine

Songs: Welcome to L A (Carradine)
       City of the One Night Stands (Baskin)
       The Best Temptation of All (Baskin)
       At the Door (Baskin)
       Welcome to L A (reprise) (Carradine)
---   The Best Temptation of All (reprise) (Carradine)
       When the Arrow Flies (Baskin)
       The Best Temptation of All (reprise) (Carradine)
       Night Time (Baskin)
       The Best Temptation of All (reprise) (Carradine)
       After the End (Baskin)
       City of the One Night Stands (reprise) (Carradine)

WE'RE NOT DRESSING (Paramount, 1934)

Columbia C2L 43 (two records) mono 'Bing Crosby in Hollywood'

Music: Harry Revel; lyrics: Mack Gordon; musical direction:
Nat W Finston, others

Cast: Bing Crosby

Songs: Love Thy Neighbor (Crosby)
       Once in A Blue Moon (Crosby)
       Good-Night, Lovely Little Lady (Crosby)
       May I? (Crosby)
       (She Walks Like You - She Talks Like You) She Reminds
          Me of You (Crosby) musical direction: Jimmie Grier

Note: Soundtrack selection on LP: Encore ST 101 'Merman in the
        Movies':

        It's A New Spanish Custom (Ethel Merman, Leon Errol)

        The following selection was originally intended for
        'We're Not Dressing' but instead was used in 'The
        Big Broadcast of 1936':

Brunswick (78rpm) 7491 It's the Animal in Me (Merman) LP:
                       Columbia CL 2751

WEST SIDE STORY (United Artists, 1961)

Columbia OS 2070 (soundtrack) stereo

Music: Leonard Bernstein; lyrics: Stephen Sondheim; musical
direction: Johnny Green

cast: Jim Bryant (for Richard Beymer), George Chakiris, Marni
        Nixon (for Natalie Wood), Tucker Smith, Russ Tamblyn,
        Betty Wand (for Rita Moreno)

Songs: Prologue (orchestra)
        Jet Song (Tamblyn, Jets)
        Something's Coming (Bryant)
        Dance at the Gym (orchestra)
            1) Blues
            2) Promenade
            3) Jump
        Maria (Bryant)
        America (Wand, Chakiris, Sharks, girls)
        Tonight (Bryant, Nixon)
---   Gee, Officer Krupke! (Tamblyn, Jets)
        I Feel Pretty (Nixon, girls)
        One Hand, One Heart (Bryant, Nixon)
        Quintet (Bryant, Nixon, Wand, Tamblyn, Chakiris, Jets,
            Sharks)
        The Rumble (orchestra)
        Cool (Smith, Jets)
        A Boy Like That (Wand)
        I Have A Love (Nixon)
        Somewhere (Finale) (Bryant, Nixon)

WHEN THE BOYS MEET THE GIRLS (MGM, 1965)

MGM SE 4334 (soundtrack) stereo   reissued: MCA 25013

Music: George Gershwin, others; lyrics: Ira Gershwin, others;
musical direction: Fred Karger

Cast: Louis Armstrong, Connie Francis, Herman's Hermits,
        Liberace, Harve Presnell, Sam and the Pharaohs

Songs: When the Boys Meet the Girls (Francis, chorus) music,
          lyrics: Jack Keller, Howard Greenfield
        Monkey See, Monkey Do (Sam, Pharaohs) music, lyrics:
          Johnny Farrow
        Embraceable You (Presnell)
        Throw It Out of Your Mind (Armstrong) music, lyrics:
          Louis Armstrong, Bill Kyle
        Mail Call (Francis, chorus) music, lyrics: Fred Karger,
          Ben Weisman, Sid Wayne
        I Got Rhythm (Francis, Presnell, chorus)
---   Listen People (Hermits) music, lyrics: Graham Gouldman
        Bidin' My Time (Hermits)
        Embraceable You (reprise) (Francis)
        Aruba Liberace (Liberace) music, lyrics: Liberace
        But Not for Me (Francis, Presnell)
        I Got Rhythm (reprise) (Armstrong)

WHERE DO WE GO FROM HERE? (Twentieth Century-Fox, 1945)

Ariel KWH 10 (soundtrack) mono

Music: Kurt Weill; lyrics: Ira Gershwin; musical direction:
Emil Newman

cast: Herman Bing, Fortunio Bonanova, June Haver, Joan Leslie,
        Fred MacMurray, Carlos Ramirez, Gene Shelton

Songs: Where Do We Go from Here? (chorus)
        Morale (Haver, chorus)
        All at Once (MacMurray)
        If Love Remains (MacMurray, Leslie)
        Song of the Rhineland (Haver, Bing, chorus)
        Christopher Columbus (The Mutiny) (Ramirez, Bonanova,
          men)
        The Nina, the Pinta, the Santa Maria (MacMurray)
        All at Once (reprise) (MacMurray, Leslie)
        Finale (MacMurray, Leslie, Haver, Shelton)

WHITE CHRISTMAS (Paramount, 1954)

Decca DL 8083 mono   reissued: MCA (British) MCL 1777

Music, lyrics: Irving Berlin; musical direction: Joseph J Lilley

Cast: Bing Crosby, Danny Kaye, Peggy Lee (not in film), Trudy
        Stevens (not in film)

Songs: The Old Man (Crosby, Kaye)
       Gee, I Wish I Was Back in the Army (Crosby, Kaye, chorus)
       Sisters (Lee, Stevens)
       The Best Things Happen While You're Dancing (Kaye, chorus)
       Snow (Crosby, Lee, Kaye, Stevens)
       Blue Skies (Crosby, Kaye)
       A Minstrel Show (Crosby, Kaye)
       Mandy (Crosby, Kaye, chorus)
---   Choreography (Kaye, Crosby, chorus)
       Count Your Blessings Instead of Sheep (Crosby)
       Love, You Didn't Do Right by Me (Lee)
       What Can You Do with A General? (Crosby)
       White Christmas (Crosby, Lee, Kaye, Stevens, chorus)

WHITE CHRISTMAS (Paramount, 1954)

Columbia CL 6338 mono

Musical direction: Buddy Cole, Percy Faith, Paul Weston

Cast: Betty Clooney (not in film), Rosemary Clooney

Songs: White Christmas (Rosemary Clooney)
       Mandy (Rosemary Clooney)
       Snow (Rosemary Clooney)
       Gee, I Wish I Was Back in the Army (Rosemary Clooney)
---   Love, You Didn't Do Right by Me (Rosemary Clooney)
       Sisters (Betty Clooney, Rosemary Clooney)
       The Best Things Happen While You're Dancing (Rosemary
          Clooney)
       Count Your Blessings Instead of Sheep (Rosemary Clooney)

WILD ON THE BEACH (Twentieth Century-Fox, 1965)

RCA LSP 3441 (soundtrack) stereo

Music, lyrics: "By" Dunham, Bobby Beverly, others; musical
direction: Jimmie Haskell

Cast: The Astronauts, Jackie and Gayle, Cindy Malone, Sandy
       Nelson, Frankie Randall, Sonny and Cher

Songs: The Yellow Haired Woman (Randall) music, lyrics: "By"
          Dunham, E Davis (not from film)
       Rock the World (Astronauts) music, lyrics: "By" Dunham,
          E Davis
       Run Away from Him (Malone)
       Drum Dance (Nelson) music, lyrics: Joe Saraceno, Frank P
          Warren
       The Gods of Love (Randall)
       It's Gonna Rain (Sonny and Cher) music, lyrics: Sonny Bono

--- Little Speedy Gonzales (Astronauts) music, lyrics:
    Stan Ross, Bobby Beverly
   Pyramid Stomp (Astronauts) music, lyrics: "By" Dunham,
    Jimmie Haskell
   The House on the Beach (Randall)
   Snap It (Astronauts) music: Jimmie Haskell
   Winter Nocturne (Jackie and Gayle) music, lyrics: "By"
    Dunham, E Davis

WILLY WONKA AND THE CHOCOLATE FACTORY (Paramount, 1971)

Paramount PAS 6012 (soundtrack) stereo reissued: MCA 37124

Music: Anthony Newley; lyrics: Leslie Bricusse; musical
direction: Walter Scharf

Cast: Frank Albertson, Julie Dawn Cole, Peter Ostrum, Diana
   Sowle, Gene Wilder, Aubrey Wood

Songs: Main Title (Golden Ticket / Pure Imagination) (orchestra)
   The Candy Man (Wood, chidren)
   Charlie's Paper Run (spoken)
   Cheer Up, Charlie (Sowle)
   Lucky Charlie (orchestra)
   (I've Got A) Golden Ticket (Albertson, Ostrum)
   Pure Imagination (Wilder)
--- Oompa Loompa (chorus)
   The Wonderous Boat Ride (Wilder, cast)
   Everlasting Gobstoppers (orchestra, sound effects)
   Oompa Loompa (reprise) (chorus)
   The Bubble Machine (orchestra, sound effects)
   I Want It Now (Cole)
   Oompa Loompa (reprise) (chorus)
   Wonkamobile, Wonkavision (sound effects, dialog)
   Oompa Loompa (reprise) (chorus)
   Wonkavator (sound effects)
   End Title (Pure Imagination) (chorus)

Note: The above recording includes spoken dialog. Vocals
   are uncredited.

WITH A SONG IN MY HEART (Twentieth Century-Fox, 1952)

Capitol L 309 (10") mono reissued: Capitol T 309 (12")

Music, lyrics: various; musical direction: George Greeley

Cast: Jane Froman (for Susan Hayward)

Songs: Opening (With A Song in My Heart) (chorus)

It's A Good Day (Froman, chorus) music, lyrics: Peggy
  Lee, Dave Barbour
Tea for Two (Froman) music: Vincent Youmans; lyrics:
  Irving Caesar
Blue Moon (Froman, chorus) music: Richard Rodgers;
  lyrics: Lorenz Hart
Embraceable You (Froman) music: George Gershwin; lyrics:
  Ira Gershwin

--- Get Happy (Froman, chorus) music: Harold Arlen; lyrics:
  Ted Koehler
I'll Walk Alone (Froman) music: Jule Styne; lyrics:
  Sammy Cahn
They're Either Too Young or Too Old (Froman) music:
  Arthur Schwartz; lyrics: Frank Loesser
An American Medley:
  America, the Beautiful (Froman, chorus) music:
    Samuel A Ward; lyrics: Katharine Lee Bates
  It's A Good Day (reprise) (Froman)
  Give My Regards to Broadway (Froman) music, lyrics:
    George M Cohan
  Carry Me Back to Old Virginny (Froman) music,
    lyrics: James A Bland
  The Eyes of Texas (Froman, chorus) music: anon;
    lyrics: John L Sinclair
  Dixie (Froman, chorus) music, lyrics: Dan D Emmett
  America, the Beautiful (reprise) (Froman, chorus)
With A Song in My Heart (reprise) (Froman, chorus)
  music: Richard Rodgers; lyrics: Lorenz Hart

Note: Additional selections on 12" reissue:

That Old Feeling (Froman) music: Sammy Fain; lyrics:
  Lew Brown
I'm Through with Love (Froman) music, lyrics: Matty
  Malneck, Fud Livingston, Gus Kahn

WITH A SONG IN MY HEART (Twentieth Century-Fox, 1952)

Legends 1000/3 (soundtrack) mono 'Susan Hayward'

Musical direction: Alfred Newman

Cast: Richard Allan, Jane Froman (for Susan Hayward)

Songs: Main Title (orchestra)
       That Old Feeling (Froman)
       Jim's Toasted Peanuts (Froman, men)
       I'm Through with Love (Froman)
       Get Happy (Froman)
       Blue Moon (Froman, chorus)
       On the Gay White Way (Froman, chorus) music: Ralph Rainger;
         lyrics: Leo Robin

The Right Kind (Froman)
With A Song in My Heart (Froman, Allan, chorus)
Embraceable You (Froman, chorus)
Tea for Two (Froman)
It's A Good Day (Froman)
They're Either Too Young or Too Old (Froman)
--- I'll Walk Alone (Froman)
An American Medley:
    America, the Beautiful (Froman, chorus)
    Wonderful Home Sweet Home (Froman, chorus)
    Give My Regards to Broadway (Froman)
    Chicago (Froman, chorus) music, lyrics: Fred Fisher
    California, Here I Come (Froman, chorus) music, lyrics:
      Joseph Meyer, Al Jolson, Buddy DeSylva
    Carry Me Back to Old Virginny (Froman)
    Maine Stein Song (Froman, chorus) music: E A Fenstad;
      lyrics: Lincoln Colcord
    Back Home Again in Indiana (Froman) music: James F
      Hanley; lyrics: Ballard MacDonald
    Alabamy Bound (Froman, chorus) music: Ray Henderson;
      lyrics: Buddy DeSylva, Bud Green
    Deep in the Heart of Texas (Froman, chorus) music:
      Don Swander; lyrics: June Hershey
    Dixie (Froman, chorus)
    America, the Beautiful (reprise) (Froman, chorus)
With A Song in My Heart (reprise) (Froman, chorus)

Note: The above recording includes spoken dialog.

THE WIZ (Universal, 1978)

MCA 2-14000 (two records - soundtrack) stereo

Music, lyrics: Charlie Smalls, others; musical direction:
Quincy Jones

Cast: Thelma Carpenter, Lena Horne, Michael Jackson, Mabel
      King, Theresa Merritt, Richard Pryor, Diana Ross, Ted
      Ross, Nipsy Russell

Songs: Overture (orchestra)
      The Feeling That We Have (Merritt, chorus)
      Can I Go On?(D Ross) music, lyrics: Quincy Jones, Nick
        Ashford, Valerie Simpson
      Glinda's Theme (chorus) music, lyrics: Quincy Jones
      He's the Wizard (Carpenter, chorus)
      March of the Munchkins (chorus) music, lyrics: Quincy
        Jones
      Soon As I Get Home / Home (D Ross)
---   You Can't Win (Jackson, chorus)

Ease on Down the Road (Jackson, D Ross, chorus)
What Would I Do If I Could Feel? (Russell, girls)
Slide Some Oil to Me (Russell)
Now Watch Me Dance (orchestra) music: Quincy Jones
Ease on Down the Road (reprise) (Russell, D Ross, Jackson)
(I'm A) Mean Ole Lion (T Ross)
Ease on Down the Road (reprise) (T Ross, Russell, Jackson, D Ross)
Poppy Girls (orchestra) music: Quincy Jones, Anthony Jackson
--- Be A Lion (D Ross, T Ross, Russell, Jackson)
End of the Yellow Brick Road (orchestra) music: Quincy Jones, Nick Ashford, Valerie Simpson
Emerald City Sequence (chorus) music, lyrics: Quincy Jones, Charlie Smalls (Pryor, spoken)
So You Want to See the Wizard (Pryor) spoken
A Sorry Phony (Pryor, cast) spoken; music: Quincy Jones
Is This What Feeling Gets? (Dorothy's Theme) (D Ross) music, lyrics: Quincy Jones, Nick Ashford, Valerie Simpson
--- Don't Bring Me No Bad News (King, chorus)
Liberation Agitato (orchestra) music: Quincy Jones
A Brand New Day (Everybody Rejoice) (cast) music, lyrics: Luther Vandross
Liberation Ballet (orchestra) music: Quincy Jones
A Brand New Day (reprise) (chorus)
Believe in Yourself (D Ross)
The Good Witch Glinda (chorus) music: Quincy Jones (dialog: Pryor, Horne)
Believe in Yourself (reprise) (Horne)
Home (reprise) (D Ross)
Is This What Feeling Gets? (reprise) (orchestra)

THE WIZARD OF OZ (MGM, 1939)

Decca DL 5152 mono

Music: Harold Arlen; lyrics: E Y Harburg; musical direction: Victor Young

Cast: Judy Garland

Songs: Over the Rainbow (Garland)
       The Jitterbug (Garland, chorus) cut from film
       Munchkinland (chorus)
---   If I Only Had A Brain (chorus)
       If I Only Had A Heart (chorus)
       The Merry Old Land of Oz (chorus)
       We're Off to See the Wizard (chorus)

THE WIZARD OF OZ (MGM, 1939)

MGM E 3996 ST (soundtrack) mono   reissued: MCA 39046 CD

Musical direction: Herbert Stothart, George Stoll

Cast: Ray Bolger, Lorraine Bridges (for Billie Burke), Judy
        Garland, Jack Haley, Burt Lahr

Songs: Overture (orchestra)
       Over the Rainbow (Garland)
       Munchkinland - Ding-Dong! The Witch Is Dead (Bridges,
           Garland, Munchkin chorus)
       Follow the Yellow Brick Road (Munchkin chorus)
       We're Off to See the Wizard (Munchkin chorus)
       If I Only Had A Brain (Bolger)
       We're Off to See the Wizard (reprise) (Bolger, Garland)
       If I Only Had A Heart (Haley)
       We're Off to See the Wizard (reprise) (Bolger, Garland,
           Haley)
       If I Only Had the Nerve (Lahr)
       We're Off to See the Wizard (reprise) (Bolger, Garland,
           Haley, Lahr)
---   If I Were King of the Forest (Lahr - with Garland, Haley,
           Bolger)
       End Credits (orchestra)

Note: The above recording includes spoken dialog.

WONDER BAR (Warner Bros, 1934)

Hollywood Soundstage 402 (soundtrack) mono

Music: Harry Warren; lyrics: Al Dubin; musical direction:
Leo F Forbstein

Cast: Ricardo Cortez, Delores Del Rio, Al Jolson, Dick Powell

Songs: Opening Music (orchestra)
       Vive La France (Jolson)
---   Don't Say Goodnight (Powell, chorus)
       Dark Eyes (Ochye Tchornia) (Jolson, chorus) trad
       Wonder Bar (Powell)
       Why Do I Dream Those Dreams (Powell)
       Tango del Rio (Cortez, Del Rio) spoken
       Goin' to Heaven on A Mule (Jolson, chorus)
       Closing Scene (orchestra)

Note: The above recording includes spoken dialog. Studio
       recordings by Dick Powell (all on LP: Columbia C2L 44):

Brunswick (78rpm) 6792 Why Do I Dream Those Dreams?
Wonder Bar
Brunswick (78rpm) 6793 Don't Say Good Night

WORDS AND MUSIC (MGM, 1948)

MGM E 505 (soundtrack) mono   reissued: MCA 25029 CD

Music: Richard Rodgers; lyrics: Lorenz Hart; musical direction:
Lennie Hayton

Cast: June Allyson, The Blackburn Twins, Judy Garland, Betty
        Garrett, Lena Horne, Mickey Rooney, Ann Sothern

Songs: I Wish I Were in Love Again (Garland, Rooney)
        Johnny One Note (Garland)
        Where or When (Horne)
        The Lady Is A Tramp (Horne)
        There's A Small Hotel (Garrett)
        Manhattan (Rooney, chorus)
        Where's That Rainbow (Sothern, chorus)
        Thou Swell (Allyson, The Blackburn Twins)
        Slaughter on Tenth Avenue (orchestra)

Note: 'Slaughter on Tenth Avenue' included only on reissues.
        Additional recordings by cast members:

        RCA 47-3229 (45rpm) Blue Room (Perry Como)
                        With A Song in My Heart (Perry Como)
        Capitol (78rpm) 15428 Blue Moon (Mel Torme)
        Out Takes (LP) OTF-1 Way Out West (Garrett) cut from film
        Out Takes (LP) OTF-2 It Never Entered My Mind (Garrett)
                        cut from film

XANADU (Universal, 1980)

MCA 6100 (soundtrack) stereo

Music, lyrics: John Farrar, Jeff Lynne

Cast: (the voices of) The Electric Light Orchestra (singing
        group), Gene Kelly, Olivia Newton-John, Cliff Richard
        (not in film), (the voices of) The Tubes (singing group)

Songs: Magic (Newton-John, chorus) music, lyrics: Farrar
        Suddenly (Newton-John, Richard, chorus) music, lyrics:
          Farrar
        Dancin' (The Tubes) music, lyrics: Farrar
        Suspended in Time (Newton-John) music, lyrics: Farrar
        Whenever You're Away from Me (Newton-John, Kelly)

              music, lyrics: Farrar
---   I'm Alive (The Electric Light Orchestra) music, lyrics:
              Lynne
          The Fall (The Electric Light Orchestra) music, lyrics: Lynne
          Don't Walk Away (The Electric Light Orchestra) music,
              lyrics: Lynne
          All Over the World (The Electric Light orchestra) music,
              lyrics: Lynne
          Xanadu (Newton-John, The Electric Light Otchestra) music,
              lyrics: Lynne

YANKEE DOODLE DANDY (Warner Bros, 1942)

Curtain Calls 100/13 (soundtrack) mono

Music, lyrics: George M Cohan, others; musical direction:
Leo F Forbstein

Cast: James Cagney, Jeanne Cagney, Rosemary DeCamp, Walter
       Huston, Frances Langford, Joan Leslie, Irene Manning

Songs: Main Title (orchestra)
       Dancing Master (and Vaudeville Routine) (Huston, James
           Cagney, DeCamp, Jeanne Cagney) trad
       I Was Born in Virginia (cast)
       The Warmest Baby in the Bunch (Leslie)
       Harrigan (James Cagney, Leslie)
       Yankee Doodle Boy (James Cagney, chorus)
       Goodbye Johnny (chorus)
       All Aboard for Old Broadway (chorus) music: M K Jerome;
           lyrics: Jack Scholl
       Give My Regards to Broadway (James Cagney, chorus)
---   Oh You Wonderful Girl (chorus)
       The Belle of the Barber's Ball (cast)
       Mary (James Cagney, Leslie)
       45 Minutes from Broadway (James Cagney, cast)
       Mary (reprise) (Manning)
       So Long Mary (Manning, chorus)
       You're A Grand Old Flag (and war medley) (James Cagney,
           chorus)
       Come Along with Me Away (chorus)
       Over There (James Cagney, Langford, chorus)
       Medley (Langford):
           Love Nest
           Little Nellie Kelly
           The Man Who Owns Broadway
           Molly Malone
           Billie
       Off the Record (James Cagney) music: Richard Rodgers;
           lyrics: Lorenz Hart

Over There (chorus)
End Titles (orchestra)

Note: The above recording includes spoken dialog.

YELLOW SUBMARINE (United Artists, 1968)

Capitol SW 153 (soundtrack) stereo   CD

Music, lyrics to songs: John Lennon, Paul McCartney, George
Harrison; musical score, direction: George Martin

Cast: (the voices of) The Beatles: George Harrison, John Lennon,
        Paul McCartney, Ringo Starr

Songs: Yellow Submarine (The Beatles)
        Only A Northern Song (The Beatles) music, lyrics: George
           Harrison
        All Together Now (The Beatles)
        Hey Bulldog (The Beatles)
        It's All Too Much (The Beatles) music, lyrics: George
           Harrison
        All You Need Is Love (The Beatles)
---   Pepperland (orchestra)
        Sea of Time & Sea of Holes (orchestra)
        Sea of Monsters (orchestra)
        March of the Meanies (orchestra)
        Pepperland Laid Waste (orchestra)
        Yellow Submarine in Pepperland (orchestra)

YENTL (United Artists / MGM, 1983)

Columbia JS 39152 (soundtrack) stereo   CD

Music: Michel Legrand; lyrics: Alan and Marilyn Bergman;
musical direction: Michel Legrand

Cast: Barbra Streisand

Songs: Where Is It Written? (Streisand)
        Papa, Can You Hear me? (Streisand)
        This Is One of Those Moments (Streisand)
        No Wonder (Streisand)
        The Way He Makes Me Feel (Streisand)
        No Wonder (pt 2) (Streisand) dialog with Amy Irving
---   Tomorrow Night (Streisand) with dialog
        Will Someone Ever Look at Me That Way? (Streisand)
        No Matter What Happens (Streisand)
        No Wonder (reprise) (Streisand)
        A Piece of Sky (Streisand)

The Way He Makes Me Feel (studio version) (Streisand)
    musical direction: Dave Grusin
No Matter What Happens (studio version) (Streisand)
    musical direction: Dave Grusin

YES, GIORGIO (MGM / United Artists, 1982)

London PFV 9001 (soundtrack) stereo

Music, lyrics: various; musical direction: Emerson Buckley, others

Cast: Leona Mitchell, Luciano Pavarotti, David Romano

Songs: If We Were in Love (Pavarotti) music: John Williams;
            lyrics: Alan and Marilyn Bergman; musical direction:
            Herbert Spencer
        Overture (orchestra) music: Michael J Lewis
        Santa Lucia (Pavarotti, Romano) trad; arranged by
            Alexander Courage
        Mattinata (Pavarotti) music: Leoncavallo; musical
            direction: Arthur Luck
        Comme Facette Mammeta (orchestra) music, lyrics: Capaldo,
            Gambardella; arranged by Alexander Courage
        O Sole Mio (Pavarotti) music, lyrics: Russo, Di Capua
        L'Elisir d'Amore: Una Furtiva Lagrima (Pavarotti) Music:
            Donizetti
        Rigoletto: La Donna e Mobile (Pavarotti) music: Verdi
        Ave Maria (Pavarotti) music: Schubert
---   I Left My Heart in San Francisco (Pavarotti) music:
            George Cory; lyrics: Douglas Cross
        This Heart of Mine (orchestra) music: Harry Warren
        Did I Remember (orchestra) music: Walter Donaldson
        If We Were in Love (reprise) (orchestra)
        La Gioconda: Cielo e Mar (Pavarotti) music: Ponchielli
        Aida: Ballet Music (orchestra) music: Verdi
        Manon Lescaut: Donna non Vidi Mai (Pavarotti) music:
            Puccini
        Turandot: Excerpts (Pavarotti, Mitchell, chorus) music:
            Puccini
        Turandot: Nessun Dorma (Pavarotti) music: Puccini
        End Titles (orchestra) musical direction: Herbert Spencer

YOLANDA AND THE THIEF (MGM, 1945)

Hollywood Soundstage 5001 (soundtrack) mono

Music: Harry Warren; lyrics: Arthur Freed; musical direction:
Lennie Hayton

Cast: Fred Astaire, Trudy Erwin (for Lucille Bremer), Ludwig

Stoessel

Songs: Main Titles (orchestra)
This Is A Day for Love (Stoessel - spoken) (children)
Angel (Erwin)
Dream Ballet (orchestra)
Will You Marry Me (Erwin, chorus)
Yolanda (Astaire)
--- Coffee Time (chorus)
End Titles (orchestra)

Note: The above recording includes spoken dialog.

YOU CAN'T RUN AWAY FROM IT (Columbia, 1956)

Decca 8396 (soundtrack) mono

Music: Gene de Paul; lyrics: Johnny Mercer; musical direction:
Morris Stoloff

Cast: June Allyson, (the voices of) The Four Aces, Stubby
Kaye, Jack Lemmon

Songs: You Can't Run Away from It (The Four Aces)
Howdy Friends and Neighbors (Allyson, Lemmon, Kaye,
chorus)
Thumbin' A Ride (Allyson, Lemmon)
Temporarily (Allyson, Lemmon)
Scarecrow Ballet (chorus, orchestra)
You Can't Run Away from It (End Titles) (chorus)

YOU WERE NEVER LOVELIER (Columbia, 1942)

Curtain Calls CC 100/24 (soundtrack) mono

Music: Jerome Kern, others; lyrics: Ira Gershwin, others;
musical direction: Leigh Harline

Cast: Fred Astaire, Xavier Cugat Orchestra, Lina Romay,
Nan Wynn (for Rita Hayworth)

Songs: Main Title (orchestra)
Chiu Chiu (Romay, chorus, Cugat Orchestra) music, lyrics:
Niconar Molinare
Dearly Beloved (Astaire, Wynn)
Audition Dance (chorus, Cugat Orchestra)
I'm Old Fashioned (Astaire, Wynn)
The Shorty George (Astaire, chorus, Wynn)
Wedding in the Spring (Romay, chorus)

You Were Never Lovelier (Astaire)
These Orchids (quartet, Cugat Orchestra)
You Were Never Lovelier (finale) (chorus)

Note: The above recording includes spoken dialog.   Studio
        recordings by cast members:

Decca (78rpm) 18489 On the Beam (Astaire)
                    You Were Never Lovelier (Astaire)
Decca (78rpm) 18490 I'm Old Fashioned (Astaire)
                    Wedding in the Spring (Astaire)
Decca (78rpm) 18491 The Shorty George (Astaire)
                    Dearly Beloved (Astaire)

        All of the above (except 'Wedding in the Spring') on
        Vocalion LP: VL 3716.

Columbia (78rpm) 36637 I'm Old Fashioned (Xavier Cugat)
                       Dearly Beloved (Xavier Cugat)
Columbia (78rpm) 36660 You Were Never Lovelier (Xavier Cugat)
Columbia (78rpm) 36651 Chiu Chiu (Xavier Cugat)
Columbia (78rpm) 36681 Bim Bam Bum (Xavier Cugat Orchestra)

YOU'LL NEVER GET RICH (Columbia, 1941)

Hollywood Soundstage 5001 (soundtrack) mono

Music, lyrics: Cole Porter; musical direction: Morris Stoloff

Cast: Fred Astaire, The Delta Rhythm Boys , Martha Tilton

Songs: Main Titles (orchestra)
       Boogie Barcarolle (orchestra) with dialog
       Dream Dancing (orchestra)
       Shootin' the Works for Uncle Sam (Astaire, chorus)
       Since I Kissed My Baby Goodbye (The Delta Rhythm Boys)
       A-stairable Rag (jazz group)
       So Near and Yet So Far (Astaire)
       Wedding Cake Walk (Tilton, chorus)
       End Titles (orchestra)

Note: The above recording includes spoken dialog with Rita
        Hayworth and Fred Astaire. Studio recordings by cast:

Decca (78rpm) 18187 So Near and Yet So Far (Astaire)
                    Since I Kissed My Baby Goodbye (Astaire,
                        The Delta Rhythm Boys)
Decca (78rpm) 18188 Dream Dancing (Astaire)
                    The Wedding Cake Walk (Astaire)

Note: All of the above (except 'Since I Kissed My Baby Goodbye')
         on Vocalion LP: VL 3716.

YOUNG AT HEART (Warner Bros, 1954)

Columbia CL 6339 mono

Music, lyrics: various; musical direction: Percy Faith, others

Cast: Doris Day, Frank Sinatra

Songs: Till My Love Comes to Me (Day) music: Ray Heindorf;
             lyrics: Paul Francis Webster
         Ready, Willing and Able (Day) music: Al Rinker; lyrics:
             Floyd Huddleston
         Hold Me in Your Arms (Day) music: Ray Heindorf; lyrics:
             Charles Henderson, Donald Pippin
         Just One of Those Things (Day) music, lyrics: Cole Porter
         There's A Moon Rising (Day)
         You My Love (Day) music: James Van Heusen; lyrics:
             Mack Gordon
         Someone to Watch Over Me (Sinatra) music: George Gershwin;
             lyrics: Ira Gershwin; musical direction: Axel Stordahl
         One for My Baby (Sinatra) music: Harold Arlen; lyrics:
             Johnny Mercer; musical direction: Axel Stordahl

YOUNG AT HEART (Warner Bros, 1954)

Capitol (45/EP) EAP 1-571

Cast: Frank Sinatra

Songs: Someone to Watch Over Me (Sinatra)
         You My Love (Sinatra)
         Just One of Those Things (Sinatra)
         Young at Heart (Sinatra) music: Johnny Richards; lyrics:
             Carolyn Leigh

Note: Soundtrack selection on WB 3XX2736 'Fifty Years of Film
         Music':

         Just One of Those Things (Sinatra)

THE YOUNG GIRLS OF ROCHEFORT (Les Demoiselles de Rochefort)
(Parc, 1967) (in USA: Warner Bros, 1968) French

Philips 70.407/408 (two records - soundtrack) stereo CD

Music: Michel Legrand; lyrics: Jacques Demy; musical direction:
Michel Legrand

Cast: Jose Bartel (for Grover Dale), Georges Blanes (for Michel
        Piccoli), Donald Burke (for Gene Kelly), Danielle
        Darrieux, Anne Germain (for Catherine Deneuve), Claude
        Parent (for Francoise Dorleac), Jacques Revaux (for
        Jacques Perrin), Romuald (for George Chakiris), Jean
        Stout (for Jacques Riberolles)

Songs: Le Pont Transbordeur (orchestra)
        Arrivee des Camionneurs (chorus)
        Chanson des Jumelles (Germain, Parent)
        Chanson de Maxence (Revaux, chorus)
        De Delphine a Lancien (Germain, Stout, chorus)
---   Nous Voyageons de Ville en Ville (Bartel, Romuald)
        Chanson de Delphine (Germain)
        Chanson de Simon (Blanes)
        Marins, Amis, Amants ou Maris (cast, chorus)
        Andy Amoureux (Burke)
        Chanson d'Yvonne (Darrieux)
        Chanson de Maxence (reprise) (Revaux)
---   Chanson de Solange (Parent)
        de Hambourg a Rochefort (cast)
        La Femme Coupee en Morceaux (chorus)
        Les Rencontres (cast)
        La Chanson d'Andy (Burke)
---   Kermesse
            Madison (orchestra)
            Basket Ball (orchestra)
            Coeurs d'Enfants (chorus)
            Les Femmes Grenouilles (orchestra)
            L'homme a la Moto (cast)
        La Chanson d'un Jour d'Ete (Germain, Parent)
        Toujours - Jamais (cast)
        Concerto (orchestra)

Note: Vocals are unidentified on the above recording. An English
        language one record album was also issued by Philips (SBL
        7792), with vocals also unidentified. Gene Kelly seems to
        be the voice of 'Andy' but the Danielle Darrieux vocal has
        been dubbed by another.

YOUNG MAN WITH A HORN (Warner Bros, 1950)

Columbia CL 582 mono reissued: CBS/Sony 32DP911 CD

Music, lyrics: various; musical direction: Harry James

Cast: Doris Day, (the sound of) Harry James

Songs: I May Be Wrong (Day) music: Henry Sullivan; lyrics:
        Harry Ruskin

           The Man I Love (James) music: George Gershwin
           The Very Thought of You (Day) music, lyrics: Ray Noble
           Melancholy Rhapsody (James) music: Ray Heindorf
---   Too Marvelous for Words (Day) music: Richard Whiting;
             lyrics: Johnny Mercer
           Get Happy (James) music: Harold Arlen
           Limehouse Blues (James) music: Philip Braham
           With A Song in My Heart (Day) music: Richard Rodgers;
             lyrics: Lorenz Hart

Note: The above recording includes some other selections not
       from the film. A soundtrack selection included on
       WB 3XX2736 'Fifty Years of Film Music':

       With A Song in My Heart (Day)

THE YOUNG ONES (Associated British, 1961)

Music for Pleasure (British) MFP 5823 stereo CD

Music, lyrics: Peter Myers, Ronald Cass, others; musical
direction: Stanley Black

Cast: Grazina Frame, Cliff Richard

Songs: Friday Night (chorus)
       Got A Funny Feeling (Richard) music, lyrics: Hank B
          Marvin, Bruce Welch
       Peace Pipe (orchestra) music: Norrie Paramor
       Nothing's Impossible (Richard, Frame)
       The Young Ones (Richard) music, lyrics: Sid Tepper,
          Roy C Bennett
       All for One (Richard, chorus)
       Lessons in Love (Richard) music: Sy Soloway; lyrics:
          Shirley Wolfe
---   No One for Me but Nicky (Frame)
       What D'You Know, We Got A Show (Richard, chorus)
       Vaudeville Routine:
          Have A Smile for Everyone You Meet (chorus) music,
            lyrics: Bert Rule, Cunningham, Brennan
          Tinkle, Tinkle, Tinkle (female vocal) music, lyrics:
            Harry M Woods
          The Eccentric (orchestra)
          Algy the Piccadilly Johnny (chorus) music, lyrics:
            Harry B Norris
          Captain Ginjah (men) music, lyrics: Leigh, Boston
          Joshuah (female vocal) music, lyrics: Bert Lee, George
            Arthurs
          Where Did You Get That Hat? (chorus) music, lyrics:
            Rolmaz
          What D'You Know, We've Got A Show (reprise) (Richard,

    chorus)
        Living Doll (Richard) music, lyrics: Lionel Bart
    When the Girl in Your Arms Is the Girl in Your Heart
        (Richard, chorus) music: Roy C Bennett; lyrics:
        Sid Tepper
    Mambo: Just Dance (chorus)
        Mood Mambo (orchestra) music: Stanley Black
    The Savage (orchestra) music: Norrie Paramor
    We Say Yeah (Richard, chorus) music, lyrics: Gormley,
        Bruce Welsh, Hank B Marvin

Note: The above vaudville routine includes spoken dialog.

YOUNG PEOPLE (Twentieth Century-Fox, 1940)

Fox 3045 (soundtrack) mono 'More Little Miss Wonderful'

Music: Harry Revel; lyrics: Mack Gordon; musical direction:
Alfred Newman

Cast: Charlotte Greenwood, Jack Oakie, Shirley Temple

Songs: Fifth Avenue (Temple, Greenwood, Oakie)
        Young People (Temple, children)
        Tra-La-La-La (Temple, Greenwood, Oakie)

YOUR CHEATIN' HEART (MGM, 1964)

MGM 4260 (soundtrack) stereo

Music, lyrics: Hank Williams; musical direction: Fred Karger

Cast: Hank Williams, Jr (for George Hamilton)

Songs: Your Cheatin' Heart (Williams)
        Hey Good Lookin' (Williams)
        I Saw the Light (Williams)
        Jambalaya (Williams)
        Ramblin' Man (Williams)
        I'm So Lonesome I Could Cry (Williams)
---   Jambalaya (reprise) (Williams)
        Cold, Cold Heart (Williams)
        Kaw-Liga (Williams)
        I Can't Help It (Williams)
        Hey Good Lookin' (reprise) (Williams)
        Lone Gone Lonesome Blues (Williams)
        You Win Again (Williams)

ZIEGFELD FOLLIES OF 1946 (MGM, 1946)

Curtain Calls CC 100/15-16 (two records - soundtrack) mono

Music: Harry Warren, others; lyrics: Arthur Freed, others;
musical direction: Lennie Hayton

Cast: Edward Arnold, Fred Astaire, Marion Bell, Fanny Brice,
        Hume Cronyn, William Frawley, Judy Garland, Kathryn
        Grayson, Lena Horne, Gene Kelly, Harriet Lee, James
        Melton, Victor Moore, Virginia O'Brien, William Powell,
        Red Skelton

Songs: Main Title (orchestra, Powell) spoken (includes bit of
            Fanny Brice singing 'I'm A Indian')
        Bring on the Beautiful Girls (Astaire, O'Brien, chorus)
            music, lyrics: Roger Edens, Earl Brent
        This Heart of Mine (orchestra)
---   Pay the Two Dollars (Moore, Arnold) spoken
        La Traviata: Libiamo ne lieti calici (Melton, Bell,
            chorus) music: Verdi
        This Heart of Mine (reprise) (Astaire, chorus)
---   Sweepstakes Ticket (Brice, Cronyn, Frawley) spoken
        Love (Horne, chorus) music, lyrics: Hugh Martin, Ralph
            Blane
        When Television Comes (Skelton) spoken
        Limehouse Blues (Lee) music: Philip Braham; lyrics:
            Douglas Furber
---   The Interview (Garland, men) music, lyrics: Roger Edens,
            Kay Thompson
        The Babbitt and the Bromide (Astaire, Kelly) music:
            George Gershwin; lyrics: Ira Gershwin
        There's Beauty Everywhere (Grayson)

Note: Studio recordings (LP: Vocalion VL 3716):

        Decca (78rpm) 23388 This Heart of Mine (Astaire)
                            If Swing Goes, I Go Too (Astaire)
                            unused in film

ZIEGFELD GIRL (MGM, 1941)

Classic International Filmusicals C I F 3006 (soundtrack) mono

Music, lyrics: Roger Edens, others; musical direction: Herbert
Stothart

Cast: Judy Garland, Tony Martin, Al Shean, Charles Winninger

Songs: Overture (chorus, orchestra)
        Laugh? I Thought I'd Split My Sides (Garland, Winninger)

       You Stepped Out of A Dream (Martin, chorus) music:
          Nacio Herb Brown; lyrics: Gus Kahn
       I'm Always Chasing Rainbows (Garland) music: Harry Carroll;
          lyrics: Joseph McCarthy
---   Caribbean Love Song (Martin, chorus) lyrics: Ralph Freed
       Minnie from Trinidad (Garland, chorus)
       Mr Gallagher and Mr Shean (Winninger, Shean) music, lyrics:
          Ed Gallagher, Al Shean
       Finale:
          Ziegfeld Girls (Garland, chorus)
          You Gotta Pull Strings (Garland, chorus) music: Walter
             Donaldson; lyrics: Harold Adamson
          You Never Looked So Beautiful Before (orchestra)
             music: Walter Donaldson; lyrics: Harold Adamson
          We Must Have Music (Garland, Martin, chorus) music:
             Nacio Herb Brown; lyrics: Gus Kahn (cut from film)
          You Stepped Out of A Dream (reprise) (Martin)
          You Never Looked So Beautiful Before (reprise)
             (Garland, chorus)
       End Titles (orchestra)

Note: The above recording includes spoken dialog. Studio
       recordings by cast members:

Decca (78rpm) 3593 I'm Always Chasing Rainbows (Garland) LP:
                      Decca DXB 172
Decca (78rpm) 3645 You Stepped Out of A Dream (Martin)
                      Too Beautiful to Last (Martin) LP: Ace of
                      Hearts AH 68

ZOOT SUIT (Universal, 1981)

MCA 1522 (soundtrack) stereo

Music, lyrics: Daniel Valdez, others; musical direction:
Shorty Rogers

Cast: Edward James Olmos, Daniel Valdez

Songs: Zoot Suit Boogie (Valdez, chorus):
          Oh Babe (additional music, lyrics: Milton Kabak,
             Louis Prima)
          Two O'Clock Jump (music: Harry James, Benny Goodman,
             Count Basie)
       Handball (Valdez, chorus)
       Chucos Suaves (Valdez, chorus) music, lyrics: Lalo Guerrero
       Marijuana Boogie (Olmos, chorus) music: Lalo Guerrero
       Vamos A Bailar (chorus) music, lyrics: Lalo Guerrero
       Zoot Suit for My Sunday Gal (female trio) music, lyrics:
          Ray Gilbert, Bob O'Brien

---   Perdido (Lost) (orchestra) music: Juan Tizol, Lengsfelder,
         Drake
      In the Mood (orchestra) music: Joe Garland
      Sleepy Lagoon (orchestra) music: Eric Coates
      Bugle Call Rag (orchestra) music: Jack Pettis
      American Patrol (orchestra) music: F W Meacham
      St Louis Blues March (orchestra) music: W C Handy
      Zoot Suit Theme (orchestra)

Note: Vocals on above recording are uncredited.

A D D E N D A

THE BELLE OF NEW YORK (MGM, 1952)

MGM E 108 (soundtrack) mono   reissued: MCA 39082

Music: Harry Warren; lyrics: Johnny Mercer; musical direction:
Adolph Deutsch

Cast: Fred Astaire, Anita Ellis (for Vera-Ellen)

Songs: When I'm Out with the Belle of New York (chorus)
       Oops! (Astaire)
       Naughty but Nice (Ellis)
       Bachelor Dinner Song (Astaire, chorus)
---   Baby Doll (Astaire)
       Bride's Wedding-Day Song (Thank You Mister Currier,
          Thank You, Mister Ives) (Ellis)
       Seeing's Believing (Astaire)
       I Wanna Be A Dancin' Man (Astaire)

CARNEGIE HALL (United Artists, 1947)

Columbia ML 2113 mono 'A Night at Carnegie Hall'

Music, lyrics: various

Cast: Raoul Jobin (not in film), Ezio Pinza, Lily Pons,
        Rise Stevens

Songs: Lakme: The Bell Song (Pons) music: Delibes
       Carmen: Seguidilla and Duet (Stevens, Jobin) music: Bizet
       Samson et Dalila: Mon Coeur s'ouvre a ta voix (Stevens)
          music: Saint-Saens
---   Simon Boccanegra: Il Lacerato Spirito (Pinza) music: Verdi
       Don Giovanni: Finch' han dal vino (Pinza) music: Mozart
       Don Giovanni: Serenata (Pinza) music: Mozart

Note: additional studio recording:

RCA Victor (78rpm) 20-2084 Beware My Heart (Vaughn Monroe)

THE NIGHT THE LIGHTS WENT OUT IN GEORGIA (Avco Embassy, 1981)

Mirage/Atlantic WTG 16051 (soundtrack) stereo

Music: David Shire, others; lyrics: Carol Connors, others;
musical coordinator: Gene Armond

Cast: Kristy McNichol, Dennis Quaid, (the voices of Glen

Campbell, George Jones, Billy Preston, Syreeta, Tanya
Tucker, Tammy Wynette)

Songs: The Night the Lights Went Out in Georgia (Tucker) music,
       lyrics: Bobby Russell
       I Love My Truck (Campbell) music, lyrics: Joe Rainey
       Rodeo Girl (Tucker) music, lyrics: Joe Rainey
       A Little Gettin' Used To (Jones) music, lyrics: Jerry
           Taylor
       Imaginary Arms (Wynette) music, lyrics: Sue Richards
---   Amanda (Quaid) music, lyrics: Dennis Quaid
       I Need You Strong for Me (McNichol)
       Hangin' Up the Gun (McNichol, Quaid) music, lyrics:
           Keith Allison, Kathy Wakefield
       Melody's Melody (instrumental)
       It's So Easy (Preston, Syreeta)

Chronology of Films

The films represented by albums included in this directory are
here arranged chronologically with foreign contributions noted
and studios that presented them.

1927

      The Jazz Singer   Warner Bros

1928

      The Singing Fool   Warner Bros

1929

The Broadway Melody	MGM
The Cocoanuts	Paramount
Gold Diggers of Broadway	Warner Bros
Honky Tonk	Warner Bros
Innocents of Paris	Paramount
The Love Parade	Paramount
Say It with Songs	Warner Bros
Untamed	MGM

1930

Big Boy	Warner Bros
The Blue Angel (Germany)	UFA / Paramount
The King of Jazz	Universal
Mammy	Warner Bros
New Moon	MGM
No, No Nanette	First National
The Rogue Song	MGM

1931

      The Threepenny Opera (Germany)   Nero

1932

The Big Broadcast	Paramount
Love Me Tonight	Paramount

One Hour with You	Paramount

1933

Broadway Through A Keyhole	Twentieth Century
College Humor	Paramount
Dancing Lady	MGM
Flying Down to Rio	RKO
Footlight Parade	Warner Bros
42nd Street	Warner Bros
Going Hollywood	MGM
Gold Diggers of 1933	Warner Bros
I'm No Angel	Paramount
Roman Scandals	Goldwyn
This Week of Grace (Britain)	Real Art
Too Much Harmony	Paramount

1934

Belle of the Ninties	Paramount
The Cat and the Fiddle	MGM
Dames	Warner Bros
Evergreen (Britain)	Gaumont
The Gay Divorcee	RKO
Happiness Ahead	First National
Here Is My Heart	Paramount
Kid Millions	Goldwyn
The Merry Widow	MGM
Moulin Rouge	Twentieth Century
Princess Charming (Britain)	Gaumont
She Loves Me Not	Paramount
Wake Up and Dream	Universal
We're Not Dressing	Paramount
Wonder Bar	Warner Bros

1935

Broadway Gondolier	Warner Bros
Every Night at Eight	Twentieth Century-Fox
Go Into Your Dance	Warner Bros
Gold Diggers of 1935	First National
I Dream Too Much	RKO
In Person	RKO
King of Burlesque	Twentieth Century-Fox
Mississippi	Paramount
Naughty Marietta	MGM
Roberta	RKO
Sanders of the River (Britain)	Korda
Top Hat	RKO
Two for Tonight	Paramount

1936

Anything Goes	Paramount
Born to Dance	MGM
Captain January	Twentieth Century-Fox
Charlie Chan at the Opera	Twentieth Century-Fox
Dimples	Twentieth Century-Fox
Everything Is Rhythm (Britain)	Astor
Follow the Fleet	RKO
Gold Diggers of 1937	First National
The Great Ziegfeld	MGM
It's Love Again (Britain)	Gaumont
The King Steps Out	Columbia
Pennies from Heaven	Columbia
Pigskin Parade	Twentieth Century-Fox
Poor Little Rich Girl	Twentieth Century-Fox
Rhythm on the Range	Paramount
Rose Marie	MGM
San Francisco	MGM
Show Boat	Universal
Song of Freedom (Britain)	Lion
Swing Time	RKO
This'll Make You Whistle (Britain)	Wilcox

1937

Broadway Melody of 1938	MGM
A Damsel in Distress	RKO
Double or Nothing	Paramount
Head Over Heels (Britain)	Gaumont
Hollywood Hotel	Warner Bros
On the Avenue	Twentieth Century-Fox
Shall We Dance	RKO
The Singing Marine	Warner Bros
Snow White and the Seven Dwarfs	Disney
Varsity Show	Warner Bros
Waikiki Wedding	Paramount
Wake Up and Live	Twentieth Century-Fox

1938

Alexander's Ragtime Band	Twentieth Century-Fox
Big Broadcast of 1938	Paramount
Carefree	RKO
Doctor Rhythm	Paramount
The Great Waltz	MGM
Happy Landing	Twentieth Century-Fox
Little Miss Broadway	Twentieth Century-Fox
Rebecca of Sunnybrook Farm	Twentieth Century-Fox
Sing You Sinners	Paramount

1939

Babes in Arms	MGM
Broadway Serenade	MGM
East Side of Heaven	Universal
First Love	Universal
Paris Honeymoon	Paramount
Rose of Washington Square	Twentieth Century-Fox
Shipyard Sally (Britain)	Twentieth Century-Fox
The Star Maker	Paramount
The Underpup	Universal
The Wizard of Oz	MGM

1940

The Boys from Syracuse	Universal
Broadway Melody of 1940	MGM
Down Argentine Way	Twentieth Century-Fox
If I Had My Way	Universal
It's A Date	Universal
New Moon	MGM
Pinocchio	Disney
Rhythm on the River	Paramount
Road to Singapore	Paramount
Second Chorus	Paramount
Spring Parade	Universal
Strike Up the Band	MGM
Tin Pan Alley	Twentieth Century-Fox
Young People	Twentieth Century-Fox

1941

Babes on Broadway	MGM
Birth of the Blues	Paramount
Blood and Sand	Twentieth Century-Fox
The Chocolate Soldier	MGM
Dumbo	Disney
The Great American Broadcast	Twentieth Century-Fox
Lady Be Good	MGM
Las Vegas Nights	Paramount
Nice Girl?	Universal
Road to Zanzibar	Paramount
Smilin' Through	MGM
Sun Valley Serenade	Twentieth Century-Fox
That Night in Rio	Twentieth Century-Fox
Weekend in Havana	Twentieth Century-Fox
You'll Never Get Rich	Columbia
Ziegfeld Girl	MGM

1942

Bambi	Disney
Cairo	MGM
The Fleet's In	Paramount
For Me and My Gal	MGM
Holiday Inn	Paramount
My Gal Sal	Twentieth Century-Fox
Orchestra Wives	Twentieth Century-Fox
Road to Morocco	Paramount
Saludos Amigos	Disney
Ship Ahoy	MGM
Springtime in the Rockies	Twentieth Century-Fox
Star Spangled Rhythm	Paramount
Yankee Doodle Dandy	Warner Bros
You Were Never Lovelier	Columbia

1943

Cabin in the Sky	MGM
The Desert Song	Warner Bros
The Gang's All Here	Twentieth Century-Fox
Girl Crazy	MGM
Hello, Frisco, Hello	Twentieth Century-Fox
Higher and Higher	RKO
His Butler's Sister	Universal
Phantom of the Opera	Universal
Presenting Lily Mars	MGM
Reveille with Beverly	Columbia
Riding High	Paramount
The Sky's the Limit	RKO
Stage Door Canteen	United Artists
Stormy Weather	Twentieth Century-Fox
Sweet Rosie O'Grady	Twentieth Century-Fox
Thank Your Lucky Stars	Warner Bros
This Is the Army	Warner Bros
Thousands Cheer	MGM

1944

And the Angels Sing	Paramount
Can't Help Singing	Universal
Cover Girl	Columbia
Follow the Boys	Universal
Four Jills in A Jeep	Twentieth Century-Fox
Going My Way	Paramount
Here Come the Waves	Paramount
Hollywood Canteen	Warner Bros
Jam Session	Columbia
Knickerbocker Holiday	United Artists
Lady in the Dark	Paramount
Meet Me in St Louis	MGM

Song of the Open Road	United Artists
Step Lively	RKO
The Three Caballeros	Disney
Two Girls and A Sailor	MGM
Up in Arms	Goldwyn

1945

Anchors Aweigh	MGM
The Bells of St Mary's	RKO
Delightfully Dangerous	United Artists
The Dolly Sisters	Twentieth-Century-Fox
Out of This World	Paramount
Rhapsody in Blue	Warner Bros
State Fair	Twentieth Century-Fox
Thrill of A Romance	MGM
Where Do We Go from Here?	Twentieth Century-Fox
Yolanda and the Thief	MGM

1946

Blue Skies	Paramount
Centennial Summer	Twentieth Century-Fox
Gilda	Columbia
The Harvey Girls	MGM
Holiday in Mexico	MGM
The Jolson Story	Columbia
Make Mine Music	Disney
Night and Day	Warner Bros
No Leave No Love	MGM
Song of the South	Disney
Three Little Girls in Blue	Twentieth Century-Fox
Till the Clouds Roll By	MGM
Two Sisters from Boston	MGM
Ziegfeld Follies of 1946	MGM

1947

Carnegie Hall	United Artists
Down to Earth	Columbia
Fun and Fancy Free	Disney
Good News	MGM
It Happened in Brooklyn	MGM
Mother Wore Tights	Twentieth Century-Fox
My Wild Irish Rose	Warner Bros
Northwest Outpost	Republic
Perils of Pauline	Paramount
The Shocking Miss Pilgrim	Twentieth Century-Fox
Something in the Wind	Universal
Song of Scheherazade	Universal
The Unfinished Dance	MGM

Welcome Stranger   Paramount

1948

Big City   MGM
Casbah   Universal
A Date with Judy   MGM
Easter Parade   MGM
The Emperor Waltz   Paramount
The Kissing Bandit   MGM
Lulu Belle   Columbia
One Touch of Venus   Universal
La Parisienne (France)   United Artists
The Pirate   MGM
Rachel and the Stranger   RKO
Road to Rio   Paramount
So Dear to My Heart   Disney
A Song Is Born   Goldwyn
Summer Holiday   MGM
Words and Music   MGM

1949

The Barkleys of Broadway   MGM
Cinderella   Disney
A Connecticut Yankee in King   Paramount
         Arthur's Court
In the Good Old Summertime   MGM
Jolson Sings Again   Columbia
On the Town   MGM
Red, Hot and Blue   Paramount
A Royal Affair (Le Roi) (France) Discina
Take Me Out to the Ball Game   MGM
That Midnight Kiss   MGM
Top O' the Morning   Paramount

1950

Annie Get Your Gun   MGM
Grounds for Marriage   MGM
Mr Music   Paramount
Nancy Goes to Rio   MGM
Pagan Love Song   MGM
Riding High   Paramount
Summer Stock   MGM
Tea for Two   Warner Bros
Three Little Words   MGM
The Toast of New Orleans   MGM
Two Weeks with Love   MGM
Young Man with A Horn   Warner Bros

1951

Alice in Wonderland	Disney
An American in Paris	MGM
Double Dynamite!	RKO
The Great Caruso	MGM
Here Comes the Groom	Paramount
I'll See You in My Dreams	Warner Bros
Lullaby of Broadway	Warner Bros
Mr Imperium	MGM
On Moonlight Bay	Warner Bros
Painting the Clouds with Sunshine	Warner Bros
Rich, Young and Pretty	MGM
Royal Wedding	MGM
Show Boat	MGM
Sunny Side of the Street	Columbia
Two Tickets to Broadway	RKO

1952

Aaron Slick from Punkin Crick	Paramount
April in Paris	Warner Bros
Because You're Mine	MGM
The Belle of New York	MGM
Everything I Have Is Yours	MGM
Hans Christian Andersen	Goldwyn
Just for You	Paramount
Lovely to Look At	MGM
The Merry Widow	MGM
Rainbow Round My Shoulder	Columbia
Singin' in the Rain	MGM
Somebody Loves Me	Paramount
The Stooge	Paramount
The Story of Robin Hood	Disney
With A Song in My Heart	Twentieth Century-Fox

1953

The Band Wagon	MGM
By the Light of the Silvery Moon	Warner Bros
Calamity Jane	Warner Bros
Call Me Madam	Twentieth Century-Fox
The Desert Song	Warner Bros
Gentlemen Prefer Blondes	Twentieth Century-Fox
I Love Melvin	MGM
The Jazz Singer	Warner Bros
Kiss Me Kate	MGM
Lili	MGM
Little Boy Blue	Paramount
Melba	United Artists
Peter Pan	Disney

Road to Bali	Paramount
So This Is Love	Warner Bros
The Stars Are Singing	Paramount
3 Sailors and A Girl	Warner Bros
Tonight We Sing	Twentieth Century-Fox
Torch Song	MGM

1954

As Long As They're Happy (Britain)	Rank
Athena	MGM
Brigadoon	MGM
Carmen Jones	Twentieth Century-Fox
The Country Girl	Paramount
Deep in My Heart	MGM
The Eddie Cantor Story	Warner Bros
Flame and the Flesh	MGM
The French Line	RKO
Knock on Wood	Paramount
The Last Time I Saw Paris	MGM
Living It Up	Paramount
Miss Sadie Thompson	Columbia
New Faces	Twentieth Century-Fox
Red Garters	Paramount
River of No Return	Twentieth Century-Fox
Rose Marie	MGM
Seven Brides for Seven Brothers	MGM
A Star Is Born	Warner Bros
The Student Prince	MGM
There's No Business Like Show Business	Twentieth Century-Fox
White Christmas	Paramount
Young At Heart	Warner Bros

1955

Artists and Models	Paramount
Gentlemen Marry Brunettes	United Artists
Guys and Dolls	Goldwyn
Hit the Deck	MGM
Interrupted Melody	MGM
It's Always Fair Weather	MGM
King's Rhapsody (Britain)	Lion
Kismet	MGM
The Lady Is A Tramp	Disney
Love Me or Leave Me	MGM
Oh, Rosalinda! (Britain)	Associated British
Oklahoma!	Magna
Pete Kelly's Blues	Warner Bros
The Seven Little Foys	Paramount

So This Is Paris	Universal
Three for the Show	Columbia

1956

Anything Goes	Paramount
The Best Things in Life Are Free	Twentieth Century-Fox
Bundle of Joy	RKO
Carousel	Twentieth Century-Fox
The Court Jester	Paramount
Friendly Persuasion	Allied Artists
High Society	MGM
Hollywood or Bust	Paramount
I'll Cry Tomorrow	MGM
The King and I	Twentieth Century-Fox
Love Me Tender	Twentieth Century-Fox
Meet Me in Las Vegas	MGM
Pardners	Paramount
Rock, Rock, Rock	Dist Corp of America
Serenade	Warner Bros
The Vagabond King	Paramount
You Can't Run Away from It	Columbia

1957

An Affair to Remember	Twentieth Century-Fox
April Love	Twentieth Century-Fox
Beau James	Paramount
A Face in the Crowd	Warner Bros
Funny Face	Paramount
The Girl Most Likely	RKO
Les Girls	MGM
The Good Companions (Britain)	Associated British
The Helen Morgan Story	Warner Bros
Jailhouse Rock	MGM
Let's Be Happy (Britain)	Pathe
Loving You	Paramount
The Pajama Game	Warner Bros
Pal Joey	Columbia
Rock, Pretty Baby	Universal
Seach for Paradise	Cinerama
Silk Stockings	MGM
Sing Boy Sing	Twentieth Century-Fox
Ten Thousand Bedrooms	MGM
This Could Be the Night	MGM
The Tommy Steele Story (Britain)	Anglo

1958

The Big Beat	Universal
Damn Yankees	Warner Bros

The Duke Wore Jeans (Britain)	Insignia
Folies-Bergere (France)	Films Around the World
Gigi	MGM
King Creole	Paramount
Mardi Gras	Twentieth Century-Fox
Merry Andrew	MGM
Nachts im Grunen Kakadu (Germany)	Real
St Louis Blues	Paramount
Seven Hills of Rome	MGM
South Pacific	Twentieth Century-Fox
Summer Love	Universal
Tom Thumb	MGM

1959

Black Orpheus (Brazil)	Lopert
The Blue Angel	Twentieth Century-Fox
Expresso Bongo (Britain)	Lion
The Five Pennies	Paramount
Follow A Star (Britain)	Rank
For the First Time	MGM
The Heart of A Man (Britain)	Rank
Hey Boy! Hey Girl!	Columbia
Idle on Parade (Britain)	Warwick
The Lady Is A Square (Britain)	Associated British
Li'l Abner	Paramount
Porgy and Bess	Goldwyn
Say One for Me	Twentieth Century-Fox
Serious Charge (Britain)	Eros
The Sleeping Beauty	Disney
Some Like It Hot	United Artists
1001 Arabian Nights	Columbia
Tommy the Toreador (Britain)	Pathe

1960

Bells Are Ringing	MGM
Can-Can	Twentieth Century-Fox
Cinderfella	Paramount
G I Blues	Paramount
Hound-Dog Man	Twentieth Century-Fox
It Started in Naples	Paramount
Journey to the Center of the Earth	Twentieth Century-Fox
Let's Make Love	Twentieth Century-Fox
Pepe	Columbia
Pollyanna	Disney

1961

All Hands on Deck	Twentieth Century-Fox
Babes in Toyland	Disney

Blue Hawaii	Paramount
Flower Drum Song	Universal
The Parent Trap	Disney
Road to Hong Kong	United Artists
West Side Story	United Artists
The Young Ones (Britain)	Associated British

1962

Billy Rose's Jumbo	MGM
Follow That Dream	United Artists
Gay Purr-ee	Warner Bros
Girls! Girls! Girls!	Paramount
Gypsy	Warner Bros
Hey, Let's Twist!	Paramount
How the West Was Won	MGM
In Search of the Castaways	Disney
Jessica	United Artists
The Music Man	Warner Bros
State Fair	Twentieth Century-Fox
Summer Magic	Disney

1963

Beach Party	American International
Bye Bye Birdie	Columbia
Follow the Boys	MGM
Fun in Acapulco	Paramount
Hootenanny Hoot	MGM
I Could Go on Singing	United Artists
It Happened at the World's Fair	MGM
Kid Galahad	United Artists
Marilyn	Twentieth Century-Fox
Palm Springs Weekend	Warner Bros
Summer Holiday (Britain)	American International
The Sword in the Stone	Disney
The Threepenny Opera (Germany)	Gloria
Two Tickets to Paris	Columbia

1964

Every Day's A Holiday (Britain) (Seaside Swingers)	Grand National
Get Yourself A College Girl	MGM
A Hard Day's Night	United Artists
Kissin' Cousins	MGM
The Lively Set	Universal
Looking for Love	MGM
Mary Poppins	Disney
Muscle Beach Party	American International
My Fair Lady	Warner Bros
Pajama Party	American International

Robin and the Seven Hoods	Warner Bros
Roustabout	Paramount
The Umbrellas of Cherbourg (France)	Parc
The Unsinkable Molly Brown	MGM
Viva Las Vegas	MGM
Your Cheatin' Heart	MGM

1965

Beach Blanket Bingo	American International
Girl Happy	MGM
Harum Scarum	MGM
Having A Wild Weekend	Warner Bros
Help!	United Artists
How to Stuff A Wild Bikini	American International
I'll Take Sweden	United Artists
The Pleasure Seekers	Twentieth Century-Fox
The Sound of Music	Twentieth Century-Fox
Tickle Me	Allied Artists
Uncle Tom's Cabin (Germany)	Hallmark
Viva Maria! (France)	United Artists
When the Boys Meet the Girls	MGM
Wild on the Beach	Twentieth Century-Fox

1966

The Christmas That Almost Wasn't	Childhood Productions
The Daydreamer	Embassy
Frankie and Johnny	United Artists
A Funny Thing Happened on the Way to the Forum	United Artists
Hold On!	MGM
A Man Called Adam	Embassy
Paradise, Hawaiian Style	Paramount
The Silencers	Columbia
The Singing Nun	MGM
Spinout	MGM
Stop the World I Want to Get Off	Warner Bros
The Swinger	Paramount

1967

Camelot	Warner Bros
Clambake	United Artists
C'mon Let's Live A Little	Paramount
Doctor Dolittle	Twentieth Century-Fox
Double Trouble	MGM
Easy Come, Easy Go	Paramount
The Fastest Guitar Alive	MGM
Good Times	Columbia
Half A Sixpence	Paramount

The Happiest Millionaire	Disney
How to Succeed in Business Without Really Trying	United Artists
The Jungle Book	Disney
Privilege	Universal
Red and Blue (Britain)	United Artists
Smashing Time (Britain)	Paramount
Thoroughly Modern Millie	Universal
Valley of the Dolls	Twentieth Century-Fox
The Young Girls of Rochefort (France)	Parc

1968

Chitty Chitty Bang Bang	United Artists
Finian's Rainbow	Warner Bros
Funny Girl	Columbia
Head	Columbia
Oliver!	Columbia
The One and Only Genuine Original Family Band	Disney
The Producers	Embassy
Speedway	MGM
Star!	Twentieth Century-Fox
Sweet Charity	Universal
Tell Me Lies (Britain)	Mira
Tevye and his Daughters (Israel)	Israel
A Time to Sing	MGM
Yellow Submarine	United Artists

1969

Alice's Restaurant	United Artists
The Aristocats	Disney
A Boy Named Charlie Brown	National General
Can Heironymus Merkin Ever Forget Mercy Humppe and Find True Happiness?	Universal
Darling Lili	Paramount
Gaily, Gaily	United Artists
Goodbye, Mr Chips	MGM
Hello, Dolly!	Twentieth Century-Fox
The Night They Raided Minsky's	United Artists
Oh! What A Lovely War	Paramount
On A Clear Day You Can See Forever	Paramount
Paint Your Wagon	Paramount

1970

Bombay Talkie (India)	Merchant Ivory
Norwood	Paramount

Pufnstuf	Universal
Scrooge	National General
Song of Norway	ABC

1971

Bedknobs and Broomsticks	Disney
Fiddler on the Roof	United Artists
Willy Wonka and the Chocolate Factory	Paramount

1972

Alice's Adventures in Wonderland	American National
The Boy Friend	MGM
Cabaret	Allied Artists
The Great Waltz	MGM
Lady Sings the Blues	Paramount
Man of La Mancha	United Artists
1776	Columbia
Snoopy, Come Home	National General

1973

Charlotte's Web	Paramount
Godspell	Columbia
Jesus Christ Superstar	Universal
Kazablan (Israel)	MGM
Lost Horizon	Columbia
The Optimists	Paramount
Tom Sawyer	United Artists

1974

Blazing Saddles	Warner Bros
Catch My Soul	Cinerama
The Day of the Locust	Paramount
Huckleberry Finn	United Artists
Jacques Brel Is Alive and Well and Living in Paris	American Film Theatre
Journey Back to Oz	Filmation
The Little Prince	Paramount
Mame	Warner Bros
Paesano - A Voice in the Night	Mediterraneo
Phantom of the Paradise	Twentieth Century-Fox
That's Entertainment	MGM

1975

At Long Last Love	Twentieth Century-Fox
Dick Deadeye	Intercontinental
Funny Lady	Columbia

Lisztomania	Warner Bros
Nashville	ABC
The Rocky Horror Show	Twentieth Century-Fox
Tommy	Columbia

1976

Bound for Glory	United Artists
Bugsy Malone	Paramount
Lucky Lady	Twentieth Century-Fox
The Slipper and the Rose	Universal
A Star Is Born	Warner Bros
That's Entertainment, part 2	MGM

1977

The First Nudie Musical	Northal
New York, New York	United Artists
Pete's Dragon	Disney
Raggedy Ann and Andy	Twentieth Century-Fox
The Rescuers	Disney
Welcome to L A	United Artists

1978

The Buddy Holly Story	Columbia
Every Which Way but Loose	Warner Bros
Grease	Paramount
High Anxiety	Twentieth Century-Fox
A Little Night Music	New World
The Magic of Lassie	International Picture
Sgt Pepper's Lonely Hearts Club Band	Universal
Thank God It's Friday	Columbia
The Wiz	Universal

1979

All That Jazz	Twentieth / Columbia
Hair	United Artists
Just A Gigolo	United Artists
The Muppet Movie	Associated Film
Rock 'n' Roll High School	New World
The Rose	Twentieth Century-Fox
'10'	Orion

1980

Any Which Way You Can	Warner Bros
The Blues Brothers	Universal
Bronco Billy	Warner Bros
Can't Stop the Music	EMI

Coal Miner's Daughter	Universal
Fame	MGM
Honeysuckle Rose	Warner Bros
The Idolmaker	United Artists
The Jazz Singer	Assoc Film Distributors
Popeye	Disney / Paramount
Xanadu	Universal

1981

The Great Muppet Caper!	Universal
Hard Country	Universal
The Night the Lights Went Out in Georgia	Avco
Zoot Suit	Universal

1982

Annie	Columbia
The Best Little Whorehouse in Texas	Universal / RKO
Grease 2	Paramount
Honkytonk Man	Warner Bros
The Pirate Movie	Twentieth Century-Fox
Victor / Victoria	MGM
Yes, Giorgio	MGM / United Artists

1983

To Be or Not to Be	Twentieth Century-Fox
Yentl	United Artists / MGM

1984

The Cotton Club	Orion
The Muppets Take Manhattan	Tri Star
Purple Rain	Warner Bros
Rhinestone	Twentieth Century-Fox

1985

A Chorus Line	Columbia
Opera Do Malandro (Brazil)	Austra
Sweet Dreams	Tri Star
That's Dancing!	MGM

1986

An American Tail	Universal
Little Shop of Horrors	Warner Bros
Under the Cherry Moon	Warner Bros

1987

Back to the Beach	Paramount
La Bamba	Columbia
Hearts of Fire	Lorimar
Light of Day	Tri Star
Three Amigos!	Orion

Performer Index

Dates following various titles indicate which of several films
of the same title the performer is included on the recording.
Check main entries to ascertain if performer was actually in
the film.

ABBOTT, DIAHNNE
  New York, New York
ACKLAND, JOSS
  The Little Prince
ADAMS, INDIA
  The Band Wagon
  That's Entertainment
  Torch Song
ADAMS, JONATHAN
  The Rocky Horror Show
ADAMS, NEILE
  This Could Be the Night
ADDISON, ADELE
  Porgy and Bess
ADIARTE, PATRICK
  Flower Drum Song
ADRIAN, MAX
  The Boy Friend
AEROSMITH
  Sgt Pepper's Lonely Hearts..
ALBANESE, LICIA
  Serenade
ALBERSTEIN, CHAVA
  Tevye and his Daughters
ALBERT, CARLOS
  Down Argentine Way
ALBERTSON, FRANK
  Willy Wonka and the Choc...
ALDERSON, JOHN
  My Fair Lady
ALLAN, RICHARD
  With A Song in My Heart
ALLEN, GRACIE
  The Big Broadcast
  A Damsel in Distress
  Two Girls and A Sailor
ALLEN, PENNY
  Oh! What A Lovely War

ALLEN, PETER
  All That Jazz
ALLEN, RAE
  Damn Yankees
ALLEN, STEVE
  Mardi Gras
ALLER, MICHELE
  Lady Sings the Blues
ALLYSON, JUNE
  Girl Crazy
  Good News
  That's Entertainment
  Thousands Cheer
  Till the Clouds Roll By
  Two Girls and A Sailor
  Words and Music
  You Can't Run Away from It
ALTIERI, ANNE
  A Boy Named Charlie Brown
ALVAREZ, CARMEN
  Li'l Abner
AMARAL, NESTOR
  The Three Caballeros
AMECHE, DON
  Alexander's Ragtime Band
  Down Argentine Way
  That Night in Rio
ANDERSON, CARL
  Jesus Christ Superstar
ANDERSON, EDDIE 'ROCHESTER'
  Cabin in the Sky
  Star Spangled Rhythm
ANDERSON, JOHN
  Honkytonk Man
ANDES, KEITH
  The Girl Most Likely
ANDRE, ANNETTE
  A Funny Thing Happened...

ANDREWS, DANA
  State Fair (1945)
ANDREWS, HARRY
  Man of La Mancha
ANDREWS, JULIE
  Darling Lili
  Mary Poppins
  The Sound of Music
  Star!
  '10'
  Thoroughly Modern Millie
  Victor / Victoria
ANDREWS, PATTI
  The Country Girl
THE ANDREWS SISTERS
  Follow the Boys (1944)
  Here Come the Waves
  Hollywood Canteen
  Just for You
  Make Mine Music
  Mr Music
  Road to Rio
ANGELI, PIER
  Merry Andrew
THE ANIMALS
  Get Yourself A College Girl
ANN-MARGRET
  Bye Bye Birdie
  The Pleasure Seekers
  State Fair (1962)
  The Swinger
  Tommy
ANTHONY, RAY (ORCHESTRA)
  This Could Be the Night
ARDEN, EVE
  Night and Day
  One Touch of Venus
ARLEN, ROXANNE
  Gypsy
ARMEN, KAY
  Hey, Let's Twist!
  Hit the Deck
  That's Entertainment
ARMITAGE, GRAHAM
  The Boy Friend
ARMSTRONG, LOUIS
  Cabin in the Sky
  The Day of the Locust
  The Five Pennies
  Hello, Dolly!
  High Society
  Jam Session

  A Man Called Adam
  Pennies from Heaven
  A Song Is Born
  When the Boys Meet the Girls
ARNAU, BRENDA
  Finian's Rainbow
ARNOLD, EDWARD
  Ziegfeld Follies of 1946
ARNOLD, TICHINA
  Little Shop of Horrors
ARTHUR, BEATRICE
  Mame
ARTHUR, MAURICE
  Oh! What A Lovely War
ASPARAGUS, FRED
  Three Amigos!
ASTAIRE, FRED
  The Band Wagon
  The Barkleys of Broadway
  The Belle of New York
  Blue Skies
  Broadway Melody of 1940
  Carefree
  A Damsel in Distress
  Dancing Lady
  Easter Parade
  Finian's Rainbow
  Flying Down to Rio
  Follow the Fleet
  Funny Face
  The Gay Divorcee
  Holiday Inn
  Roberta
  Royal Wedding
  Second Chorus
  Shall We Dance
  Silk Stockings
  The Sky's the Limit
  Swing Time
  That's Dancing!
  That's Entertainment
  That's Entertainment, pt 2
  Three Little Words
  Top Hat
  Yolanda and the Thief
  You Were Never Lovelier
  You'll Never Get Rich
  Ziegfeld Follies of 1946
THE ASTRONAUTS
  Wild on the Beach
ATCKISON, RICHARD
  Grounds for Marriage

MORGAN, ALEXANDRA
    The First Nudie Musical
MORGAN, DENNIS
    The Desert Song (1943)
    Hollywood Canteen
    My Wild Irish Rose
    Painting the Clouds with Sun..
    Thank Your Lucky Stars
MORGAN, FRANK
    Annie Get Your Gun
    Summer Holiday (1948)
MORGAN, GARY
    Pete's Dragon
MORGAN, HELEN
    Go Into Your Dance
    Show Boat (1936)
MORGAN, MICHELE
    Higher and Higher
MORGAN, PAT
    Somebody Loves Me
MORSE, ELLA MAE
    Reveille with Beverly
MORSE, ROBERT
    How to Succeed in Business...
MOSTEL, JOSHUA
    Jesus Christ Superstar
MOSTEL, ZERO
    A Funny Thing Happened...
MOTEN, ELLA
    Flying Down to Rio
MOUNT, PEGGY
    Oliver!
MUHLHARDT, KURT
    The Threepenny Opera (1963)
MULLEN, KATHRYN
    The Muppet Movie
MUNRO, PAULINE
    Tell Me Lies
MUNSEL, PATRICE
    Melba
MUNSHIN, JULES
    On the Town
    Silk Stockings
    Take Me Out to the Ball Game
MURPHEY, MICHAEL
    Hard Country
MURPHY, BRIAN
    The Boy Friend
MURPHY, GEORGE
    Broadway Melody of 1938
    Broadway Melody of 1940
    For Me and My Gal

    Kid Millions
    Little Miss Broadway
    Step Lively
    This Is the Army
MYERS, PAMELA
    The Day of the Locust
MYHERS, JOHN
    How to Succeed in Business...
    1776
MYLETT, JEFFREY
    Godspell
NABORS, JIM
    The Best Little Whorehouse...
NAISH, J CARROL
    Down Argentine Way
NAISMITH, LAURENCE
    Scrooge
NASH, CLARENCE
    Fun and Fancy Free
    The Three Caballeros
NATHAN, STEPHEN
    The First Nudie Musical
    1776
NATURAL JUICES (GROUP)
    Thank God It's Friday
NATWICK, MILDRED
    At Long Last Love
NEAGLE, ANNA
    King's Rhapsody
NEAL, JOSEPH
    Jacques Brel Is Alive and...
NEELEY, TED
    Jesus Christ Superstar
NEFF, HILDEGARD
    The Threepenny Opera (1963)
NELSON, GENE
    Oklahoma!
    So This Is Paris
    Tea for Two
NELSON, JERRY
    The Great Muppet Caper!
    The Muppet Movie
    The Muppets Take Manhattan
NELSON, SANDY
    Wild on the Beach
NELSON, WILLIE
    Honeysuckle Rose
NEVE, SUZANNE
    Scrooge
NEWELL, JAMES
    The Great American Broadcast

SANDS, TOMMY
  Babes in Toyland
  The Parent Trap
  Sing Boy Sing
SANKAR, M
  Naughty Marietta
SARANDON, SUSAN
  The Rocky Horror Picture Show
SARNE, MIKE
  Seaside Swingers
SARNO, ALBERTO
  Paesano, A Voice in the Night
SAUNDERS, TERRY
  The King and I
SAVAGE, JOHN
  Hair
SCARGILL, KAREN
  Scrooge
SCHACKMAN, AL
  Alice's Restaurant
SCHEIDER, ROY
  All That Jazz
SCHLAMME, MARTHA
  The Threepenny Opera (1963)
SCHOLL, DANNY
  Nancy Goes to Rio
SCHOLLIN, CHRISTINA
  Song of Norway
SCOTT, HAZEL
  Rhapsody in Blue
SCOTT, JANETTE
  The Good Companions
SCOTT, LESLIE
  Porgy and Bess
SCOTTI, TONY
  Valley of the Dolls
SECOMBE, HARRY
  Oliver!
  Song of Norway
SEDAN, ROLF
  Love Me Tonight
SEELY, JEANNIE
  Honeysuckle Rose
SEGAL, VIVIENNE
  The Cat and the Fiddle
SELLERS, PETER
  Alice's Adventures in Wonder...
  The Optimists
SETZER, BRIAN
  La Bamba
THE SHADOWS
  Summer Holiday (1963)

SHAFER, ROBERT
  Damn Yankees
SHA-NA-NA (GROUP)
  Grease
SHANLEY, ROBERT
  This Is the Army
SHAPIRO, DEBBIE
  The First Nudie Musical
SHARIF, OMAR
  Funny Girl
SHARKEY, RAY
  The Idolmaker
SHAW, ARTIE (CLARINET)
  Second Chorus
SHAW, OSCAR
  The Cocoanuts
SHAW, RETA
  The Pajama Game
SHAW, WINI
  Gold Diggers of 1935
  That's Dancing!
SHAWN, DICK
  The Producers
SHEAN, AL
  The Great Waltz (1938)
  Ziegfeld Girl
SHELDON, GENE
  Roberta
  Where Do We Go from Here?
SHEPHERD, CYBILL
  At Long Last Love
SHERIDAN, ANN
  Thank Your Lucky Stars
SHIGETA, JAMES
  Flower Drum Song
SHIRLEY, BILL
  My Fair Lady
  The Sleeping Beauty
SHORE, DINAH
  Aaron Slick from Punkin...
  Follow the Boys (1944)
  Fun and Fancy Free
  Thank Your Lucky Stars
  That's Entertainment, part 2
  Till the Clouds Roll By
  Two Tickets to Broadway
  Up in Arms
SHORT, MARTIN
  Three Amigos!
SHOWALTER, MAX
  '10'

WELCH, ELISABETH
  Song of Freedom
WELD, TUESDAY
  I'll Take Sweden
WELFORD, NANCY
  Gold Diggers of Broadway
WEST, MAE
  Belle of the Ninties
  I'm No Angel
WEST, SHELLY
  Any Which Way You Can
  Honkytonk Man
WHEELER, BERT
  Las Vegas Nights
WHEELER, JOHN
  Sgt Pepper's Lonely Hearts...
WHITAKER, JOHNNY
  Tom Sawyer
WHITE, SAMMY
  Show Boat (1936)
WHITE, SHEILA
  Oliver!
WHITE, TONY JOE
  Catch My Soul
WHITEMAN, PAUL (ORCHESTRA)
  The King of Jazz
  Rhapsody in Blue
  Strike Up the Band
WHITMIRE, STEVE
  The Great Muppet Caper!
  The Muppet Movie
  The Muppets Take Manhattan
WHITMORE, JAMES
  Kiss Me Kate
  Oklahoma!
THE WHO
  Tommy
WICKES, MARY
  Higher and Higher
WILD, JACK
  Oliver!
  Pufnstuf
WILDE, CORNEL
  Centennial Summer
WILDE, DAVID (PIANO)
  Lisztomania
THE WILDE TWINS
  Till the Clouds Roll By
WILDER, GENE
  The Little Prince
  Willy Wonka and the Choc...

WILDER, JO
  The Threepenny Opera (1963)
WILLIAMS, BLINKY
  Lady Sings the Blues
THE WILLIAMS BROTHERS
  Going My Way
WILLIAMS, CARA
  Meet Me in Las Vegas
WILLIAMS, CINDY
  The First Nudie Musical
WILLIAMS, ESTHER
  Pagan Love Song
  Take Me Out to the Ball Game
WILLIAMS, FRANCES
  Broadway Through A Keyhole
WILLIAMS, HANK, JR
  A Time to Sing
  Your Cheatin' Heart
WILLIAMS, LIBERTY
  Bugsy Malone
WILLIAMS, MICHAEL
  Tell Me Lies
WILLIAMS, PAUL
  Bugsy Malone
  Phantom of the Paradise
WILLIAMS, ROBIN
  Popeye
WILLIAMS, TREAT
  Hair
WILLIAMS, TUDOR
  Charlie Chan at the Opera
WILLIS, VICTOR
  Hair
WILSON, DOOLEY
  Higher and Higher
WILSON, EILEEN
  The Five Pennies
  Gentlemen Marry Brunettes
  Marilyn
  One Touch of Venus
  Valley of the Dolls
WILSON, JULIE
  This Could Be the Night
WILSON, RON
  The Lively Set
WINDSOR, BARBARA
  The Boy Friend
WINFIELD, PAUL
  Huckleberry Finn
WINNINGER, CHARLES
  State Fair (1945)
  Ziegfeld Girl

Technical Index

Dates following various titles indicate which of several films
of the same title the person's contribution is included on the
recording. (M) indicates composer of the music; (L) indicates
the lyricist; (MD) indicates the musical director. Only persons
who have contributed to the majority of the songs are included.

AARONSON, IRVING
  She Loves Me Not (MD)
ADAMS, LEE
  Bye Bye Birdie (L)
  The Night They Raided... (L)
ADAMSON, HAROLD
  An Affair to Remember (L)
  Dancing Lady (L)
  Four Jills in A Jeep (L)
  Higher and Higher
  Paesano, A Voice in the...(L)
ADDISON, JOHN
  Smashing Time (M,L,MD)
ADLER, RICHARD
  Damn Yankees (M.L)
  The Pajama Game (M,L)
AGER, MILTON
  The King of Jazz (M)
  Honky Tonk (M)
ALEXANDER, VAN
  The Best Things in Life..(MD)
ALMAGOR, DAN
  Kazablan (L)
AMFITHEATROF, DANIELLE
  Song of the South (MD)
ANDERSON, MAXWELL
  Knickerbocker Holiday (L)
ANSELL, ERIC
  Song of Freedom (M,MD)
ANTHONY, RAY
  This Could Be the Night (MD)
ARDEN, VICTOR
  Broadway Gondolier (MD)
ARLEN, HAROLD
  Cabin in the Sky (M)
  Casbah (M)
  The Country Girl (M)
  Gay Purr-ee (M)
  Here Come the Waves (M)

  Mr Imperium (M)
  Out of This World (M)
  The Sky's the Limit (M)
  A Star Is Born (1954) (M)
  Star Spangled Rhythm (M)
  Up in Arms (M)
  The Wizard of Oz (M)
ARMBRUSTER, ROBERT
  Big City (MD)
  The Chocolate Soldier (MD)
  Make Mine Music (MD)
  Northwest Outpost (MD)
  The Unsinkable Molly...(MD)
ARMOND, GENE
  The Night the Lights... (MD)
ARNAUD, LEO
  One Touch of Venus (MD)
ASCHER, KENNY
  The Muppet Movie (M.L)
  A Star Is Born (1976) (M,L)
ASKEY, GIL
  Lady Sings the Blues (MD)
ARUNDELL, DENNIS
  Oh, Rosalinda! (L)
ASHMAN, HOWARD
  Little Shop of Horrors (L)
BACHARACH, BURT
  Lost Horizon (M,MD)
BAKALEINKOFF, CONSTANTIN
  The French Line (MD)
  Higher and Higher (MD)
  Step Lively (MD)
BARAVALLE, VICTOR
  Carefree (MD)
  A Damsel in Distress (MD)
  Show Boat (1936) (MD)
BARRY, JEFF
  The Idolmaker (M,L)

BRODSZKY, NICHOLAS
    Flame and the Flesh (M)
    Let's Be Happy (M)
    Meet Me in Las Vegas (M)
    Rich, Young and Pretty (M)
    Serenade (M)
    Ten Thousand Bedrooms (M)
    The Toast of New Orleans (M)
BROOKS, HARVEY
    I'm No Angel (M)
BROOKS, JACK
    Artists and Models (L)
    Cinderfella (L)
    Song of Scheherazade (L)
BROOKS, MEL
    Blazing Saddles (M,L)
    High Anxiety (M,L)
    The Producers (M,L)
    To Be or Not to Be (M,L)
BROWN, LEW
    The Best Things in Life,,,(L)
    Good News (L)
    The Singing Fool (L)
BROWN, NACIO HERB BROWN
    The Broadway Melody (M)
    Broadway Melody of 1938 (M)
    Going Hollywood (M)
    The Kissing Bandit (M)
    Singin' in the Rain (M)
BRUNS, GEORGE
    Babes in Toyland (MD)
    The Jungle Book (MD)
    The Sleeping Beauty (MD)
BRYAN, AL
    No, No Nanette (L)
BUARQUE, CHICO
    Opera do Malandro (M,L)
BUCKLEY, EMERSON
    Yes, Giorgio (MD)
BULLOCK, WALTER
    Little Miss Broadway (L)
BURGER, JULIUS
    Song of Scheherazade (MD)
BURKE, JOE
    Gold Diggers of Broadway (M)
BURKE, JOHN(NY)
    And the Angels Sing (L)
    A Connecticut Yankee...(L)
    Double or Nothing (L)
    Doctor Rhythm (L)
    East Side of Heaven (L)
    The Emperor Waltz (L)

Going My Way (L)
If I Had My Way (L)
Little Boy Lost (L)
Mr Music (L)
Pennies from Heaven (L)
Rhythm on the River (L)
Riding High (1950) (L)
Road to Bali (L)
Road to Morocco (L)
Road to Rio (L)
Road to Singapore (L)
Road to Utopia (L)
Road to Zanzibar (L)
Sing You Sinners (L)
Top O' the Morning (L)
Welcome Stranger (L)
BURKE, SONNY
    The Lady and the Tramp (M)
BURNS, RALPH
    All That Jazz (M,MD)
    Annie (MD)
    Cabaret (MD)
    A Chorus Line (MD)
    Lucky Lady (M,MD)
    The Muppets Take Manhattan (MD)
    New York, New York (M,MD)
BUTLER, ARTIE
    The Rescuers (MD)
BUTTOLPH, DAVID
    Pigskin Parade (MD)
CAESAR, IRVING
    Tea for Two (L)
CAHN, SAMMY
    Anchors Aweigh (L)
    Anything Goes (1956) (L)
    April in Paris (L)
    The Court Jester (L)
    Double Dynamite! (L)
    It Happened in Brooklyn (L)
    Journey Back to Oz (L)
    Let's Make Love (L)
    Meet Me in Las Vegas (L)
    Pardners (L)
    Peter Pan (L)
    The Pleasure Seekers (L)
    Rich, Young and Pretty (L)
    Road to Hong kong (L)
    Robin and the Seven Hoods (L)
    Say One for me (L)
    Serenade (L)
    Step Lively (L)
    Ten Thousand Bedrooms (L)

DEMY, JACQUES
   The Umbrellas of Cherbourg (L)
   The Young Girls of...(L)
DePAUL, GENE
   Li'l Abner (M)
   Seven Brides for Seven...(M)
   A Song Is Born (M)
   You Can't Run Away from It (M)
DeSYLVA, BUDDY (B G)
   The Best Things in Life...(L)
   Good News (L)
   The Singing Fool (L)
DEUTSCH, ADOLPH
   Annie Get Your Gun (MD)
   The Band Wagon (MD)
   The Belle of New York (MD)
   Funny Face (MD)
   Les Girls (MD)
   Pagan Love Song (MD)
   Seven Brides for Seven...(MD)
   Show Boat (1951) (MD)
   Take Me Out to the Ball..(MD)
   Torch Song (MD)
DEUTSCH, HELEN
   Lili (L)
DeVOL, FRANK
   The Jazz Singer (1953) (MD)
DIAMOND, NEIL
   The Jazz Singer (1980) (M,L)
DIETZ, HOWARD
   The Band Wagon (L)
DIXON, MORT
   Happiness Ahead (L)
DOLAN, ROBERT EMMETT
   Aaron Slick from Punkin...(MD)
   Blue Skies (MD)
   Holiday Inn (MD)
   Lady in the Dark (MD)
   Star Spangled Rhythm (MD)
DONALDSON, WALTER
   The Great Ziegfeld (M)
   Kid Millions (M)
DONNELLY, DOROTHY
   Deep in My Heart (L)
   The Student Prince (L)
DORFF, STEVE
   Any Which Way You Can (MD)
   Bronco Billy (MD)
   Every Which Way but Loose (MD)
   Honkytonk Man (MD)
THE DORSEY BROTHERS
   Two for Tonight (MD)

DORSEY, TOMMY
   Ship Ahoy (MD)
DRAGON, CARMEN
   Holiday in Mexico (MD)
   Lovely to Look At (MD)
DUBIN, AL
   Broadway Gondolier (L)
   Dames (L)
   Footlight Parade (L)
   42nd Street (L)
   Go Into Your Dance (L)
   Gold Diggers of Broadway (L)
   Gold Diggers of 1933 (L)
   Gold Diggers of 1935 (L)
   Gold Diggers of 1937 (L)
   Moulin Rouge (L)
   Roman Scandals (L)
   The Singing Marine (L)
   Stage Door Canteen (L)
   Wonder Bar (L)
DuBOIS, GLADYS
   I'm No Angel (L)
DUCLOUX, WALTER
   Interrupted Melody (MD)
DUKE, VERNON
   April in Paris (M)
   Cabin in the Sky (M)
DUNHAM, 'BY'
   I'll Take Sweden (M)
   Wild on the Beach (M,L)
DUNNING, GEORGE
   1001 Arabian Nights (M)
EBB, FRED
   Cabaret (L)
   Funny Lady (L)
   Lucky Lady (L)
   New York, New York (L)
EDENS, ROGER
   Deep in My Heart (L)
   Take Me Out to the Ball...(M)
   Ziegfeld Girl (M,L)
EDWARDS, GUS
   The Star Maker (M)
EDWARDS, SHERMAN
   G I Blues (M)
   Kid Galahad (M)
   1776 (M,L)
EGE, HENRIK
   Song of Freedom (L)
ELISCU, EDWARD
   Flying Down to Rio

ELLINGTON, DUKE
   Belle of the Ninties (MD)
   The Cotton Club (M)
ELLIOTT, JACK
   The Happiest Millionaire (MD)
   The One and Only Genuine.(MD)
ELLISON, BEN
   I'm No Angel (L)
ETTINGER, AMOS
   Kazablan (L)
EVANS, RAY
   Aaron Slick from Punkin...(M,L)
   All Hand on Deck (M,L)
   Here Comes the Groom (L)
   Red Garters (M,L)
   Somebody Loves Me (M,L)
   The Stars Are Singing (M,L)
FAIN, SAMMY
   Alice in Wonderland (M)
   April Love (M)
   Calamity Jane (M)
   Footlight Parade (M)
   The Jazz Singer (1953) (M)
   Hollywood or Bust (M)
   Mardi Gras (M)
   Peter Pan (M)
   The Sleeping Beauty (M)
   Three Sailors and A Girl (M)
FAIRCHILD, EDGAR
   Can't Help Singing (MD)
FAITH, PERCY
   Love Me or Leave Me (MD)
   White Christmas (MD)
   Young at Heart (MD)
FARNON, ROBERT
   Expresso Bongo (M,L)
   Gentlemen Marry Brunettes (MD)
   Road to Hong Kong (M,MD)
FARRANT, TREVOR
   The Pirate Movie (L)
FARRAR, JOHN
   Xanadu (M,L)
FEUER, CY
   King of Burlesque (MD)
   Wake Up and Live (MD)
FIEDLER, ARTHUR
   The Desert Song (1953) (MD)
FIELDS, DOROTHY
   Every Night at Eight (L)
   I Dream Too Much (L)
   In Person (L)
   The King Steps Out (L)

Mr Imperium (L)
Roberta (L)
Sweet Charity (L)
Swing Time (L)
FIELDS, IRVING
   The Big Beat (M)
FINE, SYLVIA
   The Court Jester (M,L)
   The Five Pennies (M,L)
   Knock on Wood (M,L)
FINSTON, NAT W
   Love Me Tonight (MD)
   One Hour with You (MD)
   We're Not Dressing (MD)
FISCHER, GUNTHER
   Just A Gigolo (MD)
FISHER, DORIS
   Down to Earth (M,L)
   Gilda (M,L)
FORBES, LOU
   The Singing Marine (MD)
   Varsity Show (MD)
FORBSTEIN, LEO F
   Dames (MD)
   Footlight Parade (MD)
   42nd Street (MD)
   Go Into Your Dance (MD)
   Gold Diggers of 1933 (MD)
   Gold Diggers of 1935 (MD)
   Hollywood Hotel (MD)
   This Is the Army (MD)
   Wonder Bar (MD)
   Yankee Doodle Dandy (MD)
FORREST, GEORGE (CHET)
   Broadway Serenade (L)
   The Great Waltz (1972) (L)
   Kismet (M,L)
   Song of Norway (M,L)
FOX, CHARLES
   Pufnstuf (M,L)
FRASER, IAN
   Scrooge (MD)
FREEBAIRN-SMITH, IAN
   The Muppet Movie (MD)
FREED, ARTHUR
   Broadway Melody (L)
   Broadway Melody of 1938 (L)
   Going Hollywood (L)
   Pagan Love Song (L)
   Singin' in the Rain (L)
   Yolanda and the Thief (L)
   Ziegfeld Follies of 1946 (L)

FREED, FRED
  A Royal Affair (M,L)
FREEMAN, ERNIE
  The Silencers (MD)
FRIEDHOFER, HUGO
  An Affair to Remember (MD)
FRIML, RUDOLF
  Northwest Outpost (M)
  Rose Marie (M)
  The Vagabond King (M)
GAMLEY, DOUGLAS
  The Little Prince (MD)
GANNON, KIM
  Song of the Open Road (L)
GASSO, BERNARD
  The Big Beat (L)
GERSHENSON, JOSEPH
  The Lively Set (MD)
  Rock, Pretty Baby (MD)
  So This Is Paris (MD)
  Summer Love (MD)
  Sweet Charity (MD)
GERSHWIN, GEORGE
  An American in Paris (M)
  A Damsel in Distress (M)
  Funny Face (M)
  Girl Crazy (M)
  Lady Be Good (M)
  Porgy and Bess (M)
  Rhapsody in Blue (M)
  Shall We Dance (M)
  The Shocking Miss Pilgrim (M)
  When the Boys Meet...(M)
GERSHWIN, IRA
  An American in Paris (L)
  The Barkleys of Broadway (L)
  The Country Girl (L)
  Cover Girl (L)
  A Damsel in Distress (L)
  Funny Face (L)
  Girl Crazy (L)
  Lady Be Good (L)
  Lady in the Dark (L)
  Porgy and Bess (L)
  Rhapsody in Blue (L)
  Shall We Dance (L)
  The Shocking Miss Pilgrim (L)
  A Star Is Born (1954) (L)
  When the Boys Meet...(L)
  Where Do We Go from Here? (L)
  You Were Never Lovelier (L)

GIANT, BILL
  Girl Happy (L)
  Harum Scarum (L)
  Kissin' Cousins (L)
  Paradise, Hawaiian Style (L)
GILBERT, HERSCHEL BURKE
  Carmen Jones (MD)
GILBERT, RAY
  Song of the South (L)
  The Three Caballeros (L)
GILBERT, W S
  Dick Deadeye (L)
  The Pirate Movie (L)
GIMBEL, NORMAN
  Pufnstuf (M,L)
GLAZER, TOM
  A Face in the Crowd (M)
GLOVER, HENRY
  Hey, Let's Twist! (M)
  Two Tickets to Paris (M)
GOMEZ, VINCENTE
  Blood and Sand (M,L,MD)
GOOD, JACK
  Catch My Soul (L)
GOODHART, AL
  This'll Make You Whistle (M.L)
GORDON, MACK
  Broadway Through A Keyhole (L)
  Bundle of Joy (L)
  The Dolly Sisters (L)
  Down Argentine Way (L)
  The Gay Divorcee (L)
  The Great American Broadcast (L)
  Head Over Heels (L)
  I Love Melvin (L)
  Mother Wore Tights (L)
  Orchestra Wives (L)
  Poor Little Rich Girl (L)
  She Loves Me Not (L)
  Springtime in the Rockies (L)
  Summer Stock (L)
  Sun Valley Serenade (L)
  Sweet Rosie O'Grady (L)
  That Night in Rio (L)
  Three Little Girls in Blue (L)
  Two for Tonight (L)
  Wake Up and Live (L)
  Weekend in Havana (L)
  We're Not Dressing (L)
  Young People (L)
GORE, MICHAEL
  Fame (M,MD)

HARDIN, CHARLES
  The Buddy Holly Story (M,L)
HARLINE, LEIGH
  Pinocchio (M,MD)
  The Sky's the Limit (MD)
  Snow White and the...(M,MD)
  You Were Never Lovelier (MD)
HARNICK, SHELTON
  Fiddler on the Roof (L)
HARRISON, GEORGE
  Yellow Submarine (M,L)
HART, LORENZ
  Babes in Arms (L)
  Billy Rose's Jumbo (L)
  The Boys from Syracuse (L)
  Gentlemen Marry Brunettes (L)
  Love Me Tonight (L)
  The Merry Widow (1934) (L)
  Mississippi (L)
  Pal Joey (L)
  Words and Music (L)
HARTLEY, RICHARD
  The Rocky Horror Picture..(MD)
HASKELL, JIMMIE
  Wild on the Beach (MD)
HASSALL, CHRISTOPHER
  King's Rhapsody (L)
HAYES, ELTON
  The Story of Robin Hood (M,L)
HAYMAN, EDWARD
  Northwest Outpost (L)
HAYTON, LENNIE
  The Barkleys of Broadway (MD)
  Going Hollywood (MD)
  Good News (MD)
  The Harvey Girls (MD)
  Hello, Dolly! (MD)
  On the Town (MD)
  The Pirate (MD)
  Singin' in the Rain (MD)
  Star! (MD)
  Summer Holiday (1948) (MD)
  Till the Clouds Roll By (MD)
  Words and Music (MD)
  Yolanda and the Thief (MD)
  Ziegfeld Follies of 1946 (MD)
HEFER, HAIM
  Kazablan (L)
  Tevye and his Daughters (L)
HEINDORF, RAY
  Calamity Jane (MD)
  Damn Yankees (MD)

The Eddie Cantor Story (MD)
Finian's Rainbow (MD)
The Music Man (MD)
Night and Day (MD)
The Pajama Game (MD)
Rhapsody in Blue (MD)
A Star Is Born (1954) (MD)
Serenade (MD)
1776 (MD)
So This Is Love (MD)
Thank Your Lucky Stars (MD)
Up in Arms (MD)
HEMRIC(K), GUY
  Beach Blanket Bingo (M,L)
  How to Stuff A Wild Bikini (M,L)
  Pajama Party (M,L)
HENDERSON, CHARLES
  The Dolly Sisters (MD)
  The Gang's All Here (MD)
  I'll Cry Tomorrow (MD)
  Hello Frisco Hello (MD)
  State Fair (1945) (MD)
  Sweet Rosie O'Grady (MD)
HENDERSON, JOE
  Idle on Parade (M,L)
HENDERSON, RAY
  The Best Things in Life..(M)
  Good News (M)
  The Singing Fool (M)
HENEKER, DAVID
  Half A Sixpence (M,L)
HERBERT, VICTOR
  Babes in Toyland (M)
  Naughty Marietta (M)
HERMAN, JERRY
  Hello, Dolly! (M,L)
  Mame (M,L)
HEYMAN, EDWARD
  Delightfully Dangerous (L)
  The Kissing Bandit (L)
HEYWARD, DU BOSE
  Porgy and Bess (L)
HILLIARD, BOB
  Alice in Wonderland (L)
  Living It Up (L)
HIRSCHHORN, JOEL
  Pete's Dragon (M,L)
HIRT, CHARLES
  My Wild Irish Rose (MD)
HODEIR, ANDRE
  La Parisienne (M,L)

MELICHAR, ALEIS
  Oh, Rosalinda! (MD)
MELLY, GEORGE
  Smashing Time (L)
MENKEN, ALAN
  Little Shop of Horrors (M)
MERCER, JOHNNY
  The Belle of New York (L)
  Darling Lili (L)
  The Fleet's In (L)
  The Harvey Girls (L)
  Here Come the Waves (L)
  Hollywood Hotel (L)
  Li'l Abner (L)
  Merry Andrew (L)
  Out of This World (L)
  Second Chorus (L)
  Seven Brides for Seven...(L)
  The Sky's the Limit (L)
  Star Spangled Rhythm (L)
  Variety Show (L)
  You Can't Run Away...(L)
MERKIN, ROBBY
  Little Shop of Horrors (MD)
MERRICK, MAHON
  Every Night at Eight (MD)
MERRILL, BOB
  Funny Girl (L)
MESKELL, JACK
  Everything Is Rhythm (L)
MILLER, GLENN
  Orchestra Wives (MD)
  Sun Valley Serenade (MD)
MILLER, ROBIN
  Dick Deadeye (L)
MILLS, IRVING
  The Cotton Club (L)
MITCHELL, ADRIAN
  Tell Me Lies (L)
MITCHELL, SIDNEY D
  Pigskin Parade (L)
MONACO, JAMES V
  The Dolly Sisters (M)
  Doctor Rhythm (M)
  East Side of Heaven (M)
  If I Had My Way (M)
  Rhythm on the River (M)
  Road to Singapore (M)
  Sing You Sinners (M)
  Stage Door Canteen (M)
MONNOT, MARGUERITE
  Jessica (M)

MOODY, PHIL
  So This Is Paris (M,L)
MOONEY, HAROLD
  Pete Kelly's Blues (MD)
MORAES, CH. DE
  Opera do Malandro (MD)
MORALI, JACQUES
  Can't Stop the Music (M)
MORE, JULIAN
  Red and Blue (L)
MOREY, LARRY
  Bambi (L)
  Snow White and the Seven...(L)
MORLEY, ANGELA
  The Slipper and the Rose (MD)
MORRIS, JOHN
  Blazing Saddles (MD)
  High Anxiety (M,MD)
  The Producers (M,MD)
  To Be or Not to Be (M,MD)
MORROS, BORIS
  The Big Broadcast of 1938 (MD)
MOSS, JEFF
  The Muppets Take Manhattan (M,L)
MURPHEY, MICHAEL
  Hard Country (M,L)
MURRY, TED
  Follow the Boys (1963) (M,L)
MYERS, PETER
  Summer Holiday (1963) (M,L)
  The Young Ones (M,L)
MYROW, JOSEF
  Bundle of Joy (M)
  I Love Melvin (M)
  Mother Wore Tights (M)
  Three Little Girls...(M)
NASCIMBENE, MARIO
  Jessica (M)
NASH, OGDEN
  One Touch of Venus (L)
NEGULESCO, DUSTY
  Jessica (L)
NELSON, WILLIE
  Honeysuckle Rose (M,L)
NEWBORN, IRA
  The Blues Brothers (MD)
NEWELL, NORMAN
  Melba (L)
NEWLEY, ANTHONY
  Can Heironymous Merkin...(M)
  Idle on Parade (M,L)

PITCHFORD, DEAN
  Fame (L)
PLEIS, JACK
  Bye Bye Birdie (MD)
PLUMB, ED
  Bambi (M)
  Peter Pan (MD)
POKRASS, SAMUEL
  Happy Landing (M)
POLLACK, LEW
  Captain January (M)
  Pigskin Parade (M)
POPP, ANDRE
  Folies-Bergere (MD)
PORTER, COLE
  Anything Goes (M,L)
  At Long Last Love (M,L)
  Born to Dance (M,L)
  Broadway Melody of 1940 (M,L)
  Can-Can (M,L)
  The Gay Divorcee (M,L)
  Les Girls (M,L)
  High Society (M,L)
  Kiss Me Kate (M,L)
  Night and Day (M,L)
  The Pirate (M,L)
  Silk Stockings (M,L)
  You'll Never Get Rich (M,L)
POST, MIKE
  Rhinestone (MD)
PRATT, MICHAEL
  The Duke Wore Jeans (M,L)
  The Tommy Steele Story (M,L)
  Tommy the Toreador (M,L)
PRESLEY, ELVIS
  Love Me Tender (M,L)
PREVIN, ANDRE
  Bells Are Ringing (MD)
  Gigi (MD)
  It's Always Fair Weather (MD)
  Jesus Christ Superstar (MD)
  Kismet (MD)
  Kiss Me Kate (MD)
  My Fair Lady (MD)
  Paint Your Wagon (MD)
  Pepe (MD)
  Porgy and Bess (MD)
  Silk Stockings (MD)
  Thoroughly Modern Millie (MD)
  Three Little Words (MD)
  Valley of the Dolls (MD)

PREVIN, CHARLES
  The Boys from Syracuse (MD)
  Nice Girl? (MD)
  Spring Parade (MD)
  Two Sisters from Boston (MD)
  The Underpup (MD)
PREVIN, DORY
  see: Langdon, Dory
PRIMA, LOUIS
  Hey Boy! Hey Girl! (MD)
PRINCE
  Purple Rain (M,L)
  Under the Cherry Moon (M,L)
RADO, JAMES
  Hair (L)
RAGNI, GEROME
  Hair (L)
RAINGER, RALPH
  The Big Broadcast (M)
  The Big Broadcast of 1938 (M)
  Here Is My Heart (M)
  My Gal Sal (M)
  Paris Honeymoon (M)
  Riding High (1943) (M)
  Waikiki Wedding (M)
RALKE, DON
  C'mon Let's Live A...(MD)
  Snoopy, Come Home (MD)
RALSTON, ALFRED
  Oh! What A Lovely War (MD)
RAPOSO, JOE
  The Great Muppet Caper! (M,L,MD)
  Raggedy Ann and Andy (M,L,MD)
RAUBER, FRANCOIS
  Jacques Brel Is Alive...(MD)
RAY, CYRIL
  Everything Is Rhythm (M)
RAYE, DON
  A Song Is Born (L)
REDMAN, DON
  St Louis Blues (MD)
REINHARDT, STEPHEN
  Godspell (MD)
RENE, HENRI
  Aaron Slick from Punkin...(MD)
  New Faces (MD)
  Two Tickets to Broadway (MD)
  The Vagabond King (MD)
RENTZETTI, JOE
  The Buddy Holly Story (MD)

RUSSELL, HENRY
  Lulu Belle (MD)
RUSSELL, TONY
  Tell Me Lies (MD)
ST LOUIS, LOUIS
  Grease 2 (M,MD)
SALTER, HANS
  His Butler's Sister (MD)
SAMMES, MIKE
  The Aristocats (MD)
SAMOSSUD, JACQUES
  Knickerbocker Holiday (MD)
SANDLOFF, PETER
  The Threepenny Opera (1963) (MD)
SAVINA, CARLO
  For the First Time (MD)
  It Started in Naples (M)
SCHARF, WALTER
  Cinderfella (M,MD)
  The French Line (M)
  Funny Face (MD)
  Journey Back to Oz (MD)
  Living It Up (MD)
  Willy Wonka and the...(MD)
SCHERTZINGER, VICTOR
  The Fleet's In (M)
  The Love Parade (M,MD)
SCHOEN, VIC
  The Court Jester (MD)
  Knock on Wood (MD)
  Road to Morocco (MD)
  Road to Rio (MD)
SCHULBERG, BUDD
  A Face in the Crowd (L)
SCHWARTZ, ARTHUR
  The Band Wagon (M)
  Cairo (M)
  Thank Your Lucky Stars (M)
SCHWARTZ, STEPHEN
  Godspell (M,L)
SCOTT, WALDO
  Rachel and the Stranger (L)
SCOTT, WALLY
  The Heart of A Man (MD)
  The Lady Is A Square (MD)
SEELEN, JERRY
  The Jazz Singer (1953) (L)
SELTZER, DOV
  Kazablan (M,MD)
  Tevye and his Daughters (M,MD)

SHAW, ARTIE
  Second Chorus (M,MD)
SHAW, ROLAND
  The Duke Wore Jeans (MD)
  The Great Waltz (1972) (MD)
  Song of Norway (MD)
SHEPHERD, BILL
  Idle on Parade (MD)
SHERMAN, GARRY
  Alice's Restaurant (MD)
SHERMAN, RICHARD M / ROBERT B
  The Aristocats (M,L)
  Bedknobs and Broomsticks (M,L)
  Charlotte's Web (M,L)
  Chitty Chitty Bang Bang (M,L)
  The Happiest Millionaire (M,L)
  Huckleberry Finn (M,L)
  In Search of the Cast...(M,L)
  The Jungle Book (M,L)
  The Magic of Lassie (M,L)
  Mary Poppins (M,L)
  The One and Only Genuine (M,L)
  The Parent Trap (M,L)
  The Slipper and the Rose (M,L)
  Snoopy, Come Home (M,L)
  Summer Magic (M,L)
  The Sword in the Stone (M,L)
  Tom Sawyer (M,L)
SHERRELL, PONY
  So This Is Paris (M,L)
SHILKRET, NATHANIEL
  Shall We Dance (MD)
  Swing Time (MD)
SHIRE, DAVID
  The Night the Lights...(M)
SIGLER, MAURICE
  This'll Make You Whistle (M,L)
SILVERS, LOUIS
  Captain January (MD)
  Dancing Lady (MD)
  Dimples (MD)
  Happy Landing (MD)
  The Jazz Singer (1927) (MD)
  Little Miss Broadway (MD)
  Poor Little Rich Girl (MD)
  Rose of Washington Square (MD)
  Wake Up and Live (MD)
SINATRA, RAY
  Paesano, A Voice...(M,MD)
  The Toast of New Orleans (MD)

The Cat and the Fiddle (MD)
The Merry Widow (1934) (MD)
Naughty Marietta (MD)
New Moon (MD)
The Rogue Song (MD)
Rose Marie (1936) (MD)
San Francisco (MD)
Smilin' Through (MD)
The Unfinished Dance (MD)
The Wizard of Oz (MD)
Ziegfeld Girl (MD)
STRANGE, STANISLAUS
The Chocolate Soldier (L)
STRAUS, OSCAR
The Chocolate Soldier (M)
One Hour with You (M)
STROUSE, CHARLES
Annie (M)
Bye Bye Birdie (M)
The Night They Raided...(M)
STRAUSS, JOHANN
The Great Waltz (M)
Oh, Rosalinda! (M)
STYNE, JULE
Anchors Aweigh (M)
Bells Are Ringing (M)
Double Dynamite! (M)
Funny Girl (M)
Gentlemen Prefer Blondes (M)
Gypsy (M)
It Happened in Brooklyn (M)
Living It Up (M)
Step Lively (M)
Two Tickets to Broadway (M)
STYNER, JERRY
Beach Blanket Bingo (M,L)
Pajama Party (M,L)
How to Stuff A Wild Bikini (M,L)
SUKMAN, HARRY
The Singing Nun (MD)
SULLIVAN, ARTHUR
Dick Deadeye (M)
The Pirate Movie (M)
SULLIVAN, PETER
The Pirate Movie (MD)
TCHAIKOVSKY, PETER
The Sleeping Beauty (M)
TEPPER, SID
Blue Hawaii (L)
Clambake (M,L)
Frankie and Johnny (L)
Fun in Acapulco (L)

Girls! Girls! Girls! (L)
It Happened at the World's (L)
Roustabout (L)
Speedway (L)
Spinout (L)
TEURS, FRANK
The Cocoanuts (MD)
THOMAS, LOWELL
Search for Tomorrow (L)
THOMAS, PETER
Uncle Tom's Cabin (M,MD)
THORNE, KEN
A Funny Thing...(MD)
Head (M,MD)
TIOMKIN, DIMITRI
Friendly Persuasion (M)
Search for Paradise (M)
TORRE, JANICE
Tom Thumb (L)
TOWNSHEND, PETER
Tommy (M,L)
TRIPP, PAUL
The Christmas That...(M,L)
TROTTER, JOHN SCOTT
A Boy Named Charlie Brown (MD)
The Bells of St Mary's (MD)
Blue Skies (MD)
Birth of the Blues (MD)
Double or Nothing (MD)
Doctor Rhythm (MD)
East Side of Heaven (MD)
Going My Way (MD)
Here Come the Waves (MD)
Here Comes the Groom (MD)
Holiday Inn (MD)
If I Had My Way (MD)
Little Boy Lost (MD)
Out of This World (MD)
Paris Honeymoon (MD)
Rhythm on the River (MD)
Road to Singapore (MD)
Road to Utopia (MD)
Road to Zanzibar (MD)
Sing You Sinners (MD)
The Star Maker (MD)
Welcome, Stranger (MD)
TUNICK, JONATHAN
A Little Night Music (MD)
USHER, GARY
Muscle Beach Party (M,L)
VALDEZ, DANIEL
Zoot Suit (M,L)

About the Compiler

RICHARD CHIGLEY LYNCH was Assistant Curator of the Billy Rose Theatre Collection of the New York Public Library. He compiled *Musicals! A Directory of Musical Properties Available for Production, Broadway on Record: A Directory of New York Cast Recordings of Musical Shows, 1931-1986,* and is a regular contributor to *Show Music*. His articles have also appeared in *Kastlemusick Monthly Bulletin, Record Collectors Journal,* and other periodicals in the music and recording field.